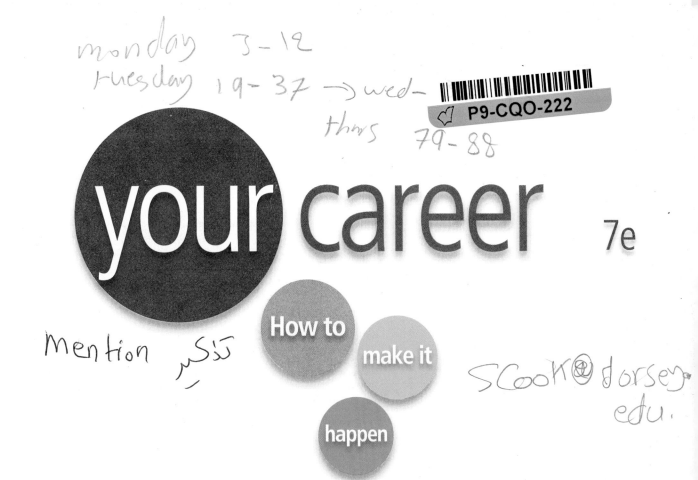

your career 7e

How to make it happen

Julie Griffin Levitt

Business Consultant, Trainer
and National Presenter

Former Supervisor
with Boise State University
Boise, Idaho

Lauri Harwood

Business Consultant and Trainer
Cincinnati, Ohio

SOUTH-WESTERN
CENGAGE Learning™

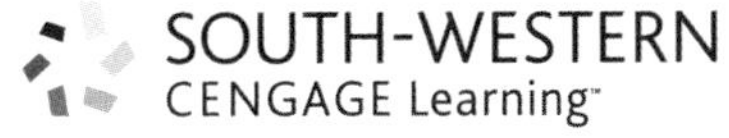

Australia • Brazil • Japan • Korea • Mexico • Singapore • Spain • United Kingdom • United States

Your Career: How to Make It Happen, 7e
Julie Griffin Levitt and Lauri Harwood

Vice President of Editorial, Business: Jack Calhoun

Vice President/Editor in Chief: Karen Schmohe

Acquisitions Editor: Jane Phelan

Senior Development Editor: Penny Shank

Consulting Editor: Vandalay Group, Inc.

Marketing Manager: Linda Kuper

Senior Media Editor: Mike Jackson

Manufacturing Coordinator: Kevin Kluck

Senior Content Project Manager: Cliff Kallemeyn

Senior Art Director: Tippy McIntosh

Internal Designer: Ke Design, Mason OH

Cover Designer: Ke Design, Mason OH

Cover Image: ballyscanlon/Getty Images

ISBN-13: 978-0-538-73099-0

ISBN-10: 0-538-73099-4

South-Western Cengage Learning
5191 Natorp Boulevard
Mason, OH 45040
USA

Cengage Learning products are represented in Canada by Nelson Education, Ltd.

For your course and learning solutions, visit **www.cengage.com**

Purchase any of our products at your local college store or at our preferred online store **www.ichapters.com**

Printed in the United States of America
3 4 5 6 7 8 13 12 11 10

Brief Table of Contents

Table of Contents

Introducing *Your Career 7e*...

Helping You Stand Out!

*Y**our Career: How to Make It Happen** 7e has a brand new look! This new edition is sharp and focused, and it targets the best practices in today's job search and career-development process. **Your Career** provides everything you need to deliver top-quality instruction and help your students stand out in a crowd.*

Helping Students Stand Out... ORGANIZED FOR SUCCESS

PART OPENERS...

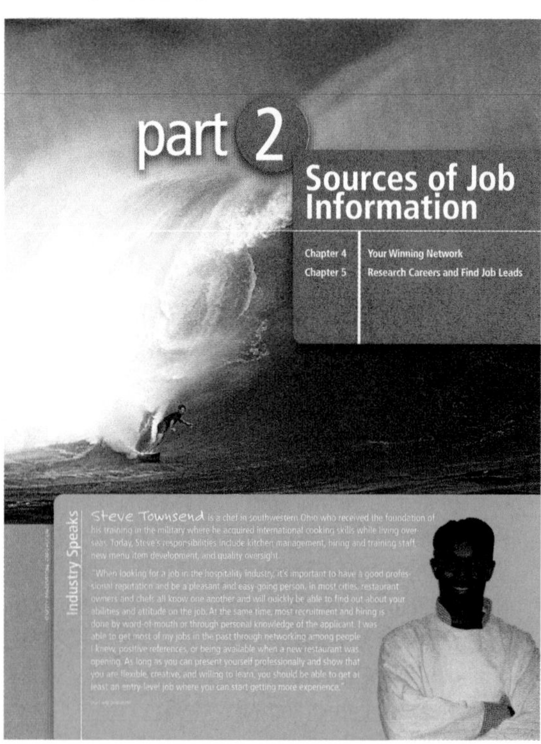

***Parts begin with** Industry Speaks — an interview with an industry professional that focuses on job-hunting advice and career development topics.*

CHAPTER OPENER...

***Objectives** — a quick review of the chapter goals and what will be learned.*

***Overview** — the learning outcomes and achievement expectations of the chapter.*

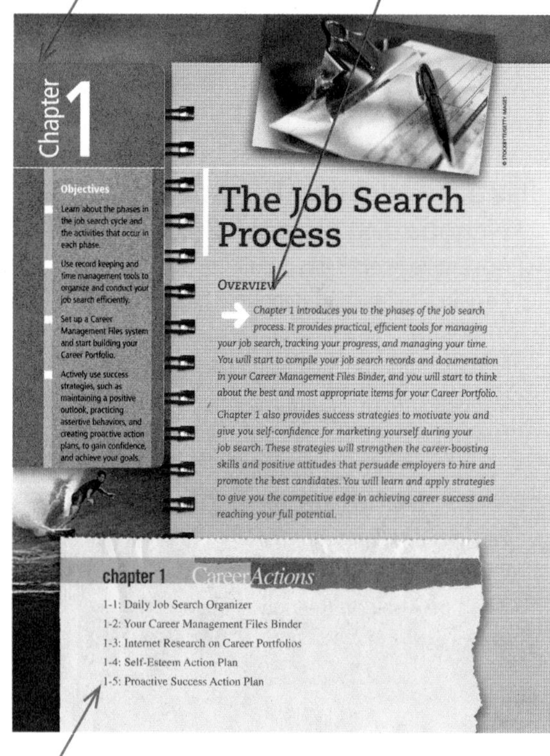

***Career Actions** — an at-a-glance list of the Career Action hands-on assignments found in the chapter taking students beyond the classroom into the business world.*

CAREER-FOCUSED FEATURES

GETTING STARTED...

Jump Start Your Job Search Knowledge

Consider a job you have held recently or currently hold. If you have not had full-time employment, think about part-time or seasonal work you have had in the past. Answer the following questions to start thinking about how you handled the job search process in the past.

- Why did you want the job? Why did you think you were suited for the job?
- How did you learn about the job opening?
- What steps did you follow to apply for and get the job?
- Why do you think you were hired? What was the most important factor in your hiring?
- What experience did you develop in the job that will serve you in your future career?

© DIGITAL VISION/GETTY IMAGES

NEW! Jump Start Your Career *challenges students to analyze careers of interest and questions associated with them and conduct research to get the answers.*

Successful companies view employee differences as assets to their business.

© DIGITAL VISION/GETTY IMAGES

Success Tips *offer motivational messages with excellent advice for achieving job satisfaction and reaching career potential.*

© PHOTODISC/GETTY IMAGES

Watch Out
Don't Lock Yourself Into Only One Option

Successful career planning requires flexibility. Changing technologies and a global economy cause some careers to become obsolete or vastly changed. Broaden your job options. Prepare to qualify for two or more closely related career targets that require related education, training, and general capabilities.

Which transferable career competencies do you have that qualify you for jobs within and between career clusters? Ask a knowledgeable career counselor to help you identify multi-career goals appropriate for your interests and abilities.

To make sure you have plenty of options for success, continue to develop your career flexibility and pursue lifelong learning.

NEW! Watch Out *warns about career taboos and mistakes to prevent.*

NEW! Make It a Habit *provides information about job etiquette, manners, and behavior.*

MAKE IT A HABIT

Form the Habit of Positive Thinking

Deliberately motivate yourself every day. Think of yourself as successful, and expect positive outcomes for everything you attempt.

Project energy and enthusiasm. Employers hire people who project positive energy and enthusiasm. Develop the habit of speaking, moving, and acting with these qualities.

Practice this positive expectation mind-set until it becomes a habit. Applicants who project enthusiasm and positive behavior generate a positive chemistry that rubs off. Hiring decisions are influenced largely by this positive energy.

Focus on past successes. Focusing on past successes to remind yourself of your abilities will help you attain your goals. For example, no one is born knowing how to ride a bicycle or use a computer. Through training, practice, and trial and error, you master new abilities. During the trial-and-error phases of development, remind yourself of past successes; look at mistakes as part of the natural learning curve. Continue until you achieve the result you want, and remind yourself that you have succeeded in the past and can do so again. You fail only when you quit trying!

© DIGITAL VISION/GETTY IMAGES

BEYOND THE CLASSROOM...

complete CareerActions

2-4 Career Competencies Inventory

Career Actions *direct students to complete the appropriate Career Action assignment located at the end of the chapter.*

APPLICATIONS FOR SUCCESS

END OF CHAPTER...

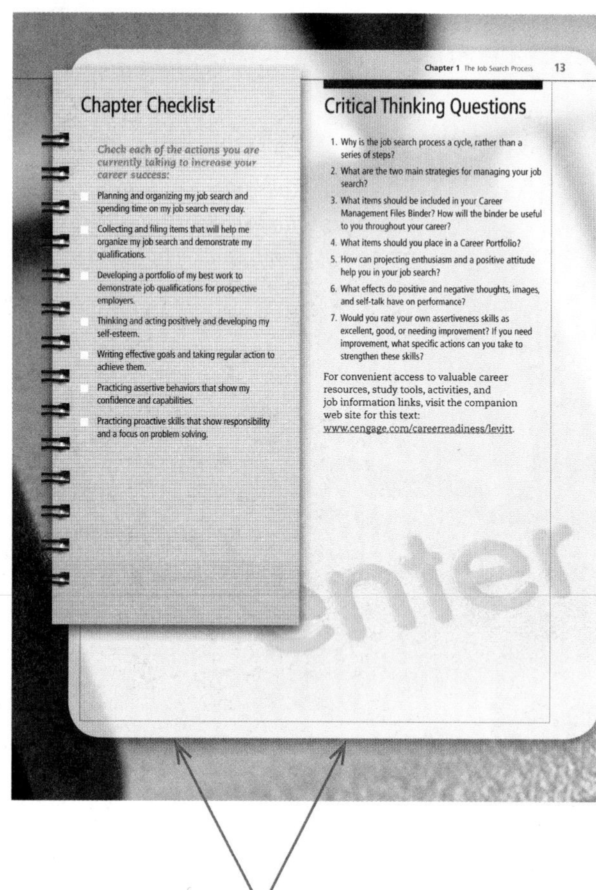

Chapter 1 The Job Search Process 13

Chapter Checklist

Check each of the actions you are currently taking to increase your career success:

- Planning and organizing my job search and spending time on my job search every day.
- Collecting and filing items that will help me organize my job search and demonstrate my qualifications.
- Developing a portfolio of my best work to demonstrate job qualifications for prospective employers.
- Thinking and acting positively and developing my self-esteem.
- Writing effective goals and taking regular action to achieve them.
- Practicing assertive behaviors that show my confidence and capabilities.
- Practicing proactive skills that show responsibility and a focus on problem solving.

Critical Thinking Questions

1. Why is the job search process a cycle, rather than a series of steps?
2. What are the two main strategies for managing your job search?
3. What items should be included in your Career Management Files Binder? How will the binder be useful to you throughout your career?
4. What items should you place in a Career Portfolio?
5. How can projecting enthusiasm and a positive attitude help you in your job search?
6. What effects do positive and negative thoughts, images, and self-talk have on performance?
7. Would you rate your own assertiveness skills as excellent, good, or needing improvement? If you need improvement, what specific actions can you take to strengthen these skills?

For convenient access to valuable career resources, study tools, activities, and job information links, visit the companion web site for this text: www.cengage.com/careerreadiness/levitt.

NEW! Trial Run ***interactive or role-playing activities model the desired outcomes of the chapter. Each activity requires peer or self-evaluation.***

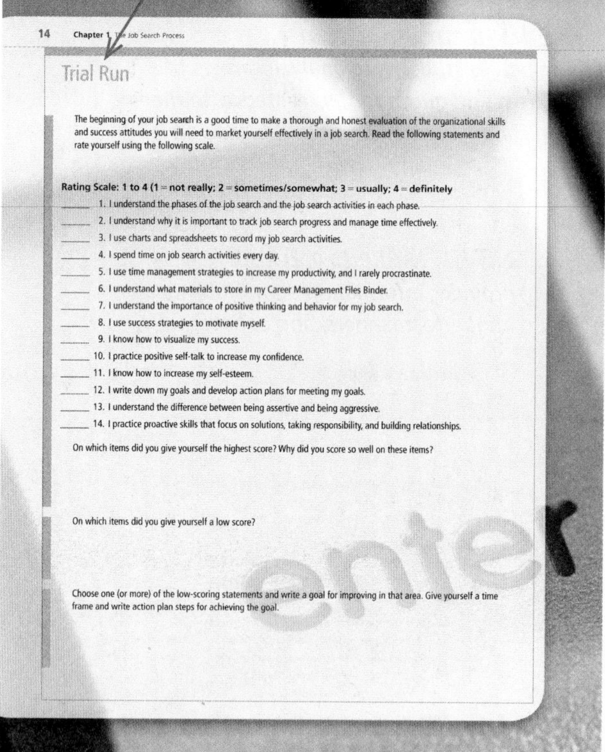

14 Chapter 1 The Job Search Process

Trial Run

The beginning of your job search is a good time to make a thorough and honest evaluation of the organizational skills and success attitudes you will need to market yourself effectively in a job search. Read the following statements and rate yourself using the following scale.

Rating Scale: 1 to 4 (1 = not really; 2 = sometimes/somewhat; 3 = usually; 4 = definitely

_____ 1. I understand the phases of the job search and the job search activities in each phase.
_____ 2. I understand why it is important to track job search progress and manage time effectively.
_____ 3. I use charts and spreadsheets to record my job search activities.
_____ 4. I spend time on job search activities every day.
_____ 5. I use time management strategies to increase my productivity, and I rarely procrastinate.
_____ 6. I understand what materials to store in my Career Management Files Binder.
_____ 7. I understand the importance of positive thinking and behavior for my job search.
_____ 8. I use success strategies to motivate myself.
_____ 9. I know how to visualize my success.
_____ 10. I practice positive self-talk to increase my confidence.
_____ 11. I know how to increase my self-esteem.
_____ 12. I write down my goals and develop action plans for meeting my goals.
_____ 13. I understand the difference between being assertive and being aggressive.
_____ 14. I practice proactive skills that focus on solutions, taking responsibility, and building relationships.

On which items did you give yourself the highest score? Why did you score so well on these items?

On which items did you give yourself a low score?

Choose one (or more) of the low-scoring statements and write a goal for improving in that area. Give yourself a time frame and write action plan steps for achieving the goal.

Checklist and Critical Thinking Questions ***highlight key chapter concepts and apply them directly to students' career goals.***

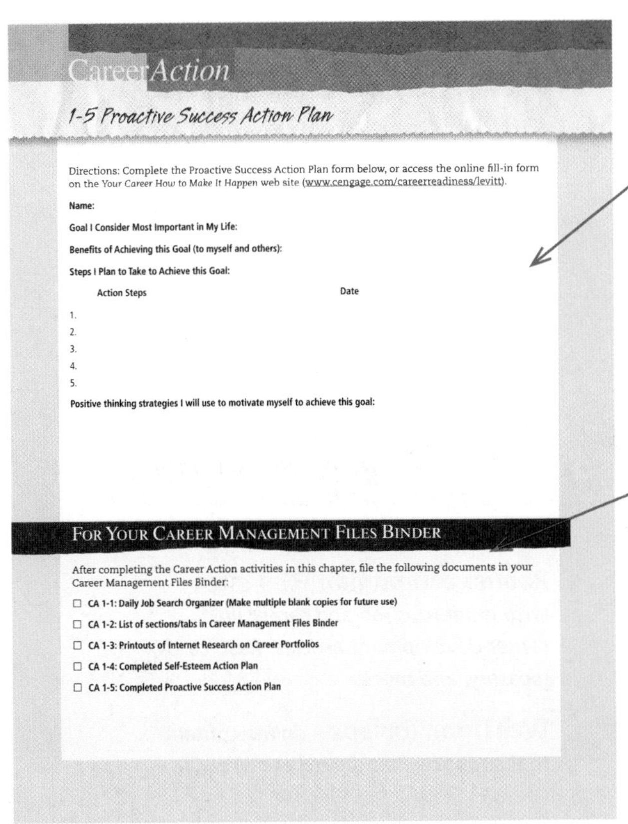

Career Action

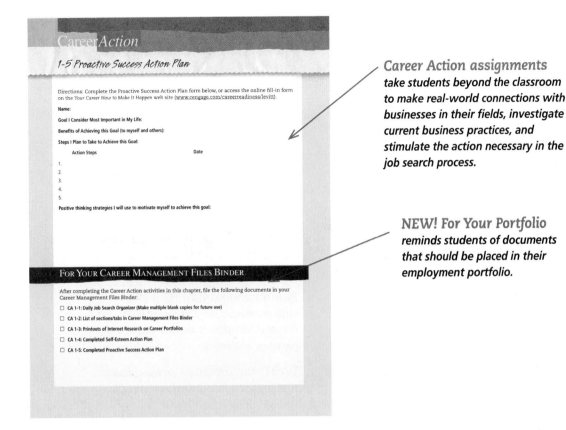

1-5 Proactive Success Action Plan

Directions: Complete the Proactive Success Action Plan form below, or access the online fill-in form on the *Your Career How to Make It Happen* web site (www.cengage.com/careerreadiness/levitt).

Name:

Goal I Consider Most Important in My Life:

Benefits of Achieving this Goal (to myself and others):

Steps I Plan to Take to Achieve this Goal:

Action Steps	Date
1.	
2.	
3.	
4.	
5.	

Positive thinking strategies I will use to motivate myself to achieve this goal:

FOR YOUR CAREER MANAGEMENT FILES BINDER

After completing the Career Action activities in this chapter, file the following documents in your Career Management Files Binder:

- ☐ CA 1-1: Daily Job Search Organizer (Make multiple blank copies for future use)
- ☐ CA 1-2: List of sections/tabs in Career Management Files Binder
- ☐ CA 1-3: Printouts of Internet Research on Career Portfolios
- ☐ CA 1-4: Completed Self-Esteem Action Plan
- ☐ CA 1-5: Completed Proactive Success Action Plan

Career Action assignments *take students beyond the classroom to make real-world connections with businesses in their fields, investigate current business practices, and stimulate the action necessary in the job search process.*

NEW! For Your Portfolio *reminds students of documents that should be placed in their employment portfolio.*

ADDED VALUE and GREATER CONVENIENCE

your career

Job Search
Quick Reference

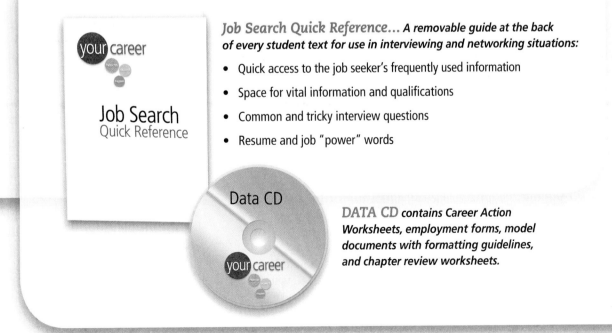

Job Search Quick Reference... ***A removable guide at the back of every student text for use in interviewing and networking situations:***

- Quick access to the job seeker's frequently used information
- Space for vital information and qualifications
- Common and tricky interview questions
- Resume and job "power" words

Data CD

DATA CD *contains Career Action Worksheets, employment forms, model documents with formatting guidelines, and chapter review worksheets.*

Helping Instructor's Stand Out...
TEACHING RESOURCES

Instructor's Resource CD ***offers complete and customizable content:***

- Teaching Suggestions
- Course Management and Schedules
- Assessment Strategies
- Teaching Masters
- Career Development Resources List
- PowerPoint Slides
- Case Studies with Solutions
- Printable Chapter Resources: Career Action forms, blank employment forms and examples, critical thinking questions and solutions.
- ExamView Chapter Tests and Solutions

Robust companion Web site ***with numerous job and career links, career development articles, flash cards, glossary, and more.***

WebTutor Toolbox *- online content that supports Blackboard and WebCT.*

Reviewers

Christian Blum
Bryant & Statton College
Getzville, NY

Larry Bohn
Sullivan University
Global e-Learning
Louisville, KY

Frances A. Brar
Brown Mackie College
Merrillville, IN

Fred J. Dorn
University of Mississippi
Lafayette, MS

Penny R. Janson
Bryant & Stratton College
Buffalo, NY

Kelley A. Mansfield
Kaplan College
Merrillville, IN

Kathy S. Marra-Wert
Marian College
Indianapolis, IN

William McAndrews
PROGRESS High School
for Professional Careers
New York, NY

Nancy Porretto
Katherine Gibbs School
Melville, NY

Krista Dabakis Price
Heald College
Portland, OR

Pat Sorcic
Bryant & Stratton College
Milwaukee, WI

Arlie Thompson
Gibbs College
Norwalk, CT

D. Ross Thomson
Bryant & Stratton College
Albany, NY

Stacy Dee Zager
Briarcliffe College
Bethpage, NY

CareerAction Assignments

Part 1 Starting Your Career

Chapter 1 The Job Search Process

TO DO

Chapter 2 Know What Employers Expect

TO DO

Chapter 3 Know Yourself to Market Yourself

TO DO

Part 2 Sources of Job Information

Chapter 4 Your Winning Network

TO DO

Chapter 5 Research Careers and Find Job Leads

TO DO

Part 3 Essential Job Search Communications

Chapter 6 Resumes

TO DO

part 1

Starting Your Career

Industry Speaks

Katie Thoman-Godshalk, RN, Certified Pediatric Nurse Practitioner, loves her work with teens and young adults who have developmental disabilities. "Being happy at your job is the best way to be a productive employee. I'm lucky my job is a good fit because I was so excited about the job that I was afraid to ask too many questions in the interview."

Katie has these tips for the first two weeks and the first year. "People make themselves the most available when someone is new, so the first two weeks are a good time to listen and observe. In the first year, so much of your job will be new, and having a mentor is very important. If you aren't assigned a mentor, ask someone who has a similar job or who has experience that will help you develop in your job to mentor you.

"If you have the required credentials you should feel confident applying for a job even if you lack experience in one area. Make it clear during the interview that you are eager to learn. If nothing else, you will get a chance to practice the interviewing process."

Chapter 1

The Job Search Process

Objectives

- Learn about the phases in the job search cycle and the activities that occur in each phase.
- Use record keeping and time management tools to organize and conduct your job search efficiently.
- Set up a Career Management Files system and start building your Career Portfolio.
- Actively use success strategies, such as maintaining a positive outlook, practicing assertive behaviors, and creating proactive action plans, to gain confidence, and achieve your goals.

© STOCKBYTE/GETTY IMAGES

Overview

Chapter 1 introduces you to the phases of the job search process. It provides practical, efficient tools for managing your job search, tracking your progress, and managing your time. You will start to compile your job search records and documentation in your Career Management Files Binder, and you will start to think about the best and most appropriate items for your Career Portfolio.

Chapter 1 also provides success strategies to motivate you and give you self-confidence for marketing yourself during your job search. These strategies will strengthen the career-boosting skills and positive attitudes that persuade employers to hire and promote the best candidates. You will learn and apply strategies to give you the competitive edge in achieving career success and reaching your full potential.

chapter 1 Career*Actions*

1-1: Daily Job Search Organizer

1-2: Your Career Management Files Binder

1-3: Internet Research on Career Portfolios

1-4: Self-Esteem Action Plan

1-5: Proactive Success Action Plan

Jump Start Your Job Search Knowledge

Consider a job you have held recently or currently hold. If you have not had full-time employment, think about part-time or seasonal work you have had in the past. Answer the following questions to start thinking about how you handled the job search process in the past.

- Why did you want the job?
- Why did you think you were suited for the job?
- How did you learn about the job opening?
- What steps did you follow to apply for and get the job?
- Why do you think you were hired?
- What was the most important factor in your hiring?
- What experience did you develop in the job that will serve you in your future career?
- What will you do differently in future jobs?

The Job Search Cycle: Where to Start?

The job search process can be daunting and difficult to navigate, even for someone with plenty of work experience. It helps to think of the process as an ongoing cycle rather than a series of steps. The cycle of preparing, assessing yourself, networking, documenting your skills, and following up with employers is an important part of your work life, not only for your first job but for the entire length of your career. Constantly revisiting these phases to stay current with your job goals, skills, and documentation will save time and help you manage your career. The basic job search cycle consists of five main phases with specific activities.

These following five phases correspond to the five main Parts of this book. In each Part, you will participate in the job search activities for that phase, building experience and creating the documents that you will need to progress through the job search cycle.

Phase 1: Preparation In the preparation phase, you will learn about the workplace and employer expectations, plan for your career, assess your own skills and characteristics, and determine your career target(s).

Phase 2: Finding Job Leads In this phase, you will network, search for job leads, and conduct research using a variety of job sources, including the Internet, your contacts, and print resources.

Phase 3: Applying for Jobs In this phase, you will market yourself by preparing effective resumes, cover letters, applications, and online forms.

Phase 4: The Interview In the interview phase, you will use strategies for getting interviews, prepare and practice for different types of job interviews and interview questions, practice effective interviewing techniques, and write effective thank you letters.

Phase 5: Follow Up and Evaluation In this phase, you will follow up with employers and learn negotiation strategies. You will evaluate and consider offers and make decisions. During this phase, a job seeker accepts a job offer or returns to an earlier phase to seek a different job.

The Job Search Cycle

Phase 1: Preparation
- Career Planning
- Self-Assessment

Phase 2: Finding Job Leads
- Research
- Networking

Phase 3: Applying for Jobs
- Resumes
- Letters and Applications

Phase 4: The Interview
- Preparation and Practice
- Interviewing Techniques

Phase 5: Follow Up and Evaluation
- Follow Up with Employers
- Accept Offer or Restart Cycle

Job Search Management

The job market is not always organized, so it is important to have a system in place when you start a job search. Employers use a variety of hiring techniques and processes. Their processes may be simple or complex, well or poorly organized, short or long. You, the job applicant, must be well organized—even if the job market is not. As you progress through this book, your collection of job-seeking tools will grow. Use them to develop an efficient, speedy, and successful job-seeking campaign.

The energy you put into organizing your job search directly affects the speed and success of your search. The techniques that follow will help you maximize your efforts.

Track Your Progress

One of the most useful things you can do as a job seeker is to keep track of everything you do for your job search. You may be applying for multiple jobs at the same time, so this can become a challenge. Keep a daily written log or enter updates in a simple spreadsheet or document. Write down employer contacts and research sources (including web sites and passwords and key words used so you can find information again easily). Keep track of skills assessments, possible job leads, resumes sent, applications completed/submitted, calls made, e-mails sent, online classes taken, and other activities. To get started, use the form in Career Action 1-1.

Establish Good Job Search Practices

If you are just finishing school, you will be competing with other recent graduates for employment. The sooner you start your job search, the greater your advantage will be. Employers sometimes view a long delay between school or your last job and application for employment as a lack of initiative or a lack of employability. The following tips will help you manage your job search effectively:

- ☐ Set up an organized job search headquarters so you can easily lay your hands on anything you need and follow up on leads effectively. Use labeled file folders for your job search schedules, job lead lists, prospective employer records, and so on.
- ☐ Prepare a weekly job search schedule. Use a monthly calendar to schedule your activities one or more weeks in advance. Record the hours you spend on your search each day.
- ☐ Prepare a daily job search plan. Use the Daily Job Search Organizer on your Data CD or the worksheet on page 15 to plan your daily goals.

- ☐ If possible, begin your job search while still a student or employed part- or full-time. (Employers consider students and employed applicants to be more employable than the unemployed. Why? Being employed is proof that you can do a job well enough to keep it.)
- ☐ If you are not employed, begin your search the moment you know that you need to get a job. If you graduate in June and will need a job then, start your search preparations in January—or before!
- ☐ Report for work on your search as you would for a job. Procrastination is the job seeker's biggest enemy. Establish a routine and work on your job search every day.
- ☐ Never be late. Employers expect you to be punctual for all scheduled appointments.
- ☐ Follow up on every job lead immediately. A delay can cost you the job you are seeking.

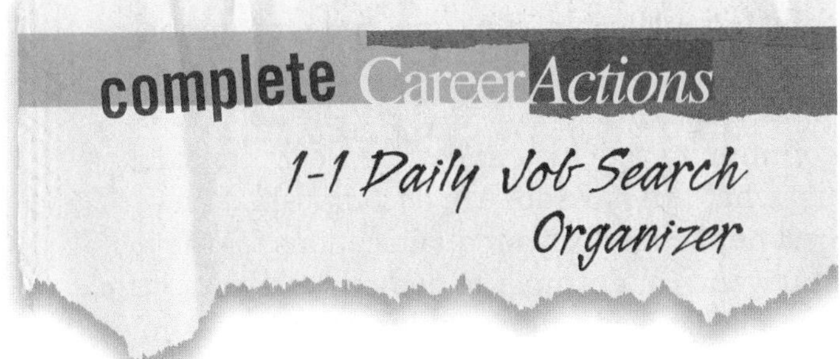

Job Search Files and Portfolios

One of the keys to a successful job search is careful record keeping and documentation of your skills. Two important record keeping tools are recommended to help you reach your full career potential and manage your work in this textbook: (1) Career Management Files Binder and (2) a Career Portfolio.

Career Management Files Binder

To help you assess your learning and prepare for job search and career success, *Your Career: How to Make It Happen* guides you through the development of your own career management files. Your **Career Management Files Binder** will include career development and job search documents (self-assessments, records of experience and skills developed, draft resumes, letters, job search organizational aids, and more). This collection of materials will become a personal record of your job search experience and a resource that you can consult throughout your career each time you seek a promotion, a new job, or a career change. Career Action 1-2 is the first step in organizing this essential career information.

Report for work on your search as you would for a job. Procrastination is the job seeker's biggest enemy. Establish a routine and work on your job search every day.

In using this textbook, you will develop information and documents you can use throughout your life to help achieve each new job and career goal. This material will consist of information you record in your Career Actions as well as drafts of job search documents you create in these assignments, such as your resume, cover letter, networking lists, and more. Altogether, this valuable career data will form your Career Management Files Binder and provide the essential base of career information you will need throughout your career. This information will also be in a format that is easy to retrieve and update any time you seek a new position in your career.

1. **Create a Career Management Files Binder.** Set up a system for collecting, organizing, and updating your career information. You will need most of this data whenever you seek a new job, an advancement, or a new career. Use a ring binder to serve as your Career Management Files Binder. Include divider tabs, labeled Chapter 1 through Chapter 14 with several extra sections for notes, examples, etc. You can also use tabs with topic labels, such as "network list," "references," "resume," "cover letter," and so on.
2. **File Completed Career Actions.** As you complete the activities in this text, place all completed Career Action forms and other written assignments (such as your resume, cover letter, and other career documents you develop) behind the corresponding chapter tab in your Career Management Files Binder. You can use the Career Action worksheets in the book or print them from the Data CD.
3. **Back Up Your Career Action Work.** If you complete the Career Action worksheets using electronic files, be sure to back them up and save them on a CD, flash drive, or hard drive along with all other documents you create for this course (resume, cover and other letters, reference sheet, and so forth). Much of this information will be valuable to you throughout your career for use in revising and updating your career documents and reference data. Keep your Data CD and backup files CD along with the printouts of your assignments in your Career Management Files Binder. In this way, you will be creating an electronic "Career-to-Go" you can take with you and easily update or revise any time you seek a promotion or a job or career change.

complete Career Actions

1-2 Your Career Management Files Binder

Career Portfolio

A **career portfolio** is an organized collection of documents and other items that you will show to a prospective employer to demonstrate your skills, abilities, achievements, experience, and qualifications. Such documents include your final resume, list of references, work samples, letters of recommendation, awards, and samples of your best work. The work in your portfolio showcases your talents and also demonstrates important organizational skills that employers seek: critical thinking, analyzing, planning, and preparation.

Portfolio items can be from paid or volunteer work, internships, cooperative education, clubs, community activities, and more. Begin considering what you have done or accomplished that best demonstrates your qualifications for the job you want. For example, to demonstrate your computer skills, you could include transcripts listing related coursework or a CD or portable flash drive containing examples of multimedia presentations or programming code you have developed. To demonstrate a strong background in foreign languages, you could include transcripts listing appropriate coursework and a letter of recommendation from an instructor or employer who is familiar with your language skills.

You will likely want to file original documents, such as school transcripts, in your Career Management Files Binder and include copies of these documents in your Career Portfolio. This way you will retain a clean master and still have a copy to show during interviews.

Identifying Items for Your Portfolio Begin by identifying your skills and experiences that relate directly to your job target. Then consider carefully what you have done or accomplished that best demonstrates those qualifications.

For example, if you are seeking an accounting job, include your transcripts listing appropriate course work; a CD with samples of budgets you developed or accounts receivable or accounts payable reports you prepared (remove all confidential information, of course); a letter of recommendation from an employer for bookkeeping or accounting work you performed; and so forth. A comprehensive list of appropriate items and ideas for building your portfolio appears on page 8. Consider additional items for your portfolio in Career Action 1-3.

Career Management Files	Career Portfolio
For personal use in record keeping and organizing during a job search	To show to prospective employers during interviews
Documents your job search progress and learning and serves as a reference tool	Showcases your skills and qualifications through high-quality documents and work samples
Includes all research, notes, document drafts, contacts, and work that is pertinent to your job search	Is a collection of your best work that represents your accomplishments and qualifications (including cover letter, resume, references, and work samples)

Assembling Your Portfolio For a traditional portfolio, use a professional-looking three-ring binder or leather folder that holds 8½- by 11-inch pages. File and categorize all of your portfolio documents behind tabbed sections if you use a binder. Use sheet protectors, CD inserts, and other accessories to display and protect your portfolio items. Larger portfolios (17 by 22 inches) are appropriate for art designers, journalists, advertising specialists, and technical writers to store and categorize oversized documents, work samples, and credentials.

Using Portfolio Items During Your Interview

Before an interview, arrange the portfolio items in the order that best demonstrates how your abilities relate specifically to the employer's needs. Ask if the interviewer would like to see samples from your portfolio before displaying anything. Even if the interviewer prefers not to review them, having a portfolio with you makes a good impression and conveys that you are professional and organized.

During the interview, you may still have an opportunity to offer a portfolio sample if the topic suggests it. Simply turn to (or take out) the appropriate portfolio items that demonstrate your qualifications. This tangible evidence of abilities often gives candidates a winning edge in competing for a job. When employers ask questions about your resume, you can use your portfolio items to support your responses. Do not misrepresent yourself in the portfolio items; the work must be your own. Be prepared to provide copies of the work if requested to do so.

Online Career Portfolio Option An online presence is increasingly important for job seekers. If you have access to space on a web site, you should also consider developing an online, web-based portfolio. An **online career portfolio** contains your portfolio documents formatted for display on the Internet. Virtually everything you could assemble in a standard portfolio (described above) can be formatted as pages of a web portfolio. However, a web-based format also allows for enhanced graphics and video and audio files. Include a link to your web portfolio on resumes, business cards, and cover letters, and employers can access the portfolio and review the documents at their convenience. In Career Action 1-3, research services for developing and hosting web-based portfolios.

complete *CareerActions*

1-3 Internet Research on Career Portfolios

Sample Portfolio Items

Examples of items for your portfolio include:

- ☐ Paper documents (including an attractive and professional cover sheet with list of portfolio contents)
- ☐ CD with text-based documents, audio and/or video files, artwork, and similar items
- ☐ Videotapes/audiotapes
- ☐ Artwork/photographs
- ☐ Other work-related items that demonstrate your qualifications and experience

To help you assemble your portfolio, look at this list of suggested items. The Data CD has a more complete list. Use your imagination and aim for a close match with your target job!

Work Experience, Work Performance, and Credentials

- **Resume:** Error-free copies of your resume printed on quality paper. Your resume should be the first item in your portfolio (after the cover sheet). Also, include a CD or flash drive with a resume file.
- **Employer or Internship Performance Reviews:** Copies of all favorable reviews.
- **Licenses:** For professions requiring a license to work in the field.
- **List of References:** References' names, addresses, and phone numbers and their association to you. Past employers, direct supervisors, and instructors are all good references.
- **Letters of Recommendation/Commendation:** Include these letters since they speak for themselves.

Education, Training, Degrees, and Certificates

- **Diploma/Degree:** Put a copy of your diploma(s) or degree(s) in your portfolio; place originals in your Career Management Files Binder (or frame them!).
- **Transcripts:** If your academic performance was good, keep copies of transcripts to demonstrate this strength. Place original transcripts in your Career Management Files Binder.
- **Certificates and Licenses:** Include professional certification (CPS, CET, PE, teaching certificates, and so on) and certificates of completion for continuing education, specialized training, workshops, and/or seminars.
- **Awards:** For perfect attendance on the job and in school; academic accomplishments; employee of the month, and so on. Awards are proof of accomplishments and are of interest to employers.

Samples of Work, Use of Technology, and Information

- **Design Work:** Computer or manual drawings to prove technical ability in mechanical, architectural, structural, or electrical designs.
- **Artwork:** Sketches, drawings, and paintings; photographs or video footage; computer-generated items.
- **Writing Samples:** Showcase your best work if you are an author, an editor, or a reporter. Include samples of technical writing, reports, articles, business plans, training materials, and so on. The ability to communicate is important to employers.
- **Software-Generated Documents:** Include your best examples from school if you lack related job experience (spreadsheets, presentations documents, newsletters, and so on). If you have on-the-job work experience, include relevant copies of your actual work. (Verify that you can share this work outside the company; a potential employer will not trust you if you share confidential information from other jobs.)

Other

- **Military Records:** List your military service with awards and badges.
- **Community Service:** Include any materials that demonstrate active involvement in community service.
- **Forms of Identification:** Front and back photocopies of a valid driver's license, social security card, or photo ID. Many employers request at least two forms of identification to process your application.
- **Proof of Citizenship.** Copies of your birth certificate, passport, visas, and/or immigration forms. These documents show you are eligible to work.

Success Strategies for Marketing Yourself

A job search is hard work and can be overwhelming. Persistence and a positive outlook are key to your success. Review and use the following strategies to help achieve your full career potential.

Maintain a Positive Outlook

Research has shown that a positive outlook can have a powerful impact on personal performance, confidence, and even health.

Positive Thinking and Behavior **Positive thinking** is making a conscious effort to think with an optimistic attitude and anticipate positive outcomes. Positive behavior means purposely acting with energy and enthusiasm. When you think and behave positively, you guide your mind toward your goals and generate matching mental and physical energy. Positive thinking causes the brain to generate positive chemical and physical responses, such as increased mental alertness and physical energy, improved respiration and circulation, and increased beneficial endorphins. This actually boosts your ability to perform and to project enthusiasm, energy, competence, and confidence—the qualities interviewers look for when they hire and promote candidates.

Visualization **Positive visualization** is purposely forming a mental picture of your successful performance and recalling the image frequently. Athletic champions and successful people throughout the world use positive visualization to boost their performance and achieve goals. The act of visualizing the successful performance of any skill or activity in detail actually increases learning and skill development. This is because visualization serves as a form of mental practice or rehearsal that strengthens performance. Practice creating a mental picture of yourself achieving your career goal with confidence and ease. This mental "rehearsal" can strengthen your actual performance.

MAKE IT A HABIT

Form the Habit of Positive Thinking

Deliberately motivate yourself every day. Think of yourself as successful, and expect positive outcomes for everything you attempt.

Project energy and enthusiasm. Employers hire people who project positive energy and enthusiasm. Develop the habit of speaking, moving, and acting with these qualities.

Practice this positive expectation mind-set until it becomes a habit. Applicants who project enthusiasm and positive behavior generate a positive chemistry that rubs off. Hiring decisions are influenced largely by this positive energy.

Focus on past successes. Focusing on past successes to remind yourself of your abilities will help you attain your goals. For example, no one is born knowing how to ride a bicycle or use a computer. Through training, practice, and trial and error, you master new abilities. During the trial-and-error phases of development, remind yourself of past successes; look at mistakes as part of the natural learning curve. Continue until you achieve the result you want, and remind yourself that you have succeeded in the past and can do so again. You fail only when you quit trying!

© STOCKBYTE/GETTY IMAGES

Build Self-Esteem

- Believe in your abilities and make a commitment. Remember how positive thinking positively influences your subconscious!
- Identify your strengths in writing, and focus on past successes.
- Set written goals for improvement, and take action.
- Surround yourself with a positive environment (positive people and positive reading, viewing, and listening materials).
- Look good and stay fit. Looking your best boosts your confidence, and others respond positively to a good appearance. Take care of your body, mind, and spirit. Exercise, eat properly, rest, and balance work with other life activities.

Positive Self-Talk **Positive self-talk** means purposely giving yourself positive reinforcement, motivation, and recognition—just as you would do for a friend. Congratulate yourself when you do well, and remind yourself of your abilities, accomplishments, strengths, and skills. Keep a to-do list, check off accomplishments, and review your progress periodically.

What you habitually say to yourself can have a profound impact on your self-image, your self-esteem, and your performance and success. Your subconscious triggers physiological responses that match the pictures and thoughts you have of yourself to make them happen. Make this work for you by keeping your self-talk positive. For example, "I did a good job on that report," or "I can do this." Avoid sabotaging your positive attitude with self-critical or uncertain language such as "I'm too nervous," or "I'll try." Focus on the positive in goal statements, self-talk, and all communications.

Self-Esteem Projecting confidence requires a healthy **self-esteem** (belief in your abilities and your worth). Think about how easy it is to project a confident, competent image when you feel good about yourself. Because life experiences may change your level of self-esteem, you need to work deliberately at strengthening and maintaining self-esteem. Negative self-esteem and fear of failure can keep you from meeting your full potential.

complete *CareerActions*

1-4 Self-Esteem Action Plan

Get Ahead with Dynamic Goal Setting

Career goal setting involves recording clear objectives and the actions required to achieve them. The main reason people don't achieve goals is that they don't set any goals to begin with. When you take regular action (no matter how small) and make progress toward goals, you create real evidence of achievement. This increases confidence and creativity and boosts your momentum. Action fuels more action! Deliberately plan and regularly work toward your goals to maximize your success.

Use the following steps to focus your efforts and maximize your goal achievement. You can also use this process to set team or group goals.

Define your goals clearly in writing Writing down your goals increases by 80 percent your likelihood of achieving them. It increases your sense of commitment, clarifies required steps in the achievement process, and helps you remember important details.

Define purpose and benefit of your goals Link your goals to a realistic, practical, specific purpose that benefits you. To boost your own motivation, base your goals on inspiration, not just logic.

Develop action plan, set deadlines, and act Establish subgoals. Divide each main goal into logical, progressive steps. Set deadlines and priorities for completing each step. Complete the steps on time.

Identify your support and resources forces Examples of supportive forces include instructors, books, training, people who encourage you to persevere, skilled coaches or mentors, and printed and online research materials. Share your goals with others to gain assistance and increase your sense of responsibility.

Record your progress As simplistic as it may seem, a long series of check marks on a calendar can motivate you by providing a sense of accomplishment. Don't let missing an occasional daily goal deter you, however. Keep focusing on the ultimate goal. Stay the course until you succeed.

Reward yourself Rewards are motivators. As you make progress toward your goals, do something nice for yourself.

Evaluate and revise as necessary Evaluate your progress. Experiment with new methods if you're not getting the results you want, and, if necessary, revise your goals.

Prioritize Your Time

Time management is an important personal and professional skill. Everyone has 24 hours in every day, but successful people learn to make the most of their time by prioritizing and organizing. Try some of these basic time management tips:

- ☐ Decide which activities are important and make sure those get done.
- ☐ Plan ahead to avoid doing everything at the last minute.
- ☐ Break large projects into small manageable steps.
- ☐ Practice using small amounts of time productively.
- ☐ Try new ways to take care of necessary but unrewarding activities in less time.
- ☐ Use a calendar or daily planner.
- ☐ Decide which activities are not important. Take control and cut back.

Develop Assertive Abilities

Assertive behavior is critical in your job search because it conveys self-esteem and capability. Employers avoid hiring people who lack confidence and have difficulty expressing themselves. They also avoid aggressive people who are overly confident, pushy, and controlling.

Employers hire people who behave confidently and who are able to convey their job qualifications clearly. Employers want employees who strengthen human relations and project competence in the workplace through assertive behavior. They hire applicants who demonstrate assertiveness in interviews, resumes, and all communications.

To reach your full career potential, be assertive and tactful in expressing yourself, and always respect the rights of others.

Look good and stay fit. Looking your best boosts your confidence, and others respond positively to a good appearance. Take care of your body, mind, and spirit. Exercise, eat properly, rest, and balance work with other life activities.

Develop Proactive Skills

In his world-acclaimed book, *7 Habits of Highly Successful People*, Stephen Covey emphasizes that the way people typically approach challenging situations and tasks is a major determinant of their career success. People who use a **proactive approach** boost their careers by focusing on solving problems, being responsible, and taking positive actions.

People who use a **reactive approach** sabotage their success by focusing on problems and avoiding difficult situations. Using proactive skills leads to many career benefits such as positive work relationships, improved work performance, better problem solving skills, more motivation, and enhanced self-esteem.

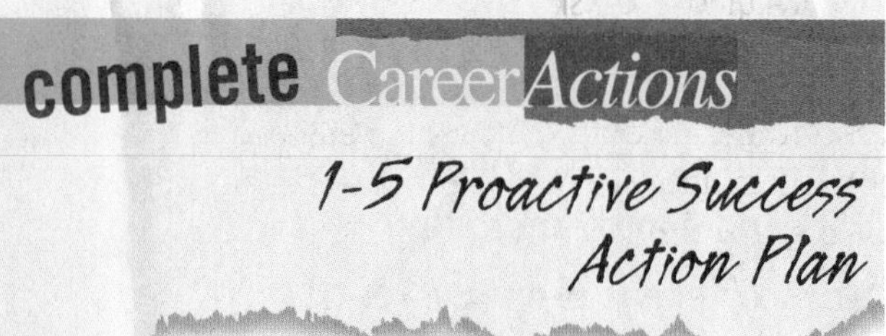

Next Steps

Complete all the Career Action assignments in this chapter to understand the phases of the job search, organize your own job search, and set up your Career Management Files Binder and Career Portfolio. These record keeping systems will be the proof of your skills and qualifications that you will use throughout your job search. File your completed work in your binder along with any important research sources you consulted.

Practice confidence boosting actions and attitudes using the success strategies emphasized in this chapter to reach your full career potential. Apply these success strategies regularly throughout your job search and career. Throughout your life, pursue your goals with an assertive belief in yourself and your rights, and practice thinking and acting positively and proactively. Success is not a one-time destination; it's a lifelong journey. In the next chapter, you will explore the world of work and begin to assess your skills in terms of an employer's expectations.

Typical Proactive Behaviors	Typical Reactive Behaviors
Focus on problem solving and personal growth	Focus on problems/difficulties of the situation (not on solutions) and have a generally negative attitude
Take responsibility for own behavior and for personal or team assignments and productivity	Blame others or circumstances for the difficulty or try to shift responsibility for solution to others
Seek synergistic solutions through productive activities	Procrastinate in the face of a difficult task or problem relationships
Employ personal motivation skills based on positive expectations	Don't seek resources for problem solving (networking, researching for useful information, and so on)
Encourage and assist others	Don't strive to motivate self or others to improve or excel
Network and strive to develop mutually beneficial relationships, share information and perspectives, and get and give support	Diminish energy of others

Chapter Checklist

Check each of the actions you are currently taking to increase your career success:

- Planning and organizing my job search and spending time on my job search every day.
- Collecting and filing items that will help me organize my job search and demonstrate my qualifications.
- Developing a portfolio of my best work to demonstrate job qualifications for prospective employers.
- Thinking and acting positively and developing my self-esteem.
- Writing effective goals and taking regular action to achieve them.
- Practicing assertive behaviors that show my confidence and capabilities.
- Practicing proactive skills that show responsibility and a focus on problem solving.

Critical Thinking Questions

1. Why is the job search process a cycle, rather than a series of steps?
2. What are two important strategies for managing your job search?
3. What items should be included in your Career Management Files Binder? How will the binder be useful to you throughout your career?
4. What items should you place in a Career Portfolio?
5. How can projecting enthusiasm and a positive attitude help you in your job search?
6. What effects do positive and negative thoughts, images, and self-talk have on performance?
7. Would you rate your own assertiveness skills as excellent, good, or needing improvement? If you need improvement, what specific actions can you take to strengthen these skills?

For convenient access to valuable career resources, study tools, activities, and job information links, visit the companion web site for this text: www.cengage.com/careerreadiness/levitt.

Trial Run

The beginning of your job search is a good time to make a thorough and honest evaluation of the organizational skills and success attitudes you will need to market yourself effectively in a job search. Read the following statements and rate yourself using the following scale.

Rating Scale: 1 to 4 (1 = not really; 2 = sometimes/somewhat; 3 = usually; 4 = definitely

______ 1. I understand the phases of the job search and the job search activities in each phase.

______ 2. I understand why it is important to track job search progress and manage time effectively.

______ 3. I use documents and spreadsheets to record my job search activities.

______ 4. I spend time on job search activities every day.

______ 5. I use time management strategies to increase my productivity, and I rarely procrastinate.

______ 6. I understand what materials to store in my Career Management Files Binder.

______ 7. I understand the importance of positive thinking and behavior for my job search.

______ 8. I use success strategies to motivate myself.

______ 9. I know how to visualize my success.

______ 10. I practice positive self-talk to increase my confidence.

______ 11. I know how to increase my self-esteem.

______ 12. I write down my goals and develop action plans for meeting my goals.

______ 13. I understand the difference between being assertive and being aggressive.

______ 14. I practice proactive skills that focus on solutions, taking responsibility, and building relationships.

On which items did you give yourself the highest score? Why did you score so well on these items?

On which items did you give yourself a low score?

Choose one (or more) of the low-scoring statements and write a goal for improving in that area. Give yourself a time frame and write action plan steps for achieving the goal.

1-1 Daily Job Search Organizer

Directions: Access this worksheet on your Data CD or make multiple copies of this page. Use this form to record your job search activities each day. Record the names of employers and contact information. List resources and web sites you used, and summarize your job search goals for the next day. Complete the last three sections of the Worksheet at the end of the day, including a summary of your progress, a list of new job leads, and any necessary follow-up (sending a thank-you note or resume, for example). Also, note whether you achieved the purpose of each contact made.

Date: _______ **Number of hours spent on job search:** _______ **From:** _______ **To:** _______

Contacts:

Employer, Name of Contact, and Job Target (include full address/phone/e-mail)	Form of Contact (personal visit, phone call, letter, e-mail contact)	Purpose of Contact (Documents sent)	Purpose Achieved (Yes/No)

Job Research Sources:

Web Site or Resource Title	Information Found	Password or log-in used	Useful Source? (Yes/No)

Other Job Search Activities:

Summary of Progress Made Today:

New Job Leads:

Follow-up/Next Steps/Goals for Tomorrow:

Career Action

1-2 Your Career Management Files Binder

Directions: Follow the instructions on page 5 to set up your own Career Management Files Binder. In this binder, store completed Career Action assignments specified throughout the book. When you have completed all of these assignments, you will have a valuable collection of career-related information that you can use throughout your life. Your completed binder will include records of your education and work experience, summaries of job- and career-related values and skills, resumes, cover letters, and more. Make a list of all the sections/tabs in your binder.

Career Action

1-3 Internet Research on Career Portfolios

Directions: Use your favorite search engine to find examples of items to include in a career portfolio. Think about the specific career area that interests you, and make a list of at least five job-specific items that you could include in a portfolio to demonstrate your work skills and qualities. (For instance, if you seek a position as a cook or chef, you might include a sample menu, recipes, and nutritional analysis.)

Also, search for articles and advice on portfolios, samples of online career portfolios, and information on online services that can host and provide templates for portfolios. Enter the search string "online career portfolio," or "web portfolio" to initiate your search. Record your findings below.

1-4 Self-Esteem Action Plan

Directions: Begin by describing yourself in writing. You may want to ask a friend or family member to help. List your positive and negative traits.

My Positive Traits **My Negative Traits**

Which list is longer? If it's your positive list, you have a good base for self-esteem. If it's your negative list, you must work harder to develop a strong sense of self-confidence. By doing so, you will strengthen your assertive abilities because having healthy self-esteem makes behaving assertively easy.

Next, identify negative images you want to change. Begin with the trait you think you should improve first. An example of a negative trait may be a lack of initiative, expressiveness, or organization. Improving your self-image often requires developing a positive habit, such as reading more to improve your vocabulary or exercising to improve fitness.

After you identify the traits you want to improve, develop an Action Plan. Write your goal in positive terms. Write your Action Plan so you can evaluate it daily. This makes progress easy to evaluate and provides reinforcement. Put a check mark on your calendar each day you make progress toward your goal. This may seem simplistic, but it is surprisingly motivational.

Goal: To improve my …

Personal Action Plan for Achieving Goal: To achieve my goal, I will complete the following steps:

Time Frame for Completing Action Plan Steps:

1-5 Proactive Success Action Plan

Directions: Complete the Proactive Success Action Plan form below, or access the online fill-in form on the *Your Career How to Make It Happen* web site (www.cengage.com/careerreadiness/levitt).

Name:

Goal I Consider Most Important in My Life:

Benefits of Achieving this Goal (to myself and others):

Steps I Plan to Take to Achieve this Goal:

Action Steps	Date
1.	
2.	
3.	
4.	
5.	

Positive thinking strategies I will use to motivate myself to achieve this goal:

For Your Career Management Files Binder

After completing the Career Action activities in this chapter, file the following documents in your Career Management Files Binder:

- ☐ **CA 1-1: Daily Job Search Organizer (Make multiple blank copies for future use)**
- ☐ **CA 1-2: List of sections/tabs in Career Management Files Binder**
- ☐ **CA 1-3: Printouts of Internet Research on Career Portfolios**
- ☐ **CA 1-4: Completed Self-Esteem Action Plan**
- ☐ **CA 1-5: Completed Proactive Success Action Plan**

Chapter 2

Know What Employers Expect

Overview

Chapter 2 is an introduction to the world of work and the employer/employee relationship. The chapter also explains the basic work attitudes and qualifications that employers focus on in making hiring decisions and that they require in their employees. In particular, you will learn about growth industries and in-demand occupations and have an opportunity to research skill qualifications for some of those jobs. The chapter activities guide you through a self-assessment from the employer's perspective. The assessment will help you identify your most important qualifications so you will be ready to present them effectively to an employer during your job search. You will also start to think about careers that might interest you, and you will consider how your skills and talents match up with the careers.

Objectives

- Learn about basic expectations in the world of work and understand the employer/employee relationship.
- Learn about growing industries and in-demand occupations and research the requirements of those careers.
- Understand the different types of skills and competencies that employers require and start to assess your skills from an employer's perspective.

chapter 2 CareerActions

2-1: Employer/Employee Relationship and Expectations

2-2: Internet Research on In-Demand Jobs

2-3: Workplace Skills and Competencies Profile

2-4: Career Competencies Inventory

Jump Start Your Workplace Knowledge

How much do you know about the world of work? Even if you have never had a job, you have probably had plenty of opportunities to observe people in different workplaces. (After all, nearly every place we go is a workplace for someone.)

Think of three different workplaces you visited this week where you interacted with an employee. Think about stores, medical offices, business offices, mechanics, child care centers, hair and nail salons, movie theaters, train stations, restaurants, schools, etc. Make a list of the qualities the employees in these three workplaces had in common. (Think about their job duties, actions, appearance, attitude, and other characteristics.) Now make a list of the qualities that were different among the employees.

© DIGITAL VISION/GETTY IMAGES

Imagine in one day you interacted with a sales clerk at a skateboard shop, a nurse at a doctor's office, and a manicurist in a nail salon. In what ways would you expect these employees to be alike? In what ways would you expect them to be different?

The World of Work: Basic Expectations

While school prepares us for work, the demands of the workplace are very different from the demands of education. A job for which you are well suited will lead to income, success, and personal fulfillment. However, success on the job can only come when employees understand the expectations and needs of the workplace. One of your first steps as a job seeker is to be sure you understand the basic requirements of the workplace.

If you have held a job in the past (even a summer or part-time job), you will have some familiarity with workplace expectations. However, if you are seeking your first job, you might be surprised to know that you will be expected to look, act, and behave very differently from the ways you act at school and in your personal life. While requirements vary across different types of careers, some basic expectations are true in most jobs.

The Employer/Employee Relationship

In the workplace, you will be expected to understand and respect the employer/employee relationship. The employer/employee relationship is an important two-way relationship and a big commitment for both parties.

- ☐ Employers rely on employees to operate their business, serve customers, and help them make a profit. They invest a great deal of money in training and paying workers.
- ☐ Employees depend on employers for their income and important benefits such as a safe work environment, health insurance, savings plans, training, and vacation pay. They invest a great deal of time and energy in performing job duties every day.

For these reasons, it is important that both parties make a good match—with the employers hiring workers who meet their needs and the employees finding a workplace that fits their career goals.

For the relationship to succeed, it is essential for the expectations of both the employer and employee to be met.

The employee must be satisfied with the pay scale, job duties, benefits, and future opportunities. The employer must be satisfied with the employee's pay scale, performance of job duties, standards of conduct, quality of work, reliability, personality, and potential for growth.

The Work Day and Work Environment

Without exception, an employer needs to know that employees will be reliable and prompt. They need to come to work every day, on time, ready to work. They need to be productive and remain on task the entire work day, from 9:00 a.m. to 5:00 p.m., or follow the work schedule as laid out by the employer.

Work environments vary greatly—from quiet offices to bustling stores and restaurants to loud factories to soothing spas, and even vehicles—but they are always places where serious work is done. Some workplaces are more creative and relaxed. Some are more formal and reserved.

Job seekers will need to be sure they are suited for the type of environment where they will be expected to spend many hours on the job.

Productivity and Performance

The main expectations on which employees are evaluated are productivity and performance. Productivity and performance refer to how well an employee completes his or her job duties. Lack of productivity results in corrective action (including pay reduction) or even loss of a job.

A job well done is important to the success of the business and to the future of the employee. Employees who take pride in their work care about quality and accomplishing their goals. They finish work on time without sacrificing quality, and they always complete work accurately and thoroughly.

Attitude and Appearance

Two of the most important expectations of employees are appearance and positive attitude. Together, they help an employee create an image of someone who is professional, trustworthy, and a pleasure to work with. This image is important for personal career success and for representing the workplace to customers and the public.

Attitude *The Advanced Learner's Dictionary of Current English* defines **attitude** as "a way of looking at life; a way of thinking, feeling or behaving." A positive attitude is represented by a pleasant demeanor, good manners, a can-do spirit, willingness to try, and an ability to get along well with others. Employees who practice a positive attitude toward work contribute to a positive work environment, which leads to better, happier, more productive employees.

> **A positive attitude** is represented by a pleasant demeanor, good manners, a can-do spirit, willingness to try, and an ability to get along well with others.

Other people want to work with (and employers want to hire) people who are polite, cooperative, and friendly. These people send a positive message to customers and do a good job representing the workplace to the public.

Appearance In any career, employees are expected at all times to present a professional, businesslike image to patients, visitors, customers, and the public. Acceptable personal appearance, like proper maintenance of work areas, is an ongoing requirement of employment.

A neat and tidy appearance is always required in the workplace and depends on good grooming and proper dress. Different types of workplaces have different dress requirements, from casual to professional to uniforms, but grooming and hygiene are essential in all types of employment. Proper hygiene and grooming require cleanliness, tidiness, neat clothing, and conservative hairstyle, makeup, and jewelry.

To facilitate safety, make sure clothing is appropriate for the work being performed. To minimize embarrassments and distractions caused by inappropriate dress, many employers have dress codes that explain appropriate workplace attire. These guidelines are generally shared with new employees at the time of hiring. If a workplace does not have a dress code, it is the employee's responsibility to observe the appropriate dress of the employer and other employees and dress accordingly. Certain types of employees may be required to wear uniforms, protective gear, identification badges, or other special dress requirements.

When it comes to image, the outer package improves the sale. Dressing for success is important on the job and critical in job interviews. See Chapter 8 for more information on appropriate attire for job interviews.

Workplace Behavior and Conduct

Proper behavior and conduct at work shows maturity and demonstrates that an employee takes his or her job seriously. At the most basic level, proper conduct involves following workplace rules. This means working hard, always following proper safety and health rules, maintaining a clean and orderly work area, and being punctual and reliable.

Etiquette Another type of behavior and conduct is known as **etiquette,** the expected professional behavior in the workplace based on common courtesy, manners, and cultural and societal norms. Etiquette requires respect, which means treating all coworkers the way you want to be treated and making others feel at ease. It also includes following social norms and rules regarding interactions with coworkers and customers. For example, many workplaces have rules against employees dating to avoid creating an uncomfortable work environment.

Etiquette also involves unwritten rules, which are sometimes tricky to navigate in the

© PHOTODISC/GETTY IMAGES

Watch Out
What Not to Wear at Work

On the TV show, "What Not to Wear," the hosts analyze a poor fashion victim's inappropriate and ill-fitting garments and then provide fashion lessons and a shopping spree for new, more appropriate attire. No such assistance exists in the workplace, but luckily, dressing for success does not require a fashion expert or a new wardrobe. By following your workplace's dress code, using good judgment, and remembering a few simple "Don'ts" you can avoid making a fashion error that could damage your reputation.

- Don't wear revealing or tight clothing such as tank tops, shorts, or low-rise jeans. Showing skin is never appropriate in the workplace.
- Don't wear athletic wear at work. If you are heading to the gym after work, pack a change of clothing.
- Don't wear t-shirts or buttons with political or religious slogans or advertisements. Such attire is inappropriate and could offend coworkers.
- Don't show body art if you can help it. Only the most creative and casual workplaces will allow visible tattoos, piercings, or excessive jewelry.
- Don't forget about neatness. Even the nicest clothes look unattractive when they are stained or wrinkled. Make sure your clothes are nicely pressed, cleaned, and always stain-free.

workplace. For example, in some restaurant kitchens, the senior-most cook prefers to be addressed as "chef," but this is not always the case. These types of rules are learned through close observation of coworkers and through the advice of trusted colleagues.

Proper conduct also involves not taking advantage of an employer. For instance, an employee who is trusted with the use of a work computer should not send personal e-mails or surf the Internet instead of working.

Honesty and Integrity Honesty and integrity are signs of a dependable and reliable employee and a trusted coworker. Working with honesty means working a full day, not being late or taking long breaks, never stealing or borrowing from the employer, and being trusted with merchandise and business finances.

Employees who are known for their honesty and integrity are trusted to follow directions, make smart business decisions, and keep business information confidential. They demonstrate responsibility through their actions and are given more opportunities because people trust them.

Financial Responsibility Managing money well is essential for achieving career success. Even if an employee does not handle cash in a job, he or she will probably have to report expenses or manage a budget in some way. Therefore, financial responsibility and money management are expected workplace behaviors.

Many employers now run credit checks on job applicants. A good personal credit rating is a sign that an employee knows how to manage money. A poor credit score is a sign that the employee is financially irresponsible or takes financial risks.

complete Career*Actions*

2-1 Employer/Employee Relationship and Expectations

In-Demand Industries and Occupations

A good way to start thinking about prospective employers and expectations that might be right for you is to consider growing industries and in-demand occupations—jobs with better wages, more job openings, and a better future. As a job seeker, you will be in demand if you target growing career areas that are going to need more workers and understand the expectations and requirements of those jobs.

The U.S. economy is undergoing a long-term shift from a manufacturing-based economy to one based in service occupations. The U.S. Bureau of Labor Statistics (BLS) Employment projections show that professional and related occupations will grow faster and add more jobs than any other major occupational group, with 6.5 million new jobs expected by 2012. Most of the job growth in this area is expected to be among hospitality careers, health care practitioners, and education occupations.

According to the BLS projections, the growing industries are:

Growing Industries	Projected Job Openings 2006–2016*
Hospitality	7,178,000
Health Care	4,883,000
Education	3,459,000
Construction	2,453,000
Transportation	2,374,000
Financial Services	2,223,000
Information Technology	1,492,000
Homeland Security	960,000
Retail	647,000
Automotive	527,000
Advanced Manufacturing	298,000
Biotechnology	144,000
Energy	131,000
Geospatial Technology	46,000
Aerospace	36,000
Other (Business & Services)	5,325,000

*Includes single-industry occupations only. Occupations that fall into more than one industry are not included.

MAKE IT A HABIT

Solving Ethical Dilemmas

Effective problem solving and critical thinking at work sometimes involve dealing with an ethical dilemma. If you are not sure what to do in a situation, start by asking yourself these questions.

- Would I be violating any laws or policies?
- Do I have the proper consent?
- Will my decision be fair and respectful?
- What are the consequences of my actions? Will anyone benefit or suffer from my actions?
- How will my decision make me feel about myself? Will I be proud of my actions?

Think over the situation carefully and gather as much information as you can. If you have any reservations about an action, don't let yourself be talked into doing it. If you do something unethical, you are the one who will have to live with the loss of reputation and with the consequences. Protect your long-term career by always demonstrating your personal integrity and ethics.

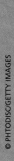

© PHTODISC/GETTY IMAGES

Online Resources for In-Demand Careers

The U.S. Departments of Education and Labor have developed comprehensive online and print resources for exploring careers and special resources for in-demand/growth careers. These resources should be a first stop for any job seeker who is actively exploring career information.

Career Voyages Online To actively promote important growth industries and help job seekers research careers, the U.S. government offers a web site called "Career Voyages." This site is designed to provide information on high growth, in-demand occupations, including average wages and information on the skills and education needed to attain those jobs.

Career Guide to Industries and Occupational Outlook Handbook The U.S. Department of Labor Bureau of Labor Statistics publishes important resources for exploring most industries and occupations, including the *Career Guide to Industries* and the *Occupational Outlook Handbook*. If you have not yet determined your career goals, spend some time perusing these resources.

Printed copies are available at libraries, and online versions are on the Bureau of Labor Statistics web site. In these resources, you will find information on dozens of industries and hundreds of occupations, including details such as:

- ☐ Occupations in the industry
- ☐ Training and advancement
- ☐ Earnings
- ☐ Working conditions
- ☐ Expected job prospects

Career Action 2-2 will give you experience in using the Bureau of Labor Statistics and Career Voyages web sites to explore career options and locate occupational information and skills requirements.

complete CareerActions

2-2 Internet Research on In-Demand Jobs

In-Demand Occupations (by Growth Industry) This table lists the occupations with the largest expected number of job openings from 2006 to 2016. The information is from the U.S. Department of Education/U.S. Department of Labor's Career Voyages web site.

Largest number of job openings, 2006–2016
*Occupation falls into more than one industry; includes numbers for multiple industries.

Hospitality	
• Waiters and Waitresses	1,537,000
• Food Preparation and Serving	927,000
• Maids and Housekeeping Cleaners	463,000
• Food Preparation Workers	451,000
Health Care	
• Registered Nurses	1,001,000
• Personal and Home Care Aides	519,000
• Home Health Aides	454,000
• Nursing Aides and Attendants	393,000
• Practical and Vocational Nurses	309,000
Education	
• Child Care Workers	646,000
• Elementary School Teachers	545,000
• Secondary School Teachers	368,000
• Teacher Assistants	350,000
• Middle School Teachers	217,000
Construction	
• Sales Representatives	476,000*
• Carpenters	348,000
• Electricians	234,000
• Construction Laborers	227,000
• First-Line Supervisors/Managers	178,000*
Transportation	
• Laborers and Material Movers	823,000
• Truck Drivers	798,000
• Shipping, Receiving, Traffic Clerks	213,000
Financial Services	
• Customer Service Representatives	1,158,000*
• Bookkeeping and Auditing Clerks	594,000
• Accountants and Auditors	450,000*
• Tellers	347,000
• Bill and Account Collectors	165,000
Information Technology	
• Computer Software Engineers	300,000
• Computer Systems Analysts	280,000
• Computer Support Specialists	242,000
• Network Communications Analysts	193,000
Homeland Security	
• Security Guards	387,000
• Police and Sheriff's Patrol Officers	243,000
• Fire Fighters	142,000
• Paramedics and EMT	62,000*
• Detectives and Criminal Investigators	42,000
Retail	
• Retail Salespersons	1,935,000*
• Customer Service Representatives	1,158,000*
• Sales Representatives, Wholesale, and Manufacturing	476,000*
• First-Line Supervisors/Managers	423,000*
• Counter and Rental Clerks	291,000*
Automotive	
• Retail Salespersons	1,935,000*
• Automotive Service Technicians and Mechanics	265,000
• First-Line Supervisors/Managers	143,000
• Sales Managers	103,000*
• Bus and Truck Service Technicians	91,000
Advanced Manufacturing	
• Team Assemblers	265,000
• Maintenance and Repair Workers	174,000*
• Sales Representatives	142,000*
• Graphic Designers	95,000*
• Industrial Engineers	89,000*
Biotechnology (emerging industry)	
• Sales Representatives, Wholesale and Manufacturing	142,000*
• Veterinary Technologists and Technicians	51,000
• Medical and Clinical Laboratory Technicians and Technologists	92,000*
Energy	
• First-Line Supervisors/Managers of	178,000*
Construction Trades and Extraction Workers	157,000*
• Plumbers, Pipefitters, and Steamfitters	142,000*
• Sales Representatives	67,000*
• Industrial Machinery Mechanics	56,000
Geospatial Technology (emerging industry)	
• Sales Representatives	142,000*
• Mechanical Engineers	58,000*
• Engineering Managers	51,000*
• Electrical Engineers	45,000*
• Architectural and Civil Drafters	40,000
Aerospace	
• Maintenance and Repair Workers	174,000*
• Sales Representatives	142,000*
• Industrial Engineers	89,000*
• Industrial Machinery Mechanics	67,000*
• Purchasing Agents	62,000*
Other (General Business & Services)	
• General Office Clerks	991,000
• Janitors and Cleaners (excluding maids/housekeeping)	802,000
• Executive Secretaries/Admin. Assistants	497,000
• Receptionists and Information Clerks	489,000
• General and Operations Managers	441,000

Teamwork Skills

Teamwork leads to a more productive and pleasant work environment and to benefits for employees and employers:

- **Collaboration.** People want to work well together and support one another because they identify with the team.
- **Communication.** Coworkers realize the importance of sharing information that others need to operate more effectively.
- **More efficient application of resources and strengths.** Team members apply themselves willingly. When one member lacks certain skills, another is there to fill the gap.
- **Sound decisions and solutions made simultaneously.** A team can generate more discussions, ideas, and solutions than a single individual can.
- **Quality.** Team members feel pride in the team effort and ensure that each member gets what he or she needs from other team members to turn out the best possible work.

4 Skills for In-Demand Jobs

Employees make or break a business, and employers want to hire people who will make their businesses more successful. The most desirable employees have the specific skills, work values, and personal qualities necessary to be successful in the employers' organizations. Sometimes known as **career competencies** or **industry skills standards**, these are the skills employees are expected to demonstrate in a job interview and/or on the job.

Academic Skills

While employers expect to have to train their new workers, they do expect employees to have the required education and qualifications for the job. Basic academic skills, especially a good grounding in math, science, and English are required, and employers expect workers to be able to read, write, listen, and speak well. They also expect employees to be able to apply their academic knowledge to on-the-job tasks. Employees who don't have to be retrained are seen as a good investment.

Education is more important than ever in today's job market. Many of the fastest-growing occupations require specific post-secondary education, on-the-job training, or a bachelor's degree. Your commitment to your education and training will be critical to your career success.

Thinking Skills

Employees in most jobs are expected to be able to solve problems and learn new tasks. These types of skills are known as thinking skills. They are important to employers because they indicate that an employee can think things through, make effective decisions, and learn new tasks quickly without retraining.

Thinking skills also show that an employee knows how to manage and use information and resources, can understand complex systems and relationships, and can prioritize and manage multiple tasks.

Communication Skills

One of the most important career competencies expected in the workplace is the ability to work well with others. Today's workplaces require frequent collaboration with others and working with teams to solve problems, develop products, share information, and perform tasks.

A complex and diverse workforce requires workers to be flexible, respect differences, and work together to increase productivity. It is increasingly important for employees to respect and value cultural, gender, and physical diversity among coworkers. Successful companies view these employee differences as assets to their business.

complete CareerActions

2-3 Workplace Skills and Competencies Profile

Critical Work Skills

Most employers expect a new employee to already know technology-related skills. Employers expect employees to stay current on their computer and technology skills so they don't have to provide as much training. Technology is essential to many jobs, and employers expect employees to be able to use and adjust to new technology quickly.

Specialized industries that require specific work skills, such as health care, hospitality, construction, transportation, and others also require specialized education and certification. Employers assume employees would have learned the required work skills in their training and education. They might require updated certification or retraining to show that the employee's skills are current.

Chapter 2 has provided you with insights into how employers view skills and competencies. Now it's time to think about your own skills from an employer's perspective. How would your skills and qualities be useful on the job?

complete CareerActions

2-4 Career Competencies Inventory

Next Steps

Complete all the Career Action assignments in this chapter to understand workplace expectations and to begin to assess your own skills from an employer's perspective.

File your completed work in your Career Management Files Binder along with any important resources you used to explore in-demand jobs and their requirements.

Knowing your own skills and strengths is the important first step in marketing yourself to an employer. In the next chapter, you will focus on identifying your skills and qualifications and setting goals for the job you want.

[Successful companies view employee differences as assets to their business.]

© DIGITAL VISION/GETTY IMAGES

Chapter Checklist

Check each of the actions you are currently taking to increase your career success:

- Understanding the employer/employee relationship and the world of work.
- Learning about basic employer expectations, including productivity, attitude, appearance, conduct, etiquette, integrity, and financial responsibility.
- Exploring growth industries and in-demand occupations.
- Using the Internet to research the occupational requirements of in-demand careers.
- Understanding the different types of skills and competencies that employers require, including academic skills, thinking skills, communication, teamwork, and critical work skills.
- Thinking about and assessing my own skills from an employer's perspective.

Critical Thinking Questions

1. Many employer surveys have shown that employers value attitude over other skills. Why would an employer prize a positive attitude over technical job skills?
2. Why do you think so many employers have dress codes for appropriate work attire?
3. Why is it important to consider growth industries when exploring careers and thinking about your job prospects?
4. What are thinking skills? Why do employers care how employees think?
5. Why do employers value employees who can work well with others?

For convenient access to valuable career resources, study tools, activities, and job information links, visit the companion web site for this text: www.cengage.com/careerreadiness/levitt.

Trial Run

Working with a partner, watch a movie or television show that takes place in a workplace (such as a hospital, office, police station, laboratory, restaurant, television station, hair salon, coffee shop, school, or any other workplace).

Identify and discuss the employee/employer relationships in the movie or show that you watched. Then, select one character who is an employee to evaluate. Evaluate the employee on the expectations and skills listed below. For each item, give an example to explain how the character earned the score.

Rating Scale: 1 to 4 (1 = poor; 2 = mediocre; 3 = adequate; 4 = strong)

- Meeting employer's expectations:
  Example:
- Reliability and promptness:
  Example:
- Work performance:
  Example:
- Professional appearance and grooming:
  Example:
- Positive attitude:
  Example:
- Workplace behavior and conduct:
  Example:
- Thinking and problem solving skills:
  Example:
- Communication and teamwork:
  Example:
- Critical work skills (using technology, equipment, medical skills, etc.):
  Example:

What advice would you give the character to improve his/her score in any areas of weakness? How could he/she improve workplace competencies to be successful on the job and in the future?

Career Action

2-1 Employer/Employee Relationship and Expectations

Directions: Think of a successful employer/employee relationship you have experienced or witnessed. Explain the workplace expectations for this job:

Why was it a successful relationship?

Now think of an unsuccessful employer/employee relationship you have experienced or witnessed. Explain the workplace expectations for this job:

Why was it not a good match?

How could the situation have been improved or avoided?

2-2 Internet Research on In-Demand Jobs

Directions: Use the Career Voyages web site to research two in-demand jobs that interest you. Search the Career Voyages web site or use the *Your Career: How to Make It Happen* web site (www.cengage.com/careerreadiness/levitt). Write a brief summary of your findings below, or use a separate sheet of paper for your report.

Occupation 1:

Job Title:

Description

Tasks

Skills

Median salary

Education required

Technology

Occupation 2:

Job Title:

Description

Tasks

Skills

Median salary

Education required

Technology

Career*Action*

2-3 Workplace Skills and Competencies Profile

Directions: Review the following skill categories and related career competencies. Check the box to the left of each skill category that applies to you in any way. Then, circle each related career competency you have developed. Think of each skill from an employer's perspective and imagine how the skill could be useful on the job. Finally, list beside "Other" any additional competencies you have that relate to each category.

Skill Category	Related Career Competencies
☐ Art	Drawing, designing, painting, sculpting, computer graphics design Other: ______________________________
☐ Athletics	Physical strength, physical ability, physical coordination, coaching, physical development, agility, team sports, individual sports Other: ______________________________
☐ Communication	Explaining/persuading, strong grammar/vocabulary, organizing thoughts clearly, communicating logically, listening, speaking, good telephone/reception skills, writing, knowledge of foreign languages Other: ______________________________
☐ Computer Technology	Computer operation, researching, training, testing, workflow analysis, evaluating, writing instructions, programming Other: ______________________________
☐ Creativity	Innovative, imaginative, idea person, bold Other: ______________________________
☐ Engineering	Researching, testing, designing, constructing, analyzing, evaluating, controlling, electronic technology Other: ______________________________
☐ Human Relations	Counseling, diplomacy, negotiating, patience, outgoing, teamwork ability, understanding, resolving conflict, handling complaints Other: ______________________________
☐ Management	Analyzing data, directing, delegating, evaluating performance, organizing people/data/things, leading, making decisions, managing time, motivating self/others, planning, budgeting money/resources, solving problems, supervising, interviewing/hiring people, owning/operating a business Other: ______________________________

☐ **Manual/Mechanical**	Good manual dexterity, building, operating, maintaining/repairing, assembling, installing, carrying, loading, lifting, cooking, driving/operating vehicles, performing precision work, assessing spatial relationships, operating heavy equipment Other: ______________________________
☐ **Mathematical**	Mathematical computations, accuracy, analyzing data, mathematical reasoning, statistical problem solving, analyzing cost effectiveness, budgeting, applying formulas, collecting money, calculating Other: ______________________________
☐ **Office**	Keyboarding, data entry, computer operation, text processing, data processing, office equipment operation, filing/retrieving records, recording data, computing data, record keeping, telephone skills, business writing Other: ______________________________
☐ **Outdoor Activities**	Animal care, farming, landscaping, grounds care, boating, navigating, oceanographic studies, forestry, logging, mining, fishing, horticulture Other: ______________________________
☐ **Performing**	Speaking, acting, dancing, singing, musical ability, comedy, conducting Other: ______________________________
☐ **Sales/Promotion**	Persuading, negotiating, promoting, influencing, selling, projecting enthusiasm, organizing, handling rejection, following up Other: ______________________________
☐ **Scientific Activities**	Investigating, researching, analyzing, systematizing, observing, diagnosing Other: ______________________________
☐ **Service/General**	Serving, referring, receiving, billing, handling complaints, good customer relations, good listening skills, patience, managing difficult people, helping others, relating to others Other: ______________________________
☐ **Service/Medical**	Nursing, diagnosing, treating, rehabilitating, counseling, consoling, sympathizing, managing stress/emergencies, good interpersonal skills Other: ______________________________
☐ **Training/Teaching**	Teaching skills/knowledge, tutoring, researching instructional content, organizing/developing content, explaining logically/clearly, demonstrating clearly, coaching others, evaluating learning, addressing all learning styles, using instructional technology Other: ______________________________

Career Action

2-4 Career Competencies Inventory

Directions: Read the following list of workplace competencies and foundation skills and personal qualities from the U.S. Department of Labor's SCANS Report on necessary work skills. As you read about each competency, check the box to the left of each skill or quality you have developed, and circle the portions of the detailed descriptions that apply to you.

WORKPLACE COMPETENCIES

RESOURCES: Identifies, organizes, plans, and manages resources

☐ **Manages Time**: Selects relevant, goal-related activities; ranks activities in order of importance; allocates time to activities; and understands, prepares, and follows schedules

☐ **Manages Money:** Uses budgets, keeps records, and makes adjustments to meet objectives

☐ **Manages Materials and Facilities:** Acquires, stores, allocates, and uses materials and/or space efficiently

☐ **Manages Human Resources:** Assesses skills and distributes work accordingly, uses coaching/mentoring skills with peers and subordinates, evaluates performance, and provides feedback

INTERPERSONAL: Works well with others

☐ **Participates as Team Member:** Contributes to group effort

☐ **Teaches Others New Skills**

☐ **Serves Clients/Customers:** Works to satisfy customers' expectations

☐ **Exercises Leadership:** Communicates ideas to justify position and persuades/convinces

☐ **Negotiates Decisions:** Works toward agreements involving exchange of resources and resolves divergent interests

☐ **Respects Cultural Diversity:** Works well with people from diverse backgrounds

INFORMATION: Acquires, organizes, interprets, and uses information

☐ **Acquires/Evaluates Information**

☐ **Organizes/Maintains Information**

☐ **Interprets/Communicates Information**

☐ **Uses Computers to Process Information**

SYSTEMS: Understands complex social, organizational, and technological systems and interrelationships

☐ **Understands Systems:** Knows how social, organizational, and technological systems work and operates effectively with them

☐ **Monitors/Corrects Performance:** Distinguishes trends, predicts impacts on system operations, diagnoses deviations in systems' performance, and corrects malfunctions

☐ **Improves/Designs Systems:** Suggests modifications to existing systems and develops new or alternative systems to improve performance

TECHNOLOGY: Works with a variety of technologies

☐ **Selects Technology:** Chooses procedures, tools, or equipment, including computers and related technologies

☐ **Applies Technology to Task:** Understands overall intent and proper procedures for setup and operation of equipment

☐ **Maintains/Troubleshoots Technology:** Prevents, identifies, or solves problems with equipment, including computers and other technologies

FOUNDATION SKILLS AND PERSONAL QUALITIES

BASIC SKILLS: Reads, writes, performs arithmetic/mathematical operations, listens, and speaks

☐ **Reading:** Locates, understands, and interprets written information, including material in documents such as manuals, graphs, and schedules

☐ **Writing:** Communicates thoughts, ideas, information, and messages in writing and creates documents such as letters, directions, manuals, reports, graphs, and flowcharts

☐ **Arithmetic/Mathematics:** Performs basic computations and approaches practical problems by choosing appropriately from a variety of mathematical techniques

☐ **Listening:** Receives, attends to, interprets, and responds to verbal messages and other cues

☐ **Speaking:** Organizes ideas and communicates orally

THINKING SKILLS: Thinks creatively, makes decisions, solves problems, visualizes, knows how to learn, and reasons

☐ **Creative Thinking:** Generates new ideas

☐ **Decision Making:** Specifies goals and constraints, generates alternatives, considers risks, facilitates group decision-making processes, and evaluates and chooses best alternative

☐ **Problem Solving:** Recognizes problems, devises and implements plan of action, and facilitates problem-solving and brainstorming discussions

☐ **Knowing How to Learn:** Uses efficient learning techniques to acquire and apply new knowledge and skills

☐ **Reasoning:** Discovers a rule or principle underlying the relationship between two or more objects and applies it when solving a problem

PERSONAL QUALITIES: Displays responsibility, self-esteem, sociability, self-management, integrity, and honesty

☐ **Responsibility:** Exerts a high level of effort, perseveres toward goal attainment, and multitasks effectively

☐ **Self-Esteem:** Believes in own self-worth and maintains a positive view of self

☐ **Sociability:** Demonstrates understanding, friendliness, adaptability, and empathy; manages conflict effectively; is polite

☐ **Self-Management:** Assesses self accurately, sets personal goals, monitors progress, works well under pressure, and exhibits self-control

☐ **Integrity/Honesty:** Chooses ethical courses

Select three skills that you identified in the checklist, and write a description of tasks you have completed where you used or developed that skill. These could be tasks from current or past jobs or school or community activities.

Skill 1:

Skill 2:

Skill 3:

For Your Career Management Files Binder

After completing the Career Action activities in this chapter, file the following documents in your Career Management Files Binder:

- ☐ **CA 2-1: Notes and examples of employee/employer relationships**
- ☐ **CA 2-2: Printouts of Internet research of in-demand jobs**
- ☐ **CA 2-3: Workplace Skills and Competencies Profile checklist**
- ☐ **CA 2-4: Career Competencies Inventory checklist and descriptions**

© STOCKBYTE/GETTY IMAGES

Chapter 3

Know Yourself to Market Yourself

Objectives

- Identify and document your education, work experience, activities, and career-related skills.
- Identify and document your values, preferences, and personal qualities so you can consider the best possible career match.
- Use the Internet to complete personal assessments for planning and confirming your career choices. Use self-assessment and career planning resources.
- Set your Career Target and prepare a Job Qualifications Profile to help you market your skills.

Overview

To achieve each step throughout your career—your first job, a promotion, a job or career change—you must sell the product: you. You must know your qualifications and be able to communicate them clearly to employers. In this chapter you will complete a thorough self-inventory to evaluate your skills and learn how well they qualify you for specific jobs. You will take a complete inventory of your education, training, experience, accomplishments, values, work preferences, and performance traits. You will use this inventory to develop or confirm your career target and create your Job Qualifications Profile.

chapter 3 Career*Actions*

3-1: Education, Training, and Activities Inventory
3-2: Experience and Skills Inventory
3-3: Potential Job References
3-4: Values, Preferences, and Personal Qualities Inventory
3-5: Self-Assessment and Career Planning Online
3-6: My Career Target
3-7: Job Qualifications Profile

Jump Start Your Workplace Knowledge

Would you hire you? Imagine that you are a manager in a field that interests you (nursing supervisor, office manager, restaurant owner, transportation supervisor, etc.), and you have to hire a new employee. What are you looking for in an employee? What type of person would you want to hire? What will the person need to be able to know and do? Make a list of at least 10 education requirements, skills, and personality characteristics that you will require and explain why these requirements are important for success in the job. How well would *you* qualify for these requirements?

Brainstorm several resources you could use to locate this information. Use at least one of those sources to try to find the answers to your questions.

Take a Personal Inventory

In this chapter, all the information you compile about yourself through the Career Action assignments will form your **personal career inventory**. This will be an important source of information when you develop your resumes, cover letters, and job applications and prepare for interviews throughout your job search.

Employers may want this information when considering you for a job. Included in this career inventory are basic personal data and information about the following:

- Education and professional training
- Work experience, skills, and accomplishments
- People who can vouch for your work and recommend you

Your Education and Training

The first step in compiling your personal career inventory is documenting your education and training, including dates, places, career-relevant courses and activities, skills, and accomplishments. You will also document your membership and achievements in organizations related to your job and career targets. This information will help you identify or confirm an appropriate career choice, develop resumes and cover letters, and prepare for job interviews.

Complete this section of your personal career inventory thoroughly and accurately. Put yourself under a microscope, and look at every detail carefully. Ask people who know you well to help you document your accomplishments. Consider scholarships, honors, and awards you have received and competitions in which you have participated.

In describing accomplishments, be as specific as possible, for example: "Member of winning team in math competition" or "Voted treasurer of the senior class."

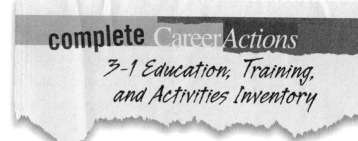

complete CareerActions

3-1 Education, Training, and Activities Inventory

Your Work Experience and Skills

In Career Action 3-2, you will document your work and other pertinent experience and record the dates and places of these experiences. You will also list the skills and knowledge you developed and any accomplishments, achievements, or recognition you received. Include any paid or volunteer work (e.g., community service projects and fund-raising), internships, and cooperative education experience. Be specific about the contributions you made, for example, "Raised 20 percent more in contributions over previous year," "Designed a bandwidth usage tracking tool that improved network efficiency by 45 percent," or "Suggested new file management procedures that reduced filing error rate by 25 percent."

When identifying the skills and accomplishments you achieved through your education, training, and organizational activities, consider two kinds of skills (or competencies) that employers are seeking: job-specific skills and transferable competencies.

Job-Specific Skills **Job-specific skills** are the technical abilities that relate specifically to a particular job. For example, in accounting, preparing a balance sheet using accounting software customized for a client is a job-specific skill. Relining brakes is a job-specific skill for an auto mechanic. Operating medical diagnostic equipment is another job-specific skill.

Employers often require employees to have certain job-specific skills (skills and technical abilities that relate to a particular job), so they do not have to provide as much training. For example, job candidates might be required to show that they know how to use specialized tools and equipment or use a specific software program.

Job candidates must be able to prove to an employer that they have these skills. When you develop a resume and career portfolio and interview for jobs, you will be expected to provide proof by examples, demonstrations, tests, grades, degrees, or certification.

Transferable Competencies **Transferable competencies** are abilities that can be applied in more than one work environment. Employers need workers who have transferable career competencies because these are the basic skills and attitudes that are important for all types of work. These skills make workers highly marketable because they are needed for a wide variety of jobs and can be transferred from one task, job, or workplace to another. Take, for example, a construction supervisor and a bookkeeper. Both must work well with others, manage time, solve problems, read, and communicate effectively. All of these are transferable competencies. Both professionals must be competent in these areas even though framing a house and balancing a set of books (a job-specific skill for each field, respectively) are not related.

Transferable skills are especially important to job seekers who have limited work experience. Students who seek entry-level jobs are often able to develop transferable competencies through coursework, volunteer activities, and part-time jobs. Think hard about your school and volunteer experiences. They may *seem* to be unrelated to your job goals, but, in reality, they are helping you build valuable transferable workplace skills that you can use to market yourself to employers. See the examples on the next page.

> Identify your job-specific skills and transferable competencies to convince employers you fit the job.

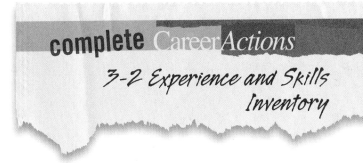

complete *CareerActions*

3-2 Experience and Skills Inventory

School/Volunteer/Part-time Job Activity	Transferable Competency for Marketing Yourself
Receiving an "A" in a business writing course...	Shows workplace writing skills
Being elected Student Government Treasurer...	Shows that the candidate is trusted and has financial skills
Selling the most advertisements for a soccer tournament program...	Shows that the candidate has marketing skills and perseveres
Receiving a perfect attendance award...	Shows that the candidate is dedicated and reliable
Receiving a positive comment card from a customer in a restaurant	Shows that the candidate has customer service skills
Participating in a committee to solve a campus parking problem	Shows that the candidate has experience working with others to solve problems
Working on a school or community newspaper	Shows that the candidate is accustomed to deadline pressures

In every occupation, transferable competencies are as important as technical expertise and job-specific skills. Strong transferable competencies are the keys to showing you have the skills to be successful in a variety of jobs. Several examples are listed below.

Job-Specific Skills	Transferable Competencies
• Taking a patient's blood pressure	• Managing budgets
• Using a specific software program	• Research skills
• Operating a forklift	• Public speaking skills
• Framing a house	• Writing skills
• Driving a truck or vehicle	• Problem solving skills
• Creating a balance sheet	• Human relations and interpersonal skills
• Giving a customer a manicure	• Interviewing skills
• Calculating a store's cash receipts	• Management skills
• Applying makeup on a television actor	• Negotiating and resolving conflicts
• Training a police dog	• Planning and managing multiple tasks
• Roasting vegetables	• Coping with deadline pressure
• Using e-mail to respond to a customer	• Maintaining a positive attitude
• Repairing the dented bumper on a car	• Teaching others
• Cleaning a hotel room	• Time management
• Teaching a toddler the alphabet	• Using resources wisely
And many more...	And many more...

Your Connections

The final step in completing your personal career inventory is identifying job references. A **job reference** is someone who can and will vouch for your capabilities, skills, and suitability for a job. References are typically people who have been your instructors and coaches in school or your supervisors or coworkers in volunteer and paid work environments. Therefore, you should review your inventory of education and work experience for potential job references.

Identify people with whom you have a good relationship and who can confirm (from firsthand observation) your good performance on the job, in school, or in other activities. Employers often want at least three job references listed on application forms. Ideally, these references are supervisors, employers, or others who know your work well. *Relatives or classmates are not appropriate references.* The more references you have available, the better prepared you are for your current and future job campaign. Be sure to ask permission to use each person as a job reference.

If you are qualified to work in two different fields, such as retail sales and accounting, you will get the best results by having one set of references targeted for each field, or a total of six references (three in the sales field and three in the accounting field). Some organizations ask for different types of references. For example, an employer may ask for **personal references** (people who vouch for your good character) as well as **professional references** (people who can vouch for your work skills and personal qualities).

Use Career Action 3-3 to identify people you can use as references. Make note of how they know you and what areas of your performance they can speak about.

complete CareerActions

3-3 Potential Job References

MAKE IT A HABIT

Update Your Skills Inventory

During your job search and throughout your career you will need to update your inventory of skills. It is important to assess yourself constantly. As you develop new skills and gain more experience, training, and education, your goals will change or expand.

Repeating the self-analysis exercises in this chapter throughout your career will help you to identify your skills and see where you fall short compared to other candidates and employees. With this knowledge, you can seek the training and experience you need to make sure you will be successful and grow in your career.

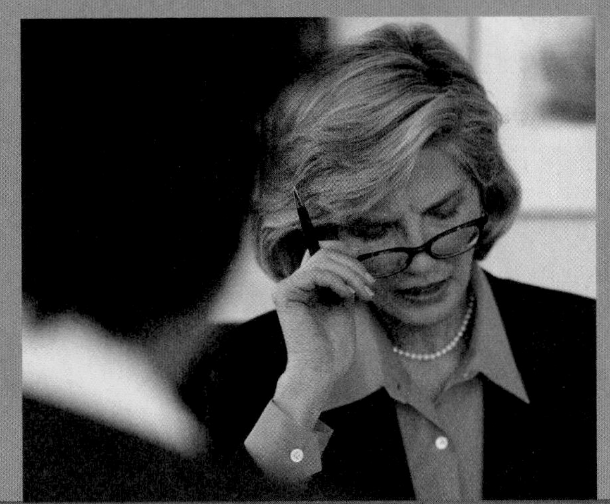

© PHOTODISC/GETTY IMAGES

Know What is Important to You

Also important in knowing yourself is an accurate assessment of your personal values, work preferences, and job-related performance traits. Understanding the personal factors that influence your performance and job satisfaction will help you make good choices when setting job and career targets and when considering specific job offers.

Values

Webster's New World Dictionary defines **value** as "that which is desirable or worthy of esteem for its own sake; the social principles, goals, or

Who Are You?

On average, Americans spend about 2,000 hours per year at work.

That really adds up! So take the time to find a job you love — work that reflects both your values and goals.

Don't be motivated by money. Many people who retire rich regret not having done work they found more meaningful.

Ask friends who know you well, volunteer, travel, read, and explore careers through temp work or a summer job before you settle for something you might regret later.

Don't skip the activities recommended in this chapter. They are designed to help you focus on finding the right career for you.

standards held or accepted by an individual." By working in a job that matches your values, you greatly increase your chances of enjoying and succeeding in the job.

Work Environment

Most people spend a lot of time in their work environment. To maximize your success, identify the work environments where you feel the most comfortable and where you perform best. For example, if you are an extrovert who is energized by working around other people, you probably won't enjoy working in an isolated environment.

Personal Qualities and Work Performance Traits

To get the job you want, you must be able to sell your personal qualities, positive job performance traits, and enthusiasm to prospective employers. Identifying your personal qualities and work performance traits will also help you decide what type of work suits you best.

In Career Action 3-4, you will identify and consider your values, preferred work environment, and personal qualities and traits to help you find a suitable job target match.

complete *CareerActions*

3-4 Values, Preferences, and Personal Qualities Inventory

Self-Assessment and Career Planning Resources

Many professional self-assessment tools and resources can speed up the process of making and confirming a successful career choice. (Note that some of these resources may have a fee attached to them.) Likewise, many convenient resources are available to speed and improve the processes of making and confirming your best career choice.

Review the resources below, and place a check mark next to those you could use to improve your career planning and self-assessment. (Comprehensive sources of job information are discussed in Chapter 5. You may want to review those now because some of them can also be used as career planning resources.)

- ☐ **Your school's career services staff and counselors.** These counselors specialize in assisting students with career planning. They provide aptitude and interest tests, and the centers have current resources for and information about the job market and occupational fields.

- ☐ **The Internet.** A wealth of career planning and job information is available through the Internet. Many sites offer online tools to help you assess your career interests and values and match the results with appropriate careers and jobs. *The Your Career: How to Make It Happen* web site (www.cengage.com/careerreadiness/levitt) links to many of these tools. See your school's career services office for recommendations for helpful web sites, and check out the career center web sites of other colleges and universities.
- ☐ **Commercial software packages.** Some commercial software packages are available on the Internet and through schools' career offices. With these systems, users complete a computerized questionnaire about their personal interests and abilities. The program then provides a list of occupations consistent with a user's answers. Check with your school's career counselor or state department of education to locate the nearest computerized system.
- ☐ **Career planning publications.** Ask your school's career services counselor or librarian for help in locating books, magazines, and articles about your field and current job target. (Many of these publications are now available online.) Your school may also have facilities or links through which you can take the Myers-Briggs Type Indicator personality test, to help you identify your personality and temperament for certain types of work.
- ☐ **People you know.** Contact people you have observed or who you know, people you admire, and people who have jobs like the one you dream of. Ask them to help you explore your readiness for a similar job or career.
- ☐ **Volunteer work.** Volunteer experience can be a big asset when applying for the job you want. It demonstrates initiative and helps you get a feel for a job and a career. You can volunteer on a part-time or temporary basis or ask about arranging an internship through your school.
- ☐ **Summer job.** Summer jobs can also offer a "taste" of a type of work you are interested in, without having to make a long-term commitment. A summer job can give you three to four months of work experience that you didn't have, and you may also find out that you enjoy this work more than the fields you were interested in before. Try retail, canvassing for the environment, tutoring a student, maintaining trails at a national park, walking dogs, or working at a landscaping store. Look online for more ideas.
- ☐ **City, county, state, and federal employment or human resources departments.** For information about government occupations, contact the employment or human resources department that manages employment in your target field.

complete CareerActions

3-5 Self-Assessment and Career Planning Online

Knowing yourself and identifying your goals are essential to a successful job search.

Your Career Target and Qualifications

To know where you would like to go in your career, you must be clear about your career goals and your qualifications. You must know what you would like to achieve, where you want to live and work, and what types of tasks you would like to do. You must also understand if and how your own skills and attributes make you a suitable candidate for the jobs you seek.

Set Your Career Target

The thoughtful self-assessment and research you have completed in this chapter have prepared you to set your career target. You may want to use the visualization skills from Chapter 1 to help you define your personal career objectives. Together with friends and associates, brainstorm appropriate careers. Think about work, hobbies, and volunteer experiences you have enjoyed in the past. What kind of work do you want to do? Where would you like to do this work? How much do you want to get paid for your work?

There are three types of career targets to set when starting your job search:

Career Target A **career target** is a job that is an ideal job for you right now. It completely suits your current qualifications and interests, matches your salary and work environment desires, and provides a challenging and interesting work situation. You have a realistic opportunity of being hired for such a job. You will probably have more than one target.

Stretch Target A **stretch target** is the hard-to-get "dream job" that you would like to have in the near future. It might be in a competitive organization or field that does not hire many candidates; it might offer exceptional salary and benefits; or it might offer a desirable location. You may not be fully qualified for the job yet, but reaching for jobs that are higher than what you think you can achieve gives you exposure and experience and helps you along the path to your future career goals.

Contingency Target A **contingency target** is your "backup plan." You could easily get this job because you are possibly over-qualified or you have a good contact. It is a "safe bet." It is not your first choice because it might lack the

© PHOTODISC/GETTY IMAGES

Watch Out
Don't Lock Yourself Into Only One Option

Successful career planning requires flexibility. Changing technologies and a global economy cause some careers to become obsolete or vastly changed. Broaden your job options. Prepare to qualify for two or more closely related career targets that require related education, training, and general capabilities.

Which transferable career competencies do you have that qualify you for jobs within and between career clusters? Ask a knowledgeable career counselor to help you identify multi-career goals appropriate for your interests and abilities.

To make sure you have plenty of options for success, continue to develop your career flexibility and pursue lifelong learning.

salary or work environment that you desire, or it might not be in your desired career area. It offers security through salary and the opportunity to develop your workplace skills, but it is usually the job you take when you have exhausted other options.

Don't let taking a contingency job be the end of your job search. If you are over-qualified or unhappy, you can leave a job for a better one without burning bridges with a contingency employer.

Always be respectful and gracious, remembering that this work is the choice of others. In the long run, you'll be adding skills that you learned at this job to your Job Qualifications Profile.

complete Career Actions

3-6 My Career Target

Job Qualifications Profile: A Snapshot to Persuade Employers

The Job Qualifications Profile organizes the qualifications information you summarized about yourself. It gives you a solid description of your abilities and how they relate to your job target. This is exactly the evidence employers need to see of a good match between the job and the applicant—you! Follow these steps to start developing this summary and preparing yourself for a successful job search:

1. **Clearly identify your career target.** If you find this difficult, a career counselor can help you. Also, refer to the other sources of career planning information and assistance listed in this chapter.
2. **Write a clear description of your targeted job.** Obtain job descriptions from prospective employers. If this isn't feasible, ask your school's career counselor or librarian to help you locate a general description of your job target in the *Dictionary of Occupational Titles,* published by the U.S. Department of Labor. For more complete descriptions of major occupations, use the printed or online version of the *Occupational Outlook Handbook.*
3. **Refer to the information you compiled in Chapters 2 and 3.** This information will help you complete the rest of the Job Qualifications Profile.
4. **Copy or print Career Action Worksheet 3-7 for multiple job targets.** Develop the broadest possible career planning base by including as many options as possible.

Your Job Qualifications Profile will be a valuable resource throughout your career for writing your resume and cover letters and for preparing for interviews for each job you target. As your career progresses, you can update the profile with your expanded skills and experiences. Your Job Qualifications Profile will result in a well-organized summary of the qualifications that relate directly to your current job target. This profile provides the snapshot of your qualifications necessary to persuade an employer to hire you for the job you want.

complete Career Actions

3-7 Job Qualifications Profile

Next Steps

Complete all the Career Action assignments in this chapter to identify your skills and qualifications and set goals for the job you want. File your completed work in your Career Management Files Binder along with any important resources you used to document your qualifications and skills. Knowing yourself and identifying your goals are essential to a successful job search. Involve your friends, relatives, coworkers, and other contacts in this process. They will be a great source of advice, motivation, and job information. In the next chapter, you will discover the importance of job search networking. You will learn strategies for building a network and using networking skills to uncover job leads.

Chapter Checklist

Check each of the actions you are currently taking to increase your career success:

- Identifying skills, abilities, work experience, values, and work preferences to achieve a good job match.
- Identifying job-specific skills and transferable career competencies to convince employers of my appropriateness for the job.
- Identifying potential references—people who are able and willing to confirm my good performance on the job, in school, or in other activities.
- Completing self-assessments to help match my interests, values, and personality style to appropriate career and job targets.
- Using career planning resources—such as school career services, career counselors, the Internet, and commercial software packages—to help validate successful career choices and goals.
- Setting career targets using visualization, brainstorming, personal reflection, and other techniques.
- Preparing to qualify for two or more closely related career targets that require similar skills and training in order to increase my career flexibility.
- Setting stretch and contingency career targets.
- Developing a Job Qualifications Profile to help in successfully marketing myself to employers.

Critical Thinking Questions

1. Why is it important in career planning and a job search to assess and document your education, training, work experience, and accomplishments?
2. How are job-specific skills different from transferable competencies? Give two examples of each.
3. What is the important role of a job reference in a job search?
4. Why is it useful to identify your work performance traits and career-related personal qualities?
5. What career planning resources will be most helpful in your job search and career planning activities? Why?
6. Why is it important to develop a broad base of skills and competencies that is flexible enough to encompass at least two fields?
7. How do you think you will be able to use your Job Qualifications Profile information in your job search and interviews?

For convenient access to valuable career resources, study tools, activities, and job information links, visit the companion web site for this text: www.cengage.com/careerreadiness/levitt.

Trial Run

After you have completed Career Actions 3-6 and 3-7, research your job target(s) in more detail. Use the career planning web sites identified in this chapter and Chapter 2 to learn salary information, work environment, tasks, job outlook, and opportunities for advancement. Also, identify the education and skills required and the personalities of people who are successful in this job. Do this work independently or work with a partner who has a similar job target and background to yours. Write a summary of your findings.

Next, identify the most important job-specific skills (such as word processing skills in an office job) and transferable competencies (such as math and problem solving skills) related to your current career target.

Job-Specific Skills:

Transferable Competencies:

Finally, evaluate yourself on how well your qualifications and values match the requirements of the job.

Rating Scale: 1 to 4 (1 = not a match; 2 = mediocre match; 3 = adequate match; 4 = excellent match)

Education	
Work Experience	
Job Skills	
Transferable Competencies	
Accomplishments and Recognition	
Values	
Work Environment Preferences	
Personal Traits and Qualities	

Overall, how well suited do you think you are for the job? Why (or why not)?

What can you do to improve your ratings and qualifications if needed?

3-1 Education, Training, and Activities Inventory

Directions: This inventory of your education and training contains three sections: (1) High School Inventory; (2) Post-Secondary Education Inventory; and (3) Seminars and Workshops Inventory. Complete each section that applies to you. List information related to your career target. Be thorough in documenting your accomplishments and achievements.

HIGH SCHOOL INVENTORY

Name of School: ______________________________

Address: ______________________________

____

Dates of Attendance: ______________ to ______________ Date of Diploma: ______________

Grade Point Average: ________ GED (Date): ______________

1. **Career-Related Courses.** List the career-related courses you completed.

____

____

2. **Career-Related and Organizational Activities.** Describe your involvement in school, extracurricular, community, and other activities (examples: clubs, sports, organizations, and volunteer work).

____

____

3. **Career-Related Skills.** List the skills you developed in high school and through other activities. Include both job-specific skills and transferable competencies (examples: operating a computer, calculating numbers, persuading others, using specific tools/equipment, leading others, and working in a team).

____

____

4. **Accomplishments, Achievements, and Recognition.** List all special accomplishments, achievements, and recognition you received in high school and through other activities (examples: selected to play lead in musical production, selected to serve on state debate team, and awarded first place in math competition). List any scholarships or honors you earned. Also, summarize praise you received from instructors, peers, and others.

____

____

POST-SECONDARY EDUCATION INVENTORY

Directions: Complete one form for each post-secondary school attended. Duplicate the form if you attended more than one post-secondary school.

Name of School: ______________________________

Address: ______________________________

____

Dates of Attendance: ____________ to ____________ Date of Diploma: ____________

Grade Point Average: ________

1. **Career-Related Courses. List the career-related courses you completed.**

2. **Career-Related and Organizational Activities.** Describe your involvement in school and extracurricular activities, in professional or other associations or organizations, in community activities, in volunteer work, and in other activities (examples: sports, clubs, offices held, volunteer work, and community projects or programs).

3. **Career-Related Skills.** List the skills you developed through your classes and other activities. Include both ***job-specific skills*** and ***transferable competencies*** (examples: operating a computer, using specific software, oral and written communication, marketing, calculating numbers, persuading and leading others, working as a team member, and researching).

4. **Accomplishments, Achievements, and Recognition.** List all special accomplishments, achievements, and recognition you received for school activities. List any scholarships or honors you earned (examples: awarded second place in state business education skills competition, won scholarship, earned service award, prepared lesson plans that were used as model for campus, and restored two-bedroom apartment).

SEMINARS AND WORKSHOPS INVENTORY

Directions: List the seminars and workshops you have attended. If necessary, add to the list of seminars and workshops by keying in the additional information (if you are using a computer for this activity) or by using additional paper (if you are handwriting this activity).

Name of Seminar/Workshop: __________

Offered by: __________ Date(s): __________

Career-related concepts or skills I learned: __________

Name of Seminar/Workshop: __________

Offered by: __________ Date(s): __________

Career-related concepts or skills I learned: __________

Name of Seminar/Workshop: __________

Offered by: __________ Date(s): __________

Career-related concepts or skills I learned: __________

Name of Seminar/Workshop: __________

Offered by: __________ Date(s): __________

Career-related concepts or skills I learned: __________

Name of Seminar/Workshop: __________

Offered by: __________ Date(s): __________

Career-related concepts or skills I learned: __________

3-2 Experience and Skills Inventory

Directions: Complete this form for each position or project you have had (cooperative work experience, internship, volunteer/paid work experience, military experience). Begin with the most recent experience, and continue in reverse chronological order. Duplicate the form for additional job experience. Complete each section of the worksheet that applies to you. Be as specific and thorough as possible.

POSITION (or ACTIVITY) TITLE: ______________________________

Name of Organization/Committee: ______________________________

Address: ______________________________

Telephone Number: ______________ Salary (if paid experience): ______________

Circle Type of Experience: (1) Cooperative (2) Volunteer (3) Internship (4) Paid Work

Dates of Employment or Involvement:

____

Supervisor Name/Title:

____

1. **Career-Related Skills.** List the ***job-specific skills, transferable competencies,*** and ***responsibilities*** you developed in this position.

   Job-Specific Skills: ______________________________

   Transferable Competencies: ______________________________

   Responsibilities: ______________________________

   ____

2. **Accomplishments and Achievements.** List your accomplishments in this position, preferably in measurable terms (examples: increased sales by 20 percent, reduced order processing time by 15 percent by developing more efficient processing methods, named employee/volunteer of the month, and supervised evening shift of five employees).

   ____

   ____

3. **Praise Received.** Summarize praise received from employers, coworkers, committee members, and customers.

   ____

   ____

Why did you leave? ______________________________

Performance rating (circle one): Excellent Very Good Good Needs Improvement Poor

3-3 Potential Job References

Directions: List at least three people who would recommend you to prospective employers. Consider potential job references from your education/training and work experience along with respected people who can be personal references. Record their names and information below. Plan to contact each reference and ask him or her to write you a letter of reference. Be sure to get their permission to use them as references during your job search. Duplicate this form to list more references if possible.

Name: ______________________________

Title and Organization: ______________________________

Mailing Address: ______________________________

Telephone Numbers: ______________________________

E-Mail Address: ______________________________

How I know this reference: ______________________________

Date I received permission to use reference: ______________________________

Date of reference letter on file: ______________________________

Date of last personal contact: ______________________________

Name: ______________________________

Title and Organization: ______________________________

Mailing Address: ______________________________

Telephone Numbers: ______________________________

E-Mail Address: ______________________________

How I know this reference: ______________________________

Date I received permission to use reference: ______________________________

Date of reference letter on file: ______________________________

Date of last personal contact: ______________________________

Name: ______________________________

Title and Organization: ______________________________

Mailing Address: ______________________________

Telephone Numbers: ______________________________

E-Mail Address: ______________________________

How I know this reference: ______________________________

Date I received permission to use reference: ______________________________

Date of reference letter on file: ______________________________

Date of last personal contact: ______________________________

3-4 Values, Preferences, and Personal Qualities Inventory

Directions: Use this form to identify and prioritize the values that are important to you. It will help you clarify the kinds of work environments you prefer. Remember, there are no wrong answers in defining what is important to you.

PART 1: VALUES

Directions: Review the values listed below, and rank the importance of each as it relates to your career and job goals (H: high, M: medium, and L: low).

Value	Ranking (H, M, L)
1. Adventure (risk taking, new challenges)	________
2. Education/Learning/Wisdom	________
3. Social needs (need for relationships with people)	________
4. Self-respect/Integrity/Self-discipline	________
5. Helping/Serving	________
6. Recognition/Respect from others	________
7. Freedom/Independence (working independently with minimal supervision)	________
8. Security (job, family, national, financial)	________
9. Spiritual needs	________
10. Expression (creative, artistic)	________
11. Responsibility (reliability, dependability)	________
12. Balance in work and personal life	________

Others (List other values below and rank each one.)

________________________	________
________________________	________
________________________	________
________________________	________
________________________	________
________________________	________
________________________	________
________________________	________
________________________	________

PART 2: WORK ENVIRONMENT PREFERENCES

Directions: In the boxes to the right, place a check mark next to each work environment condition you prefer.

Work Environment	Check Those Preferred
1. Indoor work	☐
2. Outdoor work	☐
3. Industrial/manufacturing setting	☐
4. Office setting	☐
5. Working alone	☐
6. Working with people	☐
7. Working with things	☐
8. Working with data	☐
9. Working with ideas	☐
10. Challenging opportunities	☐
11. Predictable, orderly, structured work	☐
12. Pressures at work	☐
13. Problem solving	☐
14. Standing while working	☐
15. Sitting while working	☐
16. Busy surroundings	☐
17. Quiet surroundings	☐
18. Exciting, adventurous conditions	☐
19. Safe working conditions/environment	☐
20. Creative environment	☐
21. Opportunities for professional development and ongoing training/education	☐
22. Flexibility in work structure	☐
23. Teamwork and work groups	☐
24. Opportunities to supervise, lead, advance	☐
25. Opportunities to make a meaningful difference or to help others	☐
26. Using cutting-edge technology or techniques	☐
27. Integrity and truth in work environment	☐
28. Stability and security	☐
29. High-level earnings potential	☐
30. Opportunities to participate in community affairs	☐
Others (List other conditions you are seeking in your job target.)	
______________________________	☐
______________________________	☐
______________________________	☐

______________________________ ☐
______________________________ ☐
______________________________ ☐
______________________________ ☐
______________________________ ☐
______________________________ ☐

PART 3: PERSONAL QUALITIES AND WORK PERFORMANCE TRAITS

Directions: Rate yourself on each of the personal qualities and work performance traits listed below by using a scale of high, average, or low (H, A, or L). At the bottom of the form, be sure to list other qualities or traits that are important for success in your targeted career. In developing your resume and preparing to interview well, you should be able to prove that you possess these traits by giving examples of how you have used them successfully. At the end of the form, write at least five brief positive examples of how you have used these qualities or traits.

Personal Quality or Work Performance Trait	Rating (H, A, L)
1. Initiative/Resourcefulness/Motivation	________
2. Dependability	________
3. Punctuality	________
4. Flexibility	________
5. Creativity	________
6. Patience	________
7. Perseverance	________
8. Humor	________
9. Diplomacy	________
10. Intelligence	________
11. High energy level	________
12. Ability to work well with a team	________
13. Ability to set and achieve goals	________
14. Ability to plan, organize, prioritize work	________
15. Outgoing personality	________
16. Ability to handle conflict	________
17. Optimistic attitude	________
18. Realistic attitude	________
19. Enthusiastic attitude	________
20. Willingness to work	________
21. Orderliness of work	________
22. Attention to detail	________
23. Ability to manage time well	________
24. Honesty and integrity	________
25. Ability to multitask	________

Others (List and rank other positive personal qualities or work performance traits.)

Examples: List at least five positive examples of how you have used some of these qualities and traits in the past.

Career*Action*

3-5 Self-Assessment and Career Planning Online

Directions: Use the Internet to locate and complete two or three career-related self-assessment tests that measure your interests, values, and/or personality style. Print the results for your portfolio. Some versions of tests to search for include The Career Key, a mini-Myers-Briggs Type Indicator quiz, and The Keirsey Temperament Sorter. Resources for this assignment include the following:

1. **The Your Career: How to Make It Happen** web site (www.cengage.com/careerreadiness/levitt).
2. **Your favorite search engines.** Conduct a search using a search string such as "self-assessment" or "career exploration."

Directions: Use several of the Internet resources below to search for information about your career and job targets, including descriptions of your targeted fields and jobs, salary information, employment outlook projections, and more. Prepare a written summary of your findings, or print useful information that you find. Links can be found on the *Your Career: How to Make It Happen* web site (www.cengage.com/careerreadiness/levitt).

- Bureau of Labor Statistics
- Occupational Outlook Handbook
- Career Voyages
- America's Career InfoNet
- JobStar Central
- Collegeboard
- O*Net OnLine

CareerAction

3-6 My Career Target

Directions: Answer the following questions about your current career target. When you have completed the assignment, file your worksheet in your job search portfolio.

1. **In what career field are you planning to seek employment? (Examples: accounting, office management, health care, teaching, administration, construction, and computer technology.)**

2. **What specific job or jobs are you targeting in your employment search? (List every job you are qualified for and interested in pursuing. Maximize your options by listing jobs within and between career fields or clusters that require transferable competencies you have. Don't forget to name a contingency and a stretch job.)**

3. **What specific activities are you most interested in performing in your ideal job? What energizes and excites you most?**

4. **Are you willing to travel or relocate? Explain.**

CareerAction

3-7 Job Qualifications Profile

Directions: Supply the information requested on this Job Qualifications Profile. Refer to your completed Career Actions from Chapters 2 and 3. File your completed Job Qualifications Profile in your job search portfolio.

Title of job target:

1. **Description of job:**

2. **How my education and training relate to the job target:**

3. **How my work experience related to the job target:**

4. **How my accomplishments related to the job target:**

5. **Praise or recognition I have received related to the job target:**

6. **How my skills and transferable competencies relate to the job target:**

7. **How my values relate to the job target:**

8. **How my work environment preferences relate to the job target:**

9. **How my personality traits relate to the job target:**

10. **What appeals to me about this job:**

For Your Career Management Files Binder

After completing the Career Action activities in this chapter, file the following documents in your Career Management File Binder:

- ☐ **CA 3-1: Education, Training, and Activities Inventory**
- ☐ **CA 3-2: Experience and Skills Inventory**
- ☐ **CA 3-3: Contact information for potential job references**
- ☐ **CA 3-4: Values, preferences, and personal qualities ratings**
- ☐ **CA 3-5: Printout of Internet resources for self-assessment and career planning**
- ☐ **CA 3-6: Career Target Worksheet(s)**
- ☐ **CA 3-7: Job qualifications profile**

part 2

Sources of Job Information

Industry Speaks

Steve Townsend is a chef in southwestern Ohio who received the foundation of his training in the military where he acquired international cooking skills while living overseas. Today, Steve's responsibilities include kitchen management, hiring and training staff, new menu item development, and quality oversight.

"When looking for a job in the hospitality industry, it's important to have a good professional reputation and be a pleasant and easy-going person. In most cities, restaurant owners and chefs all know one another and will quickly be able to find out about your abilities and attitude on the job. At the same time, most recruitment and hiring is done by word-of-mouth or through personal knowledge of the applicant. I was able to get most of my jobs in the past through networking among people I knew, positive references, or being available when a new restaurant was opening. As long as you can present yourself professionally and show that you are flexible, creative, and willing to learn, you should be able to get at least an entry-level job where you can start getting more experience."

Chapter 4

Objectives

- Understand the benefits and goals of successful networking.
- Develop a list of people who can act as a personal support system to motivate you in your job search and provide moral support.
- Use networking strategies and etiquette, including online networking, to expand your job search network and create opportunities for job leads.
- Gather career information and guidance through Career Information Surveys (informational interviews) with members of your network.

© STOCKBYTE/GETTY IMAGES

Your Winning Network

Overview

Statistically, the most effective resource for finding a job is networking. Chapter 4 explains how to build a powerful job search network. This chapter guides you through the development of two important support groups to help you achieve your career goals: a personal support system to motivate you and a network of people to help identify solid job leads. You will learn strategies for networking and gain important career and job advice through Career Information Survey meetings with members of your network.

chapter 4 Career*Actions*

4-1: Your Job Search Support System

4-2: Job Search Network List

4-3: Internet Research on Networking Tips and Etiquette

4-4: Career Information Survey Questions

4-5: Career Information Survey (Informational Interview)

Jump Start Your Network

Identify a job or career that you think you would like to pursue. Now, imagine that you know someone who works in that job. Think of 10 questions you could ask that person to help you find out if the job or career matches your qualifications and to learn more about how to find that type of job. (If possible, work on this activity in small groups with classmates who have similar job goals.)

Start by jotting down the 10 things you really want to know about this job or career. Then, draft questions that you could ask someone to find out that information. For instance, if you want to know about a job's hours, you might ask, "What time do you typically start and end your work day?" or "Does your job allow for different work shifts or flexible hours?"

Finally, write five more questions you could ask to gain advice about how to find a job, for example, "How did you find your job?" or "What is best strategy for finding a job in this field?"

Networking Pays Off

Because it is the No. 1 source of finding a good job, smart job seekers focus heavily on **networking**—the process of developing relationships with people who can assist with job search strategies and in finding strong job leads. Networking is the top source of job leads because employers are more likely to hire people who are referred to them personally (through networking). The larger your network, the greater your odds are of finding someone who knows a viable prospective employer. So tap into this dynamic source, build your successful network, and get the word out now.

Did you know that 65 percent of jobs are identified through networking? Successful job hunters find jobs with the help of friends, family members, and acquaintances. Only a small percentage of jobs are advertised, and most job seekers go after those few jobs. You can increase your chances if you seek unadvertised jobs that you can find through networking. The more people you make aware of your search, the more solid leads you will obtain. Through networking, you can:

- ☐ Seek career advice from many people, and make them aware of your qualifications and availability
- ☐ Tap into jobs you would not have access to without networking

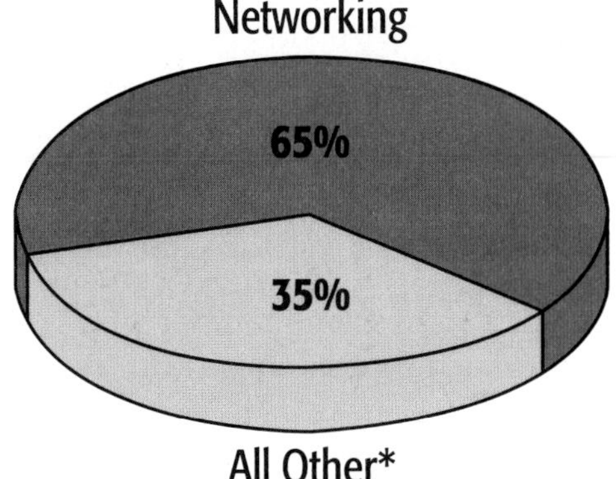

*Other includes employment agencies, ads, and miscellaneous sources.

- ☐ Gain insider information about the industry, trends, and job search and hiring processes in your field
- ☐ Gain access to information about specific employers
- ☐ Get the chance to promote yourself and make a good impression
- ☐ Practice your communication and interviewing skills
- ☐ Seek job leads and obtain referrals to other people who may help you

Your Job Search Support System

One important reason for networking is to have support, advice, and positive feedback while you undergo the challenge of looking for a job. Networking begins with your personal **job search support system.** Your support system is the group of people who can motivate, advise, and encourage you—like a personal coaching team—during your job search and throughout your career.

Good choices for your personal support system are people who are willing to provide you with motivational support, such as:

- ☐ Family
- ☐ Friends
- ☐ School, work, or social acquaintances
- ☐ Former or current employers
- ☐ Career services staff
- ☐ Instructors and counselors from school

One support system member may help boost your commitment. Another may help soothe your ego after a job rejection. Still another support system member who is skilled in writing may help you polish your resumes and cover letters. These people sustain and motivate you when you need a push and ultimately help you reach your full potential.

Select your support system members for the following qualities:

- ☐ Ability to motivate you
- ☐ Ability to help develop or edit effective job search communications (good writing skills) and ability to help you practice for interviews
- ☐ Ability to help you find solid job leads, provide job search advice, and/or share similar experiences

complete Career*Actions*

4-1 Your Job Search Support System

Your Job Search Network

The network of people who can help you with job leads and contacts is your **job search network.** This group grows exponentially with each new contact you make. A good contact is someone who is able to give you career advice, tell you about job openings, arrange an interview, or refer you to people who can help you with these things. People who know you, or have met you personally, are the most likely to help you. Your network begins with people you know who link you to others, increasing your chances of discovering good job prospects.

Starting with the suggestions on the next page, brainstorm a list of possible contacts. Who else do you know? (Don't overlook anyone.) Who do they know? Also, consider spouses and family members of people you know. Someone could have a connection exactly where you need it.

complete Career*Actions*

4-2 Job Search Network List

Strategies for Networking

You could easily have 100 to 500 acquaintances. Multiply that number by two (two referrals from each person), and the potential is astounding. This is why networking is the top source of job leads. The following guidelines will help you get the most from your networking efforts:

Create a Network List and Contact the People on It Remember that job search networking is a numbers game. The more people who know about your job search goals and qualifications, the greater your chance of finding the ideal job. Networking is a tremendous force multiplier. Focus your energies on networking to expand your job search reach and to get the word out that you are looking for a job. By doing so, you will maximize your job and career development potential.

- ☐ Contact people who can help with your career preparation and job search.
- ☐ Discuss your job target with your contacts. In planned meetings, leave a copy of your resume and a brief outline of your job target and qualifications. In spontaneous situations, follow up with this same information.
- ☐ Ask for the names of at least two other people you can contact to find job leads and information.
- ☐ Contact these two people; repeat the process.
- ☐ Follow up on every lead; be persistent.

Update your job search network list periodically to ensure that your original choices were the best ones. Eliminate people who, over time, are reluctant or have too many other commitments that prevent their involvement.

Talk about Your Job Search In your encounters with other people, go out of your way to initiate conversations about your job search. Be friendly and outgoing and introduce yourself to people. If people ask how you are doing or what you've been up to, tell them that you've been busy working on your job search. Often, that is all it takes for other people to inquire about the type of job you are seeking. You never know—they just might know someone in your field.

When you meet new people in social situations, ask what they do for a living, and don't be afraid to ask how they found their job and request their advice. In networking, getting job leads is important. Asking directly is typically not as productive as saying, "I'm looking for a/an _____ job. Do you have any advice for finding one in _____ (industry) (company) (city)?" This approach focuses on the word *advice* and makes your contacts more inclined to help. Be courteous. Also, ask for names of referrals you can contact to seek additional information.

Consider contacts where you work and socialize.

Your Job Search Network Is Larger Than You Think

- Friends, relatives, and neighbors
- Current and former employers
- Colleagues or coworkers
- People with whom you do business
- People with whom you spend leisure time
- Classmates and alumni
- Instructors, trainers, coaches, counselors
- Professionals (physicians, dentists, pharmacists, accountants)
- Service people (letter carriers, hairdressers or barbers, librarians, mechanics, clerks, others)
- People with whom your children or siblings associate

© THESUPE87/SHUTTERSTOCK

Networking During a Recent Haircut

Hair Stylist: How are you today?

Job Seeker: I'm well thanks. I've been pretty busy working on my job search.

Hair Stylist: Oh really? What kind of job are you looking for?

Job Seeker: I'm looking for an entry-level position in computer networking. Do you happen to know anyone in that field?

Hair Stylist: As a matter of fact, I do. One of my regular clients works for ABC Computer Networking.

Job Seeker: Really? Do you think he would be willing to give me advice on my job search?

Hair Stylist: He is coming in for an appointment tomorrow; why don't you leave me a copy of your resume or a business card. I'll give it to him and let him know you'd like to talk to him.

Job Seeker: Thanks so much for your help. I'll look forward to hearing from him.

OR…

Hair Stylist: Unfortunately, I don't know anyone, but I've called ABC Computer Networking for technical support for the shop. They were helpful, and they have a lot of good information on their web site. They seem like a good company.

Job Seeker: Thanks for the suggestion. I'll be sure to give them a call.

Attend Career/Job Fairs Career fairs are excellent networking opportunities because you can connect with many potential employers at one time. Check with your school's career center to find out what job fairs and other networking events are offered in your area.

These types of events call for professional attire and behavior. Practice making a good first impression. Pay attention to your appearance and practice good manners. Use positive nonverbal communication, such as an easygoing smile and eye contact that shows you are interested in what people have to say.

If you are shy or uncomfortable talking to strangers, set a goal for yourself to talk to a certain number of new people at an event. Prepare for a networking event by practicing introducing yourself. Also, prepare some questions that you can ask in any networking situation, and come with some conversation starters, such as, "What brings you to this event?" or "This is a nice location for this event." Another option is to volunteer to work at a registration table, hand out printed materials, or other tasks that will encourage you to interact with many people.

Participate Actively in Relevant Groups Join and be active in professional, trade, and other relevant associations or groups. These types of groups actively encourage people to enter their fields and are eager to offer assistance to job seekers. Nearly every career field has such a group, and most can be accessed via their web sites.

For example, a college student studying physical therapy in New York could easily find the New York Physical Therapy Association by searching online using the terms "physical therapy" and "New York." Likewise, a student working on a certificate in nail technology could quickly search for the local chapter of the International Nail Technicians Association.

The web sites of professional organizations are worth reviewing carefully. They offer valuable resources for getting job leads and keeping informed of industry developments. Many of them also offer networking opportunities and mentoring programs in which experienced members work with new members to help them work toward their goals by offering advice and guidance and by connecting them to resources and other contacts. You will learn more about these groups in Chapter 5.

Join or Start a Job Club A **job club** is a group of job seekers who meet regularly to share experiences and advice, set goals, and offer encouragement. Also known as networking or job search clubs, they can be located through newspapers, alumni and employment offices, chambers of commerce, and online. If you can't find a club that meets your needs, consider starting your own club. Recruit members online or in community newspapers.

Network Online Online social networks can be useful tools for seeking career and job search advice and referrals and for sharing information and support with other job seekers. Originally used for social networking (making friends online), many of these sites are now used regularly for job search and career networking.

Millions of college students already network socially using Facebook and MySpace. Other networking sites, such as LinkedIn, Networking for Professionals, PathConnect, and others, focus on helping members make professional contacts.

Each networking site has its own protocols and requirements, so be sure to take the online tours and follow instructions and guidelines carefully whenever you join a new network. No matter which networks you join, use the following general strategies for effective online networking:

- ☐ **Share information about yourself.** The more your network knows about your career goals, the more they will be able to help you. Fill in your profile completely, and make sure you share detailed information about your education, career goals, current and past jobs, values, and interests. Update your career information regularly to make sure it is current.
- ☐ **Be tasteful and professional.** Remember that much of what you post online is accessible to the public, and employers regularly check these sites—both for networking purposes and to check up on possible candidates. An employer who visits your Facebook site and finds unprofessional or tasteless content or photos or negative remarks about a previous employer will be unlikely to hire you. Avoid potential embarrassment and lost opportunities by always using good taste in online networks.
- ☐ **Be polite and businesslike in your communications.** Nearly everything you say online is accessible to others, and your comments will contribute to others' impressions of you. Make sure your posts and messages are well written and free from errors. Only use abbreviations and texting language if you are certain your network will understand them.
- ☐ **Follow the rules and respect members' preferences.** For example, do not repeatedly try to connect to a member if he has indicated in his profile that he does not wish to be introduced to new contacts at this time.
- ☐ **Share resources.** People will be more likely to connect with you if they think they will get something in return. A college student could be perceived as having little to offer an experienced professional. Show the network that this is not the case by reading and learning what topics are interesting to your network. Help people connect to other people in your network and send links to articles and information that will be useful to the network.
- ☐ **Join network groups with common interests and goals.** Many sites let you join groups that have similar interests or careers. Search networking sites for groups with your interests, skills, and job goals, and sign up to receive their regular e-mails and updates.
- ☐ **Look for high-quality contacts.** Thousands or millions of members in social networks make it difficult to find those members who can help you. Use the search features of the site to search for people you know and people connected to your school or places of employment. Try to find active, well-established connections by looking for members with many friends/connections and many hits on their pages. Also, try to connect with people who pay for premium memberships on networking sites. These people are likely to be very active networkers and will be more interested in connecting with you.
- ☐ **Be careful whom you connect with.** Always search members' information and postings before connecting with them. You do not want to be connected to anyone who has negative, unprofessional, or offensive content or photos in their profiles.

The online community is full of valuable resources for job seekers, and social networking is just one way to access this information. Additional online resources for job search information are covered in the next chapter.

Networking Communication and Etiquette

If possible, try to contact the members of your network in person.

Proper networking etiquette centers around effective communication with the people on your network list. Networking requires effective written communication (via letters or e-mail) and effective verbal and listening skills (via meetings, interviews, and conversations).

Job seekers have to communicate well to make contacts, request meetings, introduce themselves, participate in conversations, interview contacts, and write thank-you notes.

To get the most from networking, take advantage of the following tips:

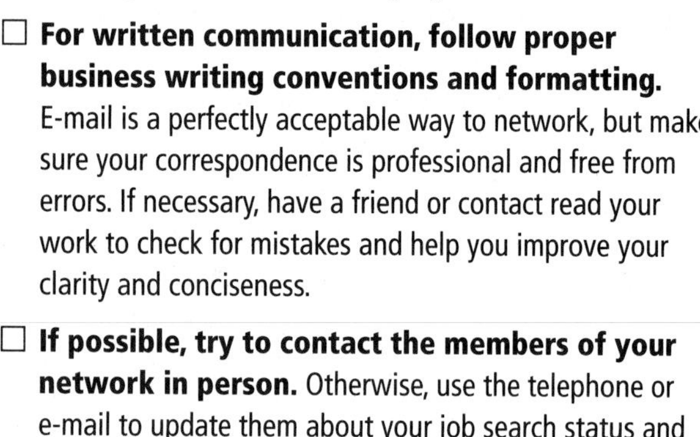

- ☐ **For written communication, follow proper business writing conventions and formatting.** E-mail is a perfectly acceptable way to network, but make sure your correspondence is professional and free from errors. If necessary, have a friend or contact read your work to check for mistakes and help you improve your clarity and conciseness.
- ☐ **If possible, try to contact the members of your network in person.** Otherwise, use the telephone or e-mail to update them about your job search status and to get additional assistance. Be professional, respectful, and friendly in all your communication.
- ☐ **Be a resource to others.** Every job hunter can use regular encouragement. If you're asked to help another job seeker who needs and deserves it, be gracious and willing to do so. Share information with members of your network and send leads to people who might be interested.
- ☐ **Be polite, but direct and to the point.** Show your contacts that you respect their authority and expertise. Ask for their opinions and ask them to recommend additional job search strategies or job leads.
- ☐ **Treat every networking contact (whether a planned or spontaneous opportunity) with professional respect.** Even if you don't believe the advice they offer is good, don't argue; just thank them for providing it. The impression you make can help or hinder the outcome.
- ☐ **Be flexible and make it easy for your contacts to meet with you.** Remember that your contacts are doing you a favor. Don't push to meet in person if they prefer a phone meeting. Don't expect contacts to change their schedule for you. Change your schedule to accommodate your contacts' needs.
- ☐ **Respect your contacts' time.** Never be late or allow a meeting to run long.
- ☐ **Business cards are essential to networking.** They look professional and allow people to stay in touch. Always exchange business cards when you meet new people. Later, write notes on the back of a card to help you remember how a contact might be helpful in your job search. Always keep plenty of your own cards on hand in networking situations.
- ☐ **Follow through with all referrals, and always thank contacts in writing.** E-mail is acceptable as long as it is professional and error-free.
- ☐ **Stay in touch throughout your search and let your contacts know when you get a job.** In today's changing work world, it is essential to build and maintain strong networking relationships throughout a career, not just during a job search.

complete *CareerActions*

4-3 Internet Research on Networking Tips and Etiquette

Sample Networking Correspondence

Whether in a printed letter or an e-mail message, correspondence with your network should always be professional and businesslike. The following writing examples demonstrate the proper tone, business writing style, and language for networking correspondence.

Example Contact Letter

Dear [Mr./Ms. Contact],

I was recently referred to you by Grace Smith of Springfield Career School. She recommended you as an excellent source of information on the physical therapy field.

I am a student about to begin a search for an entry-level position in physical therapy, and I would welcome the chance to hear your advice about the industry and your feedback on my qualifications and skills.

Do you have time to talk with me in the next two weeks? I will contact you next week about a convenient time to meet briefly or talk by phone. Thanks in advance for your insights. I look forward to meeting you.

Sincerely,
[Your Name and contact information]

Example Thank You Letter

Dear [Mr./Ms. Contact],

Thank you for taking the time to talk with me today about my career objectives. I am grateful for your insights, and I will definitely update my portfolio based on your helpful recommendations. I especially appreciate your offer to connect me to your colleagues, and I have already followed up with the contact you e-mailed me.

I look forward to reviewing the online resources you suggested, and I would welcome any additional suggestions and resources you may have. Thank you again for your assistance. I'll be sure to update you on my job search progress.

Best Regards,
[Your Name and contact information]

References

Be sure to identify people from your network who can act as your **references**. References are individuals who are willing to vouch for your qualifications and recommend you to prospective employers. These people should be able to attest to your strong performance at work, in school, or elsewhere and to your desirable character traits and values and suitability for a job. They also should be willing to write letters recommending you to employers. The more references you have available, the better prepared you are for your current and future job campaign. Add their names to the list of potential references you recorded in Career Action 3-3. Follow these additional guidelines for developing references:

- ☐ Only use references who have given you permission to use their names, and thank them for allowing you to use them.
- ☐ Only use references who would recommend you highly from firsthand knowledge and with whom you have a good relationship and regular communication.
- ☐ Because legal constraints may restrict your previous employers from giving a reference, ask former employees of a workplace. They may be more willing to give you a recommendation.
- ☐ Do not use relatives as references.
- ☐ Ask each reference to write a letter of reference that you can provide to potential employers. Keep copies of reference letters in your Career Portfolio; keep the originals in your Career Management Files Binder.
- ☐ Let your references know when you will use their names.
- ☐ Find both personal references (people who vouch for your good character) and professional references (references who vouch for your work skills and qualities).

Make sure you are in regular contact with your references. A colleague from a job you held several years ago is only a good reference if you have stayed in touch over the years and talked regularly about workplace issues and career goals.

It is inappropriate to use someone you have not spoken to in years to be a reference. He or she may not have enough information to provide

MAKE IT A HABIT

Respecting Time

Always arrive on time or early (no more than 5 or 10 minutes) for networking events and meetings. Punctuality is courteous and shows that you are responsible and prepared.

Likewise, always respect the time limits that have been set. Busy employers are not able to take much time from their workday.

Effective preparation and focused questions will help you stick to your time limit and respect your contact's time.

© PHOTODISC/GETTY IMAGES

an accurate view of your qualifications. To maintain your references, always make the effort to stay in touch via the occasional e-mail or phone call with regular updates on your job status.

Potential employers will check your previous employers *and* your references. Previous employers might only confirm your dates of employment, but references may be asked to respond to questions about your attitude, work history, job performance, ability to work with others, and work habits. Coach your references accordingly. You can't control what your references will say about you, but you should always give them information about the jobs you seek and the skills required so that they will be able to emphasize your qualifications and abilities.

In Chapter 7, you will develop a formal reference list to send with applications and resumes.

Career Information Survey

One formal form of networking is the **career information survey**. Also known as an ***informational interview,*** a career information survey is a meeting in which a job seeker interviews a contact about his or her job or career. The job seeker prepares a list of questions, makes an appointment, and behaves as if this were a job interview. The goal is for the job seeker to develop networking contacts and learn about a career or job.

Professionals in your field can provide valuable inside information and advice to help you realize your career goals. Through your meetings, you will gain:

- ☐ **Practice.** You will go directly to the business community as you research and network. You will schedule appointments and practice communicating about your career and job targets—terrific preparation for actual interviews.
- ☐ **Information.** You will obtain important current information about the scope of jobs and the hiring procedures in your field. You may even get valuable job leads.
- ☐ **Competitive Edge.** You will have the edge over applicants who do not complete these activities.

To complete your Career Information Surveys, you will contact two people who hold jobs that are similar to your job target. You will meet them at their work sites to learn about their jobs and the hiring procedures used by their employers. This will help you prepare for a successful job search in your field.

Making an Appointment for a Career Information Survey

To make a survey appointment, contact at least two organizations that employ people in your field. Making the initial contact in person is preferable. If you cannot do that, use the telephone, but first review the telephone techniques outlined in Chapter 9.

Ask to speak with someone whose job is similar to your job target. Emphasize that you are carrying out an assignment from your instructor or doing research in your field. Explain that you want to learn about your occupational field as part of your career planning research. Do not say you are looking for a job. Strangers are more likely to help you with research than with getting a job.

Guidelines for Requesting an Appointment

Follow these guidelines when making an appointment for a survey meeting.

- ☐ Be clean, neat, and properly dressed if you make the appointment in person. Be prepared by having your binder and questions with you.
- ☐ Introduce yourself. State your purpose—completing an assignment from your instructor at (name your school). If you are using this book independently, state that you are conducting career research.
- ☐ Request an appointment to ask a few questions about the person's job and the occupational field. See questions on next page and Career Action 4-4.
- ☐ Confirm the date and time. If you are making your initial contact in person, the individual may offer to meet with you immediately.
- ☐ Thank the person for his or her time and assistance.

Connecting With Hard-to-Reach Employers

Some organizations are not as accessible for career survey meetings as others. If your target employer is such an organization, follow the guidelines below to identify people with whom you can meet for a survey.

- ☐ **Turn to your network.** Ask everyone in your job search network (friends, family, school counselors, and so on) to help you identify someone who works in your targeted employment field—a person you can meet with to gather career information. Your network may provide opportunities or options otherwise not available to you.
- ☐ **Search the Internet.** Many firms have computerized hiring processes and provide application and hiring information through their company web sites or through third-party job-posting web sites. If your target employer falls in this category, obtain the company and/or third-party Internet addresses, search for the application and hiring information, and print your findings or prepare a written summary to submit as your report for Career Action 4-3.
- ☐ **Choose a closely related employer target.** If you are unable to schedule an appointment to meet with your preferred employer, schedule a meeting with a closely related organization. This will still be an opportunity to learn about the field you are investigating and whether it is right for you. Face-to-face meetings give you the valuable business communication practice necessary to outdistance your competition.

To maintain your references,
always make the effort to stay in touch
via the occasional e-mail or phone call and
with regular updates on your job status.
© BLEND IMAGES/JUPITER IMAGES

Sample Questions for Career Information Surveys

To prepare for your survey meetings, write a list of questions to ask your contacts. Following are some sample questions:

Career Information Survey Questions

Questions About Job Scope and Career Development

- Is the firm privately owned, a government agency, or a nonprofit organization?
- What are the main goals of the organization? Is it a product- or service-oriented firm?
- What skills, education, experience, and knowledge are required to qualify for a position such as yours?
- What personal qualities or traits are important in your work?
- What are your specific duties?
- What do you like the most/least about your job?
- What is the average starting salary range for a position such as yours?
- What employee benefits are offered in this position (health insurance, retirement savings programs, others)?
- What future changes do you anticipate in this field?
- What additional or ongoing education or training do you need to achieve your career goals?
- Does the employer offer on-the-job training for employees in your position? If so, what does it involve?
- Does the employer encourage continuing education for your position? If so, what kinds of programs are available, and does the employer pay the associated fees?
- Would it be possible to get a written description of your job if one is available?
- What professional or other associations would you recommend joining to stay informed about this career field?
- What publications would you recommend (books, journals, and so on)?
- Could you suggest other people to help me with my research?
- Do you have any advice for me about planning my career and job search?

Questions About Application, Interview, and Hiring Procedures

- What are the general application procedures for positions such as the one I will be seeking?
- Do you have an employment application form I could see, or may I keep a copy of one to review as a reference?
- What are the organization's typical interview procedures (one person interviews the applicant, team interviews, multiple interviews, typical length of interviews, testing)?
- What do you think is important to show in a resume for a position such as the one I will be seeking?
- What advice do you have for me about preparing and interviewing successfully?

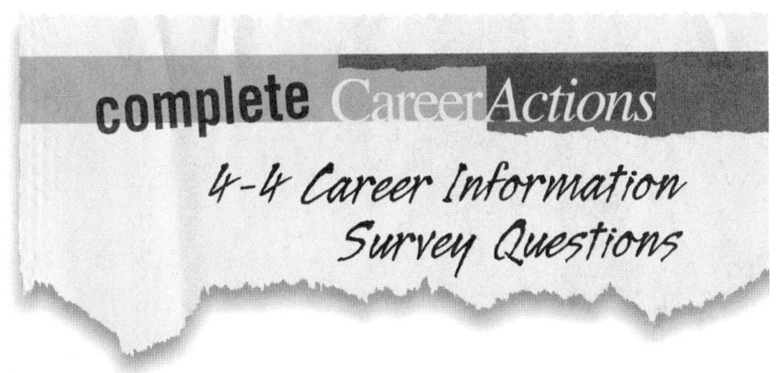

During the Career Information Survey Meeting

Your attitude, actions, and attentiveness during a career information survey meeting—especially one held in your contact's place of work—will help you gather important information about the work environment. Be professional and friendly, take notes, and most of all, be a good listener to gather as much information as possible.

Study the Work Environment Through careful observation at a job site, you can learn about the working conditions for the type of job you want. Before a survey, you should also write a list of questions about the work environment that you will answer yourself. Following are some examples:

- ☐ What type of work area does my contact have? Does my contact work at a desk, share office space, or use some other type of workspace?
- ☐ What equipment and software does my contact use?
- ☐ Is the work environment appropriate for the type of work?
- ☐ Is the environment quiet, noisy, slow paced, or fast paced?
- ☐ Does my contact interact with others? If so, with whom and how often?
- ☐ How do employees speak to each other? Are they formal or informal with each other?
- ☐ Is the dress code formal or informal?

Be on the Lookout for Prospects Be alert to the work atmosphere, and listen for revealing comments from your contacts. Employees of desirable workplaces may mention freedom, trust, pride, teamwork, fair pay and benefits, opportunities for growth, recognition, and fairness in management. Ask about and watch for these characteristics during your meetings. Keep these qualities in mind as you select your actual job prospects.

Be Professional Take your career information survey meetings seriously. If you make a strong first impression, you could gain job leads from the meetings. Some people even obtain job offers. Maximize your information-gathering sessions by following these tips:

- ☐ Be professional. Be courteous and friendly, and dress and act professionally. (See Chapter 8 for guidelines.)
- ☐ Respect your contact's time. Be prompt and respect the time limits of the meeting. You should not take more than 20 or 30 minutes of your contact's time.
- ☐ Learn your contact's name. Use it when you first meet, when you leave, and in follow-up.
- ☐ Begin by restating your reason for being there. Ask well-prepared, open-ended questions. Let your questions show that you did your homework.
- ☐ Move quickly through your prepared questions, and avoid wasting time. Take brief notes of your contact's answers, but do not try to write out every answer.
- ☐ Practice active listening, and pay attention to body language—both yours and your contact's.
- ☐ Obtain the names of other individuals you can contact.
- ☐ Be alert for job leads, and accept help enthusiastically. Do not make a direct bid for a job. (If you do, you risk offending your contact.)
- ☐ Apply the success strategies that you read about in Chapter 1. Conduct your meetings with energy, enthusiasm, and attention to detail.

Learn as Much as You Can About Interviewers Use this information to connect positively during the meeting. Ask about the interviewers' role in the organization and if you may contact them directly. If they do not offer such information, do not risk being rude by asking for it.

Watch Out

Do not ask for a job during a career information survey meeting.

A career information survey meeting is an *Informational Interview*—not a job interview. The purpose of this type of interview is to gather information and network. Always keep in mind that people who grant informational interviews are making time in their busy workday to help you with your career planning. The employer will trust that you are there to gather information and you are not going to push for a job. If you do, the employer could feel misled and may not trust you or want to help you further if a job opening becomes available.

However, you should be prepared to discuss a job opening if the *employer* brings up the topic. Sometimes, successful informational interviews do lead to job discussions, or even offers, and you should be ready and willing to consider the options that sound great to you.

© PHOTODISC/GETTY IMAGES

After the Meeting

Within one day of your survey meeting, write follow-up thank-you letters to the people who helped you. Let them know they were helpful and thank them for their time. It is always a nice touch to mention something specific the employer said and to indicate how helpful that information was. Ask the employer to keep you in mind if he or she can recommend any other people or resources that may help in your career research. Include your address, phone number, and e-mail address under your signature if it is not already in your letterhead. With any luck, it will lead to additional correspondence.

If a contact offers to help you with a job lead, hand deliver or mail a copy of your resume to him or her within a week. This person could become a key part of your job search network. (If you do not have a resume, prepare one using the guidelines in Chapter 6.)

Finally, take the time to review your notes and evaluate yourself. Consider what went well and what you could improve for your next meeting.

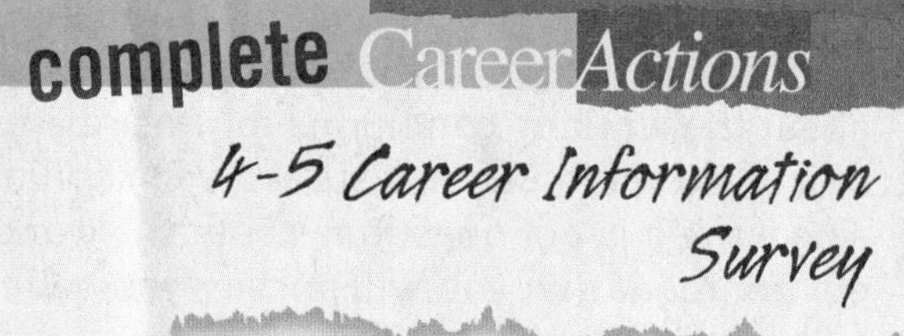

Next Steps

Complete all the Career Actions in this chapter to identify your networking contacts and practice networking strategies and career information surveys. File the completed Career Actions in your Career Management Files Binder. As you make more contacts, expand your network, and conduct more meetings, be sure to update your Career Action forms to ensure accurate records and effective follow-up. In the following chapter, you will explore web sites and other resources to continue to expand your network, conduct research, and locate current information about your field and about prospective employers and jobs.

Chapter Checklist

Check each of the actions you are currently taking to increase your career success:

- Developing a support system: people who motivate me and help me develop resumes and job search letters.
- Developing a large job search network to help me find job leads.
- Increasing my networking potential by identifying as many networking prospects as possible and considering many different networking sources.
- Getting the most from my networking efforts by approaching as many people as possible, joining job clubs and attending job fairs, networking online, and maintaining relationships.
- Conducting organized networking appointments: reviewing my job target and qualifications, leaving a resume, asking for referrals, getting references, sending thank-you letters, and following up.
- Contacting employees in the field to get current information about the scope of their jobs and their employers' hiring procedures.
- Dressing and acting professionally in all networking events and meetings to project competence and encourage job leads.
- Researching to learn about the interviewer so I can make a positive connection with him or her during the interview.
- Following up with contacts and people who participate in networking events and survey meetings by sending them thank-you letters (within one day) and copies of my resume.

Critical Thinking Questions

1. What is networking?
2. Are neighbors and fellow club members as useful for networking as instructors or coworkers are? Explain your answer.
3. Name five strategies for effective networking.
4. Why is it so important to be polite and professional in online networking?
5. How can you make sure your references will be prepared to answer potential employers' questions about you?
6. What benefits can you gain by conducting career information surveys?
7. What is the most significant information you obtained from your career information surveys?
8. What methods can you use to connect with hard-to-reach employers?

For convenient access to valuable career resources, study tools, activities, and job information links, visit the companion web site for this text: www.cengage.com/careerreadiness/levitt.

Trial Run

Working with a partner, take turns acting as interviewer and interviewee in a career information survey meeting. (Remember, in an informational interview, you—the job seeker—are the *interviewer* asking the questions; your networking contact is the *interviewee* answering the questions.) If possible, try to pair up with a student who has similar job interests or experience. Establish a time limit and use the sample questions from this chapter as well as the additional survey questions you have written. Be sure to practice:

- Introducing yourself
- Asking prepared questions in a professional and courteous manner
- Demonstrating that you have done your research
- Sticking to your time limit and closing the interview
- Thanking the interviewee for her or his time

To make this activity as realistic as possible, dress professionally and follow up with a written thank-you note. At the end of each interview, give your partner constructive feedback and suggestions using the following evaluation form:

Evaluate the interviewer on the following elements:

Rating Scale: 1 to 4 (1 = minimal; 2 = adequate; 3 = strong; 4 = outstanding)

____ Interviewer introduced himself/herself politely, stood, shook hands

____ Interviewer asked prepared questions in a professional and courteous manner

____ Interviewer demonstrated knowledge of the career/job

____ Interviewer ended the interview on time and closed the interview skillfully

____ Interviewer thanked the interviewee for his/her time

Interviewer's Strengths:

Suggestions for Improvement:

4-1 Your Personal Support System

Directions: People who boost your morale and encourage you to reach your goals should be tops on your list. Review the areas you should consider when selecting support system members. Then list the names of your personal support system members below. These people will become part of your larger job search network. File this list in your Career Management Files Binder.

Career Action

4-2 Job Search Network List

Directions: Access Career Action Worksheet 4-2 on your Data CD, or duplicate the table below. List the names of everyone you can think of for your job search network. Be sure to include the personal support system members you listed in Career Action 4-1.

Then develop a Networking Organizer with spaces to record the following for each contact: name, mailing address, e-mail address, telephone number, dates of contact, and notes of needed follow-up. Keep this organizer in your Career Management Files Binder.

Networking Organizer					
Name	Mailing Address	E-Mail Address	Telephone Number	Dates of Contact	Notes/Follow-Up

4-3 Internet Research on Networking Tips and Etiquette

Directions: Search the Internet for tips on effective job search networking. Use any of the web sites listed below (links can be found on the *Your Career: How to Make It Happen* web site), other sites you identify, or search engines. (Try using *job search networking* or *online networking* as keywords for your search.) Select at least two articles that interest you, and write a summary of each. File your research in your Career Management Files Binder.

- About.com (Job Searching)
- Career Key
- Monster
- Quintessential Careers
- The Riley Guide

4-4 Career Information Survey Questions

Directions: Develop a Career Information Survey worksheet by preparing two sets of questions:

1. **Prepare the career information questions you will ask your contact during a survey meeting (questions about the job, career development, and hiring procedures).**
2. **Prepare the work environment questions you will answer for yourself through observation.**

Some of the sample questions on page 70 may apply to your field, but you should prepare additional questions that are relevant to your field. The goal is to clarify your understanding of the particular job, the occupational field, the typical work environment, and the hiring procedures. Leave adequate space after each question to record the information you obtain. Place the questions in a professional binder to use during your surveys; projecting a professional image is important in all outside assignments. Take notes during the survey, but do not try to write out each answer completely.

1. Questions About Job Scope and Career Development Opportunities

2. Questions About Applications, Interviews, and Hiring Procedures

Career Action

4-5 Career Information Survey (Informational Interview)

Directions: In this activity, you will conduct survey meetings with people in the workplace to gather industry and job information so you can communicate well during your job search. The purposes of these meetings are to learn all you can about your career field and to identify methods of updating your industry information and skills.

Use a separate sheet of paper to write the answers to the questions you prepared in Career Action 4-4. Schedule as many of these meetings as possible; the benefits of obtaining current information and possible job leads are great. Consider contacting people in your field who screen, interview, and hire job applicants to discuss the job hiring processes in particular. This could put you closer to a future job interview if you perform impressively during your information-gathering meeting.

Small companies often have only a few employees; the owner of a company may also be the company's hiring authority.

Remember: Do not ask for a job or an interview during these meetings.

1. **Contact at least two people in your target industry who are recognized for their ability and accomplishments.** Ask your schools' career services staff, instructors, family, and friends to suggest people to contact.
2. **Call and ask whether your contacts can meet with you to discuss career development questions.** Schedule a time, date, and place to meet.
3. **Be well dressed and on time.** Such meetings can lead to referrals or job offers.
4. **Project professionalism.** Keep your neatly prepared survey questions in a professional binder. (Use the sample questions from the chapter and/or the questions you prepared in Career Action 4-4.)
5. **Be prepared to discuss your findings in class, or write a summary report.**

Follow Up and Evaluation

After the meeting, be sure to follow up with a thank-you note.

Review your notes and write out the answers to your survey questions to be sure you gathered the information you need.

Take the time to evaluate your performance. Think about what went well and what you would improve for the next time.

For Your Career Management Files Binder

After completing the Career Action activities in this chapter, file the following documents in your Career Management Files Binder:

- ☐ **CA 4-1: List of support system members**
- ☐ **CA 4-2: Network list and organizer**
- ☐ **CA 4-3: Printouts of networking articles and research**
- ☐ **CA 4-4: List of survey questions**
- ☐ **CA 4-5: Evaluation of your career information surveys**

Chapter 5

Research Careers and Find Job Leads

Objectives

- Learn how to research career fields, employers, and specific jobs.
- Sharpen your Internet research skills.
- Learn how to use Internet-based career resources and traditional resources.
- Find job leads using the Internet and traditional resources.

Overview

Chapter 5 is a springboard for you to take charge of your investigation into the world of work. You will learn why it is important to know about your prospective employers and trends in your field and how to find current information, from the Internet to more traditional research methods. This chapter also provides strategies for using your research to improve your job- and career-related vocabulary.

chapter 5 Career*Actions*

5-1: Develop Your Career-Related Vocabulary

5-2: Explore Company Web Sites

5-3: Internet Research on Job Listings and Career Information

5-4: Job Leads Source List

Jump Start Your Research Skills

How much do you know about researching a topic that interests you? Think about research projects you completed for a school assignment. How did you begin?

You have probably already chosen a prospective career; a decision you made after conducting some research of the field and completing self-assessment profiles. In this way, you used multiple routes to gain the knowledge you needed. Your career research and search for job leads will be similar because you will use many sources of information—the Internet, people, and organizations.

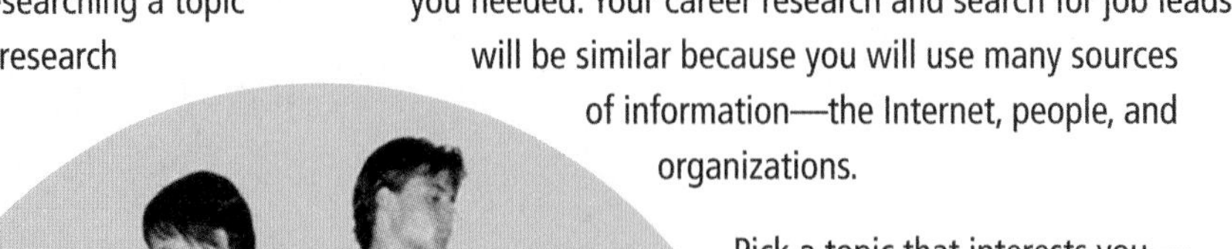

© DIGITAL VISION/GETTY IMAGES

Pick a topic that interests you—gardening, airplanes, the Rock and Roll Hall of Fame—and find as many sources of information as you can. Go online, visit the library, ask your friends, read a book, and see for yourself how many options you have to be informed.

Get an Edge through Research

When it comes to finding a job, the more you know and the better you are at finding information, the more likely you are to succeed. Researching your career field and potential employers can affect the success of your job search in many ways:

- ☐ **Competitive edge.** Employers view job applicants who don't have solid knowledge of their businesses or industry as weak choices. If you are prepared to discuss products and industry facts, you will show that you have made a sincere effort to learn about the organization and the marketplace.
- ☐ **Better career decisions.** Having current knowledge about employers, industries, and job targets allows you to make informed career decisions and assess your interest in and qualifications for specific jobs.
- ☐ **Improved ability to market your skills and get hired.** Researching employers improves your ability to discuss specifically how your qualifications match the employers' goals and needs. Employers are most willing to invest training resources in applicants who demonstrate initiative and commitment through their research of the employer and the industry.
- ☐ **Compensation for lack of experience.** Industry knowledge helps you compensate for lack of actual or extensive job experience.
- ☐ **Increased confidence.** Being well informed helps you feel more confident, communicate more clearly, and project greater competence.

Learn What You Should Know

Strengthen your employability by improving your knowledge in these areas:

1. **Information about the career field.** Learn about industry trends, educational requirements, job descriptions, growth outlook, and salary ranges.
2. **Information about prospective employers.** Learn as much as possible about the companies where you hope to work. Learn about each company's products and services; markets and customers; reputation; performance; key competitors; history and goals; corporate culture; divisions and subsidiaries; locations (U.S. and global); trends and growth indicators; number of employees and diversity; predicted job openings; and salary ranges and benefit plans.
3. **Information about specific jobs.** Get job descriptions; identify the required education and experience; and learn about working conditions, career paths, salary ranges, and benefit plans.

The information you collect through research will help you stand out when you apply for jobs and go on interviews. You will also turn up job leads in your field.

Learn about Industry Trends

Chapter 2 has government data about growth industries and occupations in the United States. The number of expected job openings in each career field is an example of an *industry trend*. There are many industry trends, such as:

- ☐ The impact of economic changes, such as fluctuations in the stock market
- ☐ The impact of social changes, such as the retirement of baby boomers
- ☐ Changes in products or services, such as the voluntary switch from the original CD and DVD format to Blu-ray format
- ☐ Changes in the business model, such as the increase in white collar jobs outsourced to developing countries
- ☐ Increased workforce diversity. Did you know that by 2042 the United States will not have a majority race? The percentage of white Americans will drop to 47%, down from 67% in 2005
- ☐ Financial statistics, such as overall industry growth and salary data
- ☐ Changes in competition, such as new competitors, better-than-expected competitor successes, mergers, and bankruptcies

Take the time to learn about current trends in your career field. Search on your career field plus the word "trends" (for example, *catering trends*). When you research specific companies, look for information about their response to these trends.

Expand Your Career-Related Vocabulary

What do *vacuum extraction, remediation system,* and *capture zone* mean? (Hint: If you know the answers, you might be an *RET.*) Every industry has its own vocabulary. Recognizing and understanding this vocabulary will help you understand your career research, write resumes and cover letters that stand out, and be informed during interviews.

Look up every unfamiliar word, acronym, and term you come across in your research. Employment directories, the Internet, and library resources have the information you need. In a search engine, enter "define *word*"; for example, *define blog*. A strong career-related vocabulary projects competence, but don't overdo it. You don't want to sound like a know-it-all or a phony.

complete *CareerActions*

5-1 Develop Your Career Development Vocabulary

Use Many Sources of Information

The exciting reality of the research process is that there are many ways to approach it, and once you get started, you'll find many people and types of online resources to help you along the way. From the campus career center to the Internet to trade journals, these resources are rich sources of information that can help you make smart decisions about career paths and jobs that match your values, interests, and qualifications.

The Indispensable Internet

The Internet affects every aspect of the job search process. It is filled with career advice, information about specific industries and employers, and job leads. Every "traditional" source of career information covered in this chapter also has an Internet presence, from your local chamber of commerce to the international professional association for your career field.

The social networking sites and job clubs in Chapter 4 are two tools for connecting with other

MAKE IT A HABIT

Remember Who You Are

At many sites, you must register as a user to have access to all of the resources. Registration is usually free. When you visit the site, you sign in with your user name and password. Keep a record of your user names and passwords in your Career Management Files Binder. To keep things simple, consider using the same user name and password at all the free information sites you use.

© TATIANA POPOVA/SHUTTERSTOCK

job seekers and people in your field. You can also search on the name of your career field plus the term "blog" or "discussion forum" or "listserv" (*oceanography listserv*, for example).

At all search engines and most large information sites, you can sign up for news alerts about the issues you are interested in. You register at the site and select the topics you want to follow, and then receive e-mails with links to newly posted articles on these topics. You can also get job alerts through e-mail and text messaging.

Don't become overwhelmed by the vast amount of information on the Internet. Use the resources in this chapter and the links at the *Your Career: How to Make It Happen* web site (www.cengage.com/careerreadiness/levitt) to find reliable sites. Take good notes and bookmark the sites you think are best.

People in the Workplace

Regardless of how up-to-date and informative a company web site is, you need to talk with current or former employees to get a "feel" for what it would be like to work there. People are strong resources for learning about the character and function of an organization and for gathering general information about an industry.

- ☐ **Employees of your target employer.** Current and former employees know about hiring procedures; employee satisfaction levels; job descriptions and responsibilities; skills, education, and experience required for jobs; company objectives; salaries; and advancement opportunities. Don't rely only on opinion, however, particularly if it's extremely negative or overly positive.
- ☐ **Your target employer.** When possible, visit your target employer to get a personal perspective. Be sure to dress appropriately. Ask for literature about the organization, such as a brochure, mission statement, strategic plan, or stockholder's report. If realistic and affordable, try the company's products or services.
- ☐ **Customers, clients, or patients.** Ask customers, clients, or patients for their opinions of the employer's service, reliability, products, and general reputation.
- ☐ **Competitors.** Research the competitors of your target employer to learn about the industry. Compare positions available, pay rates, and benefits, as well as the education, skills, and experience required.
- ☐ **Instructors, professors, and counselors.** These people often know about local employers and industries. Since they may serve as job references for you, be professional, punctual, and reliable when dealing with them.
- ☐ **Recognized people in the field.** Successful people in your field are excellent resources for learning about the industry and prospective employers. Read about career information surveys in Chapter 4.

Research Career Fields and Companies

You will not succeed in finding a job unless you are informed about the industry you want to work in and the companies you want to work for. Being smart about the career you are pursuing gives you credibility and helps you emphasize your related strengths and suitability for a job. "Insider information" is essential if you don't have real-world experience in the field.

Libraries

Your local library—public, college, or university—has extensive resources for job-seekers. Reference librarians and staff can help you locate items such as:

- ☐ Company pamphlets, brochures, and annual reports
- ☐ Dun & Bradstreet's Million Dollar Database
- ☐ Encyclopedia of Careers and Vocational Guidance
- ☐ Thomas Register of American Manufacturers
- ☐ Standard and Poor's publications, such as Industry Surveys, Stock Reports, and Register of Corporations
- ☐ Value Line Investment Survey
- ☐ Moody's Manuals
- ☐ Business Periodicals Index
- ☐ Readers' Guide to Periodical Literature
- ☐ *Occupational Outlook Handbook*, published by the U.S. Department of Labor, Bureau of Labor Statistics
- ☐ Area telephone directories
- ☐ Encyclopedia of Associations
- ☐ Newspaper and journal articles
- ☐ *Fortune* and *Forbes* magazines and *The Wall Street Journal*

Ask librarians to help locate international business information if your target employer has international holdings or is based outside the United States. The main branch of a public library will have more extensive holdings than neighborhood branches.

College Career Centers

These valuable organizations go by different names at different colleges and universities, such as the Career Resources Center or Career Planning Office. Whatever it is called at your institution, the center has a gold mine of career information, with comprehensive resources for learning about industries, companies, specific jobs, local employers, and more.

The center may have many of the library resources listed above, plus other resources directed to students, such as *Job Choices*, an excellent magazine published by the National Association of Colleges and Employers.

The staff can help with every area of a search: taking personal assessments and exploring suitable careers; help with resumes and cover letters; preparing for interviews; and possibly networking with alumni in your field.

If you have already graduated, check which services are available to alumni.

Job Information Sites

Also called career development sites, these comprehensive, "one-stop-shopping" web sites are new with the advent of the Internet. They have job banks (lists of job openings) and information on every topic related to careers and job searches. They also provide interactive tools such as appointment calendars, follow-up reminders, updates about industry trends, and networking contact lists.

Compare the resources on several sites and bookmark the sites you think are best suited to your needs. See the list of sites in Career Action 3-5, or go to the web links at the *Your Career: How to Make It Happen* web site.

Company Web Sites

The vast majority of employers have web sites where you can read about the organization and learn about available jobs and how to apply for them.

Check the sites of several organizations in your field to get a sense of the types of jobs and job titles and to view complete job descriptions

Tame the Internet Tiger

The Internet can be overwhelming. Take the time and effort to develop good research habits.

- If you are new to the Internet, take a tutorial on Internet research. There are dozens—probably hundreds—of free guides and lessons.
- Know what you are looking for. Learn how to use keywords effectively, so you don't get too many or too few "hits."
- Schedule research appointments in your calendar and set goals for each session.
- Bookmark the sites you think are best and keep a record of your user names and passwords.
- If it suits your learning style, keep a word processing file open while you work. Copy web site content into it. Be sure to copy the addresses too.
- Follow the rules. The information on these sites may be free, but it is still copyrighted; that is, someone owns the rights to publish it. Assume that all the sites you visit, except U.S. government sites, contain copyrighted information, and respect the copyrights.
- Know when to stop searching and start using the great information you find. ☺

and requirements. Try searching on each job title plus the word "jobs" to find more job listings.

If your job search is more general, such as a plan to be an administrative assistant, and the employers' business is less important to you, use the general job information sites that list openings from a broad range of industries. Chapters 6 and 7 have information about electronic resumes and applications.

Professional Associations and Industry Trade Groups

In Chapter 4, you learned about networking through professional associations and industry trade groups. The web sites of these groups are reliable sources of up-to-date information on every topic of interest in an industry. They publish online magazines and newsletters you can read at the site or receive in e-mails.

Most groups require membership to have access to all the resources, and many groups have reduced membership rates for students. To find an association, search on the name of the industry and the word "association"; for example, *occupational therapist association*. Many job information sites also have lists of associations and trade groups.

complete CareerActions
5-2 Explore Company Web Sites

Career/Job Fairs

Career fairs are a structured way to meet many potential employers in one day. Use fairs to gather company literature, talk to company recruiters about the company and its hiring requirements, pick up industry vocabulary, and maybe even schedule an interview. You can also check out your target employer's competitors to learn more about the industry. Get a list of companies before the event and research the ones that look promising.

Find Job Leads

All the resources you have learned about to this point are also sources of job leads.

- ☐ **Company web sites.** These sites list available jobs and have instructions for submitting applications and resumes.
- ☐ **Job information sites.** These sites started out to connect employers and job applicants, and extensive job banks are still central to their mission. You can post your resume, search for jobs, and apply online.

- ☐ **College career centers.** Most college career centers host recruiting events. Recruiters from a variety of companies come to campus to interview—and maybe hire—new graduates. The center may offer mock interviews. Some centers videotape the interviews and review them with you and offer suggestions.
- ☐ **Professional associations and industry trade groups.** Most of these organizations maintain job banks, and they often announce job openings during meetings and in their publications. The membership directories are great resources for finding prospective employers. Check current and back issues of printed resources or Internet archives for help-wanted ads, and look for information about employment and job market trends. Companies are impressed with applicants who know about their industry associations and publications.
- ☐ **Job/career fairs.** Employers go to community, industry, or school-sponsored career or job fairs to find new talent, so go; you have to be there to be discovered.

complete CareerActions

5-3 Internet Research on Job Listings and Career Information

Other Sources of Job Leads

The more resources you use, the more job choices you will have and the more quickly you will get results. Don't overlook these sources.

Want Ads You can find want ads for jobs (also called *help wanted ads*) in print newspapers and other print media and on the Internet.

- ☐ **Newspapers.** Look in the help-wanted section, the business section, and virtually all other sections of newspapers from locations that interest you. You can learn a lot about the hiring, expansion, downsizing, or start-up of organizations in an area. Most newspapers also post their want ads on the Internet.
- ☐ **The Internet.** Check job listings and want ads on the Internet. Search the large job information sites and smaller niche sites that focus only on your career field or specialty.
- ☐ **Journals and other publications.** Check the classified sections of printed and online professional journals in your field and other publications that target job seekers.

Human Resources Departments in Private Industry Contact the human resources department of private companies to learn about current job openings. If no openings are available, ask if you can leave your application and resume for future openings, and remember to check back in a few months to ensure that your application is still active. Some organizations have telephone recordings about current job openings.

State Employment Services Through the U.S. Department of Labor, each state has an employment agency that includes a job services or employment services office. You can call the main state information number and ask for the number of the employment services office, or look online. These offices provide career counseling, job search techniques, referrals to upgrade training or education, and information on area job openings.

Chambers of Commerce Contact the local Chamber of Commerce in each of your target geographical areas. Chambers of commerce have complete, current lists of employers and often have names and telephone numbers company executives. Most chambers also have information on new organizations coming to the area.

Local and Small Firms According to the U.S. Small Business Administration, small businesses employ more than 50 percent of the private work force. This is a clear reason to research small businesses as sources of employment. Information on openings with small businesses is available through chambers of commerce, employer directories, the want ads, and your library or campus career center.

City, County, State, and Federal Agencies
Most agencies have a civil service system that requires application and pre-employment testing through a central human resources department. Consult your local telephone directory for the numbers of these agencies, and check with your library or school's career services office. Every state has its own employment agency and web site, so you can search on line for states that interest you.

Federal agencies have a variety of positions, and many openings are projected to occur with the retirement of large groups of federal employees. Your state's employment office can refer you to the regional federal office in areas that interest you. Also look for federal job information under *U.S. Government* in major area telephone directories, and request federal job information from your library or schools' career center.

Educational Institutions To find a teaching job, contact the human resources departments of schools that interest you to learn about their application and hiring procedures. Also ask your schools' career services center staff for help in locating leads in education. Look in telephone directories and online for areas you would consider. Publications, including a Job Search Timetable for Teacher Candidates and the Employment Guide for Teacher Candidates may be available at your school's career center.

If no openings are currently available, request permission to leave your application and resume on file for future openings. Ask how you should follow up to keep your file updated and active. Also look into the possibility of becoming certified to do substitute teaching or become a teacher's assistant. This can be a good way to prove your abilities, supply you with income, and possibly work your way into a regular teaching position.

Private Employment Agencies Private contractors and employment or staffing agencies can be useful resources for finding prospective employers, particularly if the one you select specializes in your field. The operations of these organizations vary. Some focus on connecting applicants with part-time jobs, while others focus on full-time jobs.

Some employment firms connect employers and applicants to facilitate a full-time hire by the employer. Other employment firms actually serve as a permanent link between employer and employee, and the employment firm handles all human resource functions. This relieves the employer of such activities as hiring, compensation, career development, and so on. Policies vary regarding who pays fees for securing a permanent job—the applicant or the employer. Always try to negotiate in your favor.

Some employment firms focus on hiring applicants to perform contract work on a temporary or project basis. This is one of the most accessible means of reentering the job market and is a stepping stone from unemployment to employment. This arrangement has two major benefits:

- ☐ It gives the employer and the employee an opportunity to check for "a good fit" without either one having to make a permanent commitment up front.
- ☐ The employment firm takes care of the administrative details. Many people find full-time jobs this way by gaining experience through temporary jobs.

To locate this type of employment firm, look in the Yellow Pages of your telephone directory or search the Internet for employment agencies, employment contractors, employment staffing agencies, or temporary-help agencies. A specific job may not fit your career target perfectly, but it can provide some outstanding benefits, including these:

- ☐ Entry or reentry into the job market
- ☐ Experience you may lack
- ☐ References for work done well
- ☐ Additions to your list of solid job leads
- ☐ A possible full-time job
- ☐ On-the-job training and hands-on practical skill development
- ☐ Immediate income

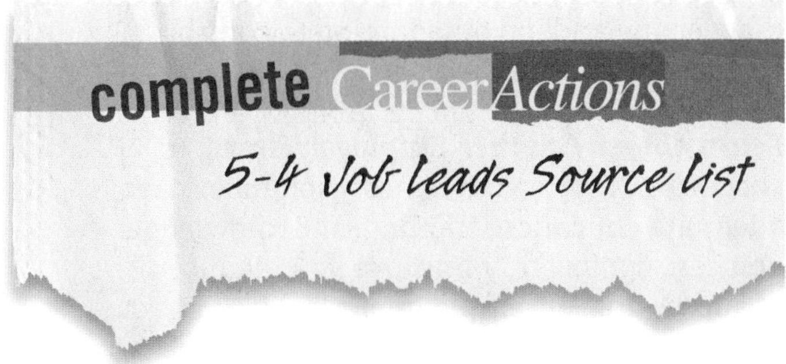

"Try Before You Buy"

Consider "practicing" in your career field to gain experience working side-by-side with people you can learn from. Cooperative education, internships, and volunteer positions are excellent opportunities for networking and can even lead to employment. Job seekers with experience have an advantage because of their familiarity with the field and because they have references who can verify their qualifications. Employers see these applicants as being able to contribute faster and needing less on-the-job training.

Cooperative Education Cooperative education programs place you in a paying job in your field while you are still studying. Students alternate between being in school and working.

Internships An internship is a period of supervised training in a workplace. Most internships are scheduled during breaks in the academic calendar. Some internships are unpaid and some provide a living stipend.

Volunteer Work Volunteering is perhaps easiest in nonprofit organizations that have limited resources to keep up with their goals and deadlines. By showing your commitment and ability to learn on the job, you will gain valuable information about the work and could even be first in line for the next available opening.

To get the most from any of these positions:

- ☐ **Demonstrate initiative.** Use your position to achieve personal and professional development goals.
- ☐ **Be flexible and enthusiastic.** Offer to take on any tasks that need to be done. If you find yourself with some free time, ask for another assignment.
- ☐ **Act like you want to be taken seriously.** Dress professionally, be punctual, never leave early, don't use office supplies or technology for personal business, and don't date or flirt with coworkers.

Watch Out
Research a private agency before signing a contract.

- Does the agency have a good reputation? Ask the staff at your school's career services center, employers who use the agency, other job seekers, and the Better Business Bureau. Don't rely on one person's word. Visit the agency.
- How long has it been in business?
- Does it have expertise in placing people in your field?
- If you would accept employment outside your local area, does the agency belong to a nationwide or regional system?
- What services will the agency provide? Get a written agreement spelling out every service you will receive.
- Do you understand the contract? Read every word, and make sure you are willing to accept the conditions. Agencies that guarantee a full refund are usually the most reputable.

MAKE IT A HABIT

Follow Current Events

During a job search, and throughout your career, it will be a challenge to keep on top of all the news and information in your field on a regular basis. Integrating personal educational habits into your daily routine is key to maintaining an edge.

In the morning, or while driving, listen to news radio programs such as NPR, for stories that affect the economy, your city, and industry. Watch the nightly news and read newspapers to "make yourself smart" on national and international topics.

You'll find that having this sort of knowledge and the ability to discuss current events with employers and coworkers will benefit you in ways you had not anticipated.

© MONKEY BUSINESS IMAGES/SHUTTERSTOCK

Should You Try Self-Employment?

Don't overlook someone who might be your dream employer: you! The popularity of self-employment continues to grow because of downsizing and job outsourcing to control costs.

Learn Under Another Employer First To succeed in your own business, you must have adequate education, training, and knowledge. You can significantly improve your chances of successful self-employment by working for someone who has succeeded in the field. Learn the ropes as an employee, not as a new business owner.

Gaining experience and achieving solid accomplishments provide the credibility you need to land contracts on your own. You need endorsements from people who are satisfied with your performance.

Research to Succeed Talk to people in your field who are successfully self-employed, and study self-employment issues. Figure out how much you need to earn enough to cover insurance and other expenses. Plan carefully and develop a formal business plan.

Networking is Essential You must network regularly with people in your field, potential clients, and customers. Market yourself by being active in professional or trade associations and clubs related to your career field.

Start Small and Build A smart way to begin self-employment is to do it part-time to develop a client base and essential references. Volunteer with groups to prove your skills. Start small, keep expenses at an absolute minimum, and expand only with demand.

Next Steps

Complete all the Career Action assignments in this chapter to increase your career research skills. Knowing where to find information and performing effective online searches will be useful and marketable abilities in both your personal and professional life. File the completed Career Actions in your Career Management Files Binder.

Chapter Checklist

Check each of the actions you are currently taking to increase your career success:

- Using many sources of current job information, including people in my field, job fairs, libraries, online sources, and associations.
- Not limiting research to published job announcements.
- Allocating time in relation to the proven success rate of the top job search strategies; networking, advertisements (print and online), and employment agencies.
- Developing and regularly expanding my job/career-related vocabulary to demonstrate competence and knowledge.

Critical Thinking Questions

1. What are the advantages of researching your occupational field?
2. What are at least two web sites you have visited that provide useful information about your field? Give at least two examples of the types of information you have found at each site.
3. How can having an internship, temporary job, and volunteer work help the job seeker?
4. What sources do you think will be most useful to you in your job search?

For convenient access to valuable career resources, study tools, activities, and job information links, visit the companion web site for this text: www.cengage.com/careerreadiness/levitt.

Trial Run

Organize Your Research

A key element in your research success is your ability to stay organized. Make a weekly research appointment calendar that includes your research topic, goals, and sources. If your goal the first week is to uncover the greatest amount of information on your career field, then outline exactly how you will do this and where you plan to look for the information. If you want to learn how to research, spend the first week mastering Google searches, taking tutorials, and reading about careers and job searching.

Complete the following calendar to organize your job research.

Week	Topic	Source 1	Source 2	Time
Goal 1: Understand skills needed, projected openings, changes in policy	Medical insurance claim industry	Internet site	*Occupational Outlook Handbook* at library	Monday 4 hours
2				
3				
4				
5				
6				
7				

5-1 Develop Your Career-Related Vocabulary

Directions: Follow these steps to create a vocabulary list. Use these terms to make your resumes, cover letters, interviews, and follow-up communications stand out.

1. **Obtain two general job descriptions for the type of job you are seeking.** Get them directly from employers, from people currently working in similar jobs, from job postings, or from the Internet. If you can't find at least two written descriptions, get verbal descriptions from people who work in your field, and write them out. Also, get one or more general job descriptions for your job target from the *Occupational Outlook Handbook.*

2. **Obtain two blank applications for the type of job you are seeking.** Note that some employers only provide applications online. Visit the web sites of these employers to obtain copies of their applications.

3. **Obtain two advertisements for positions that are similar to your job target.** Check newspapers, professional journals, the Internet, the campus career center, and other sources.

4. **Carefully read through the job target material.** Underline all action verbs (for example, *compile, analyze, operate, supervise*) and all keywords or nouns used to describe required or related skills, education, and experience, including the specific names of software programs or computer-related knowledge. Underline vocabulary, abbreviations, special terminology, and buzzwords that are unique to the field.

5. **Make a list of these terms, spelling each word correctly, and include their definitions.** If you don't know the definition of a term, find it. Categorize the terms as follows:

   - ☐ **Action verb**
   - ☐ **Keyword noun**
   - ☐ **Specialized terminology**
   - ☐ **Abbreviation**
   - ☐ **Industry buzzword**

6. **File this vocabulary list in your Career Management Files Binder, and add to it when you find new information.**

Career Action

5-2 Explore Company Web Sites

Directions: Research at least two companies that interest you. Learn about the company's products or services, objectives, locations, salaries, and trends, and research any further details that interest you. Prepare a written summary of your findings. Resources:

- *Your Career: How to Make it Happen* web site (www.cengage.com/careerreadiness/levitt)
- Career Action Worksheet 5-3 on your Data CD

Career Action

5-3 Internet Research on Job Listings and Career Information

Directions: Visit at least four of the sites listed below. File your report in your Career Management Files Binder.

1. **Describe the sites that have the most relevant information to your job target and field.**
2. **Summarize or print job listings for your field, and indicate the sources of the listings.**
3. **Summarize job trends and other useful information.**

Links to the sites below are on the *Your Career: How to Make it Happen* web site, www.cengage.com/careerreadiness/levitt.

- America's Job Bank
- The Black Collegian Online
- CareerBuilder.com
- EmploymentGuide.com
- HotJobs.com
- JobCentral.com
- Monster
- NationJob Network
- Net-Temps
- Saludos.com

You should also visit at least one specialty site in your field.

5-4 Job Leads Source List

Directions: Review each source of job information and leads in the chapter, including the web sites you used in Career Actions 5-2 and 5-3. List the sources you think would be effective in your job search. Make additional copies of this worksheet if necessary or print the worksheet on the Data CD.

Name of Source: ____________________

Address of Source: ____________________

Internet Address (URL): ____________________

E-Mail Address: ____________________ Telephone: ____________________

Action Plan for Using this Source: ____________________

____

Name of Source: ____________________

Address of Source: ____________________

Internet Address (URL): ____________________

E-Mail Address: ____________________ Telephone: ____________________

Action Plan for Using this Source: ____________________

____

Name of Source: ____________________

Address of Source: ____________________

Internet Address (URL): ____________________

E-Mail Address: ____________________ Telephone: ____________________

Action Plan for Using this Source: ____________________

____

Name of Source: ____________________

Address of Source: ____________________

Internet Address (URL): ____________________

E-Mail Address: ____________________ Telephone: ____________________

Action Plan for Using this Source: ____________________

____

Name of Source: ______________________________

Address of Source: ______________________________

Internet Address (URL): ______________________________

E-Mail Address: ______________________ Telephone: ______________________

Action Plan for Using this Source: ______________________________

____

Name of Source: ______________________________

Address of Source: ______________________________

Internet Address (URL): ______________________________

E-Mail Address: ______________________ Telephone: ______________________

Action Plan for Using this Source: ______________________________

____

For Your Career Management Files Binder

After completing the Career Action activities in this chapter, file the following documents in your Career Management Files Binder:

- ☐ **CA 5-1: Career vocabulary list**
- ☐ **CA 5-2: Information from company web sites**
- ☐ **CA 5-3: Internet job listings and career information**
- ☐ **CA 5-4: List of job leads**

part 3

Essential Job Search Communications

Industry Speaks

Shannon Ahuja is Director of Marketing and Outreach for Healthsource of Ohio, a federally qualified health center with 15 primary care offices throughout the state.

"Because it's easy to apply over the Internet, we get a lot of 'generic' resumes and cover letters, compared with the ones that are clearly tailored to the job opportunity. Your cover letter has to entice me to read your resume. You should introduce yourself, describe your overall goals, and demonstrate a clear understanding of our company and the job you are applying for. Our gut feeling is important—you have to show a high level of interest in the job.

"Here's my advice for interviews: Research the person who will interview you, and research the job opportunity you are applying for. Always go in with a list of questions you are prepared to ask. Take notes during the interview—appear interested. If you do not hear back, be sure to follow up: your persistence can you make you more interesting! Don't try to make a weakness sound like a strength. We have already asked what your greatest strength is. Answering this question is part of understanding yourself."

Chapter 6

Resumes

Objectives

- Identify the purpose and role of a resume.
- Learn the main sections of a winning resume.
- Write clear and concise resume content.
- Understand resume organization and format choices.
- Understand the different methods for distributing resumes.
- Tailor a resume to target job and employer.
- Use the Internet to research trends in resume strategies.

Overview

Chapter 6 shows you how to write and deliver resumes that get you interviews. A good resume is your key to getting an interview. Most employers consider candidates based on a quick visual screening or computerized search of the resumes they receive. Employers then look for a match between their needs and the applicants' qualifications and decide whom they wish to interview. Therefore, your resume must be organized, written, and formatted so that it passes both an initial screening and a more detailed analysis. This chapter explains how to create resumes that will pass these tests. Through the activities in this chapter you will prepare and evaluate a resume draft, make revisions, and format final print and electronic resumes.

chapter 6 CareerActions

6-1: Objective and Profile Statement

6-2: Resume Outline

6-3: Resume Power Words and Key Words

6-4: Resume Draft

6-5: Resume Evaluation

6-6: Final Print Resume

6-7: Electronic Resume Formatting

Jump Start Your Resume

To start thinking about ways to market yourself in your resume, make a list of your accomplishments. Include academic honors and awards, recognitions you have received at work, and awards you have received from your activities (such as extracurricular, volunteer, athletic, religious, military, community, and other groups).

You don't have to have received an award for something for it to be considered an accomplishment. Include anything you have done at work or school that you are especially proud of, problems you have solved, work that others have complimented, or work that has helped an individual or an organization in some way. (For example, maybe you suggested a faster system for cleaning art supplies, or maybe your boss said she appreciated that your daily reports were always thorough and on time.) Explain how each item on your list could demonstrate your value to an employer.

What Is a Resume?

A **resume** is a brief, one-page document that details your qualifications for a particular job or job target. It is a record of your *relevant* work and education experience, and it is a tool for marketing yourself to prospective employers and gaining job interviews. It is an ever-changing document that must be revised and rewritten constantly as your career goals change over time.

A winning resume is one that gets you a job interview. Consider the following typical steps an employer uses to process resumes and determine which candidates to interview:

1. A company or organization receives your resume (along with resumes from many other candidates) in response to a job advertisement—either through the mail, e-mail, or a web site. The company likely uses software to electronically scan all resumes and stores the contents in an electronic database for easy analysis, distribution, and retrieval.
2. Human resources staff members review the resumes of the candidates that appear professional and qualified. (Resumes may be read in person or may be scanned by software that searches for specific words and phrases.) Resumes of the most qualified candidates are forwarded to hiring managers for interview consideration. The other resumes are filed and stored for future consideration or discarded.
3. The hiring managers review the resumes and choose the candidates they wish to interview based on the candidates' qualifications and how they might fit in with the existing employees.

From these steps, you can infer that a winning resume achieves multiple objectives. A winning resume:

- ☐ Quickly shows that the candidate has the qualifications necessary for the job.
- ☐ Demonstrates that the candidate can meet the employer's needs.
- ☐ Offers a professional image and a quality example of written communication skills.
- ☐ Is accessible to both scanning software and human reviewers.
- ☐ Suggests that the candidate is someone who is likable and works well with others.
- ☐ Convinces prospective employers that the candidate deserves an interview.

Before You Write Your Resume

Thorough self-reflection, research, and planning are necessary to help you determine the content and format of your resume.

Before you start writing, complete the following steps:

- ☐ Complete a thorough inventory of your education, transferable competencies, and skills. (Chapters 2 and 3)
- ☐ Determine the kind of work environment in which you thrive. (Chapters 2 and 3)
- ☐ Set a career target. (Chapter 3)
- ☐ Conduct networking and perform research to identify specific companies or job titles that interest you. (Chapters 4 and 5)
- ☐ Visit your library, career center, or go online to view examples of resume organization that match your target job and experience. (Chapter 5).

If you have not already completed Chapters 1–5 of this book, do so before beginning to write your resume.

After researching an employer and a target job, you can begin to identify the experiences and qualifications that are the most important to include on your resume.

Start by listing the requirements of the position (from the job description or advertisement).

Next to each requirement, write your skills, experiences, and accomplishments that meet that requirement. This list will build on the list you started in the "Jump Start" activity and will help you form the beginnings of your resume content.

1 Plan Your Resume Content and Format

Writing a great resume that gets an interview typically does not happen on the first try. Once you find a job opening that meets your interests and qualifications, you will prepare a resume for that position by completing these carefully planned steps:

1. Identify the most appropriate resume sections.
2. Write and edit each section to showcase your marketable assets.
3. Choose the most appropriate resume organization: chronological, functional, or combination.
4. Use the most appropriate resume format: print, electronic, or web.
5. Distribute the resume using the appropriate method.
6. Tailor your resume to specific jobs.
7. Use power words (page 104).

Don't rush the process. If you skip or skimp on any steps, you will greatly diminish your chance of achieving the purpose of your resume: getting the interview and, ultimately, the job.

The rest of this chapter walks you through all the stages of preparing, writing, formatting, and submitting a winning resume.

Review these guidelines to get a sense of how to best focus the content of your resume to obtain positive results. Your goal is to use organization, writing, and formatting to create

{ **A winning resume** is one that gets you a job interview! }

a professional-looking document that can be skimmed quickly for key information and read critically to reveal impressive details.

Your Resume Sections

A common approach to organizing a resume is to use headings to separate the text into important sections that are easy to scan. For your resume, include the sections that are most appropriate for your experience, in the order that best fits your target employer's needs and best highlights your qualifications. Place your most important and impressive sections near the top of the resume.

Review the sample resumes in this chapter to see a variety of examples of how resume sections can be presented. Note also that the section names can and should be modified as needed to best fit your experience and preferences. The following sections will fulfill the resume needs of most job seekers.

Contact Information At the top of your resume (without a heading), list your name, mailing address, telephone number(s), e-mail, and web addresses (if appropriate). Note that many employers are turned off by applicants who use unprofessional e-mail or web address names. To avoid losing a job opportunity, be sure your e-mail address includes your name and is professional—never funny or crude. An address such as "john.waters@email.com" is professional and appropriate. "Sk8trBoy@email.com" is not.

Objective The next section of a resume is usually a concise job objective that describes the job you are seeking. The Objective section is especially important on resumes intended for entry-level jobs and for candidates who do not have extensive work experience. Your entire resume will be organized around this objective.

Deciding on a clear job objective, such as *Medical Laboratory Technician at ABC Healthcare Systems*, will help you determine the best way to organize your resume, select appropriate terminology, and present your experience.

The **Objective** is a statement of your employment goal. Place your objective directly below your contact information. The objective:

- ☐ Should be stated as a job title or type of work desired.
- ☐ Should reflect the needs of the employer based on your research.
- ☐ Can also include one or more of your most important job-specific skills and areas of specialization.

The objective helps employers match you to appropriate job openings. If you have more than one job objective, write a separate resume for each one.

OBJECTIVE
Server position in an exclusive restaurant where knowledge of international cuisine is an added value.

Tailor your objective as much as possible. The general objective above could be tailored to an advertisement for a waiter in a French restaurant.

OBJECTIVE
Server position in a four-star French restaurant where knowledge of the French language and cuisine is an added value.

Profile The **Profile** section is a brief statement that describes a job applicant by stating his or her most relevant experience and qualifications. The Profile is becoming more common in resume writing. It is used *instead* of the Objective when the job candidate wishes to emphasize experience and skills over goals. The Profile statement is appropriate for job seekers who have a great deal of experience. An Objective is better for job seekers who have limited experience and seek an entry-level position.

The Profile is also useful if you wish to create a generic resume that you can distribute to many employers at one time, such as at a job fair. Rather than stating a specific objective, you would provide a profile that states your most relevant experience.

PROFILE
Personable and professional Server with four years restaurant experience, in-depth knowledge of international cuisine, and excellent customer communication skills.

For job applicants with many years of relevant experience, it can be difficult to fit the experience into one statement. If this is the case, the Profile could be a bulleted list of skills or a bulleted list of several profile statements.

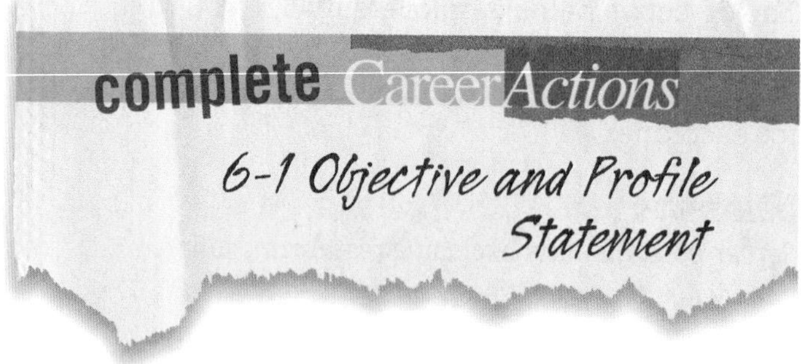

complete Career Actions
6-1 Objective and Profile Statement

Qualifications The **Qualifications** section is a bulleted list of skills that highlights why you are the ideal candidate for the job. The Qualifications section is a focal point for employers, so use it to emphasize specific, relevant skills, capabilities, and related accomplishments, such as:

- ☐ Skills with and knowledge of software/hardware
- ☐ Years of experience in a specialized field or knowledge of specialized skills
- ☐ Relevant credentials and degrees
- ☐ Relevant accomplishments in work or volunteer experiences, community involvement, and other activities

This section can also be called "Skills Summary" or "Career-Related Skills." A recent trend in business and marketing careers is to call this section "Core Competencies." Regardless of the name, this is an important section that should clearly describe your skills and show an employer why you are capable of doing the job.

Review the Career Action assignments you completed in Chapters 2 and 3 to extract qualifications, skills, desirable personal traits, and other attributes you can list to best match your job target. Present them in the qualifications section in order of importance as they relate to your job objective. For example, if your are applying for a position with a doctor's office, your courses and volunteer work in the medical or emergency response goes at the top.

Format the Qualifications section as a bulleted list to draw attention to each item; for example:

- ☐ Graphic and multimedia design, including streaming audio/video, analysis graphs, and custom web graphics
- ☐ General ledger, inventory control, and accounts receivable and accounts payable experience
- ☐ Proven team-player skills demonstrated in three successful internship projects

In the body of your resume (under the appropriate section, such as Work Experience, Education, or Related Activities), provide proof of the qualifications you have listed in the Qualifications section. If you do not have strong work experience related to your job objective, use the Qualifications summary to emphasize your accomplishments and skills in areas other than paid work experience, such as school and volunteer activities.

Work Experience In the **Work Experience** section of a resume, the jobs you have held are usually listed in reverse chronological order (most recent job first). For each job, list the employer's business name, city, and state; dates of employment; the job title; and a brief results-oriented description of the job.

Organize your descriptions so they begin with the results and benefits of your work. Give specific, measurable examples of your accomplishments, such as increased sales, decreased costs, and reduced errors. Quantify where possible (with a percentage, with a specific dollar figure, with a number of items produced or sold, and so on), for example, "Increased sales by 45 percent through skillful negotiation with automotive clients."

If you have held increasingly more responsible jobs with one employer, show this to demonstrate your reliability and your ability to learn and achieve on the job. List only new responsibilities and accomplishments for each promotion. (Continuing job duties will be assumed by the reader.) See Figures 6-12a and 6-12b on pages 138–139 for an example.

If you have little work experience, list your part-time and summer work, internships, school projects, volunteer work, and community involvement. Emphasize all your accomplishments and the skills you developed through these experiences—even if they do not relate directly to your job target. For example, if you recently graduated and you worked throughout your schooling, one accomplishment might read as follows:

> Earned 65 percent of school expenses working part-time during school year and full-time during summers.

This example demonstrates positive working ability, initiative, and potential for learning. Employers consider these qualities real pluses, particularly in entry-level applicants.

Related Experience Use this section to highlight other experience that is pertinent to your job objective. Include activities such as membership, leadership (offices held), and awards earned in professional or trade associations; honorary groups; and social, service, and school organizations. All these activities show achievement and ability to work with others.

Instead of the heading "Related Experience," consider options that may be more appropriate for your achievements and experiences, such as "Awards and Honors," "Volunteer Work," "Community Service," "Certificates Earned," "Activities," and "Professional Associations."

Education List your education in reverse chronological order (most recent first). List the technical schools, colleges, and universities you have attended, the years of attendance, and the degree(s) or certificate(s) you earned. Include relevant certifications, specialized training, and seminars.

© BLEND IMAGES/JUPITER IMAGES

Choose the right words. Use a thesaurus to find the best words to describe your capabilities and accomplishments.

Market Yourself through Accomplishment Statements

When reading resumes, employers look for applicants who show accomplishments in their work, school, and volunteer experience. To showcase your accomplishments, use specific and measurable terms (numbers, percentages, examples) to explain how you were able to:

- Increase your skills and/or knowledge
- Solve problems
- Make decisions
- Recommend solutions and track results
- Organize or plan tasks, activities, or projects
- Work well under pressure and meet deadlines
- Use technology
- Operate equipment and software proficiently
- Contribute to a team or lead others
- Train or motivate others
- Write reports and documents
- Manage money
- Cut costs or increase revenues
- Increase productivity
- Reduce errors

If you are (or will be) a recent graduate with limited work experience, list Education before Work Experience. Highlight school activities, internships, and achievements in the education section. Support your job objective by listing related major(s), minor(s), and courses. For example, a liberal arts student with courses in business will benefit from listing the business courses when applying for a business job.

If you have several years of work experience related to your job objective, emphasize your work experience by listing it before your education. Then condense the education section of your resume.

If your cumulative GPA is low but your GPA in your major is high, list your major GPA only. If your overall GPA is high and you graduated with honors, put this information on your resume. It won't hurt.

Optional Resume Sections

Add these sections if they are appropriate for your situation.

Military Service Include any military experience that is relevant to your job objective, emphasizing pertinent training, responsibilities, and accomplishments. Highlight any rapid progressions, significant promotion(s), and special commendations.

Military service is usually listed in the experience section. If you have an exemplary record, however, you can place it under a separate heading. As much as possible, avoid using military jargon that civilians would not understand.

Personal Information In most cases, resumes should not include personal information. Do not include information about height, weight, age, gender, marital status, race, religion, and so on, on your resume. Fair employment laws prohibit employers from requesting such information. Do not include a photograph of yourself. In an effort to avoid discrimination, many employers will not consider a resume with an enclosed photo. The only exception to this rule would be work that requires a certain appearance, such as modeling.

If your job target is in the field of nutrition, physical fitness, or sports and you wish to provide relevant information about your own health consciousness, fitness level, or suitability for an active job, do so in a Related Experience section named "Activities" or "Awards and Honors." In that section, you can list hobbies and/or accomplishments such as:

- ☐ Trained for and completed three marathons in 2008
- ☐ Organized a neighborhood running club
- ☐ Finalist in the 2008 Portland Vegetarian Recipe Competition
- ☐ Volunteer four hours a week at local food co-op

References Research employers to learn whether they want you to submit **references** (the names of people who can attest to your work abilities and personal qualities). Usually, you should not include references on your resume. Employers expect applicants to have references, but they differ in their preferences about when and how they want to see a reference list.

Prepare a separate reference sheet that includes the names, titles, addresses, and contact information for all your references. Take it with you to interviews and be ready to provide it to employees when they request it. (A model reference sheet is in the Model Documents folder on your Data CD.)

Do not include your photograph. To avoid discrimination, many employers will not consider a resume with an enclosed photo.

It is also unnecessary to state "References available upon request," on a resume. This is obvious and takes up valuable space that could be used for your accomplishments.

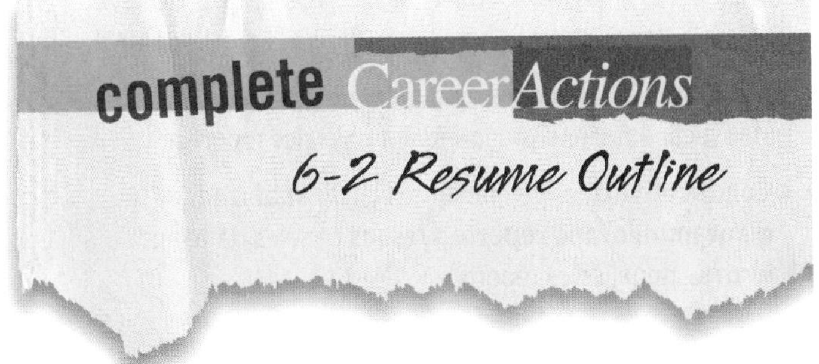

Write and Edit Your Resume

Once you have determined the appropriate sections for your resume, the next step is to write each section using professional and straightforward language and tone and excellent word choice. Your goals are to impress readers with your accomplishments through evidence and details *and* to use terminology that scanning software will identify.

Employers will also look at your resume as an example of your written communication skills. Use the following general guidelines to make sure your resume is clear, concise, and detailed.

Be Clear and Concise

A resume should be one full page unless you have extensive work experience; in that case, two pages are acceptable. Employers prefer clear, uncomplicated resumes that are quick and easy to read. Make every word count, and emphasize how you meet the employer's needs.

Convey your qualifications as clearly and concisely as possible, but do not omit pertinent information and cost yourself the interview. Use phrases, not complete sentences. You can write more concisely if you avoid clichés, dated expressions, and overly complex terms. Some common examples and alternatives follow.

Cliché/Dated	Concise
At this point in time	Now
Ballpark figure	Estimate; estimation
Explore every avenue	Explore the options
Last but not least	Finally
Left no stone unturned	Used every method
Complex/Wordy	**Concise**
Utilized	Used
Endeavor	Try
Equitable	Fair
Initiated	Started
Regarding	About

Use Numbers and Specific Examples of Accomplishments

Your resume will be clearer and more powerful if you use specific terms and examples to describe your accomplishments. Notice the more forceful impact the following specific examples have.

General/Vague	Specific
Reduced costs significantly	Reduced costs by 20 percent
The leading producer	Top producer of 30 employees

The most persuasive resumes describe the applicants' accomplishments with numbers, percentages, and dollar amounts to emphasize how the accomplishments could meet the prospective employers' needs. Use numbers whenever possible to enhance the credibility of your achievements.

Notice how the numbers in the second example below strengthen the accomplishment:

- ☐ Processed more orders than any other member of the work team.
- ☐ Processed **40 percent** more orders than any other member of the work team.

Try adding the word *that* to an accomplishment statement, as shown in the following examples. If necessary, use an estimated measurement (approximately, averaged, up to, or more than).

- ☐ Developed a new filing system that reduced filing time by 25 percent.
- ☐ Developed stock procedures that reduced backorders by 50 percent.

Use Power Words and Omit "I" and "My"

To satisfy resume-search software, you need to include terminology, usually nouns, that reflect the employer's requirements. Ultimately, however, you want a person to view your resume, so you also need to include action statements that use verbs and are persuasive to human readers. These verbs are the resume **power words.**

Action statements do not need to be complete sentences. Employers want to find the important information quickly. Omit *I, me,* and *my* to be more concise and avoid sounding like you are bragging. (The employer already knows the resume is about you.)

Use power words (action verbs and phrases) to show that you take initiative and actively participate in problem-solving and decision-making processes (wrote proposal, improved process, increased sales). Notice how the specific power words in the second example below convey a stronger image.

- ☐ My duties included reviewing marketing trends, analyzing statistical data, and preparing annual sales reports.
- ☐ **Conducted** extensive market research; **analyzed, diagrammed**, and **reported** results of sales data; and **wrote** annual sales reports.

Use a thesaurus to find just the right power words to convey your qualifications accurately and clearly. Notice the use of more specific action verbs (designed and implemented) in the second example below. Specific verbs clearly describe the applicant's scope of responsibility and convey a greater sense of accomplishment.

- ☐ **Started** the inventory-tracking system.
- ☐ **Designed** and **implemented** the inventory-tracking system.

Examples of Resume Power Words

Accelerate	Customize	Forecast	Organize	Receive	Serve
Advise	Delegate	Formulate	Originate	Recommend	Setup
Analyze	Detect	Generate	Oversee	Reconcile	Solve
Approve	Develop	Handle	Participate	Record	Start
Arrange	Diagnose	Identify	Perform	Redesign	Specialize
Assemble	Diagram	Implement	Plan	Reduce	Streamline
Assist	Direct	Improve	Prepare	Reinforce	Structure
Audit	Discover	Increase	Present	Reorganize	Study
Budget	Distribute	Influence	Prioritize	Repair	Supervise
Build	Edit	Install	Process	Report	Support
Change	Enforce	Instruct	Produce	Represent	Teach
Collaborate	Deliver	Integrate	Program	Research	Test
Collect	Demonstrate	Lead	Promote	Resolve	Track
Communicate	Design	Maintain	Propose	Respond	Train
Complete	Eliminate	Manage	Protect	Retrieve	Update
Compute	Establish	Monitor	Prove	Review	Upgrade
Conduct	Evaluate	Motivate	Provide	Revise	Write
Control	Examine	Obtain	Publish	Schedule	
Coordinate	Expand	Operate	Purchase	Select	
Create	Expedite	Order	Raise	Sell	

- ☐ **Organized** and **trained** volunteers who solicited contributions and **raised $55,000** for citywide "elder-help" campaign.
- ☐ **Coordinated** school's student-body elections and **reduced** final ballot processing time by **25 percent**.

Use Keywords Strategically

Today, many employers use web-based applicant-tracking systems or in-house software programs to electronically scan resumes into applicant- or resume-tracking databases. These programs search resumes for **keywords**—terms that represent the qualifications the company has instructed the software to search for. The purpose is to identify applicants with the required skills, knowledge, and capabilities for a position.

Employers will also search for these keywords when they read resumes. Think of keywords as the magnets that draw attention to your resume. Strive to include as many appropriate keywords in your Qualifications section as possible.

Keywords name attributes that qualified candidates must have. Appropriate keywords for your job target include industry terminology and specific words or short phrases that are "lifted" from job descriptions and ads.

Review the web sites and publications of specific companies and professional associations in your industry to identify relevant keywords. These words describe employer-valued qualifications. Use this list of sources to help identify appropriate keywords to include in your resume.

- ☐ Job titles
- ☐ Skills/specialties
- ☐ Education, certifications, licenses, and coursework
- ☐ Work and volunteer experience
- ☐ Community and other clubs/activities
- ☐ Computer/software/hardware skills and specialized tools
- ☐ Relevant personal qualities
- ☐ Industry buzzwords, jargon, and acronyms
- ☐ Accomplishments
- ☐ Industry/professional organizations
- ☐ Awards

Include keywords throughout your resume, and repeat critical keywords. The more keywords the resume-search software identifies, the more

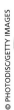

Watch Out!
Never lie or stretch the truth on a resume

If you can't prove it, it doesn't belong on your resume. It is *never* acceptable to lie or stretch the truth about your work experience. Employers can and will verify all of the facts on your resume (including degrees, job titles, dates, and salaries) and will contact your references. If you are caught in a lie, you will gain a bad reputation and will have no chance of being hired. Even if you get away with a lie and are hired anyway, the truth always has a way of coming out. When your employer discovers the truth, you could be fired immediately.

likely it is that your resume will be selected and you will be called for an interview.

Also use synonyms for keywords; employers may use different terms in their search criteria. For example, *budget* may be a synonym for *forecast*, *BA* for *Bachelor of Arts*, and *supervisor* for *manager*.

Computerized resume-search programs typically seek nouns. In searching for AutoCAD drafters, for example, the software may look for nouns (and noun synonyms) such as CAD, *engineer*, *AA degree*, *certified drafter*, *Computer-Aided Drafting*, *AutoCAD*, *wiring diagrams*, and *physics*.

The following examples are keywords that resume-tracking software would search for to fill two different positions. Remember to use your career-related vocabulary to enhance the number of keywords you use. (See Chapter 5.)

Keyword Search Samples

Position Title	Sample Keywords
Accountant	CPA, audit, accounting, accounts receivable/payable, statistics, spreadsheet, finance, systems training, computer, database, team player, B.B.A. Accounting, accurate, project leader, customer relations, accounting database, tax code, ethics, Sarbanes-Oxley compliance, data integrity
Web Specialist	HTML, web development, web hosting, web design, PHP, VB.NET, Java, SQL, Photoshop, Flash, database management, server administration, security, firewalls, FTP, Internet imaging, web design internship, American Association of Webmasters (AAWM), Western Regional Graphics Award

complete CareerActions
6-3 Resume Power Words and Key Words

Organize Your Resume

The way you organize your resume sections and details will help an employer easily identify your most important skills, qualifications, and experience. The most common resume organizations are chronological, functional, and combination. Review the following descriptions of these resume organizations to determine which one best meets your needs.

Chronological

The **chronological** organization is a traditional resume format that is widely used today. Use the chronological organization to show skills, work experience, and logical career progression that are directly related to the job target. At the top of the resume (after the contact information), place the resume section that best supports your job objective.

In this organization, you will have a large Work Experience section. (You may or may not need a Qualifications section.) List jobs one by one, specifying start and end dates. Place jobs in reverse chronological order with the most recent experience first, and stress the major accomplishments and responsibilities of each position. Avoid repeating details that are common to several positions.

Follow this same reverse chronological order in the Education and other sections. Choose this layout when you want to emphasize steady, related work experience without major employment gaps or numerous job changes. Figure 6-1 on page 118 is an example of chronological organization.

Functional

Another popular resume organization is the **functional** style of organization. Use the functional organization if you have work skills, but lack formal work experience that is directly related to your job target.

The organization is also appropriate if you have gaps in employment. Instead of showing that you have held similar jobs, this organization uses separate paragraphs to emphasize skill categories and show that you have the skills needed to do the job.

In this organization, the emphasis is on the Qualifications section of your resume. Starting with the most important skill for the job, list your skills that relate to the job objective, and substantiate them with measurable details and accomplishments. Instead of emphasizing job titles, dates, and length of employment, focus on your qualifications and transferable skills. Then, in a brief Work Experience section, list your employer names and dates of employment. Figure 6-2 on page 119 is an example of a functional resume.

Combination

The **combination** resume organization uses the best features of the chronological and functional organizations to emphasize the match between your skills and a position's requirements. Consider the combination organization if you want to emphasize your skills or if you have limited experience.

In the combination organization, the Work Experience and Qualifications sections are both emphasized. List your Qualifications section just below your objective or profile. Then incorporate your accomplishments in a reverse chronological list of Work Experience. Add credibility by linking your achievements with specific employers and time periods.

Place your education summary where it best supports your objective. If your education is more closely related to the skills required for your target job, place your educational information before your work experience information. Figure 6-3 on page 120 is an example of a combination resume.

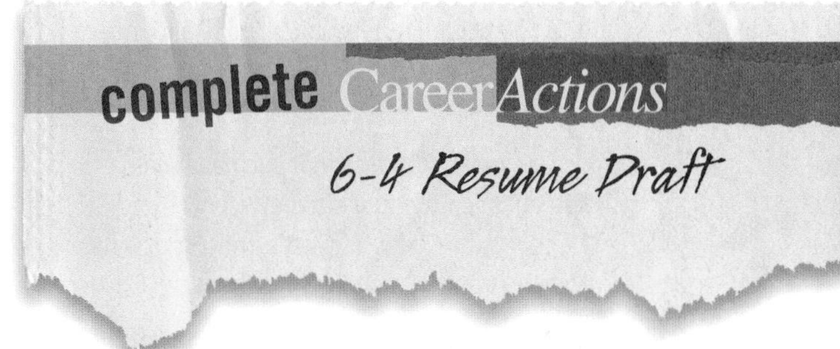

[Consider the combination organization if you want to emphasize your skills or if you have limited experience.]

 Format Your Resume

After you have developed some resume content and decided on the best organization of your sections, the next steps are to select the proper format for submitting your resume to an employer and to design the page appropriately for that format. Visual presentation of a resume is as important as the content. The appearance of your resume could be an employer's first impression of you. Even if the content is written well, an employer will not take the time to read it if it is sloppy or presented in a manner that is difficult to read or process.

As a job applicant, you need at least two resume versions: a scannable print resume and an electronic resume. In some fields, having a web resume is also an asset.

Formatting Do's for Print Resumes

- Use a clean overall format. Visual legibility is extremely important.
- Use the whole page effectively. Make sure the elements of the resume are spaced out so that they fill the entire page in an attractive layout framed by one-inch margins on all sides. Areas of white space draw attention to important parts of your resume, giving it an organized, uncrowded look.
- Use a visual hierarchy within each resume section. Use headings and subheadings to separate entries. Draw attention to headings by using capital letters and/or bold, and indent text to emphasize resume parts. (Don't overdo this, however.)
- Use a simple, standard font such as Times Roman. Keep the font size between 11 and 14 points. The ideal font sizes are 12 point for body text and 14 point for headings.
- Place important information at the top left of the page or resume sections. This is the area where readers naturally begin reading.
- Single-space the body text of your resume, and double-space or triple-space between sections or items in the resume.
- Use bulleted lists to break up lengthy paragraphs.
- Be simple and consistent. Use the same formatting for the same elements throughout the resume.
- Use only one space after periods at the end of sentences.
- Use acceptable character enhancements and codes, such as bold, centering, solid bullets, and regular and indent tabs.
- Print your resume on a laser or inkjet printer in black ink on one side of white or light-colored 8 1/2-inch by 11-inch paper.

Specific instructions for preparing each type of resume are presented later in this chapter.

Print Resume

The most common type of resume that every job applicant needs is a **print resume**. A print resume is a printed, word-processed resume designed to be:

- ☐ Visually appealing
- ☐ Delivered as an e-mail attachment, by regular mail, in person, or by fax
- ☐ Scanned clearly into a database by computer software

You will create your print resume in a word processing program. The file is typically saved as a document with full formatting (.doc file) or as a Rich Text Format (.rtf) file (RTF files are less vulnerable to viruses but may not retain full formatting). Both .doc and .rtf files can be converted to a PDF file (.pdf). A Portable Document Format file retains all formatting, is invulnerable to viruses, and is compatible across all platforms. Most users have the free software for reading PDF files, but these files may be more difficult than .doc and .rtf files to search for keywords.

A PDF file is a good choice if your word processing skills aren't tops. A person who receives a .doc or .rtf file as an e-mail attachment can view the format coding to see how skilled you are with the program. A PDF file shows the finished product, and nothing more. (If you have free time while you are looking for a job, invest some of it in advancing your software skills. You will be more efficient and more valuable on the job.)

Use the "do's and don'ts" on this page and the next page to format your print resume so it will scan clearly, present a professional and attractive image, and keep you in the running for an interview.

Revising and Final Evaluation After you have drafted your print resume and formatted it, review it, paying careful attention to every detail and marking areas for improvement.

- ☐ Rewrite sections to strengthen your qualifications.
- ☐ Eliminate unnecessary words; substitute stronger, clearer terms for weak ones, and add more power words and keywords if needed.
- ☐ Edit text and make formatting changes to fit the resume attractively and neatly on the page.

☐ Finally, check your resume against the Print Resume Checklist on the next page and make any remaining changes.

Once you have revised your resume, proceed to the critical evaluation step. Careful proofreading and evaluation are essential. Recruit help from one or two objective members of your support network who have good writing and proofreading skills. Ask these people to review and critique your resume carefully. This assistance is vital to developing a successful resume and making sure an error did not go unnoticed. Remember that a single error or typo in a resume can cost you a job by making you look careless and unqualified.

There are many examples of good print resumes in this chapter (Figures 6-4, 6-5, 6-8, 6-10, 6-11, and 6-12). Complete Career Action 6-5, Resume Evaluation

complete Career Actions
6-5 Resume Evaluation

complete Career Actions
6-6 Final Print Resume

Formatting Don'ts for Print Resumes

- Don't use the heading RESUME at the top of your document.
- Don't use excessive, decorative fonts and formatting. These elements will not scan well and will look unprofessional.
- Don't use a highly formatted style such as a newsletter layout or multiple columns. Scanner software assumes that the text reads conventionally from left to right across the page in one column.
- Don't use special justification (adjustable spacing between characters). Use the standard left-margin alignment so that each letter is clearly visible.
- Don't use underlining, italics, shadows, white letters on a black background, or colored text. These can blur or corrupt the scanned message.
- Don't use parentheses; use a hyphen after the area code of a telephone number.
- Don't include graphic images, and avoid vertical and horizontal lines and boxes. (You can use one horizontal line if you leave adequate white space above and below it so the line doesn't touch and blur any letters.)
- Don't fold or staple the resume. (Creases and staple marks can cause scanning errors.)

Electronic Resume

Many employers request that candidates submit electronic resumes. An **electronic resume** is a plain text document that is designed to be delivered via e-mail or an online form. Though you will create this type of resume as a separate file, when you send it to employers, you will likely cut and paste text from the resume into the body of an e-mail message or into the appropriate sections of an online application form.

This type of resume must be specially formatted so that the text can be transmitted electronically to employers, be easily read on screen through e-mail programs, and be transmitted directly to resume-tracking programs for processing. Because electronic resumes save employers the scanning step, many employers now require them.

ASCII Text Format The primary difference between a print resume and an electronic resume concerns the formatting. Electronic resumes are relatively plain and unattractive because they must be ASCII (also called .text, Plain Text, or Text Only) documents. These documents are stripped of all word processing codes so they can be transmitted correctly.

Print Resume Checklist

Objective or Profile

✓ Does the Objective or Profile include the job title or required abilities specified by the employer?

Qualifications

✓ Do your Qualifications contain keywords that reinforce requirements for the job?

✓ Are the Qualifications relevant to your stated job objective? Have you included all of your major strengths?

Education

✓ If your education supports your job objective better than your work experience does, have you placed the Education section first (or vice versa)?

✓ Have you emphasized courses, internships, degrees, certificates, and so forth, that best support your objective?

✓ If your GPA is impressive, have you included it (overall or major/minor related to your job objective)?

Work Experience

✓ Does each job listing contain the employer's name and address (city and state), your job title, and dates of employment?

✓ Does each job listing describe your responsibilities and specific accomplishments?

✓ In your job descriptions, have you used power words and keyword nouns to support your job objective?

✓ If your work experience is limited, have you included relevant paid and nonpaid internships and volunteer or other pertinent activities?

Related Activities

✓ Have you included your involvement in professional and other organizations that support your job objective?

✓ Have you included relevant awards, achievements, and offices held?

Overall Content and Appearance

✓ Have you included all relevant information and targeted the content to the specific job objective?

✓ Is the length of the resume appropriate for your level of experience?

✓ Is the content logically organized and presented in order of importance to your job objective?

✓ Is the resume content truthful and correct (free from all grammar, spelling, and punctuation errors)?

✓ Is the overall design visually appealing and easy to read?

✓ Have you used appropriate fonts, white space, and acceptable enhancements (boldface, bullets, indents)?

✓ Have you avoided graphic enhancements, columns, and decorative fonts?

Keyword Emphasis Using appropriate keywords throughout your electronic resume is especially important because these resumes are searched for keywords. Design your electronic resume to generate the highest possible number of keyword hits from resume-search software.

Formatting Tips for Electronic Resumes Get the edge on the competition by formatting your electronic resume correctly. Correct formatting will show your preparation and ensure that employers do not receive resume contents with wildly erratic line lengths and unreadable text. Since all word processing codes are stripped out of electronic resumes, be sure to format your resume to compensate for the loss of bold text, bullets, and other formatting capabilities. For example, use all caps for headings and dashes or asterisks for bullets. As you prepare your electronic resume, look at the samples in Figures 6-6 and 6-7, pages 126 and 128, and keep the following tips in mind:

- ☐ **Use standard section headings.** Use standard headings in all capitals, like those in a print resume—for example, OBJECTIVE, QUALIFICATIONS, EXPERIENCE, EDUCATION, and RELATED ACTIVITIES.
- ☐ **Use keywords throughout.** Using appropriate keywords throughout your electronic resume is essential. Spell all keywords correctly. (Search software will not generate positive hits on your resume if the keywords aren't spelled correctly.)
- ☐ **Emphasize nouns.** Use noun forms of industry-specific terms, such as accountant rather than accounting. Also, use nouns that describe strong interpersonal skills, such as team player. Search software frequently looks for noun forms.
- ☐ **Always back up your file.** Using a new filename, save your resume in ASCII or plain text (.txt) format so you can copy and customize it for specific employers.
- ☐ **Keep up to date on electronic resume technology.** Technology changes quickly; keep your knowledge of scanning and electronic resume technology current by verifying employers' preferences and researching the topic. Check out the Internet resources listed in this chapter and on the companion web site.

The quickest and easiest way to create an electronic resume is to save your print resume in a plain text format and adjust the formatting as needed to comply with electronic transmission requirements. In Career Action 6-7, you will follow the steps for doing this.

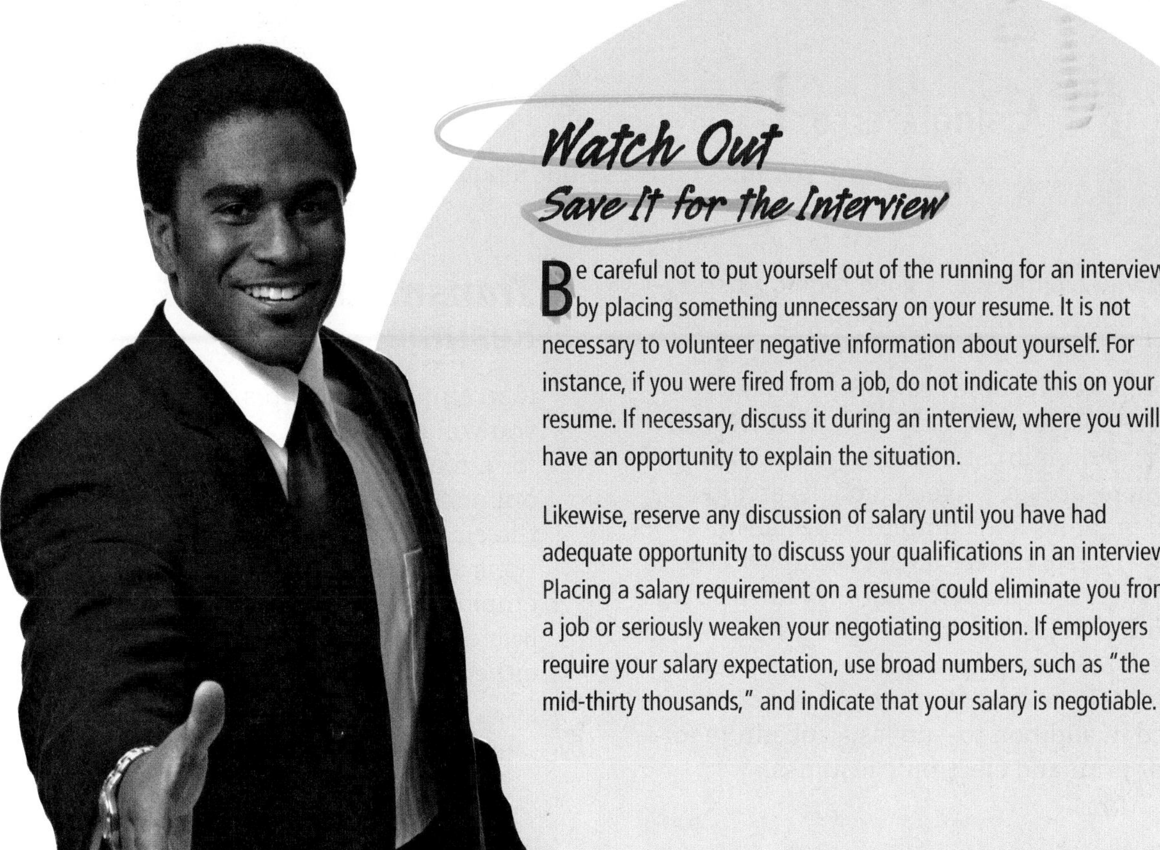

Watch Out
Save It for the Interview

Be careful not to put yourself out of the running for an interview by placing something unnecessary on your resume. It is not necessary to volunteer negative information about yourself. For instance, if you were fired from a job, do not indicate this on your resume. If necessary, discuss it during an interview, where you will have an opportunity to explain the situation.

Likewise, reserve any discussion of salary until you have had adequate opportunity to discuss your qualifications in an interview. Placing a salary requirement on a resume could eliminate you from a job or seriously weaken your negotiating position. If employers require your salary expectation, use broad numbers, such as "the mid-thirty thousands," and indicate that your salary is negotiable.

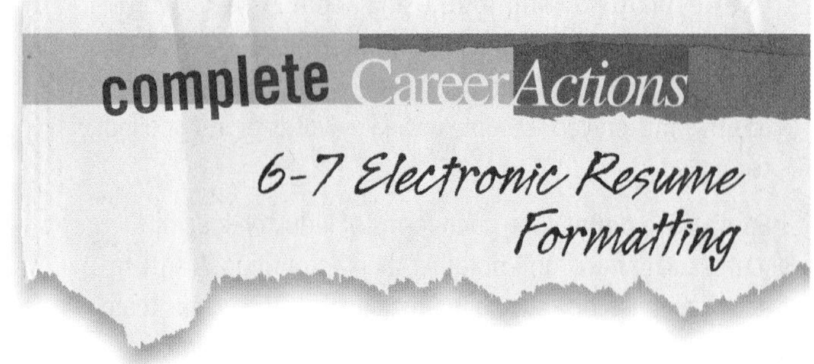

Web Resume

A **web resume** is formatted in HTML so it can be posted on the Internet as a web document. The web resume looks like an attractive print resume but can contain more sophisticated graphics. It is designed to showcase the applicant's HTML skills and may also link to a web portfolio of artistic, specialized computer, and other abilities (for example, graphic art, charts, CAD drawings, and video or musical performance clips).

A web resume is created in HTML and published to the Internet. This resume format is more flexible than the others because it supports more sophisticated elements, such as animated graphics, sound clips, and video clips. It is a good tool for displaying your expertise in computer technology (HTML, web site and graphic design, and more). Web resumes can also be creative sales tools for people who want or need to display their artistic abilities, such as photographers, artists, singers, models, architects, and graphics and computer specialists.

Web resumes are most commonly used in the high-tech industry, but they are also used in other fields. Research to determine whether a web resume is appropriate in your career field. Also, note that a web resume should be used in addition to—not as a substitute for—your print and electronic resumes.

Comprehensive information describing the purposes and benefits of web resumes; tips for writing their content; and guidelines for publishing, verifying, and distributing them are on the companion web site. Figure 6-9 on page 132 is a sample web resume.

4 Distribute Your Resume

After developing and formatting your resume, you will want to distribute it effectively to meet the preferences of employers and achieve your ultimate goal of getting interviews. If the preferred format is not specified in a job ad, ask whether you should mail a scannable print resume or attach it to an e-mail message as a backup to your electronic resume. Find out who should receive your resume and address your cover letter to that individual (see Chapter 7).

Also, give your resume to the members of your job search network in the format they prefer. Providing your resume to your network members gives them the information they need to help you find prospective employers.

[**A single error** or typo in a resume can cost you a job by making you look careless and unqualified.]

Transmitting Your Electronic Resume

If an employer requires an electronic resume, you will need to follow the requirements for e-mailing or submitting your resume online. This information is usually listed on the employer's web site. If you have questions about the procedures, call or e-mail the employers to find out the correct procedures *before* you send a resume. Generally, you will either need to:

- ☐ Paste the entire contents of your electronic resume into the body of an e-mail message.

- ☐ Paste the entire contents of your electronic resume into one blank field on a job application web site.
- ☐ Paste sections of your electronic resume into several different fields on a job application web site.

When you plan to send a resume in an e-mail message (or as an attachment), you should practice transmitting the message first. Always send your electronic resume and cover letter or e-mail introduction to a friend and to yourself to see how well the documents survive the cyberspace transfer *before* you actually send them to an employer. You may need to make modifications to repair spacing and formatting. It's not possible to practice sending resumes through an employers' web site, but you should always proofread your text thoroughly before clicking Send.

Reinforce Your Resume with a Phone Call

Do not rely on resumes alone to get interviews. It's a mistake to send out several copies of your resume and then wait for the telephone to ring. Two to three days after sending a resume, follow up with a phone call to make sure it was received. If you mail your resume, wait about a week to call. Your call reminds the receiver about you, demonstrates initiative, and increases your name recognition.

Tailor Your Resume

Do not send the same resume to every employer. Tailor your resume to individual employers by using terminology and descriptions that address the needs stated their job advertisements. Also, customize your resume for employers who specifically request your resume. Customized resumes show that you understand the specific requirements of an employer and will increase your chances of getting an interview. Tailor your resumes to specific job titles, job advertisements, and employers. The targeted resume is 100 percent more effective than the one-size-fits-all resume. Here are ways you can tailor your resume:

- ☐ Use keywords in your job objective or profile throughout your resume that match those in a job ad or job description.
- ☐ Identify the name of the company, organization, or industry in your objective.
- ☐ Use appropriate industry terminology.

When the jobs you are applying for are quite similar, the adjustments will be minimal. However, if you are applying for different types of jobs in a similar industry or making

Watch Out
International Job Applications

Resume and job application guidelines vary widely from country to country. If you are considering a job overseas, be sure to research the resume requirements of the specific country. Different countries require formats and information that can differ significantly from American resume practices. For example, in France, employers prefer handwritten cover letters. In Japan, employers require personal information on a resume along with a photograph of the applicant. Do your research, and consult resources and web sites that offer country-specific career information, such as Going Global, Transitions Abroad, JobWeb, and many others.

a career change, you will need to revise your resume to fit a new career objective. A realistic new career target is one for which you have already developed relevant, related skills. To revise a resume for a new career, refer to the following tips:

1. Make a list of all your work-related skills, knowledge, and experience.
2. Check each item on your list that matches or closely matches the needs of your new career target.
3. If necessary, change the wording of the checked items to better fit your new career target. Use a thesaurus and your research to identify appropriate keywords. For example, when changing from a career as a schoolteacher to an industry trainer, the terms *trainer*, *facilitator*, and *presenter* are more appropriate than *teacher*.
4. Create new skill and experience headings by grouping related items from your updated skills list into categories. Create a heading that describes each category.
5. Now that you have appropriate content, begin drafting and refining your new career resume. In other words, once you have completed this exercise of identifying appropriate content for a new job objective, you can begin revising your existing resume to match your new job objective.

The example below shows excerpts from a resume for a service manager position along with changes made to tailor the resume for an automotive insurance adjuster position.

Internet Resources for Resume Information

Just as no two resumes are the same, resume guidelines vary widely and are constantly changing. The Internet is a rich resource for staying on top of resume trends and locating additional resume writing and formatting suggestions. As you continue to revise and fine-tune your resumes, use your favorite search engine to:

- ☐ Research resume strategies
- ☐ Find answers to specific resume questions
- ☐ Search for writing and formatting guidelines
- ☐ Find additional resume formats—especially electronic and web formats
- ☐ Find examples of power words and industry keywords

Excerpts From "Before" Resume

Objective: Service manager in multiline dealership

Auto Repair Customer Service
Scheduled appointments, performed pre-inspections, achieved upgrade sales on 95 percent of accounts, quoted estimates, wrote work orders, performed post-repair inspections, explained statements to customers, and increased referrals from customers by 40 percent.

Parts Management
Managed ordering and stocking of mechanical and auto-body parts inventories, selected suppliers and negotiated vendor discounts that averaged 25 to 30 percent below wholesale, reconciled shipping invoices to billing statements, and approved payments.

Excerpts From "After" Resume

Objective: Insurance adjuster in automotive collision repair industry

Modified to Focus on Claims Management
Scheduled client appointments, determined mechanical and auto-body damages within 45 minutes, negotiated repairs with clients and insurance companies, prepared job documentation (pictures, work orders, billing), performed post-repair inspections, and explained statements.

Modified to Focus on Cost Containment
Obtained clients' permission to use appropriate after-market and/or rebuilt parts on 96 percent of jobs; located replacement parts; negotiated price, delivery, and discounts, averaging 25 to 30 percent below wholesale; returned unused parts for credit; reconciled billing discrepancies; approved payments.

- ☐ Access sample resumes, content ideas, and templates from different careers
- ☐ Locate resume consulting services
- ☐ Find resume-posting sites and services
- ☐ Quality sites offering useful resume development advice include the following:
  - ☐ eResumes.com
  - ☐ eResumeIQ.com (web resumes)
  - ☐ Monster
  - ☐ Purdue University Online Writing Lab (OWL)
  - ☐ Quintessential Careers
  - ☐ Susan Ireland Resumes
  - ☐ The Riley Guide

Additional links are at the *Your Career: How to Make It Happen* web site.

Next Steps

Complete all the Career Actions in this chapter to draft, evaluate, and fine-tune your print and electronic resumes. File the completed Career Actions in your Career Management Files Binder along with your Internet research from this chapter. File a copy of your final print resume in your Career Portfolio. Remember that your resume is a "living, breathing" marketing tool that must be reevaluated and revised constantly. As you seek to apply for jobs with different employers, customize your resume to show how you meet the specific job requirements.

In Chapter 7, you will continue to develop your job search package. You will explore and develop cover letters to accompany your resumes. You will also learn about and practice using online job application procedures.

Sample Resumes

The following sample resumes are on pages 118–141:

- ☐ Figure 6-1: Chronological Resume Sample (Objective: Administrative Assistant)
- ☐ Figure 6-2: Functional Resume Sample (Objective: Administrative Assistant)
- ☐ Figure 6-3: Combination Resume Sample (Objective: Administrative Assistant)
- ☐ Figure 6-4: Print Resume Sample (Objective: Health Information Technician)
- ☐ Figure 6-5: Print Resume Sample (Objective: Computerized Accounting Systems Auditor I)
- ☐ Figure 6-6: Electronic Resume Sample (Objective: Information Systems Analyst I)
- ☐ Figure 6-7: Electronic Resume Sample (Objective: Network Support Technician)
- ☐ Figure 6-8: Print Resume Sample (Objective: Receptionist)
- ☐ Figure 6-9: Web Resume Sample (Objective: Web Specialist)
- ☐ Figure 6-10: Print Resume Sample (Objective: Private Security Guard)
- ☐ Figure 6-11: Print Resume Sample (Objective: Medical Assistant)
- ☐ Figure 6-12a: Print Resume Sample, page 1 (Objective: Marketing Product Line Manager)
- ☐ Figure 6-12b: Print Resume Sample, page 2 (Marketing Product Line Manager)
- ☐ Figure 6-13: Resume Sample for Online Posting (Objective: Environmental Science Technician)

Chapter Checklist

Check each of the actions you are currently taking to increase your career success

- Writing a clear, appropriate objective or profile to focus the entire resume.
- Choosing the resume sections and organization that best support my job objective and qualifications.
- Using measurable details and accomplishment statements to market myself.
- Using appropriate power words and keywords to demonstrate a target job's required skills and knowledge.
- Preparing and evaluating the resume draft, making corrections by applying effective writing techniques, and developing a well organized, error-free final resume.
- Formatting a print resume to be visually appealing, easy to read, and scannable.
- Formatting an electronic resume carefully to ensure clear transmission to and receipt by the employer.
- Tailoring the resume to meet the needs of the employer and matching the resume to the job description by using specific terms and industry terminology.
- Using the Internet to locate resume preparation tips and to deliver an electronic resume.

Critical Thinking Questions

1. When should an applicant use separate objectives or resumes?
2. In what order should you present your resume data to best support your objective?
3. Why is it effective to include a Qualifications section immediately below the Objective on a resume?
4. Why is it essential to use power words and keywords in a resume?
5. Why is a chronological resume the preferred organization for job seekers who have a significant amount of work experience?
6. Why is the visual appearance and organization of a resume important to employers?
7. How are electronic resumes transmitted to employers?

For convenient access to valuable career resources, study tools, activities, and job information links, visit the companion web site for this text: www.cengage.com/careerreadiness/levitt.

Trial Run

A good way to get started on creating a resume is to review sample resumes online. However, these samples are only guidelines and are not intended to be used as they are. They are intended to be evaluated, revised, reorganized, and reformatted to fit a job seeker's skills and objective.

Search the Internet for free sample resumes in your career area. Choose one that is relevant to your job target and evaluate it using the Resume Checklist in the chapter. List the changes needed to make the resume better fit your qualifications and experience and to fit the formatting guidelines in this chapter.

Copy and paste the text of the sample resume into a word processing file and make the necessary revisions. Choose either a print resume or electronic resume format and make the necessary formatting changes.

Print out the revised resume and edit it carefully for mistakes and typos. Pair up with a classmate and exchange resumes for peer editing.

Evaluate resumes on the following elements:

Rating Scale: 1 to 4 (1 · not really; 2 · sometimes/somewhat; 3 · usually; 4 · definitely)

_________ 1. The Objective or Profile includes the job title or required abilities specified by the employer.

_________ 2. Qualifications contain keywords that name requirements for the job.

_________ 3. Qualifications are relevant to the stated job objective. Major strengths are included.

_________ 4. If education supports the job objective better than the work experience, it is placed first (or vice versa).

_________ 5. Candidate emphasized courses, internships, degrees, certificates, and so on, that best support the objective.

_________ 6. If GPA is impressive, it is included (overall or major/minor related to job objective).

_________ 7. Each job listing contains the employer's name and address (city and state) and job title.

_________ 8. Each job listing describes responsibilities and specific, measurable accomplishments.

_________ 9. Job descriptions use power words and keyword nouns that support the objective.

_________ 10. If work experience is limited, relevant paid and nonpaid internships and volunteer or other pertinent activities are included.

_________ 11. Candidate emphasized involvement in professional and other organizations that support the job objective.

_________ 12. Relevant awards, achievements, and offices held are included.

_________ 13. The overall design is appealing.

_________ 14. The content is correct (grammar, spelling, and punctuation).

_________ 15. The content is logically organized and presented in order of importance to the objective.

_________ 16. The resume meets all print or electronic resume formatting requirements.

KIMI R. OKASAKI
148 Barrister Avenue, Tucson, AZ 85726
520-555-0136 cell: 520-555-0137 kokasaki@provider.net

OBJECTIVE

Administrative Assistant for MegaMall Property Management Company

EDUCATION

Associate of Applied Science, 2010, Westfield Community College, Tucson, AZ
- Major: Administrative Office Technology, GPA 3.6

Related Courses and Skills
- Advanced Word Processing (Word 2007 for Windows, Word 2008 for Mac)
- Keyboarding at 75 words per minute
- Spreadsheet (Excel, Apple Numbers) and Database Management (Access and Oracle)
- Records Management
- Bookkeeping I and Computerized Bookkeeping (QuickBooks Pro)
- Ten-key at 250 strokes per minute
- Presentation Software (PowerPoint)
- Office Management
- Internet Research
- Experienced in use of PDF files and FTP

EXPERIENCE

Community Volunteer, Tucson, AZ **December 2005–December 2009**
- **National Diabetes Foundation:** Developed and customized Excel spreadsheet report to track results of three fund-raising activities, reducing reporting time by 50 percent.
- **Secretary-Treasurer, Valley Elementary School Parent-Teacher Organization:** Published electronic newsletters, answered e-mail, maintained correspondence, maintained books for two years, and satisfied yearly CPA audits. Used Word, PDF files, FTP, and QuickBooks Pro.
- **Meals on Wheels:** Using Access, designed and maintained information database to enable Meals on Wheels to study the participation of 1,200 people.

Katz Department Store, Tucson, AZ **March 2004–December 2005**
- Sales Supervisor, Part-time: Supervised four sales clerks; trained new sales employees. Computed daily cash receipts, balanced two registers, attained highest part-time sales volume, and had fewest sales returned.

Value Variety, Tucson, AZ **Summers 2002, 2003**
- Sales Clerk, Floater: Provided complete customer service in sales and returns; coordinated weekly inventory deliveries.

Figure 6-1: Chronological Resume Sample

KIMI R. OKASAKI
148 Barrister Avenue, Tucson, AZ 85726
520-555-0136 cell: 520-555-0137 kokasaki@provider.net

OBJECTIVE

Administrative Assistant for MegaMall Property Management Company

EDUCATION

Associate of Applied Science, 2010, Westfield Community College, Tucson, AZ
- Major: Administrative Office Technology, GPA 3.6

PROFESSIONAL SKILLS

Document Preparation: Expert using Word and PowerPoint (for Windows and Mac). Enter text at 75 words per minute. Integrate tabular data and graphics into documents using Access and Excel. Write, format, and proofread printed and electronic business correspondence, reports, and newsletters. Research topics on the Internet. Experienced in use of PDF files and FTP.
- Published electronic newsletters and maintained correspondence for Valley Elementary School Parent-Teacher Organization (VES-PTO) for two years.

Spreadsheet Management: Develop and maintain Excel and Apple Numbers spreadsheets.
- Developed spreadsheet to track results of three fund-raising activities for the National Diabetes Foundation that reduced reporting time by 50 percent.

Database Management: Configure, maintain, and generate reports with Access and Oracle.
- Designed and maintained an information database to enable Meals on Wheels to study the participation of 1,200 people.

Bookkeeping: Perform manual (ten-key at 250 strokes per minute) or computerized (QuickBooks Pro) bookkeeping functions from journal entry to end-of-period reports.
- Maintained books for VES-PTO for two years and satisfied yearly CPA audits.
- Computed daily cash receipts and balanced two registers as part-time sales supervisor of a department store.

Human Relations: Successfully cooperate with store managers, representatives of delivery companies and community organizations, and the general public.
- Held positions of responsibility in three community organizations over the last three years.
- Worked in two department stores: promoted to supervisor, trained new sales clerks, coordinated weekly inventory deliveries, provided customer service in sales and returns, attained highest part-time sales volume, and had fewest sales returned.

EXPERIENCE

Community Volunteer, Tucson, AZ	December 2005–December 2009
Katz Department Store, Tucson, AZ	March 2004–December 2005
Value Variety, Tucson, AZ	Summers 2002, 2003

Figure 6-2: Functional Resume Sample

KIMI R. OKASAKI
148 Barrister Avenue, Tucson, AZ 85726
520-555-0136 cell: 520-555-0137 kokasaki@provider.net

OBJECTIVE

Administrative Assistant for MegaMall Property Management Company

RELATED QUALIFICATIONS

- Advanced Word processing (Word 2007 for Windows, Word 2008 for Mac)
- Spreadsheet generation with Excel and Apple Numbers
- Database design and maintenance using Access and Oracle
- Experienced in use of PDF files and FTP
- Keyboarding at 75 words per minute
- Write and proofread printed and electronic business correspondence, reports, newsletters
- Presentation preparation using PowerPoint and Presentations software
- Internet research and e-mail correspondence using Netscape or Explorer
- Bookkeeping using QuickBooks Pro and ten-key at 250 strokes per minute
- Proven ability to work successfully with store managers, delivery companies, community organizations, and the general public

EDUCATION

Associate of Applied Science, 2010, Westfield Community College, Tucson, AZ
- Major: Administrative Office Technology, GPA 3.6

EXPERIENCE

Community Volunteer, Tucson, AZ **December 2005–December 2009**
- **National Diabetes Foundation:** Developed and customized Excel spreadsheet report to track results of three fund-raising activities, reducing reporting time by 50 percent.
- **Secretary-Treasurer, Valley Elementary School Parent-Teacher Organization:** Published electronic newsletters, answered e-mail, maintained correspondence, maintained books for two years, and satisfied yearly CPA audits. Used Word, PDF files, FTP, and QuickBooks Pro.
- **Meals on Wheels:** Using Access, designed and maintained information database to enable Meals on Wheels to study the participation of 1,200 people.

Katz Department Store, Tucson, AZ **March 2004–December 2005**
- Sales Supervisor, Part-time: Supervised four sales clerks; trained new sales employees. Computed daily cash receipts, balanced two registers, attained highest part-time sales volume, and had fewest sales returned.

Value Variety, Tucson, AZ **Summers 2002, 2003**
- Sales Clerk, Floater: Provided complete customer service in sales and returns; coordinated weekly inventory deliveries.

Figure 6-3: Combination Resume Sample

Summary of Information Emphasized in Figures 6-1 to 6-3 (chronological, functional, combination format: Okasaki)

Figures 6-1, 6-2, and 6-3 illustrate how to organize the same resume content in three different formats: chronological, functional, and combination.

Objective	Since she is applying for a specific, entry-level job Kimi uses the title of the position (from the job advertisement) as her objective.
Education	Kimi emphasizes her degree and major by placing it near the top of her resume. She has a high GPA, so she includes this as well. In the chronological resume (Figure 6-1), she also lists Related Courses and Skills that emphasize her computer skills and demonstrate her coursework that is pertinent to an Administrative Assistant position.
Experience	Kimi's chronological resume lists her experience in reverse chronological order. Because her community volunteer experience is pertinent to her job objective, she includes it in this section (using the section title "Experience" rather than "Work Experience." She describes her activities using results-oriented, measurable language. In her functional resume, Kimi emphasizes her skills over her experience by placing a short Experience section as the last item in her resume. In her combination resume, Kimi is able to emphasize both her skills and experience by including both a reverse chronological list of her experience *and* a qualifications list.
Professional Skills/ Qualifications	Kimi does not include a separate Qualifications section in her chronological resume. She calls the section "Professional Skills" in her functional resume to emphasize her skills (since her work experience is somewhat limited). Kimi emphasizes her qualifications on her combination resume by placing that section near the top of the resume. She includes keywords that would be searched for in a resume, such as technology and business terms.

SONYA REED

2332 Clovis Boulevard • Savannah, GA 31401
912-555-0109 cell: 912-555-0110 sreed@provider.net

OBJECTIVE

Health Information Technician position requiring the ability to perform detailed tasks, to change priorities quickly, and to communicate well

QUALIFICATIONS

- Registered Health Information Technician, 2010
- Family practice receptionist, 1.5 years; awarded Superior Service Certificate twice
- Five-month internship as assistant to Health Information Technician, Community Hospital
- Associate of Science, 2010

EDUCATION

Associate of Science, 2010, Savannah College of Georgia, Savannah, GA
Major: Health Information Technology GPA 3.6
Related Courses and Skills
• Medical Terminology • Clinical Classification Systems • Health Information Management
• Health Delivery Systems • Health Data • Introduction to Health Law and Ethics
• Human Disease Mechanisms • Word • Excel • Access • PowerPoint
• Explorer • Outlook • Health Care Reimbursement • Alternative Health Care Settings
• Business Communications

CERTIFICATION

Registered Health Information Technician, 2010

EXPERIENCE

- **Community Hospital, Savannah, GA** **January 2010–May 2010**
  Clinical Internship. Under the direction of the Health Information Director, assisted Health Information Technician in reviewing and assigning diagnosis codes and DRGs. Abstracted appropriate information and retrieved medical records. Assisted chiefly with Medicare/Medicaid coding for three months. Checked charts into and out of records department.

- **Family Practice Partnership, Savannah, GA** **July 2008–December 2009**
  Evening Receptionist. Answered telephone, scheduled appointments, and kept waiting room neat. Checked in patients, obtained insurance and billing information, and pulled charts for nurses. Copied requested records for transport to other medical offices. Provided cheerful, efficient service to patients; awarded Superior Service Certificate in 2008 and 2009.

ASSOCIATIONS

Community Hospital Volunteer, 2008 to Present
American Health Information Management Association, 2008 to Present

Figure 6-4: Print Resume Sample

Summary of Information Emphasized in Figure 6-4: Reed

Objective

Sonya uses an industry-standard job title to state her job objective concisely. To capture the attention of employers and to advertise her work-related characteristics, she includes job-related competencies that her targeted employers list in job postings.

Qualifications

Sonya includes several terms that both humans and resume-search software programs typically search for when filling a health information technician position. She emphasizes her Registered Health Information Technician certification first because it is a primary requirement for the job she is seeking. She also highlights her relevant work experience and her hospital internship assisting a health information technician. She includes her associate of science degree because it is a keyword that is also likely to be included in an electronic search of her resume.

Education

Sonya puts her degree near the top of the resume to reinforce her job qualifications. She worked evenings during the two years she was in school and still earned a respectable GPA, so she includes this information in her resume. In addition, she lists classes from her major that are especially pertinent to employers and includes the computer programs she knows.

Certification

Because Sonya just graduated and has limited work experience, she places her national certification in its own section of the resume to emphasize her qualifications and to show that she takes her profession seriously.

Experience

Sonya's internship through Savannah College of Georgia allowed her to work and learn at a local hospital. Because her internship lasted five months, provided hands-on experience, and is pertinent to her job objective, Sonya places it in the Experience section of her resume. Notice how Sonya describes her activities using industry-specific terminology and power words.

Although Sonya's job at the family practice clinic was at a medical facility, she did not have any responsibilities that are directly applicable to her current job objective. She puts her award for superior service at the end of her job description to demonstrate that her job performance is above average.

Associations

The associations on Sonya's resume reinforce her interest in the medical field. She adds her volunteer work because she knows her target employers value and promote community service.

DONITA SILVA

1247 Madison Road, Columbus, OH 43216 614-555-0100 cell: 614-555-1010 dsilva@provider.net

OBJECTIVE

Computerized Accounting Systems Auditor I

QUALIFICATIONS SUMMARY

- Education in accounting practices and computer systems
- Programming competence in C, C++, C#.NET, and Visual Basic.NET
- Practical experience in EDP accounting applications
- Proficient in Word, Excel, Access, and Windows
- Proven interpersonal skills in an auditing environment
- Experience in System i, Windows Server 2003 Active Directory, Microsoft Exchange Server 2007 and Novell LAN operations

EDUCATION

Bachelor of Business Administration, 2010 • Renton College, Columbus, OH
• Major: Computer Information Systems • Minor: Internal Auditing

Relevant Courses of Study:
• Analysis, Design, and Auditing of Accounting Information Systems
• Internal Auditing • Information Systems Auditing • Accounting Applications
• Database Management • Advanced Corporate Finance • Cost Accounting

Senior Internship: American Interstate Bank
Under the supervision of the managing field auditor of American Interstate Bank, performed internal audits on the safety-deposit box operations of five local branches. Reviewed the audit findings with the branch managers. Compiled final report and presented it to the managers.

EXPERIENCE

Alexander & Swartz, Columbus, OH **9/09 to Present**
Part-time Assistant Staff Auditor: Assist in audits of cash, accounts receivable, and accounts payable for midsized firms that use System i. Interface with clients and write audit reports as member of the Business Services Assurance and Advisory team.

Micronomics Company, Columbus, OH **6/06 to 9/09**
Part-time Programmer's Assistant: Designed, documented, coded, and tested C program subroutines for order-entry system. Achieved a 95 percent average program-accuracy rate on test runs. Cataloged and filed new programs and program patches for the company's software library. Used Microsoft Exchange Server 2007.

Renton College, Columbus, OH **9/04 to 6/06**
Computer Operator Aide: Using Windows Server 2003, copied files for backup. Verified accuracy of reports and scheduled print sequences. Recommended schedule changes that improved efficiency of backup procedures by 25 percent.

ASSOCIATIONS

Information Technology Management Association, 2005 to Present
Columbus Computer Club, 2004 to Present

Figure 6-5: Print Resume Sample

Summary of Information Emphasized in Figure 6-5: Silva

Note: Figures 6-5 and 6-6 illustrate how to tailor a resume for two different job objectives. Because this employer prefers it, Donita uses a one-page scannable print resume.

Objective The title Computerized Accounting Systems Auditor I is clearly understood in the field.

Qualifications Donita incorporates keywords in this section to highlight the education, specialized knowledge, and practical experience she possesses that relate directly to the Computerized Accounting Systems Auditor I job objective. She shows that she can be productive immediately.

Education Because the job Donita wants requires expertise in two fields—computer systems and accounting practices—she emphasizes the courses she took that combine the skills from both areas. She addresses the requirements of her job objective by stressing the auditing experience she obtained through the class project. She also emphasizes her proven interpersonal skills, which are critical to acquiring and retaining clients.

Experience *Alexander & Swartz.* Donita provides proof of her interpersonal skills and on-the-job auditing skills in computerized accounting. She supports the most important qualifications needed for her job objective. Throughout her Experience section, she uses power words and the accounting and technology keywords that employers seek.

Micronomics Company. By stating a measurable accomplishment, Donita shows that she gets results.

Renton College. The addition of another concrete accomplishment strengthens her credibility as an achiever.

Associations Membership in professional organizations related to the job objective demonstrates a commitment to remaining current with trends in the field. This is something employers value highly.

DONITA SILVA
1247 Madison Road
Columbus, OH 43216
614-555-0100 cell: 614-555-0101
dsilva@provider.net

OBJECTIVE

Information Systems Analyst I position in a financial environment requiring system design, programming, investigation, reporting skills

QUALIFICATIONS SUMMARY

* Education in computer systems and accounting practices
* Proven interpersonal skills and team skills in a financial setting
* Programming competence in C, C++, C#.NET and Visual Basic.NET
* Practical experience in EDP accounting applications
* Proficient in Excel, Word, Access, and Windows
* Experienced in System i, Windows Server 2003 Active Directory, Microsoft Exchange Server 2007, and Novell LAN operations

EDUCATION

Bachelor of Business Administration, Renton College, Columbus, OH, 2010
* Major: Computer Information Systems, *Minor: Internal Auditing

*Relevant Courses of Study: System Analysis and Design, Systems Development, Quantitative Analysis, Advanced Programming, Data Communications, Database Systems, Advanced Corporate Finance, Information Systems Auditing, Statistical Techniques

*Senior Internship: American Interstate Bank
Under the supervision of the managing field auditor of American Interstate Bank, performed internal audits on the safety-deposit box operations of five local branches. Reviewed the audit findings with the branch managers. Compiled final report and presented it to the managers.

EXPERIENCE

Alexander & Swartz, Columbus, OH 9/09 to Present
Part-time Assistant Staff Auditor: Assist in audits of cash, accounts receivable, and accounts payable for midsized firms that use System i. Interface with clients and write audit reports as member of the Business Services Assurance and Advisory team.

Micronomics Company, Columbus, OH 6/06 to 9/09
Part-time Programmer's Assistant: Designed, documented, coded, and tested C program subroutines for order-entry system. Achieved a 95 percent average program-accuracy rate on test runs. Cataloged and filed new programs and program patches for the company's software library. Also used Microsoft Exchange Server 2007.

Renton College, Columbus, OH 9/04 to 6/06
Computer Operator Aide. Using Windows S erver 2003, copied files for backup. Verified accuracy of reports and scheduled print sequences. Recommended schedule changes that improved efficiency of backup procedures by 25 percent.

ASSOCIATIONS

Information Technology Management Association, 2005 to Present
Columbus Computer Club, 2004 to Present

Figure 6-6: Electronic Resume Sample

Summary of Information Emphasized in Figure 6-6: Silva

Objective

The title Information Systems Analyst I is clearly understood in Donita's field, specifies the level of authority she is qualified to handle, and clarifies her area of interest and expertise. She highlights pertinent skills, implying flexibility, thoroughness, and responsibility.

Qualifications

Because computer systems and accounting practices are primary skills required in financial work, Donita highlights these skills to meet the Information Systems Analyst I job objective. Accenting mainframe languages and hardware, microcomputer software, and experience in order entry and accounting applications stresses her flexibility. She emphasizes the hardware, operating systems, and program languages with which she is experienced to demonstrate her ability to use these skills immediately.

Education

Donita highlights the courses she took that best support this job objective. The practical experience she gained in a directly related internship demonstrates her scope of knowledge and dependability. She does not include her moderate GPA of 2.9.

Experience

Alexander & Swartz. Donita uses action verbs and highlights her responsibilities and knowledge. She backs up her claim to have "proven interpersonal skills and team skills in a financial setting."

Micronomics Company. Donita's claim to be skilled in program design and coding is supported with a measurable achievement.

Renton College. Donita reinforces her image for getting results by stressing another accomplishment (25 percent increase in efficiency).

Associations

Donita's memberships demonstrate her interest in and commitment to continued professional growth.

DANIELLE RYAN
1205 Koch Lane
Seattle, WA 98115
206-555-0124 cell: 206-555-0125
dryan@provider.net

OBJECTIVE

Network Support Technician for multilocation network

QUALIFICATIONS SUMMARY

* Education in network support technology
* Competent with peer-to-peer networks, UNIX and Linux operating systems and command line utilities, TCP/IP, LAN, WAN, and Network utilities
* Familiar with menu utilities, system backups, ANSI C fundamentals, VPN (Virtual Private Network), V Standards, VNC (Virtual Network Computing), and wireless networking and security
* Practical experience with Word, Access, Excel, Windows 2007/XP/XP Professional, Windows Server 2003, and Novell
* Experienced in building wired and wireless networks and intranet and extranet technology
* Proven ability to work successfully in teams
* Excellent communication and interpersonal skills
* Highly skilled in multitasking, flexible, and adaptable

EDUCATION

Associate of Applied Science, Computer Network Support Technology, Seattle Technology College, Seattle, WA, May 2010
Related Courses and Skills
* Peer-to-Peer Networking Structures * WAN
* TCP/IP LAN Transport System * UNIX * ANSI C * Linux * Telephony
* Remote Computing * Network System Administration
* Wired and wireless networking Technologies * Client/Server Architecture
* Interpersonal Communications * Technical Report Writing

Internship, TechNet, Inc., Seattle, WA January-May 2010
Technician Internship: Assisted technicians in installing and reconfiguring multilocation wireless extranets. Assisted in implementation.

EXPERIENCE

**ComputerStop SuperStore, Seattle, WA May 2008-Present
Installation and Repair Technician, Part-time: Assemble computers, install hardware and software upgrades, provide in-store and on-site repairs to computers and peripherals. Named "Employee of the Month" three times in 18 months.

**Seattle Technology College September 2008-January 2010
Computer Lab Technician, Part-time: Assisted faculty and students with hardware- and software-related problems. Assembled, installed, and added PCs to the network throughout campus. Answered 100 percent of trouble calls within 90 minutes.

ASSOCIATIONS

Tech CORPS, Volunteer, 2008-Present
PC Users Club, 2005-Present

Figure 6-7: Electronic Resume Sample

Summary of Information Emphasized in Figure 6-7: Ryan

Danielle wants a job in a medium- or large-sized firm that has an extensive network. Many of the firms she would like to work for recruit IT (Information Technology) employees through Internet job listing sites, so Danielle prepares a cyberfriendly electronic resume. She pays particular attention to formatting:

a. Using no word processing codes.

b. Using only standard characters that are available on the keyboard.

c. Using a 12-point Courier font.

d. Saving the resume as an ASCII or Plain Text file for easy transmission.

Objective

Danielle has researched the job market and knows the types of positions that are open to people with her skills. She writes a concise, targeted job objective. Employers reviewing resumes can immediately identify which jobs match her qualifications.

Qualifications

Because Danielle knows that electronic resumes are often sorted and selected by resume-search software programs, she loads her Qualifications section with keywords that emphasize her hardware/software knowledge and experience as well as her strong interpersonal skills. She wants any resume-search program to mark her resume for further evaluation, so she includes industry-specific terms that will increase the number of hits her resume receives.

Education

In addition to her degree, Danielle lists relevant courses she has taken. Because the course names are long, she separates them with asterisks and spaces. The course listings also use industry terminology to support knowledge claims in the Qualifications section and to create other opportunities for search programs to choose Danielle's resume.

Danielle puts her internship experience in the Education section. Her exposure to a networking configuration different from the traditional wired configuration is important because it expands her capabilities in employers' eyes.

Experience

Danielle's experience is complementary to her job objective. Notice how she uses measurable accomplishments that are meaningful to employers. She knows employers want to hire people who meet deadlines and produce quality results.

Associations

Tech CORPS is made up of individuals and businesses that donate and/or install computers, software, and networks in schools and other educational institutions. Danielle's community service relates directly to her job target, shows her commitment to her community, and helps her stay current in her field.

Mike Banta
415 S. 23rd #43
Fresno, CA 93701
209-555-0152 cell: 209-555-0153 mbanta@provider net

OBJECTIVE

Seeking a receptionist position for a reliable person or organization with a strong work ethic

QUALIFICATIONS

- Windows, Word (Advanced), Outlook
- Keying at 45 words per minute
- Ten-key at 245 strokes per minute
- Excel and Access data entry
- Formatting business correspondence
- Filing: alphabetic, numeric, geographic
- Operating high-speed collating copy machine
- Multiline telephones

EDUCATION

State University, Fresno, CA
Office Occupations, Certificate, August 2010

McCaine Adult Education Center, Clovis, CA
MS Word: Levels I & II, June 2009

WORK EXPERIENCE

Fruitland West, Fresno, CA Summer 2009
Cherry Sorter
Received a raise the second day for being one of the three fastest workers. Always arrived on time; promoted to Head Sorter.

Trail Mushroom, Clovis, CA June 2005 to August 2008
Crew Leader
Promoted to Crew Leader in 2006. Calculated weekly time cards and posted daily attendance records for 16 to 20 people. Left when company closed.

Picker
Picked and sorted mushrooms 30 percent faster than the company average.

Figure 6-8: Print Resume Sample

Summary of Information Emphasized in Figure 6-8: Banta

Note: Figure 6-8 illustrates Mike's excellent job of translating personal attributes—strong work ethic and reliability—into measurable benefits for an employer.

Objective
Mike states a clear job objective and stresses his strong personal attributes that enhance his job performance.

Qualifications
Mike positions his skills at the top of his resume to assure the prospective employer that he is qualified for the entry-level job stated in his objective. Notice how the keying and ten-key skills are described in measurable terms that are meaningful to an employer.

Education
Mike lists his most current schooling first. The Education section explains where Mike learned the skills that are related to the job objective on his resume.

Work Experience
Because his work experience is limited and not directly transferable to the receptionist position he is seeking, Mike emphasizes on-the-job accomplishments that demonstrate his transferable skills such as reliability, dedication, and commitment to hard work. All of these skills are valuable to employers:

"Received a raise the second day for being one of the three fastest workers. Always arrived on time; promoted to Head Sorter."

"Promoted to Crew Leader in 2002. Calculated weekly time cards and posted daily attendance records for 16 to 20 people."

"Picked and sorted mushrooms 30 percent faster than the company average."

John Chang

jchang@provider.net

6487 West Street
Davis, CA 56915
cell: 649-555-0177

Home
Objective
Qualifications
Education
Experience
Associations
Print Resume
Contact me

Objective

Web Specialist

Qualifications Summary

- Comprehensive web site development
- Web site hosting and registration
- SQL and Access database management
- Graphic and multimedia design, including streaming audio/video, analysis graphs, maps, and custom web graphics
- Server administration in Windows 2003/XP/XP Professional, Windows Server 2003, UNIX, Linux, and Solaris

Computer Qualifications

Internet/Web Applications	Programming	Multimedia
Microsoft IIS	HTML, XML	Adobe Photoshop
SQL Server, My SQL	SQL	MPEG Video Encoding
Security and Firewalls	ColdFusion	Real Media Encoding
Adobe Acrobat	ASP, ASP.NET, VB.NET	ArcView Mapping
Dreamweaver, Flash	PHP	MP3 Compression
HTTP and FTP servers	Java	Adobe Illustrator
Multi Router Traffic Graphing	Perl	

Education/Certification

Associate of Applied Science in Internet Information Systems Technology, 2010
Twin Peaks Technical College, Twin Peaks, CA
Relevant Courses Completed: Extensive programming courses, server design, database management, network security, Internet imaging

- **Microsoft Certified Database Administrator (MCDBA)**

Work Experience

Please see web portfolio for examples of my work.

National Geographic Information Center, Boise, ID
Assistant Webmaster, Summer 2008 and Summer 2009
Updated the main databases and maintained a public Internet interface using Macromedia Dreamweaver and Active Server Pages.NET (ASP.NET). Created and more efficiently redesigned several branched sites, including photo galleries, statistics tables, and PDF document posting areas and archives. Produced geologic prediction analysis graphs using information gathered from remote automated geology stations. Designed a web interface for LAN bandwidth usage tracking, improving network efficiency by 45 percent.

- **On-the-Spot Award** received for extra effort, Geographic Festival, 2009

Perez Construction and Development, Boise, ID
Web Design Project, Summer 2007
Created entire web site for a small business in construction and land development, which included setup, design, site registration, and site hosting.

Associations

American Webmasters' Association, 2005–Present
ASP Programmers Club, 2006–Present

Other formats of this resume: Printable: (.pdf) (.doc) Electronic text: (.txt)

Figure 6-9: Web Resume Sample

Summary of Information Emphasized in Figure 6-9: Chang

Objective

The title Web Specialist is commonly understood in John's career field.

Qualifications

John summarizes his industry-specific qualifications in a bulleted list immediately following the job objective. To capture the attention of employers, he also uses an eye-catching table of key applications, programming languages, and multimedia programs to emphasize the large number of programs relevant to his job objective that he is qualified to operate.

Keywords emphasized. The names of these programs also serve as relevant keywords that are included in the downloadable electronic version of John's resume, likely generating hits by resume-search software programs.

Education

John's recent degree in Internet Information Systems Technology implies currency in the requisite knowledge base and satisfies the basic educational requirements for the position.

Experience

To provide evidence supporting his qualifications claims, John repeats important keywords and uses synonyms for keywords he listed in the Qualifications section. Examples include the following: database, Dreamweaver, ASP.NET, web site development/site registration, site hosting, web graphics/analysis graphs. He also uses power words (action verbs), such as "updated," "designed," "created," and "produced."

Measurable accomplishments. John includes a strong measurable accomplishment in the National Geographic Information Center description: "Designed a web interface for LAN bandwidth usage tracking, improving network efficiency by 45 percent." He also mentions the On-the-Spot Award for extra effort awarded to him by the Geographic Festival.

Associations

Membership in two nationally recognized professional organizations that are relevant to the job objective demonstrates John's active involvement in remaining up-to-date in the fast-changing, high-tech career field. Employers are interested in this quality when hiring for a web specialist position.

Thomas Stanley
123 Forest Drive
Springfield, NY 14201
716-555-2457 cell: 716-555-0769
tstanley@provider.net

OBJECTIVE

Private Security Guard position requiring the ability to perform safety, security, and surveillance procedures; current licensing; and excellent communication skills

QUALIFICATIONS AND CERTIFICATION

- New York State Security Guard License, 2010
- Carrying Concealed Weapons (CCW) License, 2010
- First Aid and CPR Certification, 2010
- Physical Fitness Specialist, 2010
- Fire Prevention and Safety Training, 2009
- Burglary Prevention Training, 2009
- Practical experience in closed-circuit video surveillance and switchboard operations
- Proficiency in Windows, Word, Excel, PowerPoint, and Outlook

EDUCATION

Crown Community College, Buffalo, NY
Associate of Applied Science, 2010
Major: Criminal Justice GPA: 3.75

EXPERIENCE

Buffalo Juvenile Justice Center, Buffalo, NY **Summer 2009**
Juvenile Corrections Internship
Under the direction of the Juvenile Corrections Officer, monitored and ensured the safety and security of juvenile detainees. Enforced facility safety and security rules. Escorted juvenile offenders to classes, counseling sessions, and work-release programs. Conducted security checks, searches, and pat downs. Maintained an error-free performance record with no security breaches.

County Fairgrounds, Hamburg, NY **Summer 2008**
Grounds and Maintenance Supervisor
Supervised groundskeeping and maintenance crew of eight work-released detainees for the County Sheriff's Department. Quickly resolved worker disagreements and scheduling issues using training in conflict resolution techniques. Completed evaluations and submitted thorough and timely paperwork to the Sheriff's Department.

Baker Sporting Goods, Buffalo, NY **April 2007 to May 2008**
Security Guard, Part-time
Monitored customers and employees to maintain internal and external loss-theft control. Conducted closed-circuit video surveillance of store and building exterior. Responded swiftly to all employee and customer security and safety requests. Performed switchboard operator duties. Wrote and submitted daily loss prevention reports.

Figure 6-10: Print Resume Sample

Summary of Information Emphasized in Figure 6-10: Stanley

Objective

Thomas states a clear, targeted job objective using a job title that is clearly understood in the field. To capture the attention of employers and emphasize his qualifications, he includes job-related competencies that match those listed in employers' job postings.

Qualifications and Certification

Thomas lists his qualifications and certifications in a clear, bulleted list. Because security guard positions can have several certification requirements, he is careful to include all the relevant certificates and licenses he has, along with dates to show that they are current. He uses many industry keywords and stresses experience and training that show his emphasis on safety, fitness, and security. He also lists his practical experience in video surveillance, switchboard operations, and computers because security guards are often asked to perform a variety of surveillance and communication tasks.

Education

Thomas reinforces his qualifications by placing his degree near the top of his resume. He highlights his Criminal Justice major and includes his respectable grade point average.

Experience

Thomas's work experience shows that he can be productive immediately in a job in the security field. His internship at the local Juvenile Justice Center gave him experience in juvenile corrections, and in his description, he focuses on safety and security procedures. Thomas describes his work activities using industry-specific terminology and power words. He includes an accomplishment statement that emphasizes his error-free performance record.

In his description of his summer job at the County Fairgrounds, Thomas includes an accomplishment statement emphasizing his use of conflict resolution and interpersonal skills, both of which are important security guard qualifications. He also describes his ability to complete and submit essential paperwork.

Although Thomas's job at Baker Sporting Goods was a part-time position, it gave him practical experience in a variety of common security guard tasks. He explains his activities using keywords and industry-specific language and emphasizes his ability to manage multiple surveillance and communication tasks.

Sheree Washington
5077 Pine Run
Orlando, FL 32773
407-555-8125 cell: 407-555-3468
sheree_washington@provider.net

OBJECTIVE

Medical Assistant position requiring experience in front office and back office procedures; current certification; and fluency in Spanish

QUALIFICATIONS

- Certified Medical Assistant, 2010
- Associate of Science, 2010
- Four-month Medical Assisting internship with front office administrative and back office clinical experience
- Medical records management experience in ICD-10 coding, alpha- and color-coded filing systems
- Medical terminology courses
- Medical insurance experience
- Spanish language fluency

EDUCATION

Associate of Science, 2010, College of Applied Careers, Orlando, FL Major: Medical Assisting

Related Courses and Skills

- Human Anatomy and Physiology
- Clinical and Diagnostic Procedures
- Medical Office Practices
- Patient Relations
- Phlebotomy
- Medical Law and Ethics
- Pharmacology and Medication Administration
- Laboratory Techniques
- EKG and Basic X-Ray
- Business Communications
- Medical Terminology
- Microsoft Office 2007

CERTIFICATION

- Certified Medical Assistant, 2010
- CPR/BLS Certificate, 2010
- IV Therapy and Blood Withdrawal Certificate, 2010
- Basic X-Ray Machine Operator License, 2010

EXPERIENCE

Dr. Jean Esteban, 106 Seminole Way, Sanford, FL **January 2010 to Present**
Assistant Office Manager, Part-time. Greet and register patients. Answer telephone and schedule appointments. Maintain records for all patients, including active and inactive files. Reduced report generation time by 30 percent by implementing a new system for producing reports for insurance records. Handle insurance billing and collecting. Use spreadsheet, database, word processing, and Internet software programs.

Seminole Medical Center, Orlando, FL **September 2009 to December 2009**
Medical Assisting Internship. Greeted and registered patients. Prepared patient charts. Conducted patient interviews and recorded patient history summaries. Maintained supplies and instruments, and readied examination rooms. Answered telephones and scheduled appointments. Assisted physicians with vital signs and diagnostic testing, minor laboratory testing, and EKGs. Received Standards and Procedures Award for maintaining a safe and healthy work environment.

ASSOCIATION

American Association of Medical Assistants

Figure 6-11: Print Resume Sample (Objective: Medical Assistant)

Summary of Information Emphasized in Figure 6-11: Washington

Objective

Sheree uses an industry-standard job title to state her job objective concisely and clearly. To capture the attention of employers and emphasize her qualifications, she includes job-related competencies that match those listed in employers' job postings.

Qualifications

Sheree includes several terms that readers and software programs will search for when seeking a Medical Assistant candidate. She lists her qualifications in a clear, bulleted list and emphasizes her Certified Medical Assistant certification by listing it first. She includes her practical experience in medical terminology and medical records management and highlights her ability to speak a second language, which is an increasingly important patient communication skill. She includes her degree in the Qualifications category because it is a keyword that is likely to be used in an electronic search of her resume.

Education

Sheree reinforces her qualifications by placing her degree near the top of her resume. She highlights her Medical Assisting major. She also lists classes from her major that are especially pertinent to employers and includes computer programs.

Certification

Because Medical Assistant positions can have several certification requirements, Sheree is careful to include all the relevant certificates and licenses she has along with dates to show that they are current. She places her national certification near the top of the resume to emphasize her qualifications and to show that she takes her profession seriously.

Experience

Although Sheree's current part-time job in a doctor's office is in a medical facility, her duties are mostly administrative (front office). She uses industry-specific terminology and emphasizes her contact with patients and medical records experience. She also includes a strong accomplishment statement providing evidence of her ability to save time and implement valuable new procedures.

Sheree's internship allowed her to work and learn at a local hospital. The internship lasted four months, provided hands-on experience, and is directly applicable to Sheree's job objective, so she places the description in the experience section of her resume. Note how she describes her duties in industry-specific terminology. Sheree mentions her Standards and Procedures Award at the end of the description to show that her job performance is above average and to highlight her attention to a safe and healthy environment, which is a primary job requirement.

Association

The association noted on Sheree's resume reinforces her strong interest in the medical field and shows that she takes her profession seriously.

LAURENT CHACON

1015 Cambridge Way, Houston, TX 77001
409-555-0191 cell: 409-555-2475 lchacon@provider.net

PROFILE

Marketing Manager with extensive experience in the wireless data communications industry, strategic planning experience, and proven ability to lead a team and grow a business

CORE COMPETENCIES

- Managerial and technical education: BSEE, MBA
- Strong skills in marketing strategies development and implementation
- Remote conferencing technology, Windows Live Meeting, videoconferencing
- Knowledgeable and professional interaction with customers, sales force, engineers, and manufacturing personnel
- Team leader for product line introduction
- Proven project management skills, PERT and Gantt charts, Microsoft Project
- Proficient with LANs (wired and wireless),WAN hardware and protocols, T-1, T-3 Carrier networks, analog and digital telecommunications transmissions, UNIX, C++, Visual Basic, Linux, real-time embedded software
- Skilled presenter and proficient in PowerPoint development and delivery
- Experienced in RFP and RFQ processes
- Skilled in use of Word, Excel, Access, wireless technology, VPN, Novell certification

PROFESSIONAL EXPERIENCE

NETLINK INC, Dallas, TX **2002 to Present**

- **Marketing Manager, Southwest Division** **2008 to Present**

Manage marketing operations in Texas, Nevada, Arizona, and New Mexico. Supervise a sales and service force that has an average annual growth rate of 50 percent and participate in executive-level strategic planning meetings. Direct the development and implementation of marketing plan for a banking application of LAN/WAN products; results so far include sales to 50 percent of the Southwest Division customer base. Led team whose 2008 sales strategies have doubled NETLINKs market share in the finance industry and expanded the customer base in hospitals by 80 percent.

- **Sales and Service Manager, Southwest Division** **2005 to 2008**

Supervised account executives and increased district sales by 150 percent in two years. Directed on-time, underbudget openings of offices in Houston and Dallas. Improved customer satisfaction 100 percent through systems-support teams that provide four-hour turnaround on service calls. Analyzed competitive forces in the Southwest and reported findings at quarterly planning meetings with upper management.

Figure 6-12a: Print Resume Sample, page 1 (Profile: Marketing Manager)

Laurent Chacon **(lchacon@provider.net)** **Page 2 of 2**

- **Engineering Product Development Coordinator** **2003 to 2005**

  Member of product start-up team developing ultra-fast, self-contained, secure, low-power wireless transmission technologies. Coordinated hardware and firmware integration. Supervised component testing, provided engineering support for component production, and assisted in real-time embedded software development. Acted as marketing interface during technical presentations to customers.

ABC NETWORKING, Houston, TX
Systems Support Representative **2002 to 2003**

Provided effective and consistent technical support to customers via telephone or email and live chat applications. Researched technical solutions. Reduced turnaround on service calls by an average of 2 hours per call. Maintained a technical support web page and published answers to FAQs. Received Outstanding Service Awards, 2002 and 2003.

UNIVERSITY OF SOUTH TEXAS, Houston, TX
Small Business Development Center **2000 to 2002**

- **Intern: Technical Industries**

  Guided by the Center Director, assisted small businesses specializing in technical products to establish vendor sources, design and implement testing procedures, solve production problems, and train workers in manufacturing techniques.

EDUCATION

- University of South Texas, Houston, TX — MBA, 2002
- Mid-State College, Austin, TX, cum laude — BSEE, 1999

ASSOCIATIONS

- National Association of Consulting Engineers, 2005–Present
- Information Technology Management Association, 2008–Present; President, 2009
- American Society for Quality Control, 2007–Present
- Member, Board of Directors, Texas Red Cross, 2003–Present

Figure 6-12b: Print Resume Sample, page 2 (Profile: Marketing Manager)

Summary of Information Emphasized in Figures 6-12a and 6-12b: Chacon

Note: Laurent Chacon's extensive experience justifies a two-page resume.

Profile

Laurent's Profile demonstrates that he is an experienced manager who has achieved the strong skills required by his industry. He is promoting his experience and is not seeking an entry-level position, so he uses a Profile section (in lieu of an Objective) to tell employers who he is and what he can contribute to a business.

Core Competencies

The managerial, leadership, and technical capabilities that make Laurent an effective and productive leader in this field are summarized here. These include his managerial and technical degrees, strong marketing skills, presentation skills, telecommunications and computer skills, and project-management skills. This section is full of keywords that employers seek.

Professional Experience

NETLINK INC: *Marketing Manager*. Laurent emphasizes measurable achievements because this field is very results-oriented. Laurent proves the competencies he claimed in the Qualifications section. Throughout his Professional Experience section, Laurent uses power words to clearly show his workplace activities and accomplishments.

Sales and Service Manager. Laurent documents leadership, marketing strategies, and customer service achievements. Referring to the management level of the business-planning team emphasizes the scope of responsibility he has on the job, as well as the respect he has earned.

Engineering Product Development Coordinator. This position is vital to Laurent's success because it gives him credibility with technically knowledgeable customers and with the engineering and manufacturing elements of an organization.

University of South Texas, Small Business Development Center: *Intern*. This internship is valuable because it reassures employers that Laurent understands the structure and scope of the entire business process.

Education

Laurent has credible, impressive professional experience and does not need to emphasize the specific courses he has taken. He places the Education section near the end of the resume because, at this point in his career, employers are more interested in his accomplishments than his education.

Associations

Membership in related professional organizations demonstrates a commitment to remaining current with field trends—a quality respected by employers. Employees who contribute to the business community enhance an organization's image.

ERIKA ALLEN

123 Jeffrey Street, Hoboken, NJ 07030
555-555-1234 (home) 555-555-8229 (cell) eallen@email.net

PROFILE

Registered Environmental Technician with A.S. in Environmental Sciences, OSHA Certification, knowledge of federal and state regulations, and strong technical writing abilities

CORE COMPETENCIES

- Soil and groundwater sampling and soil vapor extraction
- Environmental site mapping and assessment
- Technical writing and reporting
- GIS and AutoCAD
- Mapping and data entry
- Microsoft Word and Excel

CERTIFICATION AND TRAINING

RET – Registered Environmental Technician
Certification from National Onsite Wastewater Recycling Association 2009

Emergency First Response
Primary and Secondary Care 2009

OSHA Health & Safety Training
40-hour course 2008; 8-hour refresher course 2009

WORK EXPERIENCE

Envirocorp, Burlington, New Jersey
Environmental Technician, January 2007–present

- Survey sites and conduct field analysis and environmental site assessments
- Conduct soil and groundwater sampling
- Operate and maintain remediation systems
- Oversee drilling and excavation and monitor well installation
- Collect data and develop technical reports and maps using Word, Excel, GIS, and AutoCAD
- Three-time recipient of the Envirocorp Safety Recognition Award–2007, 2008, 2009

Environmental Consultants, Inc., Oakwood, New York
Soil and Water Extraction Technician, June 2005–December 2006

- Performed laboratory tests on water samples in accordance with schedules set by supervisor
- Performed standards for laboratory methods and followed all SOP
- Used Microsoft Word and Excel to record historical research and perform data entry

EDUCATION

New Jersey Community College, Hoboken, New Jersey
A.S. in Environmental Sciences, May 2005
GPA 3.8

Figure 6-13: Resume Sample for Online Posting

Summary of Information Emphasized in Figure 6-13: Allen

Profile

Because Erika intends to post this resume on a job listing site to apply for multiple jobs, she has used a profile of her experience rather than a specific job objective. She has also used simple formatting to make sure it will transfer cleanly when she uploads the file to the web site. She knows that she will need to check the font and formatting and modify it as needed to meet web site requirements when she posts the resume online.

Core Competencies

Erika has listed her most important qualifications, including skills that are often required in Environmental Technician positions. She has taken the time to research a variety of job descriptions and use industry keywords.

Certification and Training

Erika has important technical, regulatory, and safety certification that is preferred by many employers of environmental technicians. Therefore, she lists these near the top of her resume in its own section for emphasis. She includes dates to show that she has kept up with her training and her certification is recent.

Work Experience

In her work experience, Erika shows advancement and increased responsibility, so she emphasizes experience over her education. She uses industry specific terminology and abbreviations that employers would know. She is careful to use power words in her descriptions of her work, and she demonstrates a powerful accomplishment by including her safety awards. Through her experience and research, she knows that safety is prized in the environmental industry. Her awards are measurable proof of her commitment to safety and excellence on the job.

Education

Since Erika has pertinent work experience that is more important than her education, she lists education last. She has chosen not to list specific courses, since her skills are more important, but she does include her GPA because it is high.

Career Action

6-1 Objective and Profile Statement

Directions: Write a resume Objective for your target job. You may want to use one of the job descriptions you collected earlier as a reference for this assignment. Address the needs stated in the job description you are referencing.

Imagine that you need a generic resume to hand out to multiple employers at a job fair. Write a Profile statement that you can use in place of an Objective on that resume.

Career Action

6-2 Resume Outline

Directions: Access Career Action 6-2 on your Data CD, use this worksheet, or create a word processing document for your resume outline. Use the completed Career Actions in Chapter 3 to help with this activity.

Once you have completed the worksheet, number the sections of the outline, ranking them in order of importance and relevance to your job objective. Later, you will present the material in your final resume in this order. For example, if your education is more relevant to your job objective than your work experience, place the education information before the work experience information. Likewise, you will need to group items from your Related Experience, Activities, and Awards section in the way that best presents your accomplishments. File your completed worksheet in your Career Management Files Binder.

Name: ______________________________

Address: ______________________________

____

E-Mail Address: ______________________________

Telephone Number: ______________________________

Cell Phone Number: ______________________________

Fax Number: ______________________________

Web Site Address: ______________________________

OBJECTIVE OR PROFILE: *(Refer to sample job descriptions.)*

____

____

____

____

QUALIFICATIONS: *(Use terms and keywords that are related to your target job to describe your capabilities and accomplishments.)*

____

____

____

____

____

____

____

____

WORK EXPERIENCE: *(State your accomplishments in measurable terms, if possible. Start with the most recent job, and list each job in reverse chronological order, ending with the earliest work experience you had.)*

Dates Employed: From ____________ To ____________

Company Name: ____________

City: ____________ State ____________ ZIP ____________

Job Title and Description: ____________

____

____

____

Dates Employed: From ____________ To ____________

Company Name: ____________

City: ____________ State ____________ ZIP ____________

Job Title and Description: ____________

____

____

____

Dates Employed: From ____________ To ____________

Company Name: ____________

City: ____________ State ____________ ZIP ____________

Job Title and Description: ____________

Dates Employed: From ____________ To ____________

Company Name: ____________

City: ____________ State ____________ ZIP ____________

Job Title and Description: ____________

EDUCATION: *(If you have attended more than one school, list the schools in reverse chronological order—the most recent one first. Do not list high school if you have higher-level schooling unless the high school is considered very prestigious.)*

Name of School	City, State	Degree(s)/Certificate(s)	Years Attended

(Job seekers with little or no work experience should expand the education section and list it before the Work Experience.)

Major(s): ____________

Minor(s): ____________

GPA: ____________

Relevant Courses of Study: ____________

Certifications and Licenses: ____________

RELATED ACTIVITIES/EXPERIENCE: *(List internships, volunteer work, service clubs, and so on. List the name of the program or organization. Include a brief summary of your experience, accomplishments, and activities, as well as the dates you were involved.)*

SCHOOL-RELATED ACTIVITIES: *(Organizations, clubs, tutorial experience, class projects, honor groups, internships, leadership, and so on.)*

INTERESTS: *(List interests that are related to your job target and demonstrate well-rounded qualities, including interaction with people, manual dexterity, intellectual pursuits, artistic ability, physical fitness, strength, continuing education, and personal/professional development.)*

MILITARY SERVICE: *(If applicable, list the branch of service, your highest rank, training received, areas of specialization, major duties, skills and knowledge developed, and location of service.)*

AWARDS AND HONORS: *(If applicable, list all awards, honors, and commendations you have received. Note they do not have to be workplace awards, but they do need to be relevant to workplace skills.)*

ASSOCIATIONS AND MEMBERSHIPS: *(If applicable, list all membership or leadership in professional or trade associations, community organizations, social organizations, and volunteer groups.)*

Career Action

6-4 Resume Draft

Directions: Review the sample resumes on pages 118–141. Mark the organizational schemes and sections of the models that are useful to you. Resumes typically should contain all the standard sections listed below. The optional sections should be included when they support your main job objective or when an employer requests them. Note how the sample resumes include differences in the section headings. Mark the headings that best suit your experiences and preferences.

Standard Resume Sections:

- **Name and Contact Information (no heading)**
- **Objective or Profile**
- **Work Experience**
- **Qualifications**
- **Education**
- **Related Experience (or Activities)**

Other Resume Sections to Consider:

- **Military Service**
- **Awards and Honors**
- **Associations and Memberships**

Determine which organization is best for you. (If you have extensive work experience, the chronological organization might be best. If you have limited work experience but plenty of relevant skills, the functional or combination organization will highlight your skills.) Prepare a written or word processed rough draft of the content of your resume using the resume outline in Career Action 6-2 as a reference and starting point. Be selective about the quality and quantity of information you include. Make every word count. Emphasize your qualifications and measurable accomplishments, and include appropriate power words and keywords from Career Action 6-3. File your draft in your Career Management Files Binder.

Career Action

6-5 Resume Evaluation

Directions: Assume you are evaluating candidates for an entry-level job as an accountant for a major accounting firm. You are to write a summary comparing and evaluating the resumes of two top applicants—Alex Valenzuela and Ralph Greenwood. Their qualifications are almost identical. However, one has documented his qualifications more convincingly than the other.

Read their resumes, Figures 6-14 and 6-15 on pages 149 and 150. Determine which resume is more effective, and explain why in your summary. Be thorough, keeping in mind that your resume will be scrutinized in the same way during your job search. Use a separate sheet of paper or Career Action 6-5 on your Data CD to complete this assignment. File your summary in your Career Management Files Binder.

6-3 Resume Power Words and Keywords

Directions: Access Career Action 6-3 on your Data CD or use a separate sheet of paper to complete this activity.

1. **Prepare a comprehensive list of appropriate power words (action verbs) and keywords to use in your resumes. (Consider industry terms; acronyms; and terms describing your job positions, experience, education, skills, and so on.)**
2. **Use the list on page 104 and the Internet as a primary resource in your research.**
3. **Print a report that includes your lists of power words and keywords and a list of the resources you used to identify them.**
4. **File your summary report in your Career Management Files Binder for future reference.**

Resources for Identifying Power Words and Keywords for Your Resume:

- ***Your Career: How to Make It Happen*** **web site at www.cengage.com/careerreadiness/levitt**
- **Job advertisements and descriptions for positions you are considering (print or online)**
- **Web sites of employers you are considering**
- **Government publications such as the *Occupational Outlook Handbook* (print or online)**
- **Professional associations in your field (check their web sites, publications, and meetings)**
- **Internet searches on "resume keywords," "resume power words," and "action verbs"**
- **Online encyclopedias and dictionaries**

ALEX VALENZUELA

2440 Windom Way, Apt. 34 Los Angeles, CA 90063 213-555-0165 avalenzuela@provider.net

---

OBJECTIVE Staff Accountant, Audit Division

QUALIFICATIONS

- Experienced in invoicing, accounts receivable, accounts payable, general ledger, inventory control, Sarbanes-Oxley compliance
- Self-starter, team player, goal-oriented, willing to travel
- Attention to detail, accuracy, and deadlines
- Strong communication, problem-solving, and customer service skills
- Proficient in Word, Excel, Access, Outlook, Windows, QuickBooks Pro
- Work with PC network in client-server environment

EDUCATION

Bachelor of Business Administration, Accounting, 2010
University of Los Angeles, Los Angeles, CA GPA 3.5

Relevant courses of study:

- Analysis and Design of Accounting Information Systems
- Information Systems Auditing • Managerial Accounting
- Cost Accounting • Tax Accounting • Financial Accounting
- Intermediate Accounting I, II, III • Commercial Law

Senior Internship, 12/09 to 4/10
Project Leader: Coordinated student team analyzing inventory system of a small trailer manufacturing company. The recommended just-in-time ordering and improved parts control systems reduced yearly carrying costs by 55 percent.

EXPERIENCE

O'Keefe and Associates, Los Angeles, CA **September 08 to Present**
Part-time Bookkeeper: Use Quickbooks Pro to invoice clients, post income and expenses, process accounts payable, reconcile general ledger accounts, and prepare monthly balance sheets and P&L statements. Update expense-tracking spreadsheets for each client. Using Excel, reconcile monthly bank statement. Initiated shorter invoicing cycle and introduced discounts for prompt invoice payment; reduced A/R cycle to 35 days.

Rand and Company, Los Angeles, CA **6/06 to 8/08**
Part-time Retail Sales Clerk: Sold 175 percent of quota.
Awarded "2007 Outstanding Employee/Customer Relations" certificate.

ACTIVITIES

Vice President, Beta Alpha Psi Accounting, 2010
Member, Information Science Association, 2007 to Present
Member, Debate Team, 2006 to 2008

Figure 6-14: Resume for Career Action 6-5 (Applicant #1 for Staff Accountant position)

Ralph Greenwood
6780 Greenbriar Street, Los Angeles, CA 90067

Education:
University of Los Angeles, Los Angeles, CA
B.B.A., Accounting, June 2010
Grade Point Average: 3.5

Major Courses of Study:
Commercial Law, Cost Accounting, Economics, Principles/Management, Auditing, Statistical Techniques, Programming Systems, Principles/Finance, Managerial Accounting, Systems Analysis & Design, and Intermediate Accounting I, II, III

Experience:
January to May 2010
Department of Accounting, University of Los Angeles, Senior Internship: Coordinator of student team. Analyzed inventory system of a small retail store. Recommendations to adopt just-in-time ordering and improved stock control saved company a significant amount of time and money.

2008–Present
Westworth and Company, Los Angeles. Part-time Bookkeeper. Responsibilities include: invoicing customers, posting income and expenses, handling accounts receivable and payable; preparing income statements and balance sheets, operating PC computer in client-server network with Microsoft software and Quickbooks Pro; reconciling bank statements; and updating client expense-tracking spreadsheets. Shortened time needed to invoice clients and to receive payments.

2006–2008
Tueller's Men's Shop, Los Angeles. Part-time sales. Duties included: making retail sales; maintaining merchandise displays; assisting with inventory; assisting with cashing out; maintaining orderly stockroom.

June 2004–February 2006
Woodland General Nursery, Los Angeles. Stock maintenance staff. Duties included: unloading new merchandise; arranging merchandise in assigned locations; maintaining orderly and clean grounds; carrying and loading purchases for customers; dispensing with disposable containers and other waste. Assisting with watering, feeding, spraying, and general care of nursery items.

Other Activities:
Beta Alpha Psi—Accounting, officer; Member, *University of Los Angeles Student Center*—2008-2009; *University of Los Angeles Swim Team*, member, 2006-2008.
Hobbies: Swimming, reading, piano, travel.

References:
University of Los Angeles Career/Placement Center, 1300 J Street, Los Angeles, CA 90063

Figure 6-15: Resume for Career Action 6-5 (Applicant #2 for Staff Accountant position)

6-6 Final Print Resume

Directions: Use a word processor to prepare your final print resume. (If you hire an expert to prepare your resume, be sure to request an electronic copy so you have the file for future revisions or updates.) Use the chart below as a guide for evaluating and revising your resume. For each category that contains a question that you answered "No," revise your resume content according to the guidelines in the chapter. Proofread and edit the content until the resume is perfect. Make sure your print resume is scannable, and avoid formatting that does not scan clearly. File your resume in your Career Management Files Binder and in your Career Portfolio.

If you want more ideas for your resume, browse the links on the *Your Career: How to Make It Happen* web site. Also, check with your school's career services center, which is typically an excellent resource for help developing a resume.

	Yes	No
Objective or Profile My Objective or Profile statement includes the job title and/or the required abilities specified by the employer.		
Qualifications My Qualifications contain keywords that reinforce requirements for the job.		
My Qualifications are relevant to my stated job objective.		
I have included all of my major strengths.		
Education If my education supports my job objective better than my work experience does, I have placed the Education section first (or vice versa).		
I have emphasized courses, internships, degrees, certificates, and so forth, that best support my objective.		
I have included my overall or major/minor GPA if it is impressive; otherwise, I have left it out.		
Work Experience For each job listing, I have included the employer's name and address (city and state), my job title, and dates of employment.		
In each job listing, I have described my responsibilities and stated specific accomplishments.		
In my job descriptions, I have used power words and keyword nouns to support my job objective.		
If my work experience is limited, I have included relevant paid and nonpaid internships and volunteer or other pertinent activities.		

Related Activities		
I have included my involvement in professional and other organizations that support my job objective.		
I have included relevant awards, achievements, and offices held.		
Overall Content and Appearance		
I have included all relevant information and targeted the resume content to the specific job objective.		
I have made sure the length of the resume is appropriate for my level of experience.		
I have organized the content logically and presented it in order of importance to my job objective.		
My resume content is truthful and correct (free from all grammar, spelling, and punctuation errors).		
My resume is visually appealing and easy to read.		
I have used appropriate fonts, white space, and acceptable enhancements (boldface, bullets, indents).		
I have avoided graphic enhancements, columns, and decorative fonts.		

CareerAction

6-7 Electronic Resume Formatting

Part A: Following the formatting guidelines presented in the chapter, convert the print resume you created in Career Action 6-6 to an electronic resume. Be sure to give your electronic resume a different name so you still have the original file to use for your print resume.

Format your electronic resume carefully to ensure that the receiver views a clean-looking document. Include relevant keywords to generate as many hits as possible by resume-search programs.

Follow the instructions below to be sure your resume meets an employer's expectations.

1. **Follow the employer's directions.** Obtain and read all employer instructions for creating and sending an electronic resume. If you have questions, send an e-mail message or call to request clarification.
2. **In your word processor, open the file containing your scannable print resume.**
   a. Highlight the text, and change the font to Courier 12 point. This monospaced font is the most reliable font for accurate e-mail transmission because each character is the same width, making it possible to determine stable line lengths.
   b. Eliminate multiple columns.
   c. Limit line lengths to 65 characters, including spaces. Longer line lengths often transmit unevenly.

d. Clean up the formatting:
   - Replace bullets with asterisks or hyphens.
   - Use all capital letters for headings.
   - Use blank lines between sections to make the content more readable.
   - Eliminate special characters, such as the copyright symbol (©), the ampersand (&), and mathematical symbols.

e. Use the Save As command to give the document a new name and to save it as "Plain Text (*.txt)."

f. Close the file, and exit the word processing program.

3. **IMPORTANT: Open the document in your standard text-editing program, such as TextEdit or Notepad. (Do not open it in your word processing program.)**
   A standard text-editing program creates the cleanest electronic resume.
   a. Place your name on the first line with no other text. (Resume-search programs look only for a name on this line.)
   b. Start all lines at the left margin.
   c. Use uppercase letters for headings, but use a standard mix of uppercase and lowercase letters throughout the body of the document.
   d. Place each telephone number on a separate line. Label each one, such as "home phone," "work phone," or "cell phone."
   e. Consider the length. The specialized formatting may cause your electronic resume to become two or three pages long in your standard text-editing program. Do not worry about keeping the resume to one page in this program; however, try to limit the document to two pages.
   f. Save your resume again as a .txt document. Leave the file open.
4. **Open your e-mail program, and create a new message.**
5. **To ensure clean transmission, make sure your format is set to Plain Text format (not Rich Text or HTML).**
6. **Return to your standard text editor (TextEdit or Notepad), and select (highlight) all the resume text.** Then copy and paste it into your e-mail message window. (Or paste the text into the resume field at an employer or recruitment web site.)
7. **In the e-mail subject line, include the job title and/or the reference number of the position for which you are applying.**
8. **Insert your electronic cover letter (see Chapter 7).** In the e-mail message window that contains your electronic resume, place the cursor above your resume and paste in a copy of your electronic cover letter. Do not send a resume without a cover letter or a short message indicating that your resume is included.
9. **Key a line of asterisks under your electronic cover letter to mark the end of your cover letter message and the beginning of your resume.**
10. **Clean up any odd spacing or other formatting problems.**

Review the sample electronic resumes (Figure 6-6 on page 126 and Figure 6-7 on page 128) to see how these formatting guidelines are applied.

Figure 7-13 on page 180 shows a completed e-mail with a cover letter and resume.

Part B: Research and practice online resume posting. Access the *Your Career: How to Make It Happen* web site and choose one or more resume-posting web sites (such as Monster, America's Job Bank, The Black Collegian Online, African-American Career World, and Saludos.com) to review the instructions for creating and posting an online resume. If you prefer, use other resume-posting sites for this exercise. Practice completing an online fill-in-the-blanks resume form or pasting your electronic resume into an open resume block. Print your resume and other pertinent pages before you submit your resume, and place them in your Career Management Files Binder.

For Your Career Management Files Binder

After completing the Career Action activities in this chapter, file the following documents in your Career Management Files Binder:

- ☐ **CA 6-1: Objective and Profile statements**
- ☐ **CA 6-2: Resume outline and notes**
- ☐ **CA 6-3: List of resume power words and keywords**
- ☐ **CA 6-4: Resume first draft**
- ☐ **CA 6-5: Resume evaluation summary**
- ☐ **CA 6-6: Final print resume and electronic file (also for Career Portfolio)**
- ☐ **CA 6-7: Printout of electronic resume and electronic file**

Chapter 7

Job Applications and Cover Letters

Objectives

- Learn how to complete effective employment applications.
- Learn how to complete effective online applications.
- Learn how to write effective cover letters that get employers' attention.
- Learn how to format cover letters.
- Learn the importance of following up with employers after submitting applications and cover letters.

Overview

You will be screened into or out of an interview (and a job) based on the quality and effectiveness of your job search package: resume, cover letter, and employment application. If you carefully completed the activities in Chapter 6, your resume should be top-notch. This chapter presents tips and activities for preparing winning employment applications and cover letters. Remember: The qualified job applicant who does only an average job of preparing these documents is screened out; applicants who prepare these documents well will remain in the running for the job. Chapter 7 explains how you can market yourself by completing print and online applications correctly, writing a results-oriented cover letter, and formatting letters for print and online submission.

chapter 7 CareerActions

7-1: Completing an Employment Application

7-2: Internet Research on Cover Letter Strategies

7-3: Cover Letter Outline and Draft

7-4: Final Cover Letter

Jump Start Your Employment Application

Download three or four online job applications in your career area. Work with a partner to review them carefully and make a checklist of the common information that is requested on all of the forms or web sites (for example, name, address, available hours).

Request some printed applications from local businesses and review them the same way.

Make a second checklist of information that is requested on only one or some of the forms.

Make a third list of application questions, terminology, and abbreviations that you do not understand, and research them online to find out more information.

With your partner or as a class, discuss why you think certain information is required on all forms and other information appears on some applications but not on others.

Compare printed and online job applications. How are they alike; how are they different?

The Employment Application

An **employment application** (or **job application**) is a set of questions that employers use to get standard information from all applicants.

Many job seekers think of the application as something to get through quickly so they can get on with the interview. Wrong! Employers consider application forms, cover letters, and resumes carefully. They use these documents to select interviewees and weed out people who do not look qualified on paper.

In this section, you will learn how to complete an employment application correctly and professionally. This will help ensure that your application passes the screening process.

Application Forms

Employers design application forms to get the information they consider most important to making hiring decisions. This includes some information that applicants might omit from their cover letters or resumes. By getting the same information from all applicants, employers can compare applicants' backgrounds and qualifications.

Employers use a wide variety of application formats. The length and complexity of application forms vary greatly—from basic paper forms to sophisticated online web forms. The most important thing is to *follow the instructions exactly.*

Many employers have online applications. Others scan applications and file the information electronically. Applications are searched for information (education, work experience, and so on). If you omit important information, your application may be passed over.

Some organizations use long, complex applications with questions that require detailed answers. Some organizations ask questions that test applicants' personal values and knowledge of the job or occupational field. Treat every question seriously and answer it completely. Applicants who submit messy or incomplete applications with mistakes are the first to be eliminated. If the application is extremely long, complete it at home. Photocopy the application and fill in the copy. Check the application carefully and then transfer your data to the real application form. Take two or three days to work out the best possible answers.

Preparation and Practice

The first step is to search an employer's web site for an application you can print and use as a practice version. If you can't get one ahead of time, get one from a competitor or a related organization.

Always ask for an application you can complete at home. This will give you time to do your best work and practice wording your answers to fit in the spaces. Employers judge neatness, completeness, and the quality of answers. It usually takes more than one try to achieve the wording and effect you want.

Following directions is important to employers. Be sure to demonstrate this ability when you apply for a job! Read the entire application to see how items are interrelated and which ones require more or less detailed answers. This will help you avoid duplicating information, ensure that you write information in the right places, and learn what other information you may need.

4 Completing an Employment Application

This section has instructions for completing the major parts of a typical application.

Personal Information

In the Personal Information section, you provide your name, address, contact information, social security number, and information about any history with the organization. Respond "N/A" (not applicable) if a question does not apply to you. See Figure 7-1 for an example.

If the application asks for a current address and a permanent address, repeat your current address in the permanent address section rather than leave it blank. Always list a second phone number or cell phone number where messages can be received. Provide a working e-mail address that you check regularly.

Position Information

Figure 7-2 on page 159 shows the Position Information section of an application. Be sure to list a definite position objective, title, or number. Employers are not impressed with applicants who list "anything" as the position desired. This

ABC Company

APPLICATION FOR EMPLOYMENT

This application is used in the selection process and both pages must be completed. Attach extra sheets if necessary (references to resumes are NOT acceptable).

APPLICANT INFORMATION

Last Name	First Name	M. I.	Social Security Number	Home Phone	Alternative Phone
Martinelli	*Elizabeth*	*S.*	*999-00-0088*	*208-555-0106*	*208-555-0170*

Permanent Address – No. & Street	City	State	Zip	Date
6518 Willow Way	*Boise*	*ID*	*83706*	*01/15/--*

Have you previously ...... ☐ applied to OR ☐ been employed by ABC Company?	Where and when? *N/A*	E-mail Address *emartinelli@provider.net*

Do you have relatives working for the ABC Company? ☐Yes ☒No If yes, give names and departments where they work.

Figure 7-1: Personal Information Section

hints of desperation, a lack of confidence, or a lack of focus or direction.

If you can start work right away, write "Immediately" under Date Available. If you are currently employed, note that you will need two weeks' notice. You may be asked about your available days, hours, or shifts.

Because salary is such an influential factor in employment, use "negotiable" as the salary desired. Don't risk eliminating yourself before you have a chance to present your qualifications in an interview. Save any discussion of salary until the employer has expressed a definite interest in you. If the position is advertised at a set and nonnegotiable salary, list that figure.

Education

Your education will be covered in a section that is similar to Figure 7-3 on the next page. The sample lists one high school and one community college. If you attended more than one high school, list the most recent one you attended, and indicate the year you received your diploma. List your GPA only if it is requested or if it is high. If you have attended more than one post-secondary educational institution, list the most recent one first and work back to the first one you attended. If necessary, attach a separate list of additional schools you attended.

If space is provided to list subjects of study, research, special skills (such as a foreign language), or other activities, give examples that relate to your job objective. Check the application carefully before you fill in this section. The Employment History section may have a very similar field. Decide which information to put in each section.

Employment History

Figure 7-4 on page 160 is the employment history (or work experience) section of the sample application. List your most recent job first. If the application does not have a separate section for your military service, list it with your employment history.

Before you fill in the application, decide which information to put in the education section and which to put in the employment section.

Use brief, positive phrases to explain reasons for leaving a job and periods of unemployment: "returned to school," "changed careers," "reorganization," "employment ended," "business closed," or "took a position with more responsibility." Avoid negative language ("couldn't find a job," "quit," "personal conflict," "fired for no reason") that may lead an employer to question your abilities and judgment.

If you were fired from a job, be as brief and as positive as possible and leave longer explanations for the interview. Be prepared to describe what happened in unemotional and professional language. Take responsibility for your actions (don't blame others), explain what you learned from the situation, and explain how you could have handled the situation differently. It may help you to write out an explanation, but your best chance at getting a job will come from explaining the situation in person. It also will be essential to have a reference who will give you a solid recommendation.

References

List three professional or personal references. Whenever possible, tie your references directly to your work experience. Most prospective employers value good references from former reputable employers because former employers know firsthand how you performed at work. Notice in Figure 7-5 on page 161 how the first two references are tied to the employment history shown in Figure 7-4.

Some applications specify that references be people other than former employers or supervisors. Consider teachers, members of volunteer organizations, and other people who know your skills and qualities. This is an example of why it is so important to read every word of an application carefully.

Remember: You must talk to your references in advance and get their permission to use their names and contact information on an application.

POSITION		
Position Desired *Sales Supervisor*	Salary Desired (per month) *Negotiable*	
Willing to relocate? ☒ Yes ☐ No	Do you want ☒ Full-time ☐ Part-time	Date Available for Work *Immediately*

Figure 7-2: Position Information Section

EDUCATION						
Highest Educational Level Completed: Community College						
Name of School	Location	From	To	Degree or Diploma	Major	Minor
High School *Idaho Falls High School*	*Idaho Falls, ID*			*Diploma*		
Community College *Central Community College*	*Boise, ID*	*9/08*	*1/10*	*A.A.*	*Marketing*	
College or University						
Graduate School						
Special Training						
Languages Other Than English (if required in employment announcement):	Speak *Spanish*		Read *Spanish*		Write *Spanish*	

Figure 7-3: Education Information Section

Additional Information and Applicant Statement

This section, which sometimes appears at the beginning of an application, will ask questions about your current employment situation, eligibility to work in the U.S., ability to produce proper documentation, past felony convictions, alternate names you may have used in the past, and your willingness and ability to submit to a drug test. Always answer these questions truthfully and completely.

Request to Contact Your Current Employer
As shown in Figure 7-6 on page 161, if an application asks permission to contact your current employer, answer *yes* only if your employer is aware of your job search and approves. Otherwise, protect your current job with a reply of *no.*

Background Information Check You may be asked on an application if you are legally available for work in the United States. You may also be asked if you have a criminal history that includes a felony or misdemeanor charge. Answer these questions truthfully and indicate

EMPLOYMENT HISTORY & RELATED EXPERIENCE		
List present or most recent experience first. Include armed services experience and volunteer work.		
Employer Name Kevington's Emporium (Part-time)	Employer Address 3315 Front Street Boise, ID 83705	Dates (Mo./Yr.) From 12/08 To Present
Position Title Assistant Sales Supervisor	Supervisor Charlie Wu	Phone 208-555-0131 Ext. 125
Reason for Leaving Still employed	Salary: Start 9.00/hr End 11.58/hr	No. Hours Per Week: 20
Duties: Training, supervising, and scheduling staff of six		
Promoted to Assistant Sales Supervisor after only six months		
Employer Name Crown Sportswear (Part-time)	Employer Address 1800 Orchard Street Boise, ID 83704	Dates (Mo./Yr.) From 5/08 To 11/08
Position Title Sales Clerk	Supervisor Connie Pratt	Phone 208-555-0114 Ext. 418
Reason for Leaving Took new job	Salary: Start 8.50/hr End 8.50/hr	No. Hours Per Week: 10-15
Duties: Sales, customer service, and design and setup of all merchandise displays		
Performed managerial and closing duties for store three nights a week		
Employer Name Value Market Variety (Part-time)	Employer Address 460 Park Way Idaho Falls, ID 83402	Dates (Mo./Yr.) From 12/05 To 3/08
Position Title Sales Clerk	Supervisor Tevia Levitt	Phone 208-555-0199 Ext. 420
Reason for Leaving Moved to college location	Salary: Start 7.00/hr End 8.25/hr	No. Hours Per Week: 15
Duties: Sales, customer service, and inventory stocking tasks		
Selected "Customer Service Employee of the Month" twice in one year		

Figure 7-4: Employment History and Related Information Section

REFERENCES				
Name Charlie Wu (Kevington's Emporium)	Address 3315 Front Street Boise, ID 83705	Telephone 208-555-0131 Ext. 125	Occupation Sales Manager	Years Known 2 years
Name Tevia Levitt (Value Market Variety)	Address 460 Park Way Idaho Falls, ID 83402	Telephone 208-555-0199 Ext. 420	Occupation Supervisor	Years Known 3 years
Name Dr. Robert Cornwell	Address Business Department Central Community College 8500 College Way Boise, ID 83704	Telephone 208-555-0143	Occupation Professor, Marketing and Sales	Years Known 2 years

Figure 7-5: References Section

ADDITIONAL INFORMATION
✦Are you currently employed? ☒ Yes ☐ No ✦May we contact your employer? ☒ Yes ☐ No ✦May we contact your former employers? ☒ Yes ☐ No
Can you (if accepted for employment) provide proof of your legal right to remain and work in the U.S.? ☒ Yes ☐ No
A separate affidavit on felony and misdemeanor convictions is REQUIRED to be completed on the attached form.
I hereby certify that all statements on this application are true and complete to the best of my knowledge and belief. If employed, I understand that any untrue statements on the above record may be considered grounds for termination. Date 01/15/-- Signature Elizabeth S. Martinelli

Figure 7-6: Additional Information

"will discuss at interview." Your best option is to explain any negative history in person, where you must be prepared to take responsibility for your actions and explain what you learned.

The application will probably also notify you that the employer may procure an investigative consumer report on you as part of considering your application. If so, the investigative report could include information on your criminal record, education, credit history, driving record, and more. Any misrepresentation on your part would be identified, and you would be eliminated from consideration for the job.

Check the application for accuracy, neatness, completeness, and quality of answers. Be sure to sign the application and enter the correct date. Your signature certifies that the information in your application is true and correct.

MAKE IT A HABIT

Tips for Filling Out an Employment Application

You never get a second chance to make a good first impression, so follow these tips when completing an application:

- Read and follow directions. Prepare each section carefully.
- Write your answers neatly in blue or black ink (on a written application), or print the application after you fill it out on a computer. Make sure the application looks attractive and neat.
- Use the correct lines or spaces for your answers.
- Practice on a copy of the application, squeeze in as much positive information about yourself as possible, and abbreviate to fit the information in the spaces provided.
- Answer every question with a correct and well-phrased response. Use N/A (not applicable) if a question does not apply to you. This shows that you did not overlook the question or skip it.
- Include a cell phone number or second telephone number of a person who is readily available and willing to take messages for you.
- Be sure all information is accurate (dates, addresses, numbers, names, and so on).
- Be honest. Employers check the facts and immediately eliminate a candidate who has supplied false information.

© PHOTODISC/GETTY IMAGES

Submit Your Application at the Appropriate Time

Turn in or mail an application to the appropriate person at the correct location or submit it online. Submit it on time or ahead of time.

Once again, your research on the industry and prospective employers is essential. Resources for obtaining this information include current employees, the human resources department, knowledgeable experts in the field, and your school's career services staff.

Unless your research indicates that an employer does not want unsolicited applications, submit an application with your resume and cover letter. Some employers consider unsolicited applications to be pushy, however, so be sure to do your research first.

Look the Part and Be Ready to Interview

Never visit an employer's place of business without dressing your best and looking professional. You could be invited to interview on the spot. Prepare yourself by studying the interviewing chapters in this book and conducting practice interviews.

You could also be invited to take surveys or employment tests, so be sure you have allowed plenty of time for your visit. You would not want to miss out on an employment opportunity because you had to rush to another obligation.

4 Special Considerations for Online Job Applications

Once you find a job opening on an employer's web site or a job listing site, follow the online job application instructions carefully. Online applications are usually a mix of blank fields in which you will enter text, and pull-down menus from which you will click/select a response. They contain similar questions to paper applications, but also have some unique features.

E-mail Registration

All online job listing sites and company web sites will require you to register to fill out an application. This means providing an e-mail address and password that will be used every time you return to the web site.

If you do not have Internet and e-mail access, you can set up a free e-mail account through a service such as Yahoo! Mail and Gmail (Google) and access your account through a public computer at your school or public library. Since this will become your identification for the online application, use a professional-sounding e-mail address. Anything clever or funny is considered unprofessional and can eliminate you from consideration. Make sure you use a password that is secure enough that others will not guess it, but easy enough for you to remember easily. See Figure 7-7 on page 164.

Posting Your Resume and Cover Letter

The online application process typically includes posting your resume and cover letter. This can mean attaching or uploading the electronic files (.doc, .txt, .rtf, etc.) or cutting and pasting the text into fields on the web site.

Applying via a Company Web Site

Applying for a job on a company's web site is similar to filling out an printed job application. You will be asked to submit basic personal information such as your name, phone numbers, and address. You will also be asked some basic questions about the position and how you learned of the job.

The application may not ask for information related to your education and work experience if it requires you to attach or paste your resume and cover letter.

Be sure to attach your resume in the preferred file format that has been tailored to the specific job.

You might also be asked to answer survey questions about your work styles and preferences.

© PHOTODISC/GETTY IMAGES

Watch Out
Identity Theft

Identity theft is the crime of stealing another person's personal data for illegal purposes, such as using that person's credit card. When you apply for a job online or at a employment kiosk in a mall or store, you are asked for your birth date and social security number. Many kiosks instantly check your social security number and background.

Kiosks are here to stay, but unfortunately, it is not easy to know if a particular employer's kiosks follow the privacy laws regarding personal data. For example, you should have the opportunity to read a privacy statement before you enter your data. If you change your mind about applying, you should be able to withdraw your electronic consent for a background check while sitting at the kiosk.

The employment applications on most kiosks are identical to the ones you can fill in at the employer's web site. If you have that choice, apply through the web site.

Do not interpret this advice to mean that your data may be misused on all, or even most, kiosks. The burden falls on you to protect your information. You can read more about this sticky issue at the World Privacy Forum (www.worldprivacyforum.org).

On printed applications, it is acceptable to write "Upon hiring" in the field for the social security number.

How did you become aware of this opportunity?

* Source: --None-- Referred By:

Other Source:

Applicant Data

* First name: Street address:

* Last name: * City:

Middle: * State/Region: --

* Phone #: ZIP/Postal code:

Mobile #: * Country: United States

Email Registration

Your email address will be used as your login name allowing you to return to our website to view your status and update your profile. If you do not have an email address, you can obtain a free account at Yahoo or Gmail. Please make sure that the syntax of your email address is in the following form: *username@ispname.com*

* Email:

Please create your password

* Password:

Re-type new password:

Resume & Cover Letter

Your resume can be uploaded in any of the following formats: DOC, RTF, PDF, TXT, HTML. Files saved in .DOCX are not currently supported

* Attach resume or CV: Choose File no file selected

Cover Letter:

Please indicated the highest level of education **completed**

* Education: --Please select--

Legal Status

Are you authorized to work in the U.S.?

* Work status: --Please select--

Figure 7-7: Partial Sample of Online Employment Application

Using Job Listing Sites

A job listing site is a recruitment site that allows employers and recruiters to match your information and resume to available positions.

To access the job listings and/or post a resume on most job recruitment sites, applicants must first complete a registration or resume posting form. The applicant/job matching software used by most job listing sites requires applicant information to match to the job openings. Along with your basic personal information, history, and qualifications, this information will include:

- ☐ **Job Target Keywords.** These are search terms that describe the type of job you are seeking. Use terms that describe the skills, experience, and abilities you have that are required in jobs you want to pursue.
- ☐ **Desired employment industry.** You will typically be asked to specify the industry in which you are seeking employment.
- ☐ **Geographical preference.** You will need to specify one or more geographical areas in which you would like to work.
- ☐ **Desired salary.** Some sites require that you include the salary range you are seeking.
- ☐ **Work preferences.** Some sites ask questions about your work preferences and work styles, including working with others, preferred hours, customer service, pace of work, deadlines, and using technology.

On a job listing site where you indicate that you are open to a variety of jobs, make sure you post a generic resume that highlights your skills and accomplishments but does not have a specific objective.

Proofreading and Following Up

Fill out the application completely. Follow the employer's instructions to the best of your ability.

Do not assume that you will be able to log back in to fix mistakes. Print copies and proofread them before you click the Submit or Send button. Many sites have hotlines and online assistance for job applicants.

complete CareerActions

7-1 Completing an Employment Application

Cover Letters

A **cover letter** is a letter of inquiry or introduction that you submit with an application and/or resume. You inquire about a possible job opening and/or state your interest in a position. Most importantly, you introduce yourself to a potential employer. For this reason, a cover letter must make an excellent first impression. It must be well written, be designed to get the reader's attention and interest, and provide information that convinces the reader to interview you and consider you for employment. A cover letter should highlight your most important qualifications and stress how those qualifications can meet the employer's needs.

In most situations, employers expect a cover letter because it demonstrates the type of professionalism and initiative they want in an employee. Submitting your resume to an employer without a cover letter could cost you further consideration for employment.

Job seekers use three types of letters depending on their purpose and the type of job they seek.

- ☐ **Application cover letter.** The applicant responds to an advertised opening and states his or her interest in and qualifications for that job (Figure 7-8, page 176).
- ☐ **Prospecting Cover Letter.** The applicant writes to a potential employer to inquire about the possibility of an available position when one has not been advertised (Figure 7-9, page 177).
- ☐ **Networking Letter.** A job seeker contacts someone a member of his or her network has suggested contacting to request information or assistance with the job search. For an example of this type of letter, see Chapter 4.

Cover Letter Content

Keep your cover letter brief—four or five paragraphs and no more than one page. Follow proper business letter organization and include the sections and content described below. Figures 7-8, 7-9, and 7-10 (pages 176–178) show samples of proper cover letter formatting and content.

Address, Date, and Salutation

Place your name, address, and contact information at the top of the letter followed by the date, inside address (employer's name, title, and address), and salutation ("Dear Ms. Och:").

The Opening

Introduce yourself and state your purpose:

- ☐ Explain how you know of the employer.
- ☐ Mention the position you are applying for and explain how or where you heard about it. If you learned about it through an advertisement or announcement, include the date and where you found the notice.
- ☐ Explain why you are interested in the organization.
- ☐ State the type of job you are seeking.

If you know someone who would be influential and recognized by the reader, get that person's permission to use his or her name. Refer to any previous communication with the person you are writing.

The following excerpt is from a networking letter by Kimi Okasaki, who is seeking an administrative support position. Kimi mentions a person who is well known to the addressee:

> Carmine Garduno from the Health Services Bureau recommended that I talk with you about the possibility that you may need an administrative support person with experience in educational and community activities. Your new five-year educational and community plan is soundly developed. I am confident that my experience as a volunteer in the Valley Elementary School Parent-Teacher Organization (VES-PTO) and the Diabetes Foundation would be useful in helping you achieve success with your plan.

Your Sales Pitch

This section focuses on what you have to offer—your qualifications for the job. Persuade the reader that he or she should interview you. Emphasize your most relevant qualifications for the job.

Include two to four results-oriented descriptions of accomplishments and capabilities that show how you can benefit the employer and handle the job. Be truthful and remember that you must be able to verify these accomplishments during an interview.

Do not duplicate information exactly from your resume.

Express interest and enthusiasm for the job and focus on your strengths, experience, and achievements.

Somewhere in the letter, refer to the job description or something specific you know about the organization's activities or requirements. This demonstrates initiative and interest in the company.

This section can be presented as one to three short paragraphs or a bulleted list to highlight the qualifications you want to emphasize, for example:

> Through my volunteer work, I learned about the disease prevention techniques your department teaches to daycare workers. The potential to help families and fight disease while doing work I enjoy is irresistible. I recently completed an Associate in Science degree, majoring in Information Management Technology, with an overall GPA of 3.5. As Secretary-Treasurer of the VES-PTO, I used Excel and Word to generate and track correspondence with more than 500 student families.

Another effective way to highlight your qualifications is in a two-column, side-by-side comparison of the employer's requirements and your matching experience. This format is attractive and reader-friendly and makes your qualifications stand out. The cover letter in Figure 7-10 on page 178 illustrates the comparison-list style. The following example shows the paragraph example above in this format. (Because this format requires two-column formatting, it should be used only with printed cover letters.)

Job Requirements	My Qualifications
GPA of 3.0 or higher	Word processing and data processing experience I completed an Associate of Science degree, majoring in Information Management Technology, with an overall GPA of 3.5.
Interest in health and disease prevention	Through my volunteer work, I learned about the disease prevention techniques your department teaches to daycare workers. I am highly motivated by the desire to help families and fight disease.
Community involvement	I am actively involved in community volunteer work and serve as Secretary-Treasurer of the VES-PTO.
	I use Word and Excel to generate and track correspondence with more than 500 families.

The Closing

Ask for a meeting or an interview—not a job—and indicate how and when you will follow up. State that your resume is enclosed and include a courteous sentence that expresses appreciation or thanks. Here's a good example:

> Enclosed for your review is my resume. I would appreciate meeting with you to discuss the possibility of our working together. I will call you on Thursday to check on your availability, or you may reach me at 555-0136. I would welcome the opportunity to contribute to the exceptional community outreach efforts of the Department of Disease Prevention. Thank you for your consideration.
>
> Sincerely,
> *Kimi Okasaki*
>
> Kimi Okasaki

Tips for Writing Effective Cover Letters

Review the section on good writing style and organization in Chapter 6. These techniques also apply to writing an effective cover letter. You must be clear, follow proper business letter format, and project a friendly, motivated, and professional image.

In addition:

- ☐ **Use clear and concise wording and professional language.** Never use slang, casual, personal, or emotional words. Never plead for a job or indicate how badly you need a job.
- ☐ **Don't duplicate your resume.** Also, make sure your letter does not contradict anything in your resume.
- ☐ **Be positive.** Share your positive qualities. Project confidence and show interest in the job.
- ☐ **Don't use overblown or empty words to describe your abilities.** Use specific, measurable terms; for example, "My program increased reported customer satisfaction by 35 percent."
- ☐ **Be straightforward and relevant.** State objectives that relate to the company and the job. Relate your qualifications to the employer's needs and interests. Emphasize what you can do for the organization.
- ☐ **Be truthful.** Never misrepresent yourself or give false information. Be honest about your education, background, and experience.
- ☐ **Emphasize your skills as a team player.** Don't try to convince the employer that you are a one-person miracle worker.
- ☐ **Incorporate specialized terminology** from your industry and job target where appropriate.
- ☐ **Do your research.** Make sure you have researched the organization and/or the job enough to make informed comments. A statement that suggests you are unfamiliar with the employer would eliminate you from consideration.

MAKE IT A HABIT

Show Off Your Writing Skills

Use your cover letter to show employers that have business writing skills. In hiring surveys, many employers have noted that they consider cover letters to be examples of a job applicant's communication ability. Be sure to be concise, articulate, convincing, and—most importantly—accurate. An error-free, grammatically correct letter shows that you are conscientious and detail oriented.

Never allow slang, informal language, or texting abbreviations to sneak into your job search correspondence. Use well-crafted sentences and business-like language to demonstrate your professionalism and readiness to communicate in the workplace.

Customize the Content

Take the time to tailor the content of your cover letters to fit each employer. It is likely that you will apply for multiple jobs in different organizations, so along with changing the addressee, you will need to change the content of each cover letter to match the objectives and needs of each job. Include only information in a cover letter that is relevant to a specific job and employer.

Demonstrate Your Knowledge of the Organization or Industry Make your cover letter individual yet professional. Use your company research to personalize your letter. Mention your interest in a new or popular product of the organization; the expansion of the firm; recent organizational accomplishments; the company's reputation for reliability, quality, its product, or customer service; the firm's humanitarian efforts; or a special achievement of the person you're writing to or the organization in general.

Emphasize How You Can Meet the Employer's Needs Identify in your cover letter the employer's needs that are outlined in the job opening announcements or advertisements. If your current job target deals only with accounting, a vague listing of accounting qualifications and computer specialization will not be as effective as a reference to strong accounting abilities (with the computer specialization referenced as a backup).

If you are considering more than one position, such as an accounting technician and a computer specialist, highlight the appropriate skills, experience, and education for each job you are targeting.

Address Your Letter Appropriately

A job advertisement will indicate the address of the person or department who should receive the cover letter and resume. Use this person's full name and/or title in the inside address. If you do not know if a female recipient is married, use "Ms." rather than "Mrs."

With a prospecting cover letter, you do not always know the name of the person who should receive the letter. Some organizations do not accept unsolicited applications, resumes, or cover letters. Applicants who address communications to the human resources department may receive form letter stating that no applications are currently being accepted.

Find Out Who Hires To boost your chances of getting an interview, address a prospecting letter to the person who has hiring authority for the position. Never address your cover letter "To Whom It May Concern." This type of salutation may target your letter for the wastebasket.

How do you get the right person's name? If you do not yet know whom to address your cover letter to, consider one of these methods:

- Call your target employer and say that you are researching careers and want to write to the person who specializes in your area. Get the person's full name and title, and verify the spelling and mailing address or e-mail. When you call, introduce yourself and thank the person by name for his or her help. Always say that you are a student or are doing research. The person you speak to could possibly help you later, and using names establishes a courteous, friendly tone.
- Search the organization's web site for an organization chart or contact information. If this is not available, go to the human resources office (if your target employer has one). Ask whether there is an organizational chart you could use for your career planning class or personal research. The chart should provide you with the name of the department head to whom you should address your cover letter.

If these methods are not effective for your job search, ask members of your job search network to help you devise a workable approach. As a last resort, address the letter to a Hiring Manager, Department Head, or Human Resources Department and use the address from the organization's web site or phone book listing.

Which Department? If you send your cover letter and resume only to the human resources department, the person who heads the department you are interested in might never see them. On the other hand, if you send your letter and resume directly to the person you would work for, your chances of getting an interview will be increased, but the human resources department may resent being circumvented.

How do you handle this situation? If the employer is accepting applications, send one letter and resume to the human resources department and one letter and resume to the department head. Indicate in your letters that you have sent similar communications to each party. At worst, both letters wind up in the human resources department. If the employer is not officially accepting applications, send your cover letter and resume to the department head only. You could still get an interview.

Revise and Edit

Carefully review and edit your cover letter draft before sending it. Be choosy—or downright hypercritical—about every word you use. Every word counts! Use your computer's spell checker, but also read your letter carefully for errors. Mistakes can be costly. Any error at all in spelling, punctuation, or grammar can lead an employer to believe that you are careless and prone to mistakes.

Most people find it difficult to edit their own resumes and cover letters because they overlook important aspects (such as punctuation, omission of details, and so on) while concentrating on the wording. Ask a friend or contact who has strong communication skills and knows your background to evaluate your letter. Your contact may think of additional items you should include that you have overlooked. Choose a good writer who will give you honest criticism.

Sources for outside reviewers and critics include:

- ☐ A hiring expert you know who can tell you how your cover letter stacks up against the ones he or she reviews and suggest how you can improve yours

Tailor your cover letter to the employer's needs, and make sure that it is error free. Applicants who write good letters stay in the running!

- ☐ A friend or acquaintance who knows you and your work well enough to help you clarify confusing statements or to spot where you have left out important information or qualifications
- ☐ A professional who does not know you well who is willing to serve as a final test for your cover letter. Make it clear that the cover letter is not yet final and that you are seeking suggestions for improvement.

Consult Your Network

Employers base hiring decisions largely on trust and are more likely to consider letters that mention people they know. Members of your network are statistically the strongest source of job leads and can form the bridge to your perfect job. They can give you suggestions for improving your letters and resumes and can put you in touch with potential employers in your field. Consider the following networking options:

- ☐ **Make an appointment to meet in person.** Make appointments with the most viable of your networking members. Briefly review your job objective and ask for recommendations. Give each person a copy of your cover letter and resume and ask for feedback. Be organized; respect the person's time.
- ☐ **Call the person.** If you cannot arrange an appointment, make a telephone call. Briefly review your job objective and ask for recommendations. Ask whether you can send a copy of your cover letter and resume to get your contact's feedback.
- ☐ **Send a networking letter or e-mail.** If you cannot arrange a meeting or reach the person by telephone, send a networking letter or e-mail. Professionally and politely identify your job target and job search goals and request specific assistance or feedback on your cover letter and/or resume. See Chapter 4 for an example.

complete CareerActions
7-2 Internet Research on Cover Letter Strategies

Formatting and Submitting Cover Letters

The cover letter format depends on print or electronic delivery. Use the following guidelines for printed business letter style or e-mail transmission and web posting.

Print Cover Letter Format

If you are going to mail or fax your cover letter or send it as an e-mail attachment, format the letter using a word processing program. Consider customizing a template or sample from a job search web site, or begin with one of the templates or wizards available with Microsoft Word.

Make the letter visually appealing with a clean overall format. Follow these formatting guidelines and refer to the samples in Figures 7-8, 7-9, and 7-10 on pages 176–178:

- ☐ Use one-inch margins and center the letter on the page.
- ☐ Use one simple, standard font such as Times Roman or Arial in size 11 or 12 points. Visual legibility is extremely important.
- ☐ Single-space the body text and double space between paragraphs and sections.
- ☐ Use bulleted lists to break up lengthy paragraphs.
- ☐ Use only one space after periods at the end of sentences.
- ☐ Don't use excessive, decorative fonts and formatting (such as underlining, shadows, backgrounds, or colored text). These elements will look unprofessional.
- ☐ Use the standard left-margin alignment.
- ☐ Don't include distracting or elaborate graphics.
- ☐ Print your letter on a laser or inkjet printer in black ink on one side of white or light-colored 8 1/2-inch by 11-inch paper that matches your resume.
- ☐ Hand-sign every printed cover letter.
- ☐ Be certain the final letter is perfect—no errors! Proofread and proofread again!

Distributing Your Print Cover Letter and Resume

Once you have completed your resume and cover letter and know how to complete an employment application, you will be ready to submit a solid job search paper package (application, resume, and cover letter). How you distribute your job search documents is also important. Since employers have specific guidelines and preferences, it is essential to follow their instructions. Consider the following tips regarding distribution:

Regular Mail If you mail your documents, put them in a large envelope so you do not have to fold them. If the employer faxes or scans your letter after receiving it, any folds in the paper can cause errors.

E-Mail Attachment or Fax Some employers may specify that they want you to e-mail an attachment or fax the documents. Find out what file format they prefer and follow their instructions *exactly*. (Do not attach files to an e-mail cover letter unless requested to do so. Some organizations actually block e-mails that contain attachments.) If you fax your cover letter and resume, be sure to begin with a fax cover sheet addressed to the proper recipient. If you send them as e-mail attachments, write a brief e-mail message that indicates the files are attached (or paste your full cover letter text into an e-mail and attach only the resume file). Use an informative subject line. See Figures 7-11 and 7-12 on page 179 for examples of e-mails with attachments.

Double check everything before you send the letter, and make sure you have enclosed or attached your resume and any other required documents.

Electronic Cover Letter Format

The electronic job market has created the need for the electronic resume discussed in Chapter 6. Therefore, many employers also require electronic cover letters to be transmitted inside an e-mail message or posted in their web site application forms. Here are some of the key strategies for preparing and formatting an electronic cover letter:

- ☐ Stick with a plain text style. Use an easily readable font, in black and 12-point size, and a plain white background.
- ☐ Make sure the lines have no more than 65 characters. Longer lines may break unevenly and look fragmented on the receiver's screen.
- ☐ Keep your cover letter concise, but clear. An e-mail cover letter should be only two to three paragraphs and under 150 words. It should reveal your interest and sell the target employer on one or two of your outstanding capabilities.
- ☐ Follow standard business letter guidelines. Even though e-mail is less formal than a paper letter, you should not omit parts of the letter such as the salutation or closing.
- ☐ Entice readers with your subject line. Always include a brief, but informative, subject line that will stimulate the reader to continue reading your letter. Consider a subject line such as, "Experienced CPA for Auditing Director" rather than "Re: Job No. 3872."
- ☐ Make the most of keywords. Focus on keywords and skill sets that will increase the chances of your letter being retrieved in a database search. Because of the possibility of a database search, it is more important to use noun phrases than action verbs in an electronic cover letter. See "Using Keywords Strategically" in Chapter 6.
- ☐ Provide sufficient contact information to the prospective employer. This includes your name, address, phone number, and e-mail address.

Submitting Cover Letters and Resumes Online

Transmit your electronic cover letter in one of three ways:

- ☐ Copy and paste it into an e-mail message with the text of your electronic resume, and send it to the employer.
- ☐ Paste the text into the cover letter block in the job application section of the employer's web site as part of the online job application process.
- ☐ Upload your cover letter file (.doc, .txt, or .pdf) from your computer to the employer's web site (or job listing site) as part of the online application process.

Regardless of how the letter is sent, if it is not well written, it will not arrive at its intended destination: the hiring desk. Spell check and proofread again before you press the Send or Submit button. Check the company's web site for guidelines rather than risk sending something they do not want.

> After sending your job search package, follow up with a telephone call to increase your chances of securing an interview.

E-mail When cutting/pasting the unformatted text of your electronic resume into an e-mail message or online application form, adjust the line breaks to make the text as readable as possible. See Figure 7-13 on page 180 for an example. Placing job titles, locations, and dates on separate lines can be cleaner and easier to read than placing them all on one line. Use hyphens or asterisks instead of bullets, and use no special formatting. Use the default e-mail font. As shown in the sample, separate the cover letter text from the resume text with a row of hyphens, equal signs, or asterisks.

Web Posting Job listing and employer sites vary. Some require applicants to paste their entire resumes and/or cover letters into an open box or field on an online application. Others require applicants to build their letters and resumes online, section-by-section. In these cases, you will open your electronic cover letter and resume Word documents and cut and paste the appropriate text into the required fields on the web site. Other sites require applicants to upload their cover letter or resume files to the web sites and submit them with the online application.

Still other sites require the completion of an online application only—no resume is required in this case, though you may need to copy sections of your electronic resume into the application form. Follow each web site's instructions exactly and enter the required information. Before you click the Transmit, Send, or Submit button, print copies of all forms you have completed, proofread them carefully, and make any needed corrections. Reprint if corrections were made; then file your final forms as a reference.

complete CareerActions
7-3 Cover Letter Outline and Draft

Following Up

Applicants who follow up by calling employers after submitting cover letters and resumes are dramatically more successful in obtaining jobs. Two important reasons for this are (1) employers see follow-up as an indication of initiative and confidence, and (2) a busy employer may actually intend to call an applicant but get side-tracked. Applicants who call save the employer time and often speed the hiring decision.

Call about three or four days after the employer receives your letter, and say something like this: "This is Jennifer Ortiz calling from Raleigh. I sent you a letter and resume about the system support programming job and wanted to make sure you received it." This simple telephone call is often a deciding factor in getting an interview. Improve your odds by making this call.

With an online application, call or e-mail the employer directly. Ask for the human resources department, and state that you are responding to the company's online job posting. (Give the source of the ad, the date, the job number, and so on.) If you have applied online, ask for the name, phone number, and mailing and e-mail addresses of the hiring decision maker. Or, call and/or send an e-mail to the decision maker. Let him or her know of your application and interest in the job.

Next Steps

Complete all the Career Actions in this chapter to practice completing job applications and to draft and finalize your print and electronic cover letters. File the completed Career Actions in your Career Management Files along with your Internet research from this chapter. File a copy of your final print cover letter in your Career Portfolio. As you apply for jobs with different employers, customize your cover letter format and content to meet employers' submission requirements and to show how you meet the specific job requirements.

In Part 4, you will take the next steps in your career search by learning and practicing successful interviewing strategies.

© PHOTODISC/GETTY IMAGES

Watch Out

Did You Forget Anything?

No matter how qualified you are and how well written your cover letter and application are, if you forget something important, you will be viewed as careless and will be unlikely to get the job.

According to a Career Builder survey about cover letters, one of the most common errors made by applicants is forgetting to enclose a resume or cover letter in their envelope or neglecting to attach a document to an e-mail message. Before you send an envelope or e-mail, take a moment to make sure all of your documents are enclosed or attached. Don't forget…

Contact information. Always include phone numbers and e-mail address. Applications, cover letters, and resumes can become separated, so it is essential that contact information appear on *all* documents.

The date, salutation, or closing on the cover letter. Always use proper business letter format, and include all sections of the letter.

Your signature. On a cover letter, the signature shows your personal attention. On an application, your signature is *required* to certify and validate your information.

Chapter Checklist

Check each of the actions you are currently taking to increase your career success

- Making my print and online applications perfect.
- Tailoring my cover letters to specific employers; making sure the cover letters are error free.
- Stating the position i am applying for, listing my related abilities, and requesting a meeting or an interview.
- Getting employers' attention with results-oriented examples in my cover letter.
- Formatting my electronic cover letters correctly.
- Distributing a complete job search paper package or maximizing my online job search process.
- Consulting my network for feedback on and assistance with my cover letters and applications.
- Demonstrating initiative by following up my cover letters with telephone calls.

Critical Thinking Questions

1. What are the possible consequences of not filling out an employment application completely and according to the instructions?
2. Should you mention a salary figure in an application? Explain.
3. How is an online application different from a print application?
4. Think of a probable employer with whom you would like to interview. How can you find out to whom you should address your cover letter? Write the name, title, and address of the person in your answer.
5. What is a comparison-list cover letter? In what circumstances is it an effective format?
6. What are at least three features of an electronic cover letter?
7. What are three ways to submit a cover letter to an employer?

For convenient access to valuable career resources, study tools, activities, and job information links, visit the companion web site for this text: www.cengage.com/careerreadiness/levitt.

Trial Run

For each of the following cover letter excerpts, explain how it fails to meet the guidelines in the chapter. Rewrite the paragraphs to make them more acceptable for an effective cover letter. (Invent supporting details and evidence as needed.)

- ☐ Even though most of my experience is in retail, I think nursing is a field where I could be successful because I am totally into helping people.
- ☐ I just love to design computer graphics to enhance specialized publications. It was the only thing I liked about my last job.
- ☐ In my volunteer work with Habitat for Humanity, all my supervisors said I was one heck of a carpenter. By the age of five,
  I was already able to make a wooden birdhouse.
- ☐ I'm a talented mechanic, and I really need this job because my rent is really expensive.
- ☐ Working for Grant Brokerage Company will give me the experience I need to become a certified financial planner in the future. I don't know a lot about the stock market yet, but I'm sure I'll learn quickly on the job.

Working with a partner, use the guidelines in this chapter to create a checklist of at least 15 criteria for evaluating cover letters. (Use the resume evaluation checklist in the Trial Run in Chapter 6 as a model.) Make sure you include criteria for presentation and content, writing style, addressing letters, formatting, and distribution. Devise a rating scale (for example, 1 to 5), and use your checklist to evaluate a sample cover letter that you have written or one from an Internet resource.

KIMI R. OKASAKI

148 Barrister Avenue, Tucson, AZ 85726
520-555-0136 kokasaki@provider.net

April 20, 20—

Mr. George O'Donnell
Office Manager
MegaMall Property Management Company
P.O. Box 555
Tucson, AZ 85726

Dear Mr. O'Donnell

EXPERIENCED ADMINISTRATIVE ASSISTANT, JOB #4864

Please accept my application for the administrative assistant position advertised on the *Arizona Bugle* web site. As a Scout Leader involved in a promotional project last fall, I appreciated MegaMall's offer to let us hold our event in the center of the mall at no charge. I would welcome the chance to work in such a civic-minded organization.

I am an energetic, detail-oriented person who has strong administrative and computer skills, retail and community service experience, and the ability to work well with others. In addition, I have held positions of responsibility in four community organizations over the last eight years and was chosen as the 2009 National Diabetes Foundation Volunteer of the Year.

As you can see from my resume, I thrive in a busy atmosphere that involves many different tasks, the opportunity to work with people, the satisfaction of meeting deadlines, and the chance to excel. I would enjoy the opportunity to talk with you about how I can help MegaMall Property Management with its administrative needs. I will call you next week to request an appointment, or you may call me at your convenience at the number above. Thank you for your consideration.

Sincerely

Kimi Okasaki

Kimi Okasaki

Enclosure

Figure 7-8: Sample Application Cover Letter (Printed)

JUAN TEJADA
2440 Windom Way, Apartment 34
Los Angeles, CA 90063
213-555-0156 jtejada@provider.net

June 29, 20—

Ms. Stephanie Nolan
Manager, Auditing Staff
Nolan Henry O'Leary Public Accountants
1410 Granada Avenue, 7th Floor
San Francisco, CA 94115

Dear Ms. Nolan

Meagan Gerena at Smythe and Associates indicated that you are interested in hiring an accounting graduate with experience in the field. My degree and special interest are in Accounting/Information Systems. Please consider me for a place on your well-respected auditing team, which I noticed was recently named one of the Top 10 auditing firms in our area by the *San Francisco Business Reporter*.

During the last two years, I have worked for a CPA firm where I was able to develop a wide range of accounting and accounting-related skills. My responsibilities included:

- Performing full-charge bookkeeper duties, such as opening, posting, and closing the books; completing federal and state corporate tax returns; and creating Excel templates.
- Assisting a consultant in upgrading software for a customized accounting system.
- Creating a procedures manual that identified common operating, maintenance, and troubleshooting situations that could occur between the two operating systems and provided directions and steps for reconciling those problems in a timely and cost-effective way.

During my senior year at the University of Los Angeles, I had the chance to lead an internship research team. We studied the operations of a local accounting firm and assisted its auditors in the audit of several clients. These experiences cemented my interest in auditing as a career.

I am confident in my ability to make a positive contribution to Nolan Henry O'Leary Public Accountants and am enclosing my resume for your review. I will call next week about your interview schedule, or you may reach me at the contact information above. I look forward to meeting you.

Respectfully

Juan Tejada

Juan Tejada

Enclosure
cc: Meagan Gerena, Smythe and Associates

Figure 7-9: Sample Prospecting Cover Letter (Bullet Style)

CHRISTOPHER LIPSMEYER
846 Cameron Way
Phoenix, AZ 85012
(602) 555-0160 chris_lipsmeyer@provider.net

December 10, 20—

Mr. Gary Whaley
District Sales Manager
Computeriferals Company
1 Computer Way
Rallings City, NY 10099

Dear Mr. Whaley

Computeriferals has earned my respect. I have used and repaired peripherals from most of the leading manufacturers in my studies as a Business Systems/Computer Repair major and in my job as a sales representative at ComputerChoice. I know you build quality products, and I want to sell quality products—Computeriferals.

Careful review of my qualifications and the requirements of a sales representative at Computeriferals suggest that I am well qualified for a sales position with your organization.

Your Requirements	**My Experience**
• Ability to handle multiple prospects	• Expanded customer base from 137 to 183 accounts in the past year—a 34 percent increase
• Proven ability to meet sales goals	• Increased yearly sales from $743,000 to $1,236,000—exceeded goal by 66 percent
• Ability to expand sales in existing accounts	• Negotiated a new $250,000 service contract for an existing client with five locations
• Strong communication and follow-up skills	• Attained 100 percent customer retention through a service-first approach and frequent communication

The expanding market for Computeriferals presents an appealing challenge. Even if you have no current sales openings, I would appreciate meeting with you to discuss your requirements. My resume is enclosed for your convenience. I will call next week to request an appointment, or you may reach me at the contact information above. Thank you for your time.

Respectfully

Christopher Lipsmeyer

Christopher Lipsmeyer

Enclosure

Figure 7-10: Sample Prospecting Cover Letter (Two-Column, Comparison-List Style)

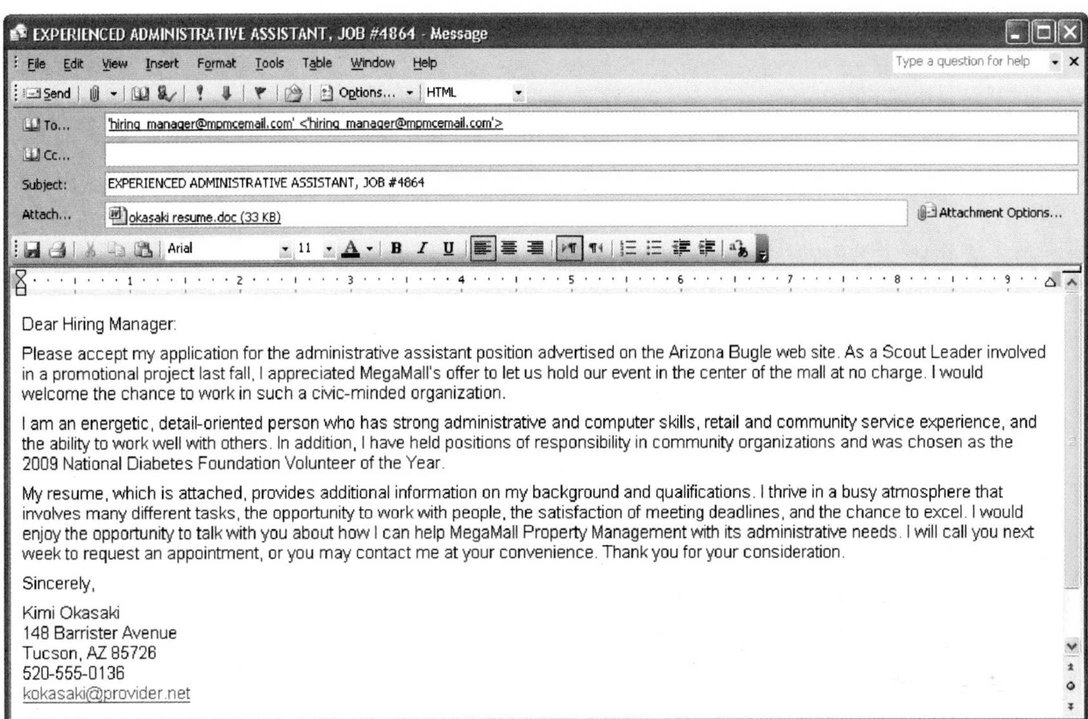

EXPERIENCED ADMINISTRATIVE ASSISTANT, JOB #4864 - Message

File Edit View Insert Format Tools Table Window Help

To... 'hiring_manager@mpmcemail.com' <hiring_manager@mpmcemail.com>

Cc...

Subject: EXPERIENCED ADMINISTRATIVE ASSISTANT, JOB #4864

Attach... okasaki resume.doc (33 KB)

Dear Hiring Manager:

Please accept my application for the administrative assistant position advertised on the Arizona Bugle web site. As a Scout Leader involved in a promotional project last fall, I appreciated MegaMall's offer to let us hold our event in the center of the mall at no charge. I would welcome the chance to work in such a civic-minded organization.

I am an energetic, detail-oriented person who has strong administrative and computer skills, retail and community service experience, and the ability to work well with others. In addition, I have held positions of responsibility in community organizations and was chosen as the 2009 National Diabetes Foundation Volunteer of the Year.

My resume, which is attached, provides additional information on my background and qualifications. I thrive in a busy atmosphere that involves many different tasks, the opportunity to work with people, the satisfaction of meeting deadlines, and the chance to excel. I would enjoy the opportunity to talk with you about how I can help MegaMall Property Management with its administrative needs. I will call you next week to request an appointment, or you may contact me at your convenience. Thank you for your consideration.

Sincerely,

Kimi Okasaki
148 Barrister Avenue
Tucson, AZ 85726
520-555-0136
kokasaki@provider.net

Figure 7-11: Sample E-mail Cover Letter with Resume Attachment

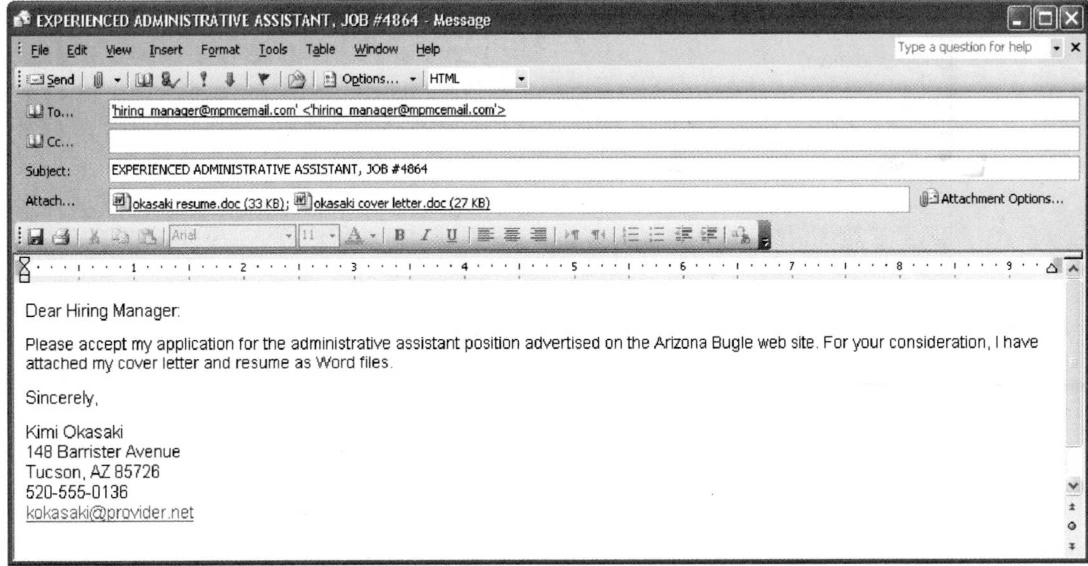

EXPERIENCED ADMINISTRATIVE ASSISTANT, JOB #4864 - Message

File Edit View Insert Format Tools Table Window Help

To... 'hiring_manager@mpmcemail.com' <hiring_manager@mpmcemail.com>

Cc...

Subject: EXPERIENCED ADMINISTRATIVE ASSISTANT, JOB #4864

Attach... okasaki resume.doc (33 KB); okasaki cover letter.doc (27 KB)

Dear Hiring Manager:

Please accept my application for the administrative assistant position advertised on the Arizona Bugle web site. For your consideration, I have attached my cover letter and resume as Word files.

Sincerely,

Kimi Okasaki
148 Barrister Avenue
Tucson, AZ 85726
520-555-0136
kokasaki@provider.net

Figure 7-12: Sample E-mail with Attached Cover Letter and Resume Files

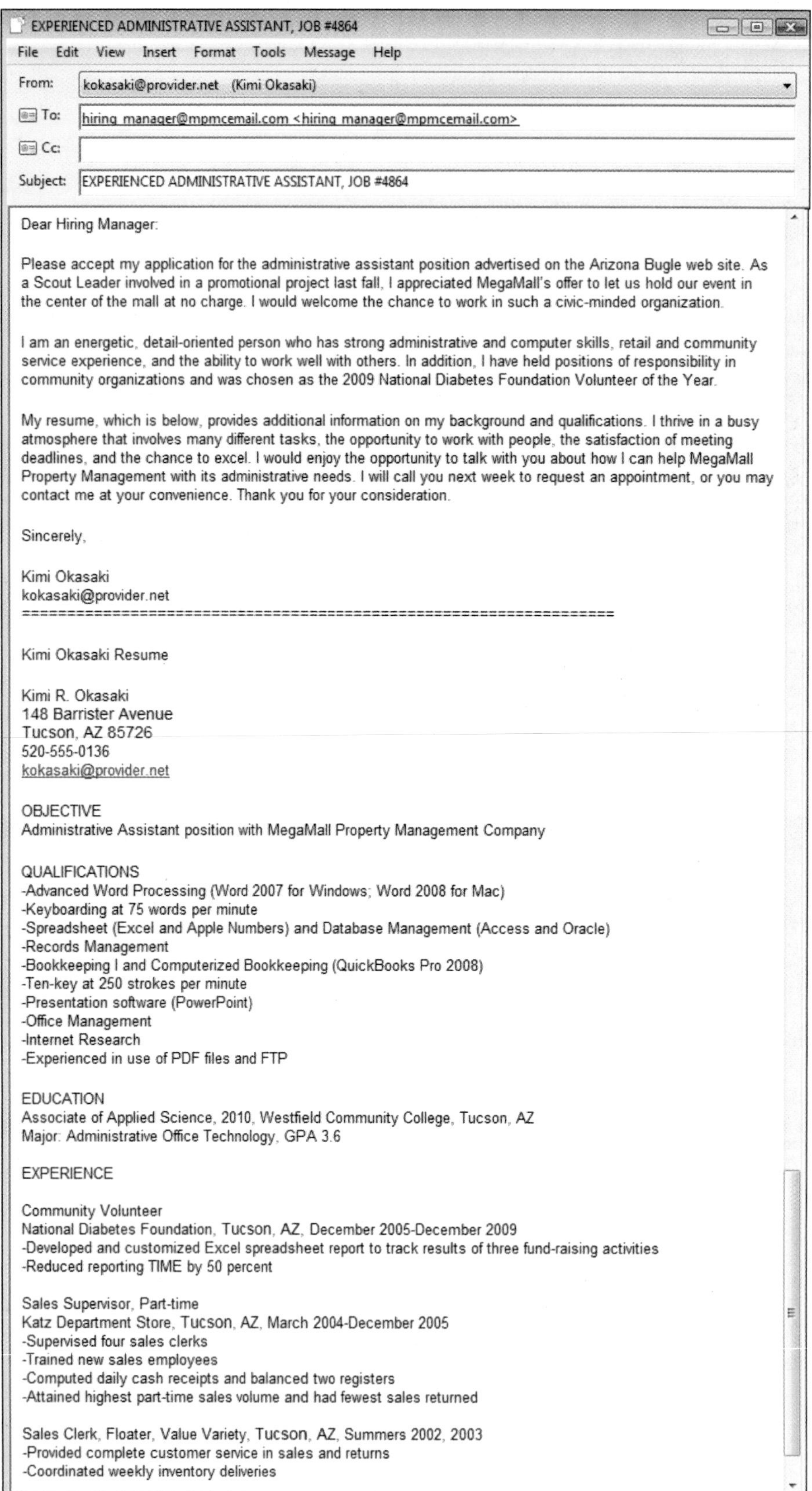

EXPERIENCED ADMINISTRATIVE ASSISTANT, JOB #4864

File Edit View Insert Format Tools Message Help

From: kokasaki@provider.net (Kimi Okasaki)

To: hiring manager@mpmcemail.com <hiring manager@mpmcemail.com>

Cc:

Subject: EXPERIENCED ADMINISTRATIVE ASSISTANT, JOB #4864

Dear Hiring Manager:

Please accept my application for the administrative assistant position advertised on the Arizona Bugle web site. As a Scout Leader involved in a promotional project last fall, I appreciated MegaMall's offer to let us hold our event in the center of the mall at no charge. I would welcome the chance to work in such a civic-minded organization.

I am an energetic, detail-oriented person who has strong administrative and computer skills, retail and community service experience, and the ability to work well with others. In addition, I have held positions of responsibility in community organizations and was chosen as the 2009 National Diabetes Foundation Volunteer of the Year.

My resume, which is below, provides additional information on my background and qualifications. I thrive in a busy atmosphere that involves many different tasks, the opportunity to work with people, the satisfaction of meeting deadlines, and the chance to excel. I would enjoy the opportunity to talk with you about how I can help MegaMall Property Management with its administrative needs. I will call you next week to request an appointment, or you may contact me at your convenience. Thank you for your consideration.

Sincerely,

Kimi Okasaki
kokasaki@provider.net
===

Kimi Okasaki Resume

Kimi R. Okasaki
148 Barrister Avenue
Tucson, AZ 85726
520-555-0136
kokasaki@provider.net

OBJECTIVE
Administrative Assistant position with MegaMall Property Management Company

QUALIFICATIONS
-Advanced Word Processing (Word 2007 for Windows; Word 2008 for Mac)
-Keyboarding at 75 words per minute
-Spreadsheet (Excel and Apple Numbers) and Database Management (Access and Oracle)
-Records Management
-Bookkeeping I and Computerized Bookkeeping (QuickBooks Pro 2008)
-Ten-key at 250 strokes per minute
-Presentation software (PowerPoint)
-Office Management
-Internet Research
-Experienced in use of PDF files and FTP

EDUCATION
Associate of Applied Science, 2010, Westfield Community College, Tucson, AZ
Major: Administrative Office Technology, GPA 3.6

EXPERIENCE

Community Volunteer
National Diabetes Foundation, Tucson, AZ, December 2005-December 2009
-Developed and customized Excel spreadsheet report to track results of three fund-raising activities
-Reduced reporting TIME by 50 percent

Sales Supervisor, Part-time
Katz Department Store, Tucson, AZ, March 2004-December 2005
-Supervised four sales clerks
-Trained new sales employees
-Computed daily cash receipts and balanced two registers
-Attained highest part-time sales volume and had fewest sales returned

Sales Clerk, Floater, Value Variety, Tucson, AZ, Summers 2002, 2003
-Provided complete customer service in sales and returns
-Coordinated weekly inventory deliveries

Figure 7-13: Sample E-mail Cover Letter with Resume Inside Message

Career Action

7-1 Completing an Employment Application

Directions: Using the guidelines presented in this chapter, print and complete the application for employment form on your Data CD. If at all possible, obtain and complete an actual application from an employer in your target industry—even one from your actual target employer. Using an application from your target industry provides the best preparation and practice. If one is not available, search the Internet for "sample job applications." Many varieties are available on web sites such as Quintessential Careers and About.com's Job Searching page. Complete the application for practice, and use it as a model when you fill out actual applications for employment.

Career Action

7-2 Internet Research on Cover Letter Strategies

Directions: Visit the sites listed below and other sites and search engines to find at least five new strategies for writing a successful cover letter. Links are at the *Your Career: How to Make It Happen* web site. Look for new ideas that may be useful to you. Print copies of the data, or write a summary of your findings. If you find new information or information that varies from that in this book, research further and discuss the topic(s) in the classroom, with your school's career services staff, and/or with interview specialists. File your research in your Career Management Files Binder.

- ☐ About.com: Job Searching (Go to Resumes/Letters)
- ☐ CareerJournal.com (Search: Cover Letter)
- ☐ CareerLab (Go to: Cover Letter Library)
- ☐ Monster (Go to: Career Advice)
- ☐ Quintessential Careers (Go to: Job Seeker/Job Search Tools)
- ☐ The Riley Guide (Go to: Resumes & Cover Letters)

7-3 Cover Letter Outline and Draft

Part A Directions: Access Career Action Worksheet 7-3 on your Data CD or use the following worksheet to organize and outline your basic cover letter (keeping in mind it should be tailored to fit each employer's needs). Don't try to write a perfect letter at this point; just work on getting the essence of your message on paper. You will refine it later. Review the sample cover letters in Figures 7-8, 7-9, and 7-10 on pages 176–178 for guidance.

Part B Directions: Using your cover letter outline and related job target research information, compose a cover letter draft. Make it concise, tailored to the employer's needs, and courteous. Most importantly, make sure it demonstrates how you can benefit the employer. File your draft in your Career Management Files Binder.

PART A: COVER LETTER OUTLINE

Your Personal Letterhead:
(Include name, address, phone number, and e-mail.) ______________________

Date: ______________________

Name, Title, Organization, and Address of Recipient: ______________________

Salutation: Dear ______________________

Paragraph 1 Opening:
(Include the name of a referral if you have one; state your position objective.) ______________________

Paragraph 2 Your Sales Pitch:
(Tailor it to the opening. Where appropriate, use bullets or side-by-side columns to highlight strong job-relevant qualifications.)

Paragraph 3 Closing:
(State that your resume is enclosed and request a meeting or an interview. Include your telephone number or refer to the contact information in your letterhead. Thank the reader.)

Complimentary Close:

Sincerely,

(Key your name here.)

Career Action

7-4 Final Cover Letter

Directions: Working in a Word file, polish your cover letter draft, emphasizing your qualifications and making the content clear and concise. Use a thesaurus to find words with just the right meaning. As you prepare your final cover letter, remember that, just as with a resume:

IT MUST BE PERFECT!

After your cover letter is complete, review it with thorough attention to detail; even one error can eliminate you in the employer's paper screening.

When you think your letter is perfect, ask an outside critic to review it one more time slowly and carefully, looking for even the smallest error. This is critical to the success of your cover letter. Print the final letter on top-quality paper.

Copy the Word file and save it with a new file name. Change the formatting of the cover letter to make it appropriate for an electronic cover letter that can be sent via e-mail or an online application.

File copies of your final print and electronic cover letters in your Career Management Files Binder and your Career Port folio.

For Your Career Management Files Binder

After completing the Career Action activities in this chapter, file the following documents in your Career Management Files Binder:

- ☐ **CA 7-1: Completed employment applications**
- ☐ **CA 7-2: Internet research on cover letter strategies**
- ☐ **CA 7-3: Cover letter outline and draft**
- ☐ **CA 7-4: Final print and electronic cover letters and files (also for Career Portfolio)**

part 4

The Job Interview

Industry Speaks

Dave Nielson heads the networking department of a regional medical diagnostic imaging organization. "I took some zigs and zags before getting this position, and I view that as a positive thing. I learned something from every job and every person (even irate customers) and I discovered my own work style. My current boss observed me for a year in a different position and asked me to interview for the job I have now.

"IT departments can be very hectic, with tight deadlines and the occasional crisis. The jobs in our department are specialized and each person has a lot of responsibility. We also do a lot of team projects. It's a challenging, fun job—for the right person.

"The people we hire have done high-level IT work in the past, but our role in medical imaging is pretty specialized and there's a lot to learn. I've learned to be skeptical of people who are overly confident about their capabilities, especially in an interview.

"If you get an interview, you've already been screened through an informal phone call. If the interview goes well, several people will talk to you over the next week, including a lunch meeting. We hire people who are excited about learning new things. We also have a rule that we only hire cheerful people."

Chapter 8

Objectives

- Apply the elements of successful interviewing
- Demonstrate enthusiasm and interest in a position and an organization
- Project professionalism with your wardrobe and positive body language
- Develop good verbal communication practices
- Develop a plan for improving your business etiquette
- Create a 60-Second Commercial to sell yourself
- Assemble your Interview Marketing Kit

Interview Essentials

Overview

You have learned how to present yourself well through your resume, cover letters, and job applications. Now it's time for what may be the most important business meeting you ever attend: the job interview. You will learn what happens in the first 30 seconds of the interview and how to create a good first impression by conveying a positive attitude, dressing like a successful professional, using positive body language, speaking well, and following proper business etiquette. You will also learn how to create a 60-Second Commercial for a very important product (you!) and assemble an Interview Marketing Kit.

chapter 8 Career*Actions*

8-1: Internet Research on Dressing for Job Interviews

8-2: Body Language Self-Inventory

8-3: Internet Research on Business Etiquette

8-4: Create Your 60-Second Commercial

8-5: Action Plan for Core Areas of Successful Interviewing

Jump Start Your Knowledge of Real Job Interviews

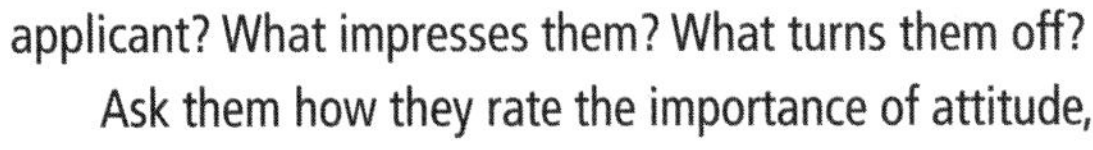

Everyone who is working had a successful job interview at some point in their career. Ask two friends or relatives about a job interview they had. How did they prepare? Were they dressed appropriately? Were there any surprises?

Talk with two friends or relatives about hiring interviews they have conducted. How do they prepare for interviews? What qualities do they look for in an applicant? What impresses them? What turns them off? Ask them how they rate the importance of attitude, appearance, body language, verbal communication, and job qualifications on a scale of one to 10, with 10 being most important.

Ask everyone for their top two tips for successful interviews. Organize the information you collect and put it in a format that will be most helpful for your classmates (a PowerPoint presentation, for example).

© DIGITAL VISION/GETTY IMAGES

1 Know the Key Elements of Successful Interviewing

No one ever gets a job without having some type of interview. The interview is the doorway that every job seeker must be prepared to walk through on the way to successful employment. Think of it as a very important business meeting—maybe the first one with your new employer. Your goal is to learn about the job and the company, and the interviewer's goal is to learn about your abilities and potential. Both of you are evaluating whether you are a good match.

Before the interview, you "exist" to the interviewer on paper or online. The interviewer has looked at your application documents and has compared your education, work experience, and qualifications with those of other applicants. The interview is your chance to "come alive" as someone who can help the organization achieve its goals and as a person others will want to work with.

A successful interview has many elements, some of which are more important than you may realize. Your attitude is the biggest factor determining your success, and it comes through in many ways, including your appearance, body language, and how you speak. Your job qualifications also count, of course, and you must be able to summarize them well.

Your Attitude—The No. 1 Factor

Attitude is the No. 1 factor that influences an employer to hire. Here are some ways you can exhibit a good attitude:

1. **Concentrate on being likable.** As simple as this may seem, research proves that one of the most essential goals in successful interviewing is to be liked by the interviewer. Interviewers want to hire pleasant people whom others will enjoy working with on a daily basis. To project yourself as highly likable, do these things (these actions are detailed later in this chapter):
   - ☐ Be friendly, courteous, and enthusiastic.
   - ☐ Speak positively.
   - ☐ Use positive body language and smile.
   - ☐ Make certain your appearance is appropriate.
2. **Project an air of confidence and pride.** Act as though you want and deserve the job—not as though you are desperate.

3. **Demonstrate enthusiasm.** The applicant who demonstrates little enthusiasm for a job will never be selected for the position.
4. **Demonstrate knowledge of and interest in the employer.** Saying "I really want this job" is not convincing. Explain why you want the position and how it fits into your career plans. You can cite opportunities that may be unique to the firm or emphasize your skills and education that are highly relevant to the position.
5. **Perform at your best every moment.** There are no "time outs" during an interview. While in the waiting area, treat the assistant or receptionist courteously; learn and use his or her name. (An interviewer often requests this person's opinion of the applicants.)
6. **An interview is a two-way street.** Project genuine interest in determining whether you and the employer can both benefit from your employment.

Dress for Success

Have you ever looked at a display of magazines or books and been drawn to one with an appealing cover? The same concept applies in interviews. Your image and appearance help determine the all-important first impression you make. Remember: By the time you have walked into the room and sat down, the interviewer has decided whether you will be considered for the position. Your image and appearance may count for as much as 25 percent of the employer's positive or negative hiring decision.

Dress Conservatively

Most interviewers expect applicants to wear businesslike clothes when they apply for office or professional positions. For men and women, a conservative suit of quality, dark fabric makes the best choice. For women, a tailored dress or coordinated skirt and blouse with matching jacket are also appropriate. Strengthen your image by using your best colors in your accessories—scarves, ties, shirts, blouses and so on.

Base your clothing choice on your research about the career field and the employer. Whenever possible, visit your target employer before the interview to observe the working atmosphere, conditions, and dress code.

The First 30 Seconds Count

People often form opinions about others within 30 seconds of first meeting them! For this reason, the first 30 seconds can make or break an interview.

Interview and interpersonal communications experts have studied what applicants can do to make a favorable first impression and project professionalism and competence during interviews.

Area	Impact on Interview
Attitude	40%
Image and Appearance	25%
Verbal and Nonverbal Communication	25%
Job Qualifications	10%

Interviewers say they form strong opinions about an applicant in the time it takes to walk across the room, say "Hello," and sit down.

A word of caution: Even if an employer permits casual dress on the job, or if employees wear uniforms or safety gear, you should still dress formally for an interview to show you take the opportunity seriously. Never dress too casually. T-shirts, jeans, tennis shoes, and other casual or faddish items may cost you the job.

Try on the outfit before the interview and appraise yourself honestly. Do you come across as the professional, competent, qualified person the employer is looking for? Consider the entire event, not just the conversation with the interviewer. For example, if you're riding a motorcycle or bike, what will you do with your helmet? If there are five feet of snow on the ground, what will you carry your shoes in and where will you put your boots?

complete CareerActions
8-1 Internet Research on Dressing for Job Interviews

Use Positive Body Language

Through our life experiences, we become experts at sending and interpreting nonverbal messages. Your nonverbal communication, or body language, actually carries more influence than the words you say. You may be speaking persuasively, but body language that conveys arrogance, lack of enthusiasm, excessive nervousness, or other negative messages will drown out your words.

To succeed in interviews, keep your body language positive.

Be Perfectly Groomed Make sure your clothes fit well and are clean and pressed. Shine your shoes and, ladies, leave behind that beloved, ancient handbag you take everywhere. If it looks like rain, take an umbrella and wear a raincoat—you do not want to walk into an interview dripping wet! Wear effective deodorant, but go easy on the after-shave lotion or cologne. Be immaculately groomed from head to toe.

Look the Part If you try to make a bold statement against business world conformity with a nose ring and pink hair, you can probably kiss the job good-bye. People who sport visible tattoos or body piercings; unnatural hair or makeup styles; ball caps and baggy pants; or too many earrings, bracelets, or rings to an interview might as well stay home. Many organizations have policies that prohibit radical hairstyles, low-cut blouses or shirts that don't cover the waist, and even open-toed shoes. Show employers that you conduct yourself professionally and dress accordingly.

Appear Relaxed

Your body language will immediately notify an employer if you are overly tense. Be well rested before an interview so you will be alert, and, if possible, exercise by running, stretching, or doing yoga on the day of the interview. Exercise is one of nature's best techniques for relaxing your body and your mind. Try to allocate adequate time in your day—especially during your job search—to do some form of exercise. And be sure to eat something light and healthy so that you don't feel hungry or tired.

During the interview, occasionally change your position in your seat; this relaxes muscular body tension and breaks the rigid feeling that nervousness can cause. Breathe deeply and don't hurry your movements; this will project confidence and will reduce your anxiety. If possible, give a genuine smile! It's an effective tension breaker for both you and the interviewer.

Develop Assertive Body Language

Concentrate on sending assertive messages with your body language. Assertive body language is relaxed, open, and confident. Your posture and gestures support your words and convey credibility and self-assurance.

- ☐ When you meet the interviewer, **give a firm handshake and make eye contact.** This immediately communicates intelligence, competence, and honesty.
- ☐ **Walk briskly.** You'll look confident and show that you're ready for the meeting.
- ☐ **Sit, stand, and walk with your head up and your back straight.** Good posture conveys that you're composed, respectable, alert, and strong. Slouching conveys that you're bored, disinterested, lazy, or unintelligent. Crossing your arms and legs may be interpreted as being closed or stubborn.
- ☐ **Make eye contact.** Making good eye contact is essential to achieving effective communication. It conveys that you really care about what the person has to say. It also conveys confidence, intelligence, competence, and honesty. This doesn't mean that you should glue your eyes to the interviewer; it means that you should look at the interviewer, especially when he or she is talking. Break eye contact at natural points in the discussion. If you are extremely uncomfortable looking directly into the eyes of the interviewer, look at his or her forehead. This gives the impression of looking into his or her eyes. In a group interview, periodically make eye contact with each person. Avoid letting your eyes dart back and forth around the room.
- ☐ **Aim for a pleasant, uplifted facial expression.** Occasionally nod your head and gesture to convey agreement and emphasis. Avoid frowning, clenching your jaw, and other negative expressions.
- ☐ **Don't fidget.** Fidgeting is distracting and makes you look nervous, self-conscious, and unsure of your

Communicate that You are Trustworthy

During an interview, it is essential to come across as a trustworthy and believable person. Conveying trust is almost entirely a nonverbal function.

Trust is an emotional response that is learned in infancy and childhood and remains embedded in the brain. As children, we learned to trust people who projected caring, competence, warmth, and self-confidence through their body language.

As adults, we evaluate trustworthiness in the same way—through positive nonverbal messages that convince our emotional brain center. Looking someone in the eye when speaking to them is the single most important thing you can do to build confidence in what you are saying. A good handshake and good posture, pleasant facial expression, and an energetic, pleasant tone of voice also affect believability.

© PHOTODISC/GETTY IMAGES

Interviewers will not hire people they think are untrustworthy.

ability to get the job. Keep your hands apart to avoid fidgeting. Rest them on the arms of the chair, and keep them still. Keep your hands relaxed, not in tight fists.

☐ **Watch the interviewer's body language.** The interviewer may lean forward, signaling you to expand on what you are saying. If the interviewer shuffles papers, looks around the room, or gives other nonverbal cues that you should finish speaking, heed the signal. Keep listening and watching to determine whether what you are saying is clearly understood. Retreat from a subject if you observe that it's not being well received.

☐ **Subtly mirror the interviewer's communication behaviors.** Some people have intense, highly energetic body language and voice qualities, while others are more relaxed. Subtly match your interviewer's style, speed, and tone of voice—but don't overdo it. Never mirror negative behavior.

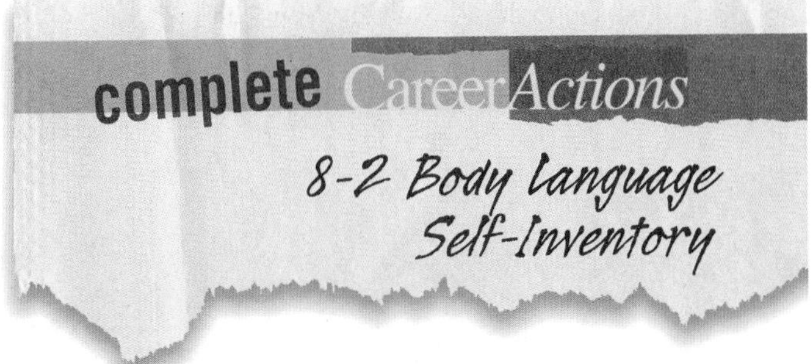

Speak Well for Yourself

You're dressed for the part, your positive attitude is shining through, and your body language shows that you're confident, relaxed, and enthusiastic. What's next? Speaking, of course. Even though research shows that body language can carry more influence than words, you need good verbal communication skills to make a strong case for yourself and get the information you need.

It's How You Say It

Follow these general tips about voice quality to build on the great first impression you made.

☐ **Start off right by greeting the interviewer by name.** This conveys respect, which enhances your likeability. If more than one person is conducting the interview, learn and use everyone's name.

☐ **State your name and the position you're seeking.** Begin with a friendly greeting and state the position you're interviewing for: "Hello, Ms. Ong, I'm Bella Reyna. I'm here to interview for the accounting position." Identifying the position is important because interviewers often interview applicants for many different positions. If someone has already introduced you to the interviewer, simply say, "Good morning, Ms. Ong."

☐ **Use an energetic, pleasant tone of voice** to convey a positive attitude and enhance your likeability.

☐ **Modulate your voice.** Don't speak in a monotone or speak too slowly or too rapidly. Speak loud enough to be heard, but not too loudly.

☐ **Don't slur your words.** Speak distinctly and clearly. No one likes to ask a person to repeat something.

☐ **Use positive words and phrases.** One of the most important interview goals is to keep the content completely positive so the interviewer's final impression is "Yes, this is the person for the job." Use a positive vocabulary, and eliminate all negative terms.

☐ **Use proper grammar.** Grammatical errors can cost applicants the job. Use correct grammar; word choice; and a businesslike vocabulary, not an informal, chatty one. Avoid slang, and never use profanity or derogatory terms. When under stress, people often use pet phrases (such as "like" and "you know") too often. Ask a friend or family member to help you identify any speech weaknesses you have. Begin eliminating these poor speech habits now.

It's What You Say

Speak professionally during your interview.

☐ **Emphasize how you fit the job.** Near the beginning of an interview, as soon as it seems appropriate, ask a question similar to this: "Could you describe the scope of the job and tell me what capabilities are most important in filling the position?" The interviewer's response will help you focus on emphasizing your qualifications that best match the needs of the employer.

☐ **Keep the interview businesslike.** Do not discuss personal, domestic, or financial problems.

- ☐ **Don't ramble.** Be concise—but not curt—with your replies. Answer questions with required information, adding anything you think is relevant or especially important; then stop talking or ask your own question.
- ☐ **Concentrate.** An interview isn't just about talking. Listen to the interviewer carefully to learn important details about the job requirements, the organization, and the department so you can respond appropriately. Chapter 10 has important tips about listening.
- ☐ **Try to demonstrate a sense of humor.** Humor is an important factor in working well with other people and is a sign of intelligence. Use humor only when appropriate, however, and don't tell jokes; they're not suitable for an interview. Never use profanity or off-color humor. Making yourself the subject of the humor is usually safe, but be careful not to make yourself look bad.
- ☐ **Emphasize your strengths—even when discussing an error you made.** Emphasize your strengths and abilities that are relevant to the job. Although you want to avoid bringing up past shortcomings, do not try to dodge one that comes out during an interview. Face it head-on, and explain what you learned from the experience. If the interviewer asks you about the circumstances, explain briefly; don't make excuses or blame others. You will create a better impression by being honest, candid, and sincere. The interviewer is human too and has made his or her share of mistakes.
- ☐ **Do not lie during an interview.**
- ☐ **Be prepared to state why you left a previous job if you're asked.** Do not speak unfavorably about your former supervisor or firm. Interviewers may believe that you would do the same after leaving their companies. Maintain your business and professional integrity throughout the interview.
- ☐ **Focus on your goal.** Keep coming back to the main purpose of the interview: determining how you and the employer can mutually benefit from your employment. If the conversation strays too far from this subject, bring it back in the right direction. Get feedback from the interviewer to determine how you're coming across. Stop and ask: "Do you think my skills in that area would be helpful to you?" If the answer is yes, you know you're on the right track. If the answer is no or unclear, clarify how you are qualified for the job.

4 Be Aware of Business Etiquette

Business etiquette is the expected professional behavior in the workplace, and it is based on common courtesy, manners, and cultural and societal norms. Etiquette blunders include leaving your cell phone ringer on during a business meeting and using your napkin to wipe your nose during a business lunch.

Watch Out

Avoid Credibility Robbers

Avoid using words and phrases that make you sound indecisive or unbelievable. Eliminate the following credibility robbers from your vocabulary:

- **Just or only.** Used as follows, "I just worked as a waiter" or "I only worked there on a part-time basis" implies that you are not proud of your work or that you don't consider the work meaningful. All work is meaningful; it demonstrates initiative. Leave out these credibility robbers.
- **I guess.** This makes you sound uncertain.
- **Little.** Don't belittle your accomplishments, as in "This is a little report/project I wrote/developed."
- **Probably.** This suggests unnecessary doubt: "The technique I developed would probably be useful in your department." This statement sounds more convincing: "I believe the technique I developed would be useful in your department."

This is a small sample of words and phrases that can diminish your image. Ask members of your support system to help you identify other verbal credibility robbers and to remind you when you use them.

Your behavior in an interview gives your potential employer clues to how you will treat clients and customers.

Culturally appropriate business etiquette is important in conducting global business successfully. An unintentional etiquette breach can quickly squash a delicate international transaction. For example, in Asia, presenting a business card using only one hand is considered rude.

complete CareerActions
8-3 Internet Research on Business Etiquette

Prepare a 60-Second Commercial

You need to convince the interviewer that you are the best qualified person for the job. If you don't, you won't be hired. At some point in every interview, you will have an opportunity to deliver a prepared "clincher" speech highlighting your best qualities and showing how they will benefit your employer.

Getting hired can be compared to making a sale. In this case, you and your capabilities are the product. You complete the "sale" by emphasizing how your capabilities can benefit the employer. To help make the sale, develop a 60-Second Commercial, a power-packed summary of the benefits you offer.

As a starting point, think of times you provided benefits to an employer or some other organization. Employers are persuaded to hire

Convincing a future employer that you are flexible and adaptable to new situations can be just as important as having one or two years of direct experience.

Transferable Competencies

Even if you are applying for your first position in your chosen field, it doesn't mean that you are entirely without experience or skills. Think about your part-time, temporary, or summer jobs and identify roles that you were called upon to play in different situations. Did you work with diverse populations? Did you learn how to use office equipment? Did you cover for your supervisor from time to time?

Don't overlook volunteer positions you have held, even if they were relatively short-term. Community service reveals a lot about an applicant's readiness for work. Sometimes volunteering can be as demanding as a paid position, requiring travel, long hours, or coordinating skills. Picture yourself in your volunteer role, and apply these qualities to potential requirements in the employer's place of business.

Don't forget skills you possess that are not specifically listed as a job requirement, such as speaking a second language.

the person who can offer advantages in one or more of these areas:

- ☐ Increasing sales/profits/productivity
- ☐ Decreasing costs
- ☐ Saving time
- ☐ Solving problems or resolving conflicts
- ☐ Increasing convenience
- ☐ Enhancing image and/or improving relationships
- ☐ Increasing accuracy or efficiency

Do not use vague language. Provide evidence of your capabilities with specific examples. Use numbers to boost your credibility when you can. ("I developed a processing system that reduced processing time by 20%.")

Since employers are looking for flexible employees who can adapt to new situations, you should also emphasize your transferable competencies, such as your ability to handle diverse responsibilities, manage yourself (attendance, punctuality, problem-solving), and work well with others. Transferable competencies were introduced in Chapter 3.

Your "master" 60-Second Commercial will be useful in many situations, such as direct requests for interviews, phone requests, networking, practice and real interviews, and thank-you letters. You can draw from it for 30-second and even 15-second "spots."

Show that You Can Work with Others

Be able to give examples that emphasize your ability to work successfully with others. Be prepared to explain the contributions you made to a group and how you were able to solve a problem or resolve group conflicts. Identify any particularly complex projects you handled in past jobs. Be ready to explain the variety of tasks you performed and how you managed multiple priorities at the same time.

Be Convincing

Follow these additional tips to develop and deliver a convincing 60-Second Commercial:

- ☐ **Be authentic.** Be sure your 60-Second Commercial represents you authentically. Don't "sell" what you can't deliver.
- ☐ **Create an opening for your Commercial.** Ask the interviewer to review the scope of the job responsibilities and the reason for the opening. Pay attention to the answers. If necessary, probe further to clarify what the employer really needs, then discuss the benefits you can offer to meet those needs. An untrained interviewer may never ask you directly about your qualifications. Be sure you present them in the interview.
- ☐ **Include measurable accomplishments.** The key to an effective 60-Second Commercial is to provide examples of your capabilities. Pick the items that best fit the needs expressed by the interviewer; Example: "I can see that *xyz* is the most crucial challenge to your organization. My skills can alleviate those problem areas because of my specific *xyz* experience."
- ☐ **Be concise.** Your interview Commercial must be short, relevant, and convincing.
- ☐ **Focus and polish the content.** Your aim is to prepare a brief, polished summary of your qualifications. The heart of your message should emphasize how you can benefit the employer. It is your interview "billboard" saying "Here's what I can do for you." This helps the interviewer focus on the strengths you have to offer.
- ☐ **Be ready for any situation.** Practice delivering the 60-second version and a 30-second version. Whenever possible, weave your Commercial into the interview—perhaps the longer version first, followed later by the shorter one. Don't overdo it, however; twice is probably enough.
- ☐ **Tailor your 60-Second Commercial to each employer.** You may need to vary your Commercial slightly to match the requirements of each job. If the job description lists computer skills first, then list yours first too. Use the wording and terms used in the job requirements.

Review the 60-Second Commercial samples in Figure 8-1. See how they focus on employer benefits and emphasize results-oriented accomplishments and transferable competencies. Notice the use of examples and concise phrases rather than complete sentences. (In an actual interview, you should use complete sentences.)

60-SECOND COMMERCIAL SAMPLE #1

Job Target: Sales representative with Axion Inc., a consumer product company

Experience Credentials: Two years in retail sales at Computer Logistics, Inc.

Education Credentials: B.A. in sales and marketing

Proof of Benefits Provided

- ▲ Increased school newspaper revenues by 22% as advertising assistant
- ▲ Voted "Most Helpful Clerk" by customers in Service Excellence contest at Ralston Pharmacy
- ▲ Received performance ratings of "excellent" in accurate, quick sales for two years at Computer Logistics

Related Job Skills/Preferences

- ▲ Highly skilled in record keeping, use of personal computers, business math
- ▲ Enjoy travel; open to relocation

Transferable Competencies

- ▲ Maintain a professional appearance and have good communication skills
- ▲ Strong interpersonal relations skills

60-SECOND COMMERCIAL SAMPLE #2

Job Target: Graphics/text specialist position with Action Publishers

Experience Credentials: Worked 18 months as graphics/text processing assistant at Westville State College Print Center

Education Credentials: Associate of Applied Business Degree, Westville State College

Proof of Benefits Provided

- ▲ Worked with team to develop priority scheduling method, resulting in 99% on-time delivery
- ▲ Developed three graphic-intensive brochures that were selected by school for national student recruitment campaign

Related Job Skills/Preferences

- ▲ Key 70 wpm
- ▲ Skilled in English usage
- ▲ Proficient in Microsoft Office and Adobe Photoshop, Illustrator, and InDesign
- ▲ Operate personal computers, printers, networks, and other office equipment
- ▲ Enjoy all aspects of document/graphic development

Transferable Competencies

- ▲ Punctual, self-starter, resourceful in information management, skilled in computer technology, excellent team skills

Figure 8-1: 60-Second Commercial Samples

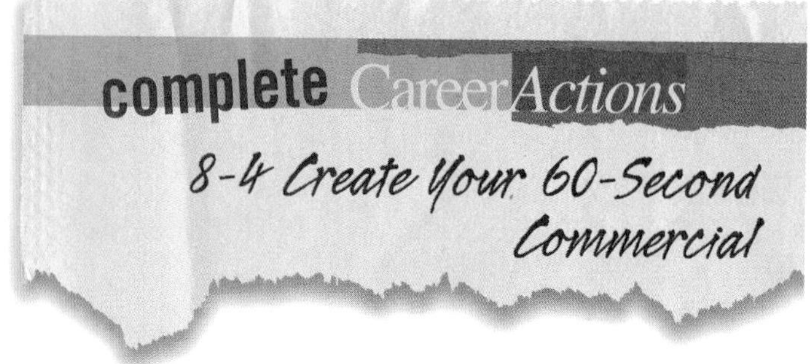

complete CareerActions
8-4 Create Your 60-Second Commercial

Prepare an Interview Marketing Kit

Job applicants who prepare well for interviews have a decided advantage over those who don't: they perform better during the interview. By performing well, you will project professionalism and organization skills and increase your own sense of readiness.

Before each interview, create an Interview Marketing Kit. Select the items that are most appropriate for the current job target from your Career Portfolio (see Chapter 1).

Put these items into a professional-looking binder or small attaché case. A regular briefcase is not recommended because interviewers may view it as overkill.

Include these items in your Interview Marketing Kit:

1. **Items from your Career Portfolio** that pertain to the interview:
   - ☐ Job-related samples of your work, if applicable
   - ☐ Required certificates, licenses, transcripts, and related documents
   - ☐ Extra copies of your resume
   - ☐ Letters of recommendation
   - ☐ Lists of references appropriate for the job
2. **A copy of your 60-Second Commercial** summarizing your qualifications for the job (skills, education, and experience)
3. **A notebook with your list of pertinent questions** you can ask during the interview
4. **Professional preparation items**
   - ☐ Pens and pencils
   - ☐ Appointment calendar

Arrange the portfolio items in the order that best shows how your abilities relate to the employer's needs.

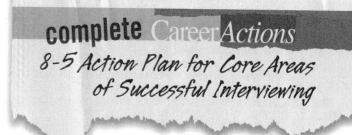

complete CareerActions

8-5 Action Plan for Core Areas of Successful Interviewing

Next Steps

Complete all the Career Actions in this chapter to ensure that you know how to apply the key elements that go into successful interviewing. These activities will help you prepare for your interviews, and this preparation will work to your advantage in many ways. You will stand out from the crowd by coming across as professional, self-confident, and competent. File the completed Career Actions in your Career Management Files Binder. Make extra copies of your master 60-Second Commercial for your Interview Marketing Kit. In the next chapter, you will learn how to ask for job interviews.

Chapter Checklist

Check each of the actions you are currently taking to increase your career success:

- ☐ Projecting enthusiasm and a positive attitude in interviews.
- ☐ Projecting professionalism; smiling, dressing neatly and appropriately, and being clean and neat.
- ☐ Using positive verbal communication; using positive terms; and avoiding grammatical errors, slang, and credibility robbers.
- ☐ Using positive body language in the first 30 seconds of and throughout the interview to project trust and credibility quickly.
- ☐ Making the sale by delivering a polished "60-Second Commercial" that emphasizes my qualifications and includes measurable accomplishments whenever possible.
- ☐ Preparing an Interview Marketing Kit that contains appropriate portfolio items.

Critical Thinking Questions

1. What aspects of the job applicant do interviewers focus on the most? Why do they do this?
2. How can a job applicant demonstrate a positive attitude during an interview?
3. What is the most important information an applicant must convey to an interviewer?
4. What negative nonverbal habits are the most important for you to eliminate to improve your interview abilities?

For convenient access to valuable career resources, study tools, activities, and job information links, visit the companion web site for this text: www.cengage.com/careerreadiness/levitt.

Trial Run

The average worker will change jobs at least ten times in his or her career. Many will not only change jobs within a specific field, but will change careers altogether. To keep current with interview styles, trends, and expectations, conduct interviews of your own with hiring managers and human resource directors across a wide variety of fields.

After requesting an interview for a class assignment, ask the following questions:

Name of Person Interviewed: ______________________________

Name of Company: ____________________ Position: ____________________

Who in your company is responsible for interviewing job candidates? ______________________________

____

How are new employees recruited? ______________________________

____

What skills are you looking for, and what types of questions do you ask in interviews to evaluate candidates?

____

____

____

How important are skills and education as compared to enthusiasm, reliability, and communication skills?

____

____

____

What advice would you give to someone seeking a job and interviewing in your field?

____

____

____

Copy this form and use it to conduct at least three interviews with employers in different fields. File in your Career Management Files Binder.

8-1 Internet Research on Dressing for Job Interviews

Directions: Read different experts' tips for looking your best at job interviews. Take an honest look at yourself in the mirror. Where can you enhance the first impression you will make? Record the most helpful advice and plan your outfit.

Relevant tips for dressing for success:

____

____

____

____

Ideas for interview outfit:

____

____

____

I already have these things:	I need to buy or do these things:

Support person who will give me an honest opinion and good advice:

____

8-2 Body Language Self-Inventory

Part 1 Directions: Review these descriptions of nonverbal communication behaviors and voice qualities, and place a check mark next to each item that describes your body language habits. You can also do this Career Action with a partner. Definitions:

- Assertive body language is relaxed, open, and confident. It agrees with and supports your words and conveys competence, self-assurance, caring, and credibility.
- Passive body language looks non-energetic and diminishes your credibility by conveying insecurity, weakness, anxiety, and a lack of self-assurance and competence.
- Aggressive body language appears brash and overbearing and sends offensive messages that convey hostility, pushiness, intimidation, and a domineering attitude.

Review your answers and circle aggressive or passive habits. In Part 2, list the habits you think are most important to change. Finally, take action to correct these habits, and ask others to remind you when you exhibit them.

POSTURE

Behavior	Style	Behavior	Style
☐ Comfortably upright	Assertive	☐ Overbearing, intimidating	Aggressive
☐ Relaxed, balanced	Assertive	☐ Wooden, tight	Passive
☐ Open, not constricted	Assertive	☐ Slumped shoulders	Passive
☐ Overly stiff	Aggressive	☐ Slumped back/spine	Passive
☐ Arms/legs crossed	Aggressive		

HANDSHAKE

Behavior	Style	Behavior	Style
☐ Appropriately firm	Assertive	☐ Held for too long	Aggressive
☐ Connect between thumb and first finger	Assertive	☐ Limp	Passive
☐ Shake from elbow through hand	Assertive	☐ Shake from wrist through hand	Passive
☐ Held for appropriate length of time	Assertive	☐ Hold too briefly	Passive
☐ "Bone-crushing" grip	Aggressive	☐ Grasping fingers only	Passive

FACIAL EXPRESSION

Behavior	Style	Behavior	Style
☐ Open, relaxed, pleasant	Assertive	☐ Clenched jaw	Aggressive
☐ Frowning	Aggressive	☐ Wrinkling forehead	Passive
☐ Moody, sulking	Aggressive	☐ Biting or licking lips	Passive
☐ Tight upper lip, pursed mouth	Aggressive	☐ Continual smiling	Passive

EYE CONTACT

Behavior	Style	Behavior	Style
☐ Comfortably direct	Assertive	☐ Constantly looking down	Passive
☐ Staring off; bored expression	Aggressive	☐ Blinking rapidly	Passive
☐ Sneering, looking down nose	Aggressive	☐ Frequently shifting focus	Passive
☐ Direct stare	Aggressive	☐ No eye contact; avoidance	Passive

VOICE QUALITIES

Behavior	Style	Behavior	Style
☐ Distinct and clear	Assertive	☐ Too loud	Aggressive
☐ Controlled, but relaxed	Assertive	☐ Arrogant or sarcastic	Aggressive
☐ Warm, pleasant tone	Assertive	☐ Dull or monotone	Passive
☐ Energized; suitable emphasis	Assertive	☐ Whiny tone	Passive
☐ Too rapid	Aggressive	☐ Too soft or too low	Passive
☐ Too demanding or urgent	Aggressive	☐ Too nasal	Passive

GESTURES

Behavior	Style	Behavior	Style
☐ Natural, not erratic	Assertive	☐ Hands on hips	Aggressive
☐ Occasional gestures to emphasize	Assertive	☐ Wooden gestures	Passive
☐ Occasional positive head nodding	Assertive	☐ Tilting head to one side	Passive
☐ Open hand (conveys trust)	Assertive	☐ Bringing hand to face	Passive
☐ Leaning toward speaker	Assertive	☐ Too much head nodding	Passive
☐ Pointing finger	Aggressive	☐ Fidgeting	Passive
☐ Clenched fists	Aggressive		

DISTRACTING NONVERBAL HABITS

Behavior	Style	Behavior	Style
☐ Drumming fingers	Passive	☐ Fiddling with any object	Passive
☐ Use of fillers (um, uh, you know)	Passive	☐ Rubbing beard or mustache	Passive
☐ Jiggling leg/arm	Passive	☐ Biting nails	Passive
☐ Fiddling with hair or glasses	Passive	☐ Scratching	Passive

OTHER HABITS (List similar habits you have)

Behavior	Style	Behavior	Style
☐		☐	
☐		☐	

Part 2 Directions: Review your self assessment; then list the negative nonverbal habits you plan to change. List them in order of importance (with the most important change first).

MY GOALS FOR IMPROVING NONVERBAL COMMUNICATION AND VOICE QUALITIES

1. ______________________________

2. ______________________________

3. ______________________________

CareerAction

8-3 Internet Research on Business Etiquette

Directions: Read about expected etiquette for job interviews. Record things you didn't know before and behaviors you can improve.

____

____

____

____

How will you practice the new behaviors before an interview?

____

____

____

Different cultures have different business etiquette rules. Record some things you learned about business etiquette in other cultures. Be sure to note the culture.

____

____

____

____

8-4 Create Your 60-Second Commercial

Directions: Follow the steps outlined below to create your own 60-Second Commercial. File your completed 60-Second Commercial in your Career Management Files Binder and put another copy in your Interview Marketing Kit.

1. **Prepare a rough draft.** On a separate sheet of paper, prepare a rough draft of your basic points.
2. **Use short phrases, not full sentences.** The goal is to say the most about your qualifications in the fewest possible words.
3. **Name your target job position and employer.**
4. **Briefly summarize your education and training.** Use your resume and Career Action 3-1 (Education, Training, and Activities Inventory) as references.
5. **Focus on "proof of benefits provided."** Provide relevant examples of your work performance and accomplishments and successful use of your job-specific skills. Whenever possible, use numbers or percentages to describe your successes. Also emphasize the benefits you can provide for the employer.
6. **List your job skills and transferrable competencies that are most relevant to the job target.** Refer to Career Actions 3-2 and 3-7 to review your job-specific skills and qualifications.
7. **Tailor each list.** Use your draft as a base, and tailor it to each target employer. Practice delivering your list aloud, but don't memorize it word for word. (You don't want to sound as though you are reading a script or lacking energy.) Take a copy of your 60-Second Commercial with you to an interview. If you have a momentary memory lapse, quickly scan the list, but don't read from it directly.

Career Action

8-5 Action Plan for Core Areas of Successful Interviewing

Directions: Develop an action plan for strengthening the interview strategies presented in Chapter 8 and applying them in your own job search.

Attitude

____

____

____

Image and Appearance

____

____

____

Nonverbal Communication

Verbal Communication

Business Etiquette

60-Second Commercial

File your action plan in your Career Management Files Binder.

For Your Career Management Files Binder

After completing the Career Action activities in this chapter, file the following documents in your Career Management Files Binder:

- ☐ **CA 8-1: Tips and plans for dressing for job interviews**
- ☐ **CA 8-2: Body language inventory and plans for improvement**
- ☐ **CA 8-3: Plans for improving specific areas of business etiquette**
- ☐ **CA 8-4: Your 60-Second Commercial**
- ☐ **CA 8-5: Action plan for successful interviewing**

© STOCKBYTE/GETTY IMAGES

Chapter 9

Ask for—and Get—the Interview

Objectives

- Develop skills and strategies for making a direct request for an interview.
- Know when and how to make an indirect request for an interview.
- Have a backup plan if your target employer isn't hiring.

Overview

In Chapter 9 you will be challenged to step outside your comfort zone and take a proactive approach to landing an interview. You will research and practice strategies for getting that all-important meeting with a target employer. You will learn the skills and styles—direct or indirect, in person or on the phone—necessary to get the opportunity you need and use it to your advantage. In this chapter you will also see the importance of taking a less-than-perfect job while you continue looking for the right one.

chapter 9 Career*Actions*

9-1: Develop Your In-Person Request for an Interview

9-2: Develop and Practice Your Telephone Request for an Interview

9-3: Internet Research on Strategies for Getting Interviews

9-4: Develop a Contingency Plan

Jump Start Asking for an Interview

Your success when asking for an interview is related to the type of work and career you are targeting. Some employers might view a direct request for an interview as aggressive, while other businesses would be grateful to find a qualified applicant.

What is the business etiquette in your field or at your target employer? Remember what you read in Chapter 8: the most important business meeting you will ever have with your employer is your job interview. Don't get off on the wrong foot, or have the door slammed in your face because you broke the unspoken rules.

Ask people who work in your target career field how they were selected for their interviews. Do they think a direct request via telephone or e-mail is acceptable? Or do they recommend asking someone in your support network to try to open a door for you?

Getting an Interview

In the best of all possible worlds, you apply for your dream job, the employer reads your resume and cover letter or application, and contacts you to schedule an interview. This happy scenario is not farfetched, but you also need to know how to take the initiative and ask prospective employers for a job interview.

- ☐ You can contact an employer directly—in person, by telephone, or through a standard letter or e-mail—to ask for an interview.
- ☐ You can use an indirect strategy to create opportunities to be asked to interview for a position.

You should be prepared to use direct and indirect strategies to get through the interview doorway. Indirect requests for interviews are especially important when job competition is high.

Every opportunity you have to meet with employers, whether for a formal interview or an informational survey, gives you important practice and keeps your job search active.

Direct Requests for Interviews

Once you have identified a promising employer prospect, your goal is to get an interview. It's best to meet face-to-face or over the telephone. Don't write when you can call, and don't call when you can make a personal visit. If you can't visit or call, a standard letter or e-mail communication is appropriate. Tailor your request for an interview to each prospective employer by emphasizing your strengths and experience that are most relevant to the employer's needs.

Apply Your Verbal Skills to Interview Requests

To increase your chance of getting an interview, focus on being courteous, likable, persuasive, and resourceful. As always, act professionally, because your interview really begins at the time of that first contact. You will be judged to be a potential candidate or not based on the first impression that you make.

Whether on the phone or in person, use a friendly tone and correct grammar. Write out a practice script beforehand if it helps you feel more confident. Speak distinctly and confidently and eliminate slang and annoying filler expressions such as *um, uh,* and *you know.*

Be courteous and respect the person's time. Most businesspeople will only have a few minutes for your visit or call. If you sense that this is not a good time, say "I would be glad to call (visit) at a more convenient time." Remain composed and professional. Do not act inconvenienced or become irritated.

Focus Your Interview Request The focus of an effective interview request should be on how your abilities can benefit—or even be essential to—the employer. Identify the advantages of your specific qualifications, and translate those advantages into benefits for the prospective employer. Communicate your message clearly and concisely and emphasize your qualifications before requesting an interview.

Conducting employer research is vital and should include finding out who is in charge of the department that could benefit the most from your abilities. This is the target person for your interview request.

Request an Interview in Person

Requesting an interview by making a personal visit is the most successful method of getting an interview. It is difficult for people to ignore you when you are standing in front of them. If you can make a good impression, you have already achieved a major goal in the interview process. Follow these guidelines:

1. **Research the firm** thoroughly beforehand.
2. **Dress for the part.** Dress and groom yourself as though you are going to an actual interview.
3. **Be prepared.** Take your Interview Marketing Kit and 60-Second Commercial (Chapter 8) and your resume (Chapter 6).
4. **Pay special attention to gatekeeper** (the person standing between you and the employer). This may be a front-line staff member, an administrative assistant, a supervisor, or a human resources staff member. Actively and courteously seek that person's help.
5. **Present the most concise, action-packed version of your 60-Second Commercial** and then request an interview.
6. **Thank your contact by name** for his or her time and consideration.

Do your homework before every interview

- Name, address, locations, contact information, hours of operation
- Type of business
- Products or services
- Advertised job openings (with salary ranges)
- Number of employees
- Departments and managers
- Competitors and customers
- Culture (dress code, desired image, philosophy)
- Reputation
- History (past successes and challenges)

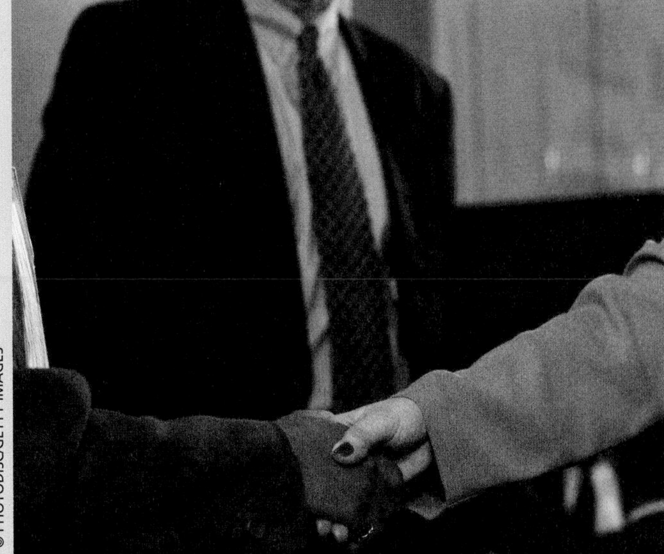

Learn as much as you can about the organization before you walk through the door.

If you don't get an interview, ask for a referral to another department or company that may need your abilities. Remain courteous and professional throughout the conversation.

Study the following example of a request for an interview made during a personal visit to an employer. The applicant is applying for an administrative support position in a medical center. Note how she highlights her qualifications, demonstrates her knowledge of the employer and the industry, and expresses her interest in a job—just the right approach.

Sample In-Person Request for an Interview

The Opening. "Hello, Mr. Washington. My name is Jaleesa Williams. My instructor Phyllis Johnston recommends your Information Services Department at St. Mary's Hospital for its well-organized systems design. I recently completed my education at Mesa College, earning two A.S. degrees – one in Information Management Technology and the second in Medical Administrative Assisting."

The 60-Second Commercial Excerpt. "I worked for 18 months as a clerical assistant in the Business Office at Lewis State College while attending school. I'm proficient in Word, Excel, Access, PowerPoint, and Outlook software and have received MOUS certification in each of these software packages. I operate personal computers, networks, and general office equipment. I also type 70 words per minute and am skilled in English usage."

The Request. "I've developed some time-saving methods for creating templates and macros that may be appropriate for your department. Would you have time for me to review them with you today, or would one day next week be more convenient?"

The Close. "Next Tuesday at 10 a.m.? I appreciate your willingness to meet with me so soon, Mr. Washington. I look forward to meeting with you then. Thank you and good-bye."

complete CareerActions

9-1 Develop Your In-Person Request for an Interview

Request an Interview Over the Phone

The telephone can be a powerful ally. Because it is "live," it demands immediate attention from the person who answers it. Because it allows for two-way communication, you can respond immediately to their questions, and they can respond to yours. Use the telephone to create a "short-list" of employers who are viable targets for employment. Follow up with personal visits to the most likely prospects.

Using the Telephone Persuasively Your telephone communication skills will affect your success throughout your career. You can develop these skills just as you develop any other skill.

Your voice is your personality over the telephone. You want to use your voice to project confidence and enthusiasm and make a positive impression. Follow these guidelines:

1. **Know why you are calling.** Is your purpose to get the name of the hiring individual? Is it to request information about the position? Is it to request an interview?
2. **Research the firm thoroughly beforehand.** Get the name of the person you need to contact before you call to request an interview. You may need to make a preliminary call to get this information.
3. **Write a script or outline before you call.** Know what you want to say before you make an important phone call. A script or outline helps you organize your message, making you sound intelligent and well prepared. You can also refer to it if you forget something. Summarize the key points you need to cover before placing the call, including the information you need to obtain from your contact. Pattern your script after the samples in this chapter and refer to your 60-Second Commercial.

4. **Don't read from the script during the call.** Not using the script during the call is just as important as writing a script or outline in the first place. Practice what you want to say before the call until you become comfortable saying it. During the call, use your script or outline to guide you from one idea to another.
5. **Speak clearly and get to the point.** Any long pauses could cause you to be put on hold or transferred to voice mail before you have had a chance to make your pitch.
6. **Don't do anything else.** Listen and respond to the person on the other end of the line. Give the phone call your entire attention. Don't chew gum or drink while talking on the phone.
7. **Stand up, speak directly into the mouthpiece, and smile while you talk.** The muscles used to smile relax your vocal cords and create a pleasant tone of voice. Standing up gives your voice more energy.

Study the telephone request for an interview that follows. Note how the applicant incorporates his qualifications, knowledge of the employer and the industry, and interest in the employer.

Sample Telephone Request for an Interview

The Opening. "Hello, Ms. Hope. This is Stephen Rogowski. I've recently completed research comparing the product quality and service records of computer network manufacturers. I'm impressed with the results XYZ Company has achieved, and I'm interested in learning about a possible sales representative position."

The 60-Second Commercial Excerpt. "I'm completing my degree in sales and marketing at Lewis State College and have two years of successful retail sales experience. I also was the advertising assistant for our school paper and increased sales by 18 percent this year."

The Request. "Would it be possible to arrange a meeting with you to discuss your sales goals and how I might contribute to them?"

The Close. "Thank you, Ms. Hope. I look forward to meeting with you next Tuesday, the 18th, at 2:30. Good-bye."

complete *CareerActions*

9-2 Develop and Practice Your Telephone Request for an Interview

Write a Letter to Request an Interview

If you are relying on your cover letter and resume to get interviews and you have prepared these documents well, you are ready to make an interview request. Review the guidelines for preparing and distributing a cover letter in Chapter 7. You may want to use e-mail and a letter. By using both media, you give extra emphasis to your message and increase the likelihood that your request will be read.

If you don't receive responses from your cover letter and resume within a week to 10 days, reinforce the request through a telephone call or personal visit.

If you call, say that you mailed a letter on a specific date and that you are calling to see if it was received, and by whom. Then ask to speak to that person to discuss your letter. You can also ask about company hiring policies or openings.

Respond to a Job Posting on the Internet

When you apply for a job on a general job listing site or a specific employer's web site, follow the instructions provided exactly. Often employers want you to e-mail or fax your resume and a cover letter. They may use a special code to identify a specific job opening; be sure to include this code in your cover letter.

They may also have an online resume form to fill out or a text block into which you can paste your resume or letter. All of these options become your "request for an interview."

© PHOTODISC/GETTY IMAGES

Sound impressive by sounding prepared

- **Identify yourself.** "Hello, this is Benjamin Bernstein." Personnel who screen calls are suspicious of callers who don't give their names or state why they are calling. Be straightforward to eliminate any suspicions instantly.
- **Explain why you are calling.** Emphasize your qualifications before you make any request so your listener has a reason to answer *yes.* Ask for an interview, or use a practiced indirect strategy for getting through to the employer.
- **Get the name of the person who answers.** Ask, "Could I please have your name in case I need to talk with you again?" Write the name down. Using this person's name may make him or her more receptive to helping you.
- **Ask if it's a good time to talk.**
- **Clarify the details.** Clarify any follow-up activities you are instructed to complete (pick up an application, supply additional information or references, keep an appointment, and so on). Verify the time and place of any meetings, and get the correct spelling and pronunciation of the names of people you will meet.

Indirect Strategies for Landing Interviews

To reach an employer, to bypass a gatekeeper, find the hidden job market, or get around the office receptionist, you may need to use an indirect strategy to land an interview.

Get Through to an Employer

When job competition is high, many employers are flooded with applicants. In response, they may issue a temporary no-hire policy, which makes personal contact difficult because employees are instructed to notify applicants that no interviews are being scheduled at that time.

In a situation like this, you need to use initiative and persistence. Develop a persuasive reason to contact the person with hiring authority in your target organization.

Using an indirect strategy can create opportunities to meet people in your target organization who can arrange an interview for you. While you should not make a direct request for a job during a meeting that is arranged indirectly, you can discuss your experience and abilities. By doing so, you may actually convince your contact that you would be an asset to the organization, which is exactly your intention. Also ask whether the employer may need your skills in the future or if your contact could suggest another organization or department that may need someone with your qualifications.

Ask for Professional Advice

One effective indirect strategy is to arrange a brief meeting or telephone call with a prospective employer to discuss professional issues and ask for advice about additional preparation to make you more employable.

Ask about Professional Organizations Ask for recommendations about professional associations, industry trade groups, and publications in your field. Consider asking the following questions:

- ☐ Which professional association(s) would keep me informed of industry developments, technological advances in the field, and emerging trends?
- ☐ Which professional publications or Internet resources deal specifically with our field?
- ☐ Who else could I speak to for further advice on this topic?

Ask for Help with Career Planning If you have not completed your education or have limited experience related to your target job, ask for help choosing your coursework or with career planning. Your conversation could be similar to this:

"Hello, Mr. Cuervo. This is Cecilia Lee. I'm completing an assignment for a career planning course and would appreciate your help with some of my research. I'm seeking opinions from people who are recognized and experienced in the field of [your field]. My skills lie in the area(s) of ______________. Could you please help me identify positions within [your career field] for which these skills would be most useful? I'd also appreciate your recommendations about any additional coursework and preparation I may need."

Ask for Help with Your Resume If you are seeking help in developing your resume into one that employers will not pass over, you can place a telephone call to an employer and ask for his or her help in the following manner:

"Hello, Ms. Pappas. This is Phuong Tran. You've been highly recommended to me by Dr. Ivarsen of the Computer Information Systems Department of Nevada College. I'm developing a professional resume and would very much appreciate your critiquing it."

Develop a Relationship with Your Target Organization

The **gatekeeper** (the administrative support person, receptionist, or human resources staff member) who must screen all job applicants can help, hinder, or ruin your chances of obtaining a job with the organization. This person's influence on your job campaign can be considerable, so you need to use good diplomacy skills when communicating with him or her. Follow these guidelines:

- ☐ Express respect for the organization, perhaps referring to its reputation for professionalism, reliability, or leadership.
- ☐ Find common ground in an effort to establish a good rapport with the gatekeeper. If this person likes and trusts you, you may learn valuable information about what the company is like to work for, and whether you will fit in.
- ☐ If it seems feasible, ask for the person's help in arranging a meeting with the appropriate staff member. Indicate your awareness of their busy schedules and ask the gatekeeper the best time to contact the employer. Ask if you could speak with someone else who could tell you more about your areas of interest.
- ☐ Thank them by name for their time and assistance before leaving.

MAKE IT A HABIT

Apply Your Networking Techniques

By far the most effective indirect strategy for getting an interview is through the continuous process of networking. Let everyone you know, even if only casually, that you are looking for a job, to change your career, or get back to work.

Employers are flooded with resumes of highly skilled individuals. If they do not immediately call perfectly qualified applicants to arrange an interview, then what are they looking for? The answer is a personal referral.

Employers would rather take a chance on someone whose name has been passed to them by someone they know, socially or professionally, than interview a perfect stranger.

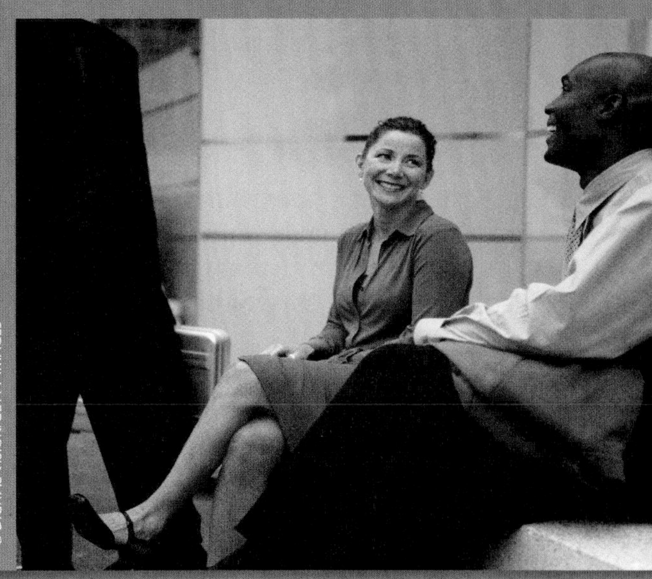

When making the first contact with a target employer, remember that, if you are successful in your job search, you will be working with the people you meet. You can never afford to be ill-mannered, unprofessional, or overbearing with anyone you come into contact with, from the first phone call or step through the door.

Uncover the Hidden Job Market

Numerous studies emphasize that 80 to 85 percent of job openings are never published and that personal searching is required to uncover them. This is the **hidden job market.** It's up to you to make an employer aware of your potential and possibly create a job in the process.

The first step to uncovering the hidden job market is researching target employers thoroughly. See the feature "Do Your Homework" on page 207 for what you should learn. Find out who is in charge of the department that can use your assets.

Next, analyze how your qualifications can be useful—or even essential—to the employer. The key is to identify how you can provide a useful service or save or make money for the organization.

Practice and polish your 60-Second Commercial. Ask a member of your support system to help you by playing the role of your contact and critiquing your presentation. Then present your qualifications for the job or service so convincingly that an employer is motivated to create a job for you. The hidden job market is uncovered through your own ingenuity.

Other Indirect Strategies

Try these tried and true strategies for getting interviews. Refer to additional sources of job leads in Chapter 5.

Go Through the Human Resources Department If your target employer has a strict policy requiring all applicants to be processed through the human resources department, follow the required procedure. You can expect the first step to be submitting an application, resume, and cover letter. If you are selected, you will be invited to a screening interview with a member of the human resources staff. This interview may be in person or over the telephone. (The screening interview is covered in Chapter 10.)

If you perform well during a screening interview and you appear to be qualified, you may be scheduled for a departmental interview. If the employer doesn't have an opening in your area, find out how to keep your file active and how you can stay informed of the hiring status for the position.

Use a Private Employment Agency If you plan to use employment or staffing agencies or employment contractors in your job search, they will arrange your job interviews. Read the agency's agreement thoroughly to be certain you are satisfied—and comfortable with—their procedures, including interviews. Clarify all the procedures carefully before agreeing to them, as advised in Chapter 5.

Visit Your College Career Center As you learned in Chapter 5, your school's career center is a gold mine of information and professional advice. Ask a staff member for advice about getting interviews.

Request Interviews at Career Fairs Employers use job fairs to show off their businesses and actively seek resumes and contacts. Job seekers can meet dozens of potential employers in one location, so bring several copies of your resume. Ask company representatives about hiring procedures, their opinion of industry trends, and what types of

> **Establish good rapport** with everyone you meet in person or talk with over the telephone.

employees they typically hire. Try to arrange a follow-up career information survey meeting with an employer, using the name of the person you meet as your contact. Be sure to keep your contact's business card, and use it to follow up within the week with a thank-you note or phone call.

Ask Successful Alumni for Help If you haven't already done so, join your college or university alumni association and participate in the social events, outings, and guest speaker engagements they sponsor. Ask for the names of alumni who are successful in your field, and request a career information survey with them or someone else in their company.

complete CareerActions

9-3 Internet Research on Strategies for Getting Interviews

While You're Waiting for that Interview

You should develop a contingency plan to fall back on if your strategies for getting interviews are taking longer than you expected. Look back at the suggestions about internships, cooperative jobs, and volunteer work in "Try Before You Buy" in Chapter 5, and consider these additional options.

Take Another Job You may need to take another job while you wait for a position to come open. This work experience can increase your value. Use the experience to polish your current skills, develop new ones, and establish a reputation as a valuable employee.

Follow Up Call your target employer when you have been in your interim job for some time and when you think that employment opportunities may have improved. Ask whether the employer would consider reevaluating your qualifications in light of your new experience.

Check Back Periodically Call the human resources department to remain informed of the hiring status and to reaffirm your interest. This may help you be first in line for openings.

If you consider more than one organization to be a prime employer, don't let one discouragement slow you down. Review the techniques in this chapter and rally your efforts toward your next target. Preparation, practice, action, and perseverance will pay off.

complete CareerActions

9-4 Develop a Contingency Plan

Next Steps

Complete all the Career Actions in this chapter to make sure you are well prepared to make both direct and indirect interview requests. Write out practice telephone scripts, and have your support network review your letters or e-mails before you send them. File the completed Career Actions in your Career Management Files Binder. As you become successful in scheduling interviews, move on to Chapter 10 to learn the styles of interviews you are likely to encounter, and to prepare answers to likely interview questions.

Chapter Checklist

Check each of the actions you are currently taking to increase your career success:

- Preparing for an in-person request for an interview as though it were an actual interview, knowing that a first impression can influence the outcome.
- Emphasizing my qualifications before I make the request, giving the interviewer a reason to answer *yes.*
- Preparing a written script or outline and practice asking for an interview before doing it in person.
- Treating gatekeepers and other staff members courteously and professionally because I know they are often the key to connecting with the hiring authority.
- Creating my own opportunities for employment by exploring the hidden job market.
- Developing a backup plan in case my strategies for getting interviews take longer than expected.

Critical Thinking Questions

1. What method of making a request for an interview do you think will be the most effective in your job search? Why?
2. What are some advantages of requesting interviews by telephone rather than by letter?
3. Why is it important to establish a good relationship with the gatekeeper and other people you meet while you wait to be interviewed? What are the strategies for doing so?
4. Get creative. Think of an employer you could realistically target for a hidden job market position. What are the needs of this employer, based on your research? What special skills and knowledge do you have that represent a hidden job you could perform to meet the employer's needs?

For convenient access to valuable career resources, study tools, activities, and job information links, visit the companion web site for this text: www.cengage.com/careerreadiness/levitt.

Trial Run

You need to be proactive and confident to use the strategies in this chapter successfully. Before you try your approach on strangers, practice with your classmates and your support team. Most of these approaches are new, so be sure to review the basic advice as a class to make sure you understand when to apply each suggestion.

Directions: Divide into teams of 3–4 students. Each team creates an interview request scenario and presents it to the class. Discuss types of employers, types of approaches, possible pitfalls, and follow-up. One student can play the role of the employer, on the phone or in person, reacting to the request for an interview.

Use this checklist to evaluate each team:

- ☐ In-person verbal skills
- ☐ Telephone skills
- ☐ Written skills
- ☐ 60-Second Commercial applicable to job
- ☐ Request style appropriate to employment target
- ☐ Reaction to rejection

Team's strengths:

Suggestions for improvement:

9-1 Develop Your In-Person Request for an Interview

Directions: Read the sample request for an interview on page 208 and write a script or outline that would be appropriate to use when requesting an interview with your prospective job target(s). File a copy in your Career Management Files Binder.

The Opening

The 60-Second Commercial Excerpt

The Request

The Close

9-2 Develop and Practice Your Telephone Request for an Interview

Part A: Write a script or outline that would be appropriate to use when making a telephone request for an interview with your prospective job target(s). File a copy in your Career Management Files Binder.

The Opening

The 60-Second Commercial Excerpt

The Request

The Close

Part B: Turn to your support system for assistance. Do some role-playing, following the guidelines below. Deliver your telephone request for an interview to your support system helper.

1. **Tape record your delivery, play it back, critique it, and improve on it where necessary.**
2. **Request your helper to ask you questions that require more information about your qualifications.**
3. **Practice responding when your helper makes excuses for not scheduling an interview.**
4. **Practice presenting your qualifications persuasively.**
5. **Practice turning objections into acceptance.**

Career Action

9-3 Internet Research Strategies for Getting Interviews

Directions: Search the Internet for additional tips for getting job interviews. You may want to look for tips on using social network sites in your job search. Look for new ideas that are especially useful to you. Summarize your findings and file your research in your Career Management Files Binder.

Career Action

9-4 Develop a Contingency Plan

Directions: Use this worksheet to discover what types of jobs you are qualified for that may not be your career target. Refer to your completed Career Actions 3-6 and 3-7 to complete the form below.

List three jobs that you are currently qualified or over-qualified to do:

____

____

____

List the benefits of working in a field related to your career target:

____

____

____

Describe your action plan for finding a "backup" job through indirect interview requests:

____

____

____

For Your Career Management Files Binder

After completing the Career Action activities in this chapter, file the following documents in your Career Management Files Binder:

- ☐ **CA 9-1: Script or outline for in-person interview request**
- ☐ **CA 9-2: Script or outline for telephone interview request**
- ☐ **CA 9-3: Strategies for getting interviews**
- ☐ **CA 9-4: Contingency plan while waiting for interviews**

Chapter 10

Interview Styles and Questions

Overview

Job interviews are either structured or unstructured. Once you have a job interview scheduled, you can improve your chance of success if you find out what style of interview will be used. This chapter helps you take control of the interview by understanding different interview styles, practicing answering interview questions, asking appropriate questions of your own, and practicing good listening skills.

Objectives

- Become familiar with and prepare for the most common interview styles.
- Review and practice answering typical interview questions.
- Gain skills to handle difficult interview questions.
- Learn to ask interview questions that count.
- Learn tactics for listening well and handling silence.

chapter 10 CareerActions

10-1: Research Interview Styles

10-2: Internet Research on Interview Question-and-Answer Tips

10-3: Create a Question-and-Answer Planning Sheet

Jump Start Your Interview Performance

Job interviews are like other situations you find yourself managing in daily life. You intuitively know how to act and speak in formal and informal situations. For example, your style of speaking with your friend's grandparents at his formal wedding is probably quite different from the way you talk with your nieces and nephews at a backyard barbecue.

Interviews call for your best performance, and part of that means matching your behavior to the structure and style of the interview.

With a partner, practice giving the most persuasive excerpt of your 60-Second Commercial in two situations: (a) a structured interview conducted by a trained interviewer from the human resources department and (b) at the close of an unstructured interview with a small business owner who did not directly ask about your qualifications for the job. Record these sessions and meet with another group. Listen to all four commercials. Identify the type of interview the person was in, point out the strongest parts of each Commercial, and offer tips for improvement.

The Interview Connection

In every interview, try to give the interviewer a picture of your personal attributes as well as your experience, skills, and other job qualifications. Make your verbal and nonverbal messages positive, using posture, facial expressions, and voice qualities that convey competence, friendliness, energy, and enthusiasm. This helps the interviewer feel comfortable and creates an open tone, which improves the chance for a successful interview.

The Structured Interview

The **structured interview** is often used by professional interviewers who work in the human resources department or who are part of a corporate interview team. The interviewer typically asks a predetermined set of questions, sometimes recording the applicant's responses on an interview rating form or checklist. This structured approach focuses on factual information and doesn't always give the interviewer adequate information about the applicant's personality and attitude.

Screening Interview

Large organizations often require applicants to be interviewed first through the human resources department. The **screening interview** is used to identify qualified applicants for the next level of interviews and to screen out those who do not have the basic qualifications for the job.

Some employers conduct screening interviews by telephone. Some screening interviews are also outsourced, especially by small companies with limited human resources staff. In these cases, the interviewers may not be able to answer all of your questions. The interviewer may use a rating sheet to evaluate each applicant. Notice the categories on the Interview Evaluation form, Figure 10-1 on page 225

Your goal in a screening interview is to be scheduled for the next required interview. Make sure that you state your qualifications clearly and concisely. Ask what to expect next, who is responsible for making a hiring decision, and when this decision will be made.

As a rule, you should expect to have no fewer than two interviews with an employer before a hiring decision is made. If you are scheduled for a follow-up interview, you are definitely in the running, so review and polish your interviewing skills. Keep your chin up, your smile broad, and go for the win!

Behavioral Interview

The behavioral interview is widely used today and is based on the premise that past performance is the best predictor of future behavior. In a **behavioral interview**, the interviewer asks questions aimed at getting the applicant to provide specific examples of how he or she has successfully used the skills required for the target job. This helps the interviewer evaluate the candidate's experience and predict future on-the-job behavior in the following areas:

- ☐ **Content skills**—work-specific skills, such as computer programming, CAD, and medical transcription.
- ☐ **Functional or transferable skills**—skills used with people, things, or information, such as good communication, organizational, or planning skills. These are valuable from one job to another.
- ☐ **Adaptive or self-management skills**—personal characteristics, such as being dependable, a team player, a self-directed worker, a problem-solver, or a decision-maker.

If you have completed the activities in Chapter 8, you are ready to handle a behavioral interview. Your 60-Second Commercial contains the proof-by-example descriptions of your capabilities that are most relevant to the target job. This is exactly what an interviewer is looking for in a behavioral interview.

To prepare for behavioral interviews, recall scenarios from your experiences that illustrate how you have performed or behaved on the job. Write out examples that demonstrate good performance. Also, be ready to describe how you have handled difficult situations. Students with little work experience should focus on class projects and group situations that illustrate their task performance and interpersonal behavior. These four steps provide a good model for your answers to behavioral questions:

1. Describe the situation.
2. Explain the actions you took.
3. Describe the outcomes.
4. Summarize what you learned from the experience.

Example: Describe an accomplishment that demonstrates your initiative.
Suggested Answer: "While I was working part-time as a computer lab technician for Seattle Technology College, our department received several complaints about service response time. I set a personal goal of answering all troubleshooting calls within 90 minutes. I recorded the exact response time for each call and maintained the 90-minute response time goal for one full semester. I was awarded the Customer Service Certificate for this performance."

Whenever possible, give positive examples that demonstrate measurable achievements. Or, when describing a less positive experience, emphasize what actions you took to correct weaknesses or poor performance. By giving specific examples, you establish credibility and believability that can translate into a job offer. See additional examples of behavioral interview questions in the section "Behavioral Questions" on page 227

Campus Interview

Campus interviews are generally scheduled through a school's career center. These are prearranged screening interviews, usually structured. The average campus interview is 20 to 30 minutes, and the schedule is closely observed.

The interviewer must evaluate each candidate quickly, so you should keep your remarks concise and to the point. Most interviewers are professionally trained and know how to guide applicants through the fact-finding process. Let the interviewer take the lead, and respond as briefly as possible without omitting pertinent information about your qualifications.

Panel or Board Interview

In a **board or panel interview**, you talk with more than one person at one time. Focus on the person questioning you at the time, but don't ignore the others. Appearing relaxed and projecting a self-assured attitude are important. The panel may have been selected to represent personalities and styles in the workplace, so take steps to ensure that your answer and mannerisms "mirror" the style of the interviewers. This may include body language, hand gestures, and tone of voice.

Before a board or panel interview, try to obtain and memorize the names of every member of the panel. During the interview, draw a diagram of the seating arrangement and label seats with interviewers' names. At the close of the interview, shake hands and thank each interviewer by name as you leave.

Team Interview

A **team interview** may be given by a group of three to five employees. In this type of interview, the applicant meets individually with each person; the team and the applicant do not meet together at one time. (If an employee will work directly with several managers, a few team members may conduct a panel interview.)

Employees who conduct team interviews are usually trained in interviewing techniques. They meet before the interview to determine the subject areas each team member will cover. A few common questions may be asked by all the team members to give the applicant more than one opportunity for adequate expression. After the interview, the team members meet to discuss the applicant's performance. Using common criteria, they assess the information from the individual sessions and their reactions before identifying the best candidate.

Team interviews give applicants a chance to meet with several people who may be their peers or supervisors on the job. This type of interview ensures a personality fit and increases the applicant's chances of establishing rapport with one or more members of the team.

Before a team interview, learn the names of the members and, if possible, learn something

Video Interview

A video interview uses two-way video to conduct a "face-to-face" interview over the Internet. Video interviews are being used to save money and time for organizations. Many major corporations, colleges, and universities are set up to offer real-time video interviewing.

Cameras are attached to computers at both locations. You may have to go somewhere to use a computer, or you may be able to use your own computer if you have the right software and equipment.

To succeed in a video interview, follow the guidelines for standard face-to-face interviews outlined in Chapter 8. Dress appropriately, project energy, and maintain eye contact with the camera. Use positive body language and good posture and avoid fidgeting.

Practice a video interview with a member of your support group to increase your comfort level.

about their areas of expertise. Use this information to enhance your performance. Be sure to give consistent answers to similar questions.

Telephone Interview

A **telephone interview** is a cost-effective screening technique. If you expect to be interviewed by telephone, prepare by getting a member of your network to role-play the interviewer. Practice delivering your 60-Second Commercial and answering typical interview questions.

If you have submitted resumes or applications, you must expect a call from an interviewer at any time. Make sure you have a businesslike outgoing voice mail message with your name and phone number, and make sure all housemates know to answer the phone professionally and take messages if necessary. Return calls promptly, and be prepared either to interview immediately or to leave a message with your full contact information and your availability. The following tips will help you succeed in a telephone interview:

1. **Be prepared to take an interview call at any time.** Post your resume and 60-Second Commercial where you can refer to them easily. Keep paper and pen handy, so you can write down names and information and keep a log of your calls. If you need a moment to collect yourself, politely ask the interviewer to hold for a moment while you move to a quiet location. Eliminate all distractions and background noise.
2. **Focus on why you are interested in working for the prospective employer,** on the basis of your research and understanding of the employer's products or services, current developments, philosophies, and so on.
3. **Be professional, courteous, and friendly;** let the caller lead the conversation, but ask questions of your own.
4. **Stand up, speak directly into the mouthpiece, and smile while you talk.** This gives your voice more energy and a pleasant tone. Never smoke, eat, or chew gum while on the telephone.
5. **Be factual in your answers; be brief yet thorough.** Avoid yes/no answers; they give no real information about your abilities.

MAKE IT A HABIT

Become a Good Listener

You may think of the interview primarily in terms of talking, but listening carefully is just as important. You need to listen to the interviewer carefully to learn important details about the job requirements, the organization, and the department so you can respond appropriately.

Follow these tips to become a more effective listener:

- Give each question your undivided attention. Don't formulate your response while you are listening.
- Nod as appropriate.
- Repeat or summarize the main ideas.
- Ask questions when you need to clarify what the interviewer means. If you don't understand a question, ask for clarification instead of talking and hoping you answered correctly.
- Listen "between the lines" for the underlying messages.
- Don't argue or interrupt.
- Maintain eye contact (but not too intensely).
- Maintain an "open" position (don't cross your arms or legs; keep your hands unclenched).
- Maintain the same eye level as the interviewer (sit or stand as appropriate).

6. **If you need time to think about a question, avoid using repetitive phrases to buy time.** Instead, simply say, "Let me think about that."
7. **Ask what skills, knowledge, and qualities the employer is looking for in filling the position.** While the interviewer answers, jot down the qualities you have that match; then describe them to emphasize how you meet the employer's needs.
8. **As you wrap up the interview, ask what the next steps are.** Tell the interviewer that you are available for a face-to-face interview at his or her earliest convenience.
9. **Follow up.** Call back one or two days later, thank the interviewer for his or her time, and restate your interest in the position. If necessary, leave this message by voice mail, or send an e-mail or a fax.

Computer-Based Interview

Some companies use **computer-based interviews** to screen applicants. The applicant logs onto a password-protected web site with instructions on how to complete the interview. The interview typically consists of 50 to 100 multiple-choice and true/false questions. Interviews are usually timed, and you cannot start and stop them once you have begun.

Some programs search for contradictions by asking you the same question in different forms, so be consistent in your answers.

The benefits of computer-based interviews include ease and cost effectiveness of data collection, consistent gathering of information from all applicants to keep the playing field level, and avoidance of personal bias from the interviewer. The primary drawback is that computers are not capable of assessing personal qualities such as attitude and enthusiasm. These qualities can be observed in follow-up interviews, however.

Some computer-based interviews include open-ended questions that are reviewed by recruitment specialists or managers. Answer questions just as you would in a face-to-face interview. Emphasize your related skills, but don't exaggerate. Be concise, avoiding overly-long responses or negative focus on a topic.

The Unstructured Interview

The **unstructured interview** is generally used by people who are not professionally trained in interviewing. It tends to be more informal and conversational than a structured interview. The unstructured approach is often used by the owners or managers of small businesses and not-for-profit organizations.

The questions in unstructured interviews are usually open-ended to encourage interviewees to express their personalities, background, and goals. Success or failure in this type of interview may be based more on communcation skills than on the content of the answers.

An untrained interviewer may not be skilled in discussing job qualifications, so the conversation may get bogged down by unimportant details. In this situation, you need to be the "professional interviewee." You can aid the interviewer by asking questions to learn about the full scope of the job and by communicating all your skills, experience, and attributes that apply to it.

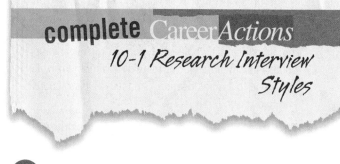

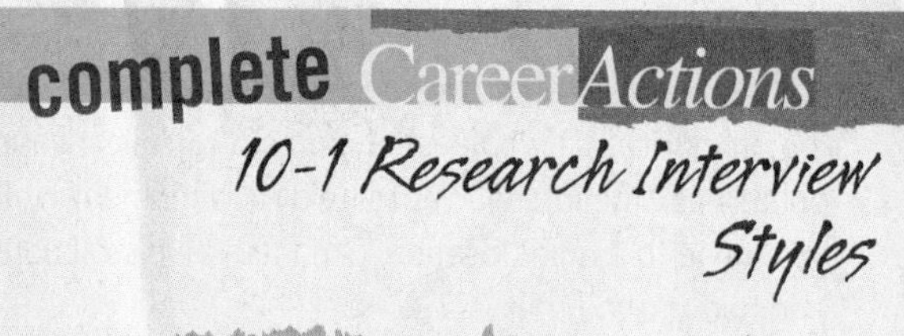

Typical Interview Questions

The core of a job interview is the question-and-answer period. It should include questions and answers from the interviewer and from you. You should generally let the interviewer take the lead. Interviewers usually consider an applicant's effort to control the interview to be rude or aggressive.

INTERVIEW EVALUATION

Applicant: ______________________ Date: ______________________

Position: ______________________

	POOR	FAIR	GOOD	VERY GOOD	EXCELLENT
Resume, Application, Cover Letter					
Attitude, Interest, Enthusiasm					
Communication Skills					
Knowledge of Job/Company					
Education/Training					
Related Experience					
Team/Interactive Skills					
Leadership Ability					
Coping Ability (stress, conflict, time demands, and so on)					
Motivation/Goals					
Judgment, Decision Making, Maturity					
Organizational/Planning Skills					
Demonstrated Performance/ Achievements					
Appearance (appropriate dress, grooming)					

Comments: ______________________

Conclusion: Considering the observations made above and the applicant's qualifications, do you think this person should be considered for the position?

Yes__ No__ Reservations: ______________________

Interviewer's Signature: ______________________

Figure 10-1: Typical Interview Rating Form

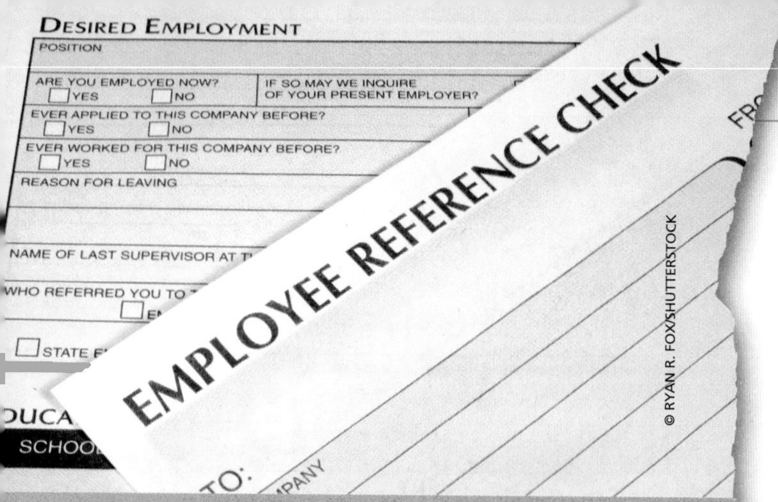

DESIRED EMPLOYMENT

POSITION

ARE YOU EMPLOYED NOW? YES NO | IF SO MAY WE INQUIRE OF YOUR PRESENT EMPLOYER?

EVER APPLIED TO THIS COMPANY BEFORE? YES NO

EVER WORKED FOR THIS COMPANY BEFORE? YES NO

REASON FOR LEAVING

NAME OF LAST SUPERVISOR AT T

WHO REFERRED YOU TO

STATE

EMPLOYEE REFERENCE CHECK

TO:

© RYAN R. FOX/SHUTTERSTOCK

Focus on Your Job Qualifications

Persuasively discussing your strengths and how they can benefit the employer requires preparation. Consider the positive capabilities and qualities your coworkers, supervisors, and instructors have recognized in you. Review your 60-Second Commercial and resume. Write out examples of your performance that relate to the target job. Choose these types of examples to showcase what you can do for the employer:

- What examples demonstrate your organizational skills and orderly mind?
- Have you developed improved methods of performing tasks or working with people?
- How can you demonstrate that you can work effectively on a team?
- Can you cite examples of effective problem solving?
- What examples demonstrate your creativity?
- Can you give examples of handling detail work well?
- Can you give examples of being dependable and flexible?
- Can you give examples of working independently without regular supervision?

You should also ask questions, for several reasons: (1) to demonstrate your interest and communication skills, (2) to show your initiative and preparation, and (3) to verify for yourself that you want to work for this employer.

Questions asked by interviewers generally fall into four categories:

☐ General information questions

☐ Behavioral questions

☐ Character questions

☐ Stress questions

Study the following lists of the most common questions and suggested answers. In Career Action 10-3, you will write your own responses. Writing and rehearsing a script or outline will help you during an interview.

General Information Questions

General information questions are asked to obtain factual information. They usually cover your skills, work experience, and so on.

1. **Why do you want this job?** (Be prepared; every employer wants to know the answer to this question.) **Suggested answer:** "My skills and experience are directly related to this position, and my interest lies especially in this field." If applicable, relate examples of your experience, education and/or training that are pertinent to the job you are seeking. Don't mention the pay or benefits.
2. **What type of work do you most enjoy?** **Suggested answer:** Play your research card; name the types of tasks that are involved in the job and demonstrate how you are qualified for the position.
3. **What are your strongest skills?** **Suggested answer:** Relate your skills directly to those required for the position.
4. **What are your long-term career goals, and how do you plan to achieve them?** **Suggested answer:** Emphasize your strengths, state that your goal is to make a strong contribution in your job, and explain that you look forward to developing the experience necessary for career growth. Employers are impressed with employees who show initiative because they perform better than those who have no plans for self-improvement. Mention your plans to continue your education and expand your knowledge to become a more valuable employee.

5. **Are you a team player?**
Suggested answer: Teamwork is highly valued in today's workplace, so a positive answer is usually a plus. Give examples of your successful team roles (as a leader, a member, or a partner) from school, previous jobs, volunteer work, or sports.

6. **Do you have a geographic preference? Are you willing to relocate?**
Suggested answer: If the job requires relocation, this question is important. If you have no objection to relocating, make this perfectly clear. If you do have objections, this could be a stress question. Be honest in your answer. If you don't like being mobile, say so; otherwise, you will undoubtedly be unhappy in the job.

7. **Under what management style do you work most efficiently?**
Suggested answer: "I am flexible and can be productive under any style. The management style I enjoy working with the most is ____________." (This answer shows that you are flexible and casts no negative connotations. It also answers the primary question.)

Behavioral Questions

Behavioral questions probe the applicant's specific past performance and behaviors. The interviewer wants details of experiences that illustrate how you perform or behave on a job or in stressful environments, and you can expect questions such as "Describe the most challenging assignment you've had. How did you handle it?" This may be followed by several more in-depth probes, such as "Explain the problems you encountered. How did you overcome them?"

Some behavioral questions probe for negative experiences. In responding to these, use the SAR technique to frame your answer: Situation–Action–Results. What happened? What did you do? What were the results? Be thorough, but keep your answer short. Focus on what you learned from the experience or what actions you took to improve the situation.

1. **Tell me specifically about a time when you worked under great stress.**
Suggested answer: Be careful to choose a relevant example that would be considered "stressful" in a work environment. Quickly describe the elements that made it stressful for you and how you maintained your cool and got the job done. If you don't have a good example, describe what you would do, or how you would handle the situation better this time.

2. **Describe an experience when you dealt with an angry customer or coworker.**
Suggested answer: Give an answer that highlights how you value communication and know that conflict can lead to personal growth and opportunity. Your reply should also include how you resolved the situation and what you would do differently in the future.

3. **Give me an example of your ability to adapt to change.**
Suggested answer: "When the new firm took over management of our site, I focused on the positive

Watch Out
"Tell Me about Yourself"

Sometimes an employer will start an interview by taking a few minutes to establish rapport or make small talk, and then say, "Tell me about yourself."

Be prepared to handle this type of interview effectively. Once the interviewer makes this request, he or she comments just enough to encourage you to keep talking. The purpose is to see whether you focus on your qualifications for the job and how the employer would benefit by hiring you. Do not ramble on about your life history; this is a sure way to disqualify yourself on the spot. Ask questions such as "What exactly do you want to know about—my work experience, educational experience, skills, or extracurricular and community activities?"

Your objective is to highlight your positive qualities (personal attributes, accomplishments, skills, pertinent training, work experience, and so on). After you think you have covered these topics, ask, "Would you like me to clarify or expand on any area for you?" This helps you focus on the information the interviewer wants.

outcomes rather than looking back and comparing management styles. I encouraged my co-workers to remain flexible and patient." This shows your leadership and maturity.

4. **Explain what problems you have encountered. How did you overcome them?**
   Suggested answer: Some behavioral questions probe for negative experiences. In responding to these, focus on what you learned from the experience or what actions you took to improve the situation.

Character Questions

Character questions are asked to learn about your personal attributes, such as integrity, personality, attitudes, and motivation.

1. **How would you describe yourself?**
   Suggested answer: Emphasize your strongest personal attributes, and focus on those that are relevant to your target job. Review your capabilities and accomplishments. Examples: "I'm punctual and dependable. At my current job, I haven't been late or missed one day in the last two years." "I get along well with others; in fact, my coworkers chose me to represent them in our company's monthly staff meetings."

   Give specific examples of your strengths. Don't just say "I'm a hard worker" or "I'm dependable." Other leads include "I learn quickly," "I like solving problems; for example . . . ," "I like contributing to a team," and "I like managing people." Be careful to use a relevant example that shows you know what's important in a work environment.

2. **What rewards do you look for in your career?**
   Suggested answer: Don't make financial rewards your prime motivator. Emphasize your desire to improve your skills, make a valuable contribution to the field, and become better educated. These answers show initiative, interest, and professionalism.

3. **What accomplishment are you most proud of, particularly as it relates to your field?**
   Suggested answer: Relate an accomplishment that shows special effort and initiative. "I recognized the need to improve communications [between two departments]. I designed a questionnaire that was completed by representatives from each department. Management made several of the changes and communications were improved in these areas."

4. **Do you work well under pressure?**
   Suggested answer: You may be tempted to answer with a simple *yes* or *no*, but don't. Yes and no answers reveal nothing specific about you. Don't miss any opportunity to sell yourself.

   Be honest in your answer. If you prefer to work at a well-defined job in an organized, calm atmosphere (rather than one that involves constant decision making and pressure), say so. Otherwise, you may end up in a job that is a constant source of tension. If you enjoy the challenge of pressure, either in decision making or in dealing with people, make this clear.

   Keep in mind that a large company may have more than one working environment. For instance, an administrative support job in the customer relations department would likely involve more interactive pressure with the public than a support job in the data processing department would.

Stress Questions

Stress questions are asked to determine how you perform under pressure (controlled and composed or nervous and unsettled). They are also used to find out whether you are good at making decisions, solving problems, and thinking under stress.

Some questions may be aimed at clarifying issues the interviewer perceives as possible problems, such as being over-qualified or under-qualified or lacking dependability (if your resume shows many different jobs).

Preparing Answers to Stress Questions

Prepare to answer any stress questions that are based on your resume or personal circumstances. Look at a stress question as an opportunity to prove that a situation is not a problem as it relates to your ability to do the job. Career Action 10-3 will help you prepare by having you write out responses to possible stress questions. Rehearse your responses. Record yourself doing the question(s) and prepared response(s) or ask a member of your support network to help you role-play the interview. Revise your responses based on the feedback you receive.

Remaining Cool Under Stress Keep your cool. Take three to five calming deep breaths; and tell yourself, "I can do this."

If you are asked a question that you are totally unprepared for, don't ramble through an answer. Use the "that's a good question, let me think about that for a minute" technique. This can buy you time to prepare a well-thought-out response. Your goal is to demonstrate that you can handle stress—that you don't just react but instead think through the situation and remain composed.

Whenever possible, give positive examples that demonstrate measureable achievements. When describing a less positive experience, emphasize what actions you took to correct weaknesses or poor performance. Specific examples help to establish credibility and believability.

3. **Why have you held so many jobs?**
   Suggested answer: Employers like to see a work history that implies stability and dependability. People often have valid reasons for holding numerous jobs that don't necessarily imply immaturity or an inability to commit. Some jobs are seasonal (agriculture and recreation), some jobs require frequent relocation (construction), and some jobs are profoundly affected by the economy. You may have held a variety of summer jobs while completing your education. Capitalize on this; it shows initiative and provides you with broad working experience. Whatever the case, emphasize that while you may previously have wanted to obtain a broad base of experience, your goal now is to apply yourself to long-term employment and developing a career.
4. **What is your greatest weakness?**
   Suggested answer: "My weakest area is accounting, so I am taking a course in beginning accounting at the community college. It's going well and I plan to take the advanced course next semester." The objective is to acknowledge a weakness that is low on the employers list and to explain your steps to improve it (through practice, education, planning, etc.)

> Your goal is to demonstrate that you think through the situation and remain composed.

1. **Why do you think you are the best candidate for the job? Or, Why should I hire you?**
   Suggested answer: Ask the interviewer to highlight the important objectives and challenges of the job. Then explain how you can handle them. Focus on how you can benefit the employer, citing examples of increasing productivity, saving money, increasing sales, and so on. Summarize your accomplishment, skills, and experience that are pertinent to the job. Then ask, "How does that fit your requirements?" This shifts the focus from you to the interviewer, helping reduce stress for you.
2. **Why do you want to leave your current job?**
   Suggested answer: This question will likely be posed to determine whether you have a problem with your current job. Accentuate the positive—you are seeking a new challenge, you have mastered your present job and are seeking advancement, you want to work for a company with stability, and so on. If you have a problem with your current job or boss, avoid discussing it. If you feel you must, describe the situation briefly and unemotionally, then return the tone to a positive one.
5. **Have you ever been fired from a job?**
   Suggested answer: If you have been fired, use terms such as *laid off, let go,* or *employment ended*; they sound less negative. Be honest about the reason for your termination. Briefly describe the situation; explain what you learned from the experience and how you could have handled the experience differently. Take responsibility for past mistakes, but end your response on a positive note.
6. **Does your current employer know you are planning to leave?**
   Suggested answer: If your current employer is aware of this fact, say so. If not, and especially if you depend on your current income, make this clear. Say that you prefer your current employer not be informed of your job search until a firm offer is made, and that you will give two weeks' notice before leaving. Consider it a good sign that they are asking this question—you are probably close to being offered a position.

Inappropriate Questions

The interview is going along well, and then it happens: "Are you considering having children?" or "How long has your family been in this country?"

On the surface, questions such as these seem innocent enough. Yet the structure and format of the questions may be illegal or, at the very least, inappropriate. When you are in a situation where the person asking the question has the power to decide whether you will get the job, this information can be used to discriminate against you or other candidates. Questions that focus on age, gender, race, marital status, language, children, criminal record, national origin, religion, or disability are inappropriate in a job interview.

So you've just been hit with an inappropriate question. What do you do? How do you respond? The risk here is that refusing to answer can count against you, even though the question is illegal. If you complain about a question being illegal or unfair, you probably won't be offered the job. You certainly have the right to refuse, but first weigh the situation. Is it worth jeopardizing the job over this question? If it is an offensive question, the answer may be "yes, I do not want to work for this company." Or, does the interviewer appear non-threatening and unaware that the question is inappropriate? Only you can decide.

The most effective approach is to answer the question in a polite, honest manner. Don't offer detailed personal information. Instead, steer the conversation back to your ability to meet the employer's expectations, as in the following examples:

Interviewer: Do you have children?
Applicant: Yes, and I'm thorough in arranging dependable child care. It pays off; I've never had to miss a day of work for childcare purposes (emphasizing planning and management skills). *Or* I am available to work the hours required of this position, including overtime and travel with advance notice.

Interviewer: Were you born in the United States?
Applicant: I have the legal right to work in the U.S., and my English language abilities are more than ample to meet the requirements of the job.

Watch Out
The Stress Interview

Stress interviews are generally reserved for jobs that involve regular pressure. They are designed to test the applicant's behavior, logic, and emotional control under pressure.

A skilled interviewer may combine some stress techniques with an unstructured interview approach to get a well-rounded picture of your personality. Some techniques used in stress interviewing include (a) remaining silent following one of your remarks, (b) questioning you rapidly, (c) placing you on the defensive with irritating questions or remarks, and (d) criticizing your responses or remarks.

Some stress questions are routinely asked in other types of job interviews—even informal ones. Every job has an occasional crisis situation. An interviewer may also use a stress technique unintentionally. Do not react negatively. Take a deep breath, demonstrate control, and be courteous.

Your Questions Count

Making the interview an effective two-way communication is important. Prepare to ask three to five well-chosen questions. Outline a list of questions that will help you to learn what you need to know about the employer, organizational culture, and the position.

Don't ask all your questions at the end of the interview. Interject them naturally at appropriate intervals throughout the meeting. Keep your questions positive, and avoid asking anything that could elicit a negative reaction. Also, never discuss salary until a job offer has been made.

Good Questions to Ask

Asking appropriate questions demonstrates interest and confidence, showcases your knowledge, and gives you an active role in the interview. Study the following sample questions carefully; then write your own questions as part of Career Action 10-2.

1. **Do you have a training program for this position? If so, would you describe it?**
   Why it works: This demonstrates interest in the job and a desire to perform it well.
2. **Would you describe the duties and tasks of this position in a typical workday?**
   Why it works: The answer to this question will help you better understand the scope of the job. It may be just what you want, or you may learn that it's not the type of work you are seeking. The information you receive will be important to you in considering a job offer.
3. **May I have a copy of the written job description?**
   Why it works: Getting a job description can help you tie your qualifications to those required for the job.
4. **Will the responsibilities of this position expand with time and experience on the job? Could good performance in this job lead to opportunities for career growth?**
   Why it works: Answers to these questions will help you determine whether this is a dead-end job or if employee career growth is encouraged.
5. **Could you tell me about the people I would work with? Who would I report to?**
   Why it works: The answers can help you assess company structure and how you might fit into the organization.
6. **Do you need any more information about my qualifications or experience?**
   Why it works: This gives you an opportunity to clear up any misunderstanding or lack of information. It also gives you another chance to run your 60-Second Commercial, once again emphasizing just how well qualified you are.

Watch Out
Silence During Interviews

Be prepared to handle silence. The interviewer asks you a question, you answer, and the interviewer does not respond. Interviewers sometimes use this technique to test applicants' confidence and ability to handle stress or uncertainty. Do not retract your statement; just wait calmly. You have no obligation to continue talking if you answered adequately. By doing this, you will pass the "test" and project a mature, confident image. Break a long silence by asking whether the interviewer needs more information or by asking a related question.

You can also use silence. If you are asked a difficult question, answering too quickly and without enough thought can be detrimental. You're entitled to think carefully about a question and prepare a response. The employer wouldn't want you to solve problems on the job without adequate thought and planning. Avoid long pauses in a telephone- or video-based interview, however; such pauses can be perceived as slow thinking abilities.

7. **When will you be making your hiring decision? May I call you if I have additional questions?**
   Why it works: These types of questions help you judge when to follow up and will keep the door open for further communication.

Turnoff Questions to Avoid

Following are some questions that are most disliked by employers. Do not ask them; they will make you sound uninformed and diminish your likability.

1. **What does this company do?**
   Why to avoid: You should have done your research well enough to know exactly what the company does. Asking this question will make you appear uninformed and unqualified. Employers are not looking for employees who know nothing about their business.
2. **How much sick leave and vacation time will I get?**
   Why to avoid: Do not ask this question during a first interview. Although employee benefits are important, asking specifically about vacation time or sick leave projects a negative attitude. You should ask this question before making a final decision about a job offer, however. Employers understand the importance of major benefits to prospective employees.
3. **Will I have an office?**
   Why to avoid: This suggests that you care more about where you will work than about what you will do.
4. **What time do I have to be at work in the morning? How long do you give for lunch?**
   Why to avoid: These questions sound immature and do not project an enthusiastic interest in the work.
5. **How long do I have to work before I am eligible for a raise?**
   Why to avoid: This question tells the employer that you are more interested in the salary than the job.

Apply Savvy Q-and-A Strategies

The following strategies for interview question-and-answer sessions are well received by employers.

- ☐ **Be enthusiastic.** Enthusiasm is a quality that employers look for when hiring.
- ☐ **Pause to think before you reply.** If you're uncomfortable with a question, go back to the familiar. Stress your assets. Use a "thinking pause" to buy time to answer the question well. For example, "Could we return to this question? I'd like to think about it for a moment" or "That's a good question" or "Let me see…" (This works if you need only a little extra time.)
- ☐ **Be candid and honest.** Be realistic when expressing your preferences and dislikes. You won't be happy in a job that isn't a good fit.
- ☐ **Do not use canned responses.** Tailor your answers to fit your goals, objectives, and personality, as well as the goals and needs of the employer.
- ☐ **Be concise.** Keep your responses to the point, but avoid being curt or too brief.
- ☐ **Answer in complete sentences, and speak correctly.** Avoid using slang, bad grammar, or repetitive terms. Speak clearly.
- ☐ **Be positive.** Positive thinking promotes positive behavior and speech, a positive image, positive responses, and a positive atmosphere. It also projects enthusiasm, self-confidence, and initiative.
- ☐ **Fill in the gaps.** If you sense that the interviewer thinks you have an area of weakness, communicate how you plan to eliminate the weakness or round out your qualifications—perhaps by completing research or coursework in the area.

complete CareerActions
10-2 Internet Research on Interview Question-and-Answer Tips

If It Doesn't Work Out

Job interviews are stressful, and many interviews do not go well for one reason or another. Follow the advice in this chapter to prepare for different types of interviews and interview questions, and keep your perspective if a specific interview falls short of your expectations.

The Bad Interview

Some interviews are not good; in fact, some are grim. After learning the details of a job, you may be convinced that you don't want it. The interviewer may be inept at interviewing, making it difficult for you to perform well. Do not stop trying. Do your best to be the professional interviewee. You can always learn something beneficial or use the opportunity to polish your interviewing skills. Don't give up during an interview; it could cost you a future reference or a good job lead from the interviewer. If you have a bad interview, chalk it up to experience.

The Unsuccessful Interview

Don't be discouraged. Most people have several interviews before a good job is offered. Keep your positive attitude after a bad interview; take what you learned to the next one and use it in your favor. Getting a top-notch job is a full-time job that usually requires several interviews and some rejections.

Remember what you learned from interviews and use it the next time. If you aren't offered a job or you sense during the interview that things have not gone well, ask the interviewer to suggest ways you could improve your interviewing skills. They may be willing to tell you if they consider you to be lacking in any area of skill, training, or experience. Attaining this information may be the starting point for an update of your skills or interviewing technique before your next interview.

complete Career *Actions*

10-3 Create a Question-and-Answer Planning Sheet

Next Steps

Complete all the Career Actions in this chapter to make sure you are prepared for any type of interview. Practice answering common and stressful interview questions, and do online research to prepare for a wide range of interview questions. File the completed Career Actions in your Career Management Files Binder. In Chapter 11, you will arrange and practice interviews with your support group or employers in your field, learn to "sell" yourself effectively, and apply self-assessment and critique skills to your job hunt.

[**Keep your positive attitude after a bad interview;** take what you learned to the next one and use it in your favor.]

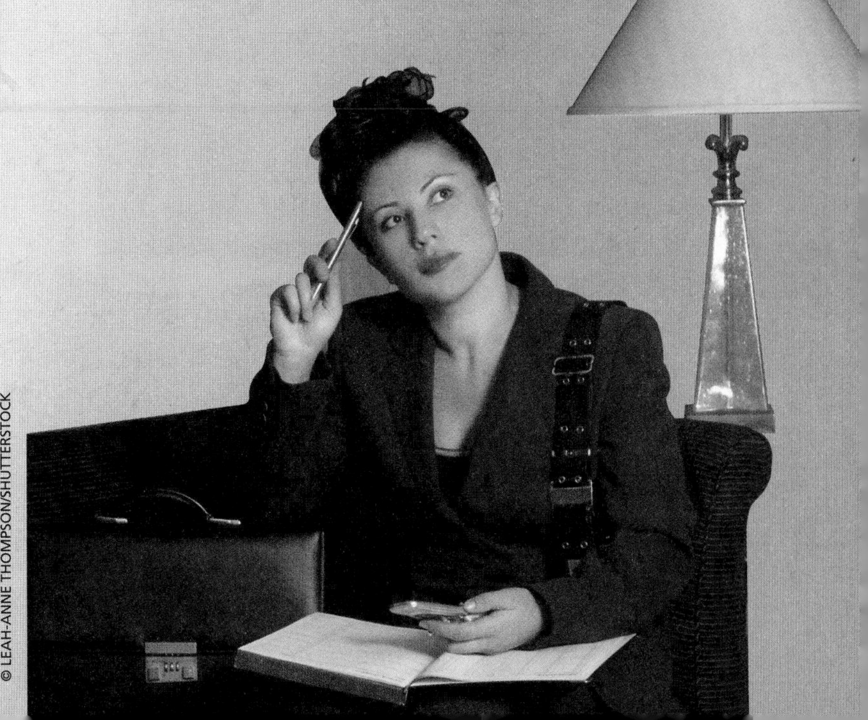

© LEAH-ANNE THOMPSON/SHUTTERSTOCK

Chapter Checklist

Check each of the actions you are currently taking to increase your career success:

- ☐ Preparing for different types of interviews.
- ☐ Focusing on responding persuasively to questions about my qualifications and abilities; citing examples of applying my abilities in work, school, and other activities.
- ☐ Preparing and rehearsing responses to typical interview questions.
- ☐ Anticipating the stress of inappropriate interview questions and practicing careful responses.
- ☐ Preparing and practicing responses to stress questions; thinking through the question and remaining composed.
- ☐ Preparing and asking appropriate questions.
- ☐ Avoiding asking questions that diminish my likability, including questions that are too direct, questions that my research should have answered, and questions that make me appear immature or uncommitted to the job.

Critical Thinking Questions

1. How will you benefit from knowing what style of interview your target employer typically uses?
2. What style(s) of interviewing do you expect to be most prevalent in your job search? What techniques do you plan to use to maximize your performance in these types of interviews?
3. What are the job applicant's main objectives during the question-and-answer portion of the interview?
4. Why is it important for an applicant to ask some questions during an interview?
5. What specific types of questions do you most need to prepare for to be ready for your interviews? List two examples, and include the answers you plan to give.
6. How will you handle an illegal or inappropriate question from an interviewer?

For convenient access to valuable career resources, study tools, activities, and job information links, visit the companion web site for this text: www.cengage.com/careerreadiness/levitt.

Trial Run

Divide into teams of four and give everyone a sheet of paper. Each person selects a type of interview question (general information, behavioral, character, or stress) and writes two questions from the lists in this chapter on a sheet of paper (one question on side A, one question on side B).

Pass the sheets to the left. Take three minutes to write a possible answer to the interview question on side A. When time is up, pass the sheets to the left again and answer the second question on Side A. Do this until each person on the team has answered all four interview questions on side A.

Repeat the exercise with the questions on side B.

Read each question and the four suggested answers out loud. Critique the answers, and discuss which answer is the best choice or how a combination of the answers would be most appropriate. Be creative.

If possible, have someone record all the questions and answers and distribute them back to the group.

Career Action

10-1 Research Interview Styles

PART 1: PERSONAL CONTACT RESEARCH

Directions: Contact atleast two organizations in your field that are similar to your target employer, and arrange a brief meeting with each to research their interview styles. Make sure they understand that this is not a request for an interview. Follow the guidelines for conducting a successful career information survey in Chapter 4, as well as the steps below.

1. **During your meetings, ask your contacts to describe the style of interviewing they use to evaluate applicants for positions similar to the one you are targeting.**
2. **Ask what criteria (skills, experience, education, personal qualities) they use to evaluate applicants.**
3. **Ask for specific examples of applicants' positive and negative actions and comments.**
4. **Take notes of any information you find useful.**
5. **As always, act professionally and thank the people who help you. Follow up by sending thank-you notes.**

PART 2: INTERNET RESEARCH

Directions: Use these sites or others to search for information on the interview styles you expect to be the most prevalent in your field (links are on the *Your Career: How to Make It Happen* web site at www.cengage.com/careerreadiness/levitt). Summarize the key points you find useful or print relevant articles. File your research in your Career Management Files Binder.

aarp.org
CareerJournal.com
Quintessential Careers
The Riley Guide
Womensjoblist.com
Yahoo! HotJobs

Career Action

10-2 Internet Research on Interview Question-and-Answer Tips

Directions: Use the Internet to search for additional tips about interview questions and answers. Summarize the key points or print the relevant articles you find. Be sure to check many sources, from sponsored links on newspaper/media sites to Yahoo! and career information sites, and use the links on the *Your Career: How to Make it Happen* web site. If you want to know more about handling inappropriate questions, include this topic in your search, directly from a search engine.

10-3 Create a Question-and-Answer Planning Sheet

Directions: Record the answers to typical questions you can expect to be asked during job interviews. Also write sample questions that you can ask during interviews. Use the suggestions in this chapter and the previous interview chapters and your 60-Second Commercial. Tailor your answers to your target job. Emphasize your qualifications for the job at every opportunity. Use positive, action-oriented words. Save the completed worksheet in your Career Management Files Binder.

GENERAL INFORMATION QUESTIONS

Why do you want this job?

What type of work do you enjoy doing the most?

What are your strongest skills?

What are your long-term career goals, and how do you plan to achieve them?

Do you think of yourself as a team player? Give examples.

Do you have a geographical preference? Are you willing to relocate?

Under what management style do you work most productively?

What is important to you in a company? What do you look for in an organization?

BEHAVIORAL AND CHARACTER QUESTIONS

What have you accomplished that demonstrates your initiative?

How do you deal with an angry customer or coworker? Describe an experience you've had.

How are you able to adapt to change? Give an example.

How would you describe yourself?

What rewards do you look for in your career?

What accomplishment are you most proud of, particularly as it relates to your field?

What do you think are the most important characteristics and abilities a person must possess to be successful? How do you rate yourself in those areas?

STRESS QUESTIONS

Why do you think you are the best candidate for this job? Why should I hire you?

Why do you want to leave your current job?

Why have you held so many jobs?

What is your greatest weakness?

Have you ever been fired from a job?

Does your current employer know you are planning to leave?

What kinds of decisions are the most difficult for you?

What is your salary range? (Although not strictly a stress question, being asked about salary expectations is always awkward. Search the Internet for advice about handling this common question. Hint: Avoid giving a direct answer.)

QUESTIONS AND TOPICS TO AVOID

List several questions to avoid asking during an interview, and explain why the questions are inappropriate:

Q-AND-A SAVVY STRATEGIES

Review "Apply Savvy Q-and-A Strategies" in this chapter. List the strategies that are most applicable to your job search. Add others you found through your Internet research.

YOUR QUESTIONS

Review the sample questions in "Your Questions Count." In your own words, write the questions you want to ask during your interviews. If necessary, ask for help from a member of your support system. Add questions that are pertinent to your job search and goals.

FOR YOUR CAREER MANAGEMENT FILES BINDER

After completing the Career Action activities in this chapter, file the following documents in your Career Management Files Binder:

- ☐ **CA 10-1: Types of interview styles**
- ☐ **CA 10-2: Interview Q&A tips from the Internet**
- ☐ **CA 10-3: Interview Q&A planning sheet**

© STOCKBYTE/GETTY IMAGES

Chapter 11

Interview Like a Pro

Objectives

- Gain a competitive advantage with interview survival skills.
- Build confidence by completing a practice interview.
- Learn new skills through interview self-assessment and critique.

Overview

Chapter 11 provides vital interview rehearsal activities, including a practice interview with a member of your support network and a dress rehearsal interview with an employer in your field. You will also learn important game strategies to prepare for interviews and close interviews in your favor. These activities will help you sharpen your interview skills, boost your confidence, and increase your competitive advantage. Chapter 11 also outlines follow-up activities you can take to tip the hiring decision in your favor.

chapter 11 CareerActions

11-1: Arrange Your Own Practice Interview

11-2: Participate in a Dress Rehearsal Interview

11-3: Summarize and Evaluate Your Interviews

11-4: Interview Critique Form

11-5: Internet Research on Interview Follow-up Tips

11-6: Follow-up Telephone Call and Letter or E-mail

Jump Start Your Interview Success

Because an interview is a dynamic exchange between two people, there will never be a list of "Interview Do's and Don'ts" that works in every situation. There are, however, three gifts you can give yourself to be at your best in interviews:

- Plenty of time to prepare so you aren't rushed or stressed right before the interview.
- Diligent, focused preparation and practice.
- The self-confidence you will gain from feeling ready for the interview.

© DIGITAL VISION/GETTY IMAGES

Go online and search on the phrase "job interview advice." Read a few articles in depth, or gather tidbits from several sites. Look for guidelines about standard business etiquette, and see if you can find any specific expectations for your career field. The Internet has the power to set standards and establish cultural norms by judging or rewarding certain behaviors, so it's important to know what's being said.

For fun, read about the worst interview blunders to make sure you don't repeat someone else's mistake.

Gain a Competitive Advantage

While some people may claim they can walk into an interview and "wing it," do not try to be one of them.

If you get an e-mail or telephone call asking you to come to a job interview, the employer is interested in *you*. You are the focus of the interview. You will be evaluated on your past successes and mistakes and on your future goals and potential. You will be expected to give concrete examples of your skills and explain how they relate to the requirements for this job.

Any nervousness that you feel about an upcoming job interview is an appropriate response to a situation that will test your interpersonal, social, professional, and verbal and nonverbal skills.

Preparation and practice can help you relax and give you a genuine competitive advantage over the other people who are interviewing for "your" position. The payoff could be just the job you are looking for.

Schedule Practice Interviews

Users of *Your Career: How to Make It Happen* emphasize that the practice interviews improve their actual interview performance by as much as 100 percent. They say that this valuable practice enhances their preparation, increases their self-confidence, improves the image of competence they project, and reduces their anxiety about the process—all of which improve their performance in actual interviews. Gain these valuable advantages yourself by doing practice interviews.

Interview with Someone in Your Support Network Schedule a practice interview with a friend, family member, or an acquaintance in your support network, preferably someone experienced in interviewing who knows you personally. Ask someone to observe the practice interview, and get recommendations from both people for improving your performance.

If possible, videotape the practice interview. This firsthand review may be the most valuable performance feedback you can get. Reread the tips in Chapter 8. Listen to your tone of voice and look at your body language.

☐ Did you speak too fast or too low? Practice improving your speaking, and above all, aim to speak in a warm, energetic tone.

☐ Using your body language self-inventory in Career Action 8-2, watch for negative, passive, or aggressive body language and try to improve.

complete Career Actions

11-1 Arrange Your Own Practice Interview

Interview with Someone in Your Career Field Once you feel comfortable with your performance in the practice interview with your support team, schedule a dress rehearsal interview with an employer in your field.

Some people receive job offers as a result of dress rehearsal practice interviews; others obtain leads that result in jobs. Everyone gains helpful interview experience.

When making an appointment for a dress rehearsal interview:

☐ Explain that the interview is a course assignment and that you would appreciate the employer's help in completing it.

☐ Say that you would like the interview to be as realistic as possible.

☐ Ask what the protocol is for real applicants, and follow each step. If there is an application form, pick it up ahead of time and complete it carefully.

☐ Take your Interview Marketing Kit (Chapter 8), and use it appropriately.

Remember that any job offer should come spontaneously from the employer. Asking directly for a job contradicts your request for help in practicing your interviewing skills. If your contact makes an offer or provides leads or suggestions, however, follow up immediately if you are interested.

MAKE IT A HABIT

Manage Your Schedule

Limit the number of interviews you schedule for one day. After two interviews, an applicant's performance level typically drops. Don't jeopardize your chances of getting a job because you are tired.

Never be late for an interview. If you know where you are going you will have one less thing to worry about. If the interview is in an unfamiliar area, be sure that you have directions and know how long it will take to get there.

If possible, go to the location a few days before, at the same time of day, to look for construction delays and traffic jams. Alternatively, take public transportation and use the time to relax and rehearse. Take your cell phone (or borrow one) so you can call the interviewer if you will be late. (Be sure to turn it off during the interview.)

Plan to arrive about ten minutes before the interview. If you are early, sit in your car or find someplace else to wait until it's time to go in.

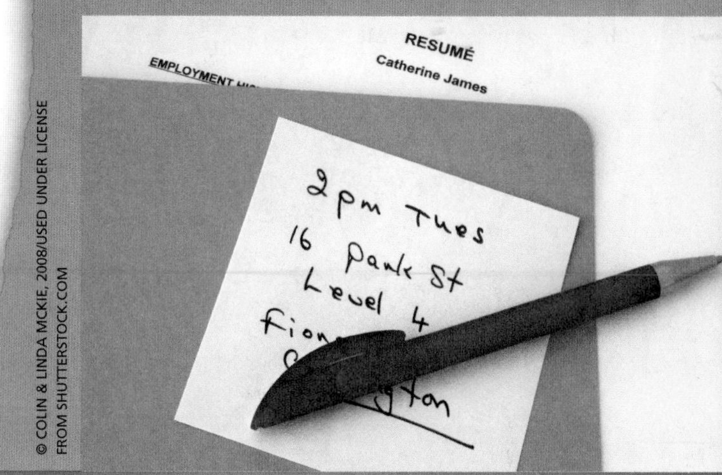

Ask everyone who interviews you to evaluate your performance. Ask them to complete the Interview Critique Form (Career Action 11-4).

Be sure to follow up with a thank-you note. See Figure 11-2 on page 250.

MAKE IT A HABIT

Practice Using Your Marketing Materials

To capture an interviewer's attention, refer first to an item that represents one of your most outstanding accomplishments. Save another exceptional item to use toward the end of the interview to leave a favorable last impression.

Practice using your Interview Marketing Kit items so the actual delivery will be smooth. Have a friend give you a mock interview, and practice referring to your portfolio items at key points during the interview.

Suppose an interviewer asks, "How important do you think it is to keep up with changing technology?" To this you can reply "I think it is very important, and I have taken several classes to update my software skills." You can then provide an appropriate example of how you have kept up to date with technology in your field. By rehearsing, you will be able to work the portfolio items into an interview naturally.

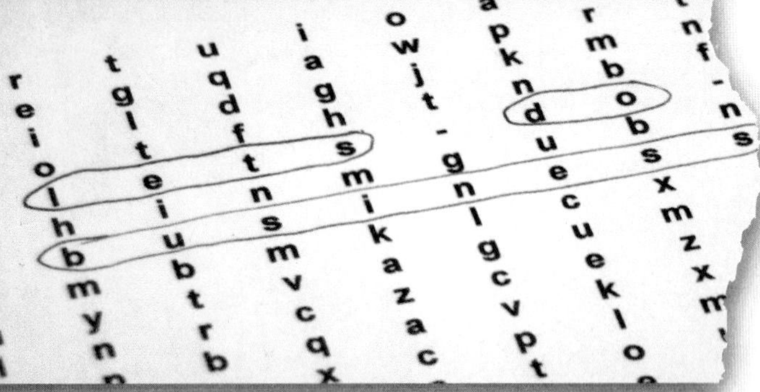

complete Career Actions

11-2 Participate in a Dress Rehearsal Interview

Prepare for the Interview

The tips in this section apply to all your job interviews. To get the most benefit from your practice interviews, prepare for them as if they were real interviews.

- ☐ Reduce your stress level by learning as much as you can about the situation, such as the type of interview, in advance.
- ☐ Study the job description or ad and match your qualifications and experience with every job requirement. Say these things out loud. Practice what you will say about your plans to fill any gaps between the job requirements and your qualifications and experience.
- ☐ Pick five likely questions and five questions you hope aren't asked. Prepare your answers and practice saying them in front of the mirror or with friends. Practice "thinking on your feet" in response to tough questions. (Chapter 10)
- ☐ Review and practice your 60-Second Commercial. (Chapter 8)
- ☐ Have you heard the advice to "make up your mind to have a good time and *then* go to the party"? Approach your interviews the same way, and see how a positive attitude can strengthen your performance. (Chapter 1 and Chapter 8)
- ☐ Try positive visualization and other techniques for managing stress. (Chapter 1)
- ☐ Look at the Interview Critique Form (Career Action 11-4) to remind yourself how you will be judged.
- ☐ Call someone on your support team for a last-minute morale boost before heading to the interview.
- ☐ Assemble your Interview Marketing Kit and take it with you. (Chapter 8)
- ☐ On the day of the interview, take the time to look your best. Eat well and be rested, immaculately groomed, and appropriately dressed. (Chapter 8)
- ☐ Use positive, assertive body language. (Chapter 8)
- ☐ Use your voice well—what you say and how you say it. (Chapter 8)
- ☐ Learn how to wrap up an interview in your favor (next page).

Prepare an Interview Survival Pack

Feeling in control is one way to keep your cool in stressful interviewing situations. If you can anticipate uncomfortable situations ahead of time, you can manage the stress they cause more effectively. With a little planning, you can avoid an interview-sabotaging experience.

Prepare a survival pack that contains items such as:

- ☐ Personal hygiene items (toothpaste and toothbrush, comb, even deodorant)
- ☐ Spare stockings or tie (in case of snags or stains)
- ☐ Spare earrings or shoelaces
- ☐ Whatever else you need to look, smell, and be your best no matter what happens

Put your gear in a zippered pouch that fits neatly into your Interview Marketing Kit. If you travel by car, store it there.

Organize Your "Props" Before the Interview

Organize the physical items you will have with you so you don't have to fumble with them during the interview.

- ☐ Review the recommended contents of the Interview Marketing Kit on page 196, and put your portfolio items in the order in which you will use them.
- ☐ Bring a businesslike pen—and make sure it works before the meeting.
- ☐ Open your notebook to your questions, and open your appointment calendar to the current week or month.

Use Your Portfolio Items Wisely

It's a mistake to rely only on your portfolio items to convince an interviewer of your qualifications. The focus of the interview is still on you. Your personal appearance, your body language, and your verbal communication skills are essential. The portfolio items are visual aids to support your qualifications. For each interview, select the items to match the specific employer and job. Do not use every item for every interview.

Some interviewers may not want to review your portfolio items while they meet with you. Ask permission before you show any portfolio items and before you take any notes.

Referring to your appointment calendar is an exception to this rule. If you need to schedule a follow-up meeting or activity, having your appointment book handy is essential so you can confirm any further appointments immediately. Doing so later could result in a lost opportunity; an interviewer may want to make a future commitment while you're still in the interview.

> **Portfolio items** are visual aids to support your qualifications. Do not use every item for every interview.

Wrap Up the Interview in Your Favor

Whether it's a practice interview or the real thing, be proactive and professional by influencing how the interview ends. For your own sake, clarify what to expect next in the process. Leave a positive impression by restating your qualifications and by closing the interview skillfully.

Clarify What to Expect Next

Before you leave the interview, clarify:

☐ What, if anything, you should do to follow up.

☐ When a decision will be made.

☐ How the interviewer prefers you to follow up (by telephone, by letter, or in person).

The following sample dialogue shows how to get this information:

You: When should I expect to hear whether I am selected for the position?

Interviewer: We'll notify all applicants of our decision within two weeks.

You: Do you mind if I check back with you?

Interviewer: I prefer that you don't until we notify you.

or

Interviewer: No, I don't mind.

You: How would you prefer I contact you?

Interviewer: Please call my assistant.

Clarifying these details underscores your image as a fellow professional who understands the importance of following through after important meetings.

Watch Out
Avoid Interview Disqualifiers

Any one of these blunders during an interview could cost you the job:

1. Don't be late. It's hard to count all the negative messages being late sends: lack of respect, lack of genuine interest, personal disorganization, and on and on.
2. Don't be abrupt or discourteous to anyone you meet.
3. Don't sit down until the interviewer invites you to; waiting is courteous.
4. Don't bring anyone else to the interview; it makes you look immature and insecure.
5. Don't invade the interviewer's personal space by reading anything on the desk or putting anything on it.
6. Don't have anything in your mouth.

Use Your Clincher

As you near the close of an interview, make a point of leaving your interviewer with a clear picture of how you fit the job. Bring the interview full circle by asking a question similar to this example in a courteous tone: "Would you please summarize the most important qualifications you're looking for in filling this position?"

Run the short version of your 60-Second Commercial to restate your skills, experience, and other assets that meet the employer's needs. This important clincher gives you one last chance to market yourself and your qualifications. People remember best what they hear first and last.

Close the Interview Skillfully

Some applicants lose the race for a job by not clearing the final hurdle: closing the interview skillfully. Don't let your posture, attitude, or verbal and nonverbal communication slip for even a moment. Use the following techniques to close an interview skillfully:

☐ Watch for signs from the interviewer that it's time to wrap up. Signs include asking whether you have any further questions, tidying up papers on the desk, pushing the chair back, or simply sitting back in the chair. Heed the cue. Don't make the interviewer impatient by droning on at this point.

☐ If the interviewer is not skilled at interviewing, help wrap up smoothly by asking, "Is there anything else you need to discuss with me? I know you are busy, and I appreciate the time you have given me for this interview."

☐ Request a commitment from the interviewer to notify you when an applicant has been selected. Imply that this is not the only job you are considering: "By what date will you make your decision on this position? I'd appreciate knowing within the next two weeks so I can finalize my plans."

☐ Before you leave, determine any follow-up activities the interviewer expects from you. If a second interview is arranged, write down the date, time, place, and names of all of the people who will be interviewing you. If you are expected to provide additional information, credentials, references, or work samples, make a note and verify what you are supposed to do before you leave.

- ☐ If you're seriously interested in the job, say so! Just as in effective sales, the person who asks is the most likely to receive. Interviewers are impressed by applicants' expressions of interest; candidates who directly express their interest strengthen their position. Offer a simple statement—for example, "I'd be pleased to be a part of this organization" or "After talking with you, I'm convinced this is the job I want, and I believe my qualifications would be an asset to the Acme Corporation. Please consider me seriously for this position."
- ☐ As you leave, remember to use the interviewer's name: "Thank you for interviewing me, Ms. Carpenter."
- ☐ If you haven't been given one, ask the interviewer for a business card. You'll need it for your thank-you note.
- ☐ Be conscious of using positive body language. Keep your shoulders back and your head up when you stand, and give a warm smile and a firm handshake. Once you leave the interviewer's office, you are still interviewing. Thank the receptionist or assistant by name, and add a brief parting greeting.

Review Figure 11-1 on the next page to reinforce your understanding of the areas that employers consider the most important during an interview.

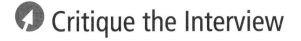

Critique the Interview

Within one hour of every interview (or at the earliest possible time), summarize and evaluate your own interview performance in writing (Career Action 11-3). Ask yourself the following questions:

- ☐ What positive impressions did I make? Why did I make these impressions?
- ☐ What negative impressions might I have left with the interviewer? Why did I make these impressions?
- ☐ Was there anything I should have said but didn't?
- ☐ What other questions would I have liked to ask?
- ☐ What questions do I wish I had answered differently? How would I have answered them differently?

MAKE IT A HABIT

Apply Interview Success Strategies

To polish your performance, practice these successful interview techniques from earlier chapters:

- **Remember: There is no "time out" from the moment you enter the building until you leave.** Maintain good posture, project energy and enthusiasm, and think good thoughts. Smile!
- **Use the interviewer's name in your greeting.** Identify yourself and the position for which you are applying.
- **Be likable and relaxed.** Be courteous and friendly, and show interest in the position.
- **Use positive body language** and voice tone throughout the interview.
- **Focus on your capabilities and accomplishments.**
- **Stress your qualifications** and your interest in benefiting the company and advancing yourself.
- **Ask a few appropriate questions.**
- **Remain calm if asked a stress question.** Allow yourself time to plan an effective answer.
- **Wrap up the interview in your favor.** Ask the interviewer to summarize the most important qualifications for the job; then stress your related abilities.

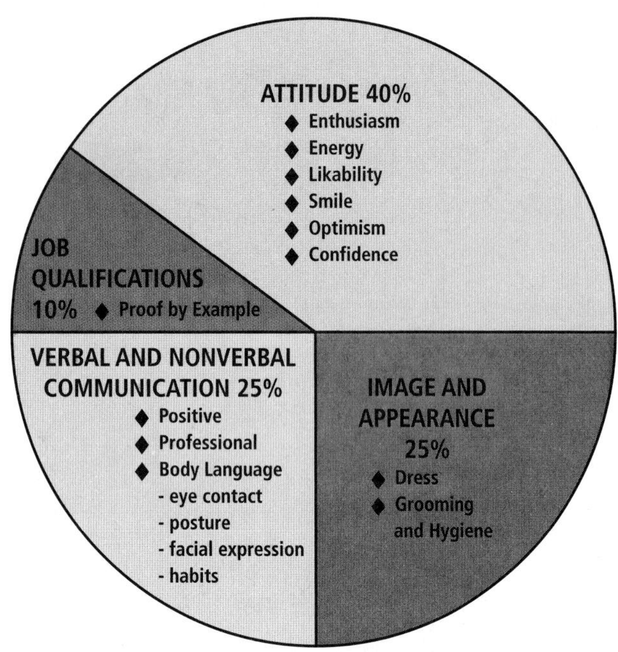

Figure 11-1: How You are Rated During an Interview

- ☐ How did I feel about the interview immediately after it concluded? How do I feel about the interview now?
- ☐ What behaviors or habits of speech distracted from my professionalism?
- ☐ Did my appearance give the impression I hoped it would?

Give everyone who conducts or observes a practice interview a copy of the Interview Critique Form (page 258). Ask them to evaluate your performance, identify your strengths and weaknesses, and suggest ways you can improve your performance. Work on your areas of weakness before you have an actual interview.

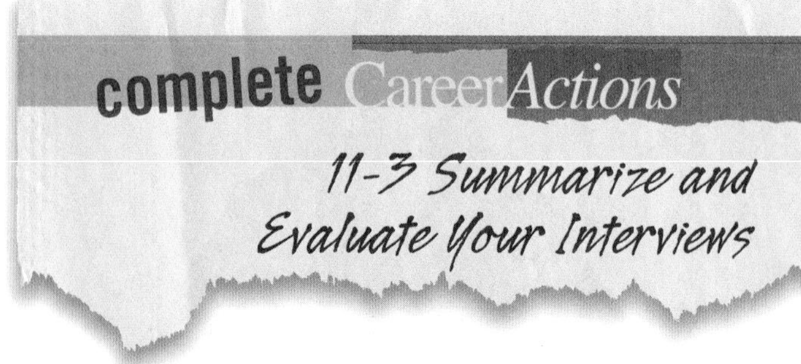

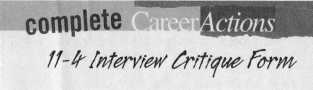

complete Career Actions

11-4 Interview Critique Form

Good Interview Follow-up Moves

Interview follow-up can increase your chances of getting the job by 30 percent or more because many applicants don't bother to do it! Interviewers see follow-up by a job seeker as a proactive step that shows initiative and interest.

Good follow-up reinforces your qualifications and helps you stand out favorably from the competition. Be patient during this stage of the job search. The hiring process often takes longer than the employer expects.

The key to follow-up is action: evaluate your interview performance (Career Actions 11-3 and 11-4) and send a follow-up message to the interviewer.

Plan Your Follow-up Strategies

Look at your completed Career Action 11-3 and circle in red any notes that require follow-up (information you need to clarify or reinforce with the employer, questions you want answered, areas of weak performance and suggestions for improving them, and specific actions you need to take).

Determine what method of follow-up is most appropriate. If you remembered to ask the interviewer how he or she wanted you to follow up, the decision has been made for you. If you forgot to ask, send a follow-up letter or e-mail rather than make a telephone call. If the interviewer approves of follow-up telephone calls, use that method. A telephone call is more personal and lively and gives you quicker feedback. If you call, you should also follow up with a letter or an e-mail because it provides a reminder of you.

Outline Your Follow-up Message Regardless of the method you choose for follow-up, outline the message first:

- ☐ List any questions you need to ask.
- ☐ Summarize pertinent information you omitted or covered inadequately in your interview.
- ☐ State specifically how the organization could benefit by hiring you (a brief rerun of or an excerpt from your 60-Second Commercial).

Make your follow-up message brief and polished. Include only the most important questions or information.

Time Your Call Make your follow-up call within two days of your interview, while your name and the interview are still fresh in the interviewer's mind. Keep in mind:

- ☐ Mondays and Fridays are the busiest business days, so call on another day.
- ☐ Just before lunch and just before the end of the day are usually inconvenient times as well.

Send a Brief Thank-You Note Too Even if you make your initial follow-up by telephone, you should send a brief thank-you letter or e-mail message within 48 hours of your interview to be sure your message is received during the decision-making stage. (The body of a thank-you e-mail is similar to that of a thank-you letter.)

You should write a thank-you note to every person who interviewed you. The letters can be basically the same, but try to vary each one in case the recipients compare notes. If you've already made a telephone call, do not restate your qualifications in this message; just thank the interviewer.

Send a thank-you note even if you're sure the job is not for you.

The thank-you letter brings your name before the interviewer in a favorable light one more time, reinforcing your name in his or her mind. It also provides a positive written record of you in the employer's files.

Review the brief thank-you letter in Figure 11-2 on page 250.

When to Send a More Complete Follow-up Letter If the interviewer wants you to follow up in writing or if you think follow-up is important to getting hired, send a more complete letter that includes the following:

- ☐ A reference to your interview and the position you are seeking.
- ☐ Clarification of any pertinent information omitted during your interview.
- ☐ A brief version of your 60-Second Commercial.
- ☐ A thank you for the interviewer's time.
- ☐ A statement of enthusiasm for the job.

Review the more complete follow-up letter in Figure 11-3 on page 251. The follow-up letter provides a permanent written record of your qualifications and professional courtesy. The employer can review it any time, making it an effective way to keep your "Commercial" running.

complete CareerActions

11-5 Internet Research on Interview Follow-up Tips

Connect with Your Support Network Again

If a member of your support network is influential with your prospective employer, contact him or her to ask for additional support. A friendly follow-up call from this person to the employer could tip the scales in your favor.

An alternative to the follow-up call by a network member is a letter of recommendation from one or more people who can confirm your qualifications. Some employers routinely request letters of recommendation from former employers, managers, or supervisors of applicants. Arranging to have such letters sent on your own demonstrates initiative—another benefit for you.

2440 Observatory Boulevard
Apartment 34
Los Angeles, CA 90063
July 2, 20—

Ms. Stephanie Nolan
Manager, Auditing Staff
Nolan Henry O'Leary Public Accountants
1410 Granada Avenue, 7th Floor
San Francisco, CA 94115

Dear Ms. Nolan:

Thank you for the opportunity to interview for the position of Staff Auditor I with you and your team. Your invitation to join the first hour of the weekly staff meeting made me feel especially welcome—and sent me to the library to brush up on the finer points of the state's tax credit program for employers who train welfare recipients!

I would enjoy being part of your team and look forward to your hiring decision. Please call me any time this week at 213-555-0128.

Sincerely,

Russell Dunbar

Russell Dunbar

Figure 11-2: Sample of a Brief Thank-You Letter

3493 Huntington Heights
Denver, CO 80202
August 23, 20—

Mr. Frederick J. Gray Wolf
Normandy Copiers, Inc.
3500 Main Street
Boulder, CO 80302-8715

Dear Mr. Gray Wolf:

The enthusiasm you shared this afternoon for the customer-centered philosophy behind the new Normandy Print Center is contagious! I know from experience how satisfying it is to break new ground and to achieve results that exceed all expectations. The Normandy management system sounds unique, innovative, and challenging.

During our meeting, we discussed how I could contribute to your marketing plan, but we didn't have time to talk about store operations. While I managed the parts and service operations of Renaissance Business Systems, our team achieved and maintained a production efficiency rate that consistently placed us in the top 5 percent of the 160 shops nationwide. Sales of maintenance contracts increased every year I was in charge, and we had the lowest return rate for products of all the centers.

Thank you for talking with me about the new opportunities at Normandy. Normandy Copiers, Inc., will be a great success in Boulder, and I would like to contribute to that success. As we agreed, I will call you next Thursday, but you can reach me before that at 303-555-0171.

Sincerely,

Francesca Elena Valdez

Francesca Elena Valdez

Figure 11-3: Sample of a More Complete Follow-up Letter

© CHRISTOPHER HALLORAN 2008/USED UNDER LICENSE FROM SHUTTERSTOCK.COM

Successful Follow-up Phone Call

If your interviewer gave the go-ahead for a follow-up call, you can set yourself apart from the competition with a well-timed, well-prepared telephone call.

- **Demonstrate courtesy.** "Do you have a moment?"
- **Begin with a greeting and self-introduction.** "Hello, Ms. Delgado. This is Greg Bell."
- **Identify the position for which you interviewed and the date.** "I want to thank you for meeting with me yesterday to discuss the Data Processing Systems Analyst I position."
- **Provide important information you omitted.** "After reviewing our meeting, I realized I hadn't mentioned some pertinent information regarding my (education, work experience, qualifications, certification, other)." Concisely give the specifics.
- **Reemphasize your qualifications.** If necessary, give a short, targeted version of your 60-Second Commercial, emphasizing exactly how your qualifications can benefit the employer.
- **If necessary, ask questions to clarify any points that were not covered adequately.** For example, a clearer description of the job responsibilities or clarification of work relationships.
- **Thank the interviewer, express your interest, and encourage a speedy hiring decision.** "Thank you again for the interview. I look forward to learning of your hiring decision soon. I believe we could benefit each other, and I'd be pleased to be a part of Mississippi Central Power Company."

Waiting-Game Strategies

Waiting to hear about a hiring decision is frustrating. Your best strategy is action.

Evaluate your performance and identify follow-up activities. After you complete your follow-up telephone call and letter, review your completed Career Action 11-3. Concentrate on the positive aspects to keep your self-image positive. Have you completed all the follow-up activities?

Call back if you don't hear about the decision by the date the interviewer indicated the hiring decision would be made. This approach does not pressure the interviewer: "Hello, Ms. Delgado. This is Greg Bell. You indicated during our meeting that you expected to make a hiring decision by July 30. I might have missed your call if you tried to get in touch with me." Be careful not to go overboard and annoy or bother the employer.

complete *Career Actions*

11-6 Follow-up Telephone Call and Letter or E-mail

Next Steps

Complete all the Career Actions in this chapter to ensure that you have given yourself a competitive edge through ample interview practice. Review and use the feedback you receive from your practice and dress rehearsal interviews. File the completed Career Actions in your Career Management Files Binder, and make extra copies of the evaluation forms to use every time you interview. In the next chapter, you learn about pre-employment tests and negotiating employment offers.

Chapter Checklist

Check each of the actions you are currently taking to increase your career success:

- Scheduling two practice interviews to improve my interview performance and confidence (an interview with someone in my support network and a dress rehearsal interview with an employer in my target field).
- Preparing for practice interviews as if they were real, participating seriously, and applying interview success strategies.
- Wrapping up interviews in my favor.
- Asking interviewers to evaluate my practice interviews.
- Summarizing every interview and evaluating my performance while it is fresh in my mind.
- Preparing a written script for a follow-up telephone call (if the interviewer said that calling is appropriate).
- Thanking every interviewer with a thank-you note or e-mail message.
- Sending a more complete follow-up letter if I need to clarify something or add information.
- Connecting with my support network after every interview.

Critical Thinking Questions

1. How have you used the success strategies described in Chapter 1 (visualization, positive self-talk, affirmation statements, goal setting, and proactive and assertive behavior) in preparing for and participating in a practice interview? Which of these strategies do you find the most useful?
2. Why is it important to prepare for and perform in a practice interview as though it were the real thing?
3. What negative nonverbal habits are the most important for you to eliminate to improve your interviews?
4. What is included in good interview follow-up?
5. What are the important topics to include in follow-up communications?
6. What strategies should you use if you are waiting to hear about a hiring decision?

For convenient access to valuable career resources, study tools, activities, and job information links, visit the companion web site for this text: www.cengage.com/careerreadiness/levitt.

Trial Run

On the first page of Chapter 1, you read that finding a job is a 5-step process: prepare (learn about today's workplace; evaluate your interests/skills), find job leads, apply for jobs, interviews, and follow-up and evaluation. If you are using the chapters in order, you have completed many activities for the first four steps, and (we hope) have found some job leads, sent out resumes, and had a practice and/or real interview. In this Trial Run, you take stock of your job search strategies.

Directions: Set aside at least two hours for this Trial Run. You will need this book, your Career Management Files Binder, your Career Portfolio, and some blank paper (or use the worksheet on your Data CD). If your completed Career Actions are on a computer, you'll need it too. Find a quiet place to do this work. (Or, work with a partner or in groups of three. Spend at least one hour evaluating each person's materials and progress and planning next steps.)

Remind yourself of the key points in Chapters 1–11 by mentally answering the questions in the end-of-chapter checklists. Look at your Career Actions for each chapter. Evaluate each area of your own job search thoughtfully and honestly.

	What have I accomplished?	What advice or activity in the book has been most helpful?	Where are the gaps?	What advice or activity in the book (that I haven't done) could I apply?
Example: *Find job leads (Chapters 4–5)*	*Everyone knows I'm looking for a job* *Contacts in Ashland & Paducah*	*Good career info conversation with Ms. Owens-Garcia; sent her thank-you note*	*Need job leads in small businesses* *Ask Henry & Jean how they found their jobs*	*Look at trade group sites & Chambers of Commerce sites*
Prepare (Chapters 1–3)				
Find job leads (Chapters 4–5)				
Apply for jobs (Chapters 6–7)				
Interviews (Chapters 8–11)				

Develop a plan for each area:

	What is the most important activity(s) I could do in this area?	What is my plan?
Example: *Find job leads*	*Attend November job fair at Campus Career Center*	• *Research companies @ fair* • *Post resume at CCC job fair page* • *Ask Mrs. Weiss about portfolio; need more samples?* • *Ask Mrs. W if I should schedule 2nd practice interview* • *Look for job fairs @ convention center web site*
Prepare		
Find job leads		
Apply for jobs		
Interviews		

Career Action

11-1 Arrange Your Own Practice Interview

Directions: Schedule a practice interview with your support network members (one interviewer and one or two observers). Use the sample questions in Chapter 10 as a guide for your practice session. You can make a copy of them for the "interviewer" and add any stress questions (or others) you want to rehearse. Encourage the interviewer to expand on the questions, if possible, tailoring them to your job target to give you relevant interview practice. If possible, arrange to have the practice interview videotaped.

Career Action

11-2 Participate in a Dress Rehearsal Interview

Directions: Contact an employer in your career field, and ask for help with a course assignment. Ask the employer to conduct a practice interview with you and to complete a copy of the Interview Critique Form.

1. **Dress appropriately.**
2. **Take a copy of the Interview Critique Form (see Career Action 10-5) with you, and ask the interviewer to evaluate your performance by completing the form during or after the interview.**
3. **After the dress-rehearsal interview, evaluate your own performance; complete a copy of the Interview Follow-up and Evaluation Form (Career Action 11-3).**
4. **Within two days of your dress rehearsal, send a follow-up thank you letter to the person who gave you the interview.**

11-3 Summarize and Evaluate Your Interviews

Directions: Summarize every practice and real interview as soon as possible to avoid forgetting important details. Duplicate and use Career Action 11-3 for your own evaluation and follow-up plans. Answer the questions as completely as possible.

Name of Organization: ______

Date of Interview: ______

Name(s) and Title(s) of Interviewer(s): ______

______

Address: ______

Telephone: ______ Fax: ______

E-Mail address: ______

SUMMARY ACTIVITIES AND QUESTIONS

On a separate sheet of paper, write every question you can remember being asked during the interview. Take your time, and be thorough. Do this before answering any of the following questions.

Based on the knowledge you gained in your interview and research, which of your qualifications would be the greatest asset in this job? Which of these qualifications should be reinforced with the prospective employer in your follow-up?

______

______

______

List any questions you think you answered inadequately. Write out the best possible answer to each question. Use additional paper if necessary.

______

______

______

Did you forget to provide important information that demonstrates your qualifications for the job? Explain in detail.

______

______

______

What questions did you intend to ask but either forgot or didn't have a chance to ask? Write them now.

______

______

______

How could you have presented yourself more effectively?

____

____

____

In what area(s) do you think you performed the best in your interview? Why?

____

____

____

In what area(s) do you think you performed poorly? What steps can you take to improve in these areas?

____

____

____

Describe information you learned about the interviewer that may be helpful in establishing greater rapport in the future (philosophy, current working projects, personal interests or hobbies, mutual goals, and so on).

____

____

____

Is there any point of confusion that needs to be clarified for the employer? Explain.

____

____

____

Are you scheduled for another interview with the organization? If so, record the date, time, place and name(s) of the interviewer(s).

____

____

Record any other activities you offered to follow up on or were specifically asked to follow up on by the interviewer (for example, provide references, transcripts, certificates, or examples of work).

____

____

How does the interviewer prefer you to follow up (by telephone, by letter, in person)?

____

____

When did the interviewer say the hiring decision would be made?

____

____

11-4 Interview Critique Form

Directions: Give copies of the Interview Critique Form to the people who help you in practice interviews. You can also ask them to look at your completed Career Action 11-3 and offer suggestions. Before you give this form to someone, complete the first two lines below.

Name of Interviewee: ______________________ **Date:** ______________________

Position Applied for: ______________________

Interviewer: Please circle the appropriate rating in each category. If desired, add any comments for each category.

Documentation (resume, cover letter, employment application)

Excellent **Very Good** **Good** **Needs Improvement**

Comments or suggestions (optional):

____

____

____

Attitude (Interested in position, self-confident, likable, pleasant tone of voice, smiling)

Excellent **Very Good** **Good** **Needs Improvement**

Comments or suggestions (optional): ______________________

____

____

____

Appearance (Generally neat and tidy, appropriately dressed, alert, good hygiene)

Excellent **Very Good** **Good** **Needs Improvement**

Comments or suggestions (optional): ______________________

____

____

____

Job Qualifications (Education, skills, and experience suitable for position; good personal attributes; human relations capability; dependable; punctual; industrious)

Excellent **Very Good** **Good** **Needs Improvement**

Comments or suggestions (optional): ______________________

____

____

____

Verbal Communication (Speaks clearly with positive tone, uses proper English, avoids slang or repetitive words, emphasizes assets, is courteous, uses name of the interviewer)

Excellent **Very Good** **Good** **Needs Improvement**

Comments or suggestions (optional): ____________________

____

____

____

Nonverbal Communication (Positive, assertive body language, good eye contact, does not fidget)

Excellent **Very Good** **Good** **Needs Improvement**

Comments or suggestions (optional): ____________________

____

____

____

Listening (Does not interrupt or respond too quickly; asks to have a question repeated, if necessary; takes time to think through important questions; calmly endures silence)

Excellent **Very Good** **Good** **Needs Improvement**

Comments or suggestions (optional): ____________________

____

____

____

Enthusiasm (Demonstrates interest/energy through verbal and nonverbal communication)

Excellent **Very Good** **Good** **Needs Improvement**

Comments or suggestions (optional): ____________________

____

____

____

Please summarize any other observations you made during the interview. Note any favorable behavior, and provide suggestions for improvement.

CareerAction

11-5 Internet Research on Interview Follow-up Tips

Directions: Search the Internet for additional tips on interview follow-up that could be useful. File your research in your Career Management Files Binder. Try searching on "interview thank-you letter" and "interview follow-up letter."

CareerAction

11-6 Follow-up Telephone Call and Letter or E-mail

Directions: Write a script for your follow-up telephone call, letter, or e-mail message. File the completed worksheet and final documents in your Career Management Files Binder.

FOR YOUR CAREER MANAGEMENT FILES BINDER

After completing the Career Action activities in this chapter, file the following documents in your Career Management Files Binder:

- ☐ **CA 11-1: Plans for a practice interview**
- ☐ **CA 11-2: Plans for a dress rehearsal interview**
- ☐ **CA 11-3: Interview summary and evaluation**
- ☐ **CA 11-4: Interview Critique Form**
- ☐ **CA 11-5: Interview follow-up tips**
- ☐ **CA 11-6: Interview follow-up communication**

part 5

Next Steps

Industry Speaks

After serving in the Marines as a Military Police Officer, Brian McNay used the GI Bill to earn a bachelor's degree in Organizational Leadership. Today he is an Administrative Assistant at Procter & Gamble. "Flexibility and agility are absolutely essential in my job. I need to be flexible enough to work on five projects at the same time, and agile enough to move between those jobs and shift gears as priorities change. I get instructions and guidelines for every project, but I'm expected to find my own way to do the work, the way that works best for me. Employees are expected to grow in their jobs, because the company promotes from within.

"The military taught me to be a close observer. If I observe the little tricks that 10 people do to make their work easier, I have 10 strategies that I can adapt to make my own. I take a notebook everywhere because I can learn from everybody."

Brian has also learned to be adaptable. "My advice to job seekers is to be patient and diligent. Work hard to find a job and get your foot in the door, and then work hard to excel in your new job."

Chapter 12

© STOCKBYTE/GETTY IMAGES

Objectives

- Use the Internet to research current salary information for your field.
- Identify employment testing procedures and compensation packages for the type of job you are seeking in your field.
- Become familiar with guidelines for negotiating the compensation package you are offered.
- Summarize how to deal effectively with job offers.

Following Up and Negotiating Offers

Overview

You may be asked to take a pre-employment screening test before you are considered for a job. Chapter 12 presents strategies to help you perform successfully when preparing for and taking different types of screening tests, including drug screening and background checks. You will also learn how to research salaries and benefit packages; how to negotiate a fair compensation package; and how to evaluate, accept, or reject job offers.

chapter 12 CareerActions

12-1: Internet Research on Salary Information

12-2: Salary and Benefits Planning Sheet

12-3: Planning for Dealing with Job Offers

Jump Start Your Knowledge of Health Care Benefits

The high cost of health care is on everyone's mind these days. You can't watch television without seeing a news story or commercial about the cost of prescription drugs or individuals going bankrupt after trying to pay for a catastrophic illness or emergency.

Most Americans get their health care coverage through their employer, but this situation is not as stable as in the past. More of us work in the service sector, where fewer employers offer health insurance. Many of us are part-time workers or contractors who are not eligible to participate in employer-sponsored health insurance.

Ask five people you know about their health care benefits. If they are comfortable talking with you for this report, ask how and why their situation has changed in the last three years. What do they expect in the future? What are their suggestions for changing the system? Try to reach a cross-section of people, such as a government employee, a self-employed friend, and a retiree. With a partner, present your findings to the class. Recommend changes.

Ace Employment Tests

Doing your homework is a sure way to improve your educational test scores, and it also helps you succeed in employment tests. As part of your research, find out if the prospective employer requires pre-employment testing. Many employers don't use pre-employment testing, but you may apply to one that does.

If a test is involved, find out whether it's a written, oral, computerized, or combination test. Does it test technical knowledge, job-related skills, manual dexterity, personality, special abilities, or other job-related capabilities? Try to find out what will be tested and how.

The Personality Test

The **personality test** is the one exception to the "do your homework" rule. Because this type of test is usually designed to determine whether your personal and behavioral preferences are well matched to the work involved, advance study doesn't apply. Technically, there are no wrong answers in these tests. Most personality tests measure things like your solitary or social tendencies, relative need for stability, preference for efficiency or creativity, style of goal achievement (flexible or fixed), and your tendency to accept others' ideas or stick to your own. Answer all questions honestly. If your personality doesn't match the job, you won't be happy in it.

The Skills Test

If the employer will test your job-related skills, start to review, practice, and improve your skills today. No matter how good your skills are, you can improve them with practice, which increases your employability. Another benefit of polishing your skills is that you'll be able to start your new job with more confidence. Stop preparing one or two days before you take a skills test, however. Cramming until the last minute increases anxiety and often results in lower performance.

The Technical Test

If you will be required to take an oral or written test for a professional position, try to get some samples of the technical questions that may be asked. Resources for learning about the types of questions are the employer's human resources department, other employees in the company, people who have taken the test, and people who have taken similar tests in your field. Libraries and bookstores also have sample tests.

If you can find sample questions or even general topics that will be covered in the technical test, write out answers to the questions. The important thing is to be as complete as possible in your answers. The purpose of a technical test is to find out how much you know about the subject.

The Computerized Pre-employment Test

The computerized pre-employment test is useful for screening large numbers of applicants because it saves time and other expenses. The test may be general in content, or it may be a skills or personality test.

Typically, you take this test at the employer's site or at an employment agency. You may also be asked to log on to an employer's web site and take the test online. You receive instructions on how to use the computerized test program and are given a specific amount of time to complete it. The results are usually scored electronically and generated in a report. They are then analyzed by human resources personnel. The best advice for performing well on a computerized pre-employment test is to do your best; don't try to outwit the test. Also, avoid using absolutes such as *never* and *always*. These words can signal an extreme personality or lying. If it is a skills test, practicing ahead of time can help improve your score.

Taking Employment Tests

Employment testing may be an important factor in an employer's hiring decision. Follow these guidelines to perform at your best:

- ☐ Eat properly before the test, and be well rested. A sluggish body and brain can diminish your test performance.
- ☐ Do some physical exercise or yoga (or a similar activity) before the test to improve your circulation and your ability to relax and concentrate.
- ☐ Arrive 10 to 15 minutes early to avoid feeling rushed or tense.
- ☐ Most firms provide more than enough time to complete a test, so don't rush into poor performance. Ask exactly how much time is allotted for the test, however.
- ☐ Before beginning, read the test carefully to clarify the instructions and to determine how many points are assigned to each question. If you run short on time, answer the questions that are assigned the largest number of points. If the points aren't indicated, ask the person monitoring the test how the questions are weighted.
- ☐ Ask whether points will be deducted for questions you don't answer. If they will, answer every question. If not, don't spend a lot of time on questions you can't answer easily. (Save those for last.)
- ☐ Many tests are objective, often including multiple choice questions. In true-false questions, extreme statements are frequently false (for example, choices that contain the words *all, never,* or *always*). Moderate statements are often true.
- ☐ Double-check to be sure you didn't skip any questions. Your first response is usually the correct one, so don't change answers unless you're sure you made a careless mistake.
- ☐ On general math tests, expect some simple addition, subtraction, multiplication, division, fraction, percentage, and decimal problems. Many math tests also include word problems.
- ☐ Advanced math tests will be geared to your field (engineering and statistical analysis, for instance). Consult others who have taken similar tests to determine what you should review. Your education and working experience are your primary preparation for advanced math tests.
- ☐ Oral tests or boards are generally given for applicants with advanced college degrees and for senior management and supervisory positions. They test an applicant's technical knowledge. Ask a colleague and/or an instructor in your field to meet

with you to review the important technical aspects of your field. Review and study the major principles before the meeting and use the meeting to summarize them.

4 Research Salary and Benefits Ahead of Time

To optimize your ability to negotiate for the best possible salary and benefits, you must become as knowledgeable as possible about the going salary ranges and the types of benefits being offered in your field. You significantly reduce your salary and benefits bargaining power if you omit this research step.

The Compensation Package

Salary is not the only important factor you should consider when assessing the value of a job. The complete compensation package includes salary, potential for earnings growth, and all other benefits. All of these are important. Base your compensation considerations on the following:

- ☐ The trends in your field (based on research)
- ☐ Your worth (the value you can offer the employer)
- ☐ The benefits that are most important to you: health/life insurance, retirement programs, flextime, dependent care, reimbursement for education or training, and so on

Research Compensation Trends in Your Field

Research the going rate. Increase your chances of being offered the best compensation package by including this topic in your employer and industry research. Talk with leaders in your field, people who hold positions that are similar to your target job, and area placement specialists. Also search the Internet for salary and benefits information.

Some employers provide printed job descriptions that include a fixed salary listing, while others offer salary information on their web sites. A job notice may include a salary range, or the salary may be open.

You may be able to find the range or approximate salary for a position from the employer's human resources department.

Some employers, however, don't give out this information. They may give you only the bottom of the range—rarely the top figure. Having a general idea of the range is better than having no idea.

Your school's career services office can help you research salary and benefits packages through local contacts and publications such as the *Job Choices* journal—an excellent publication by the National Association of Colleges and Employers.

If the salary is fixed, as may occur in some union or government jobs, you must decide whether it's acceptable to you. Research salary and benefits information online. Check the web sites of associations in your career field.

Watch Out
Take Drug Screening Seriously

Applicants who test positively for drug use or who admit to using illegal drugs may be screened out of the job immediately. Never give flippant answers to questions about drug use. They could be interpreted negatively.

Policies for drug screening vary considerably from one employer to another. As part of your employer research, find out what the drug screening procedures and requirements are. Check with employers directly and with people who work for them. Schools' career services counselors often have information about drug testing procedures and may be familiar with the procedures local employers use.

To protect yourself, before you are tested, report to the employer any prescription or over-the-counter drugs you are taking. Some of these can result in a false-positive test.

If you learn that the salary is negotiable, try for a salary at the top of the range. (You can agree to accept a salary that is lower than the top level, but if you offer to take the lowest end of the range first, that's probably what you'll get.)

Study the following section, "Negotiate for Top Salary and Benefits," and prepare to bargain your way up the pay scale.

complete *CareerActions*

12-1 Internet Research on Salary Information

Watch Out
Background Checks

A background check is a consumer report that employers use to screen potential employees. In addition to confirming your education and work history, employers may request a consumer report from a credit reporting bureau to check your social security number, credit payment record, driving record, or criminal history.

This type of background check is particularly common for jobs that require government security clearance, but it may be used for any job.

Before employers can get your consumer report, they must have your written consent, however. You always have the option of withdrawing your application if there is information you do not want to disclose.

The best way to prepare for a background check is to be truthful on all employment forms, maintain good credit, know what your references are going to say about you, and obtain copies of personnel files from past employers. If necessary, get a copy of your credit report from a credit bureau and dispute any incorrect information.

Negotiate for Top Salary and Benefits

To obtain the strongest bargaining position, try to postpone any discussion of compensation until you receive a job offer. Bringing up the topic of compensation too soon could shift the focus away from your qualifications and cost you the job. Concentrate on what the employer will gain (your skills, experience, personal strengths, and so on) before focusing on the price (your compensation). Review and apply the following strategies:

- ☐ **Whenever possible, let the interviewer bring up the topic of salary and benefits.**
- ☐ **Do not accept a job offer without discussing the salary and benefits.** You can bring up the topic by asking, "What salary range do you have in mind for the job?"
- ☐ **Aim for a salary that equals the peak of your qualifications.** The higher you start, the higher the offer is likely to be. State your requirement in a range (upper twenties, mid thirties), making it broad enough to negotiate. Don't specify a low end; if you do, the employer will likely select it.
- ☐ **If the interviewer asks what salary you want, a good response is "What figure or range is the company planning to pay?"** This gives you a starting point for negotiation. If it's higher than you expected, you help yourself by not stating a lower figure first. If it's lower, you now have a place to begin negotiations.
- ☐ **If the interviewer presses for your salary requirement, refer to your research.** "The national average for a person with my experience, education, and training is $_____. Considering the cost-of-living factors, I would expect a salary in the range of _____."
- ☐ **If the interviewer brings up the subject of salary before you adequately cover your qualifications**, delay the topic by saying,

"Actually, the position itself is more important to me than the salary. Could we discuss the position a little more?"

- ☐ **While discussing salary, return to your assets.** Review all the benefits and qualifications you have to offer the company.
- ☐ **Once you state your salary range, do not back down,** particularly if you think it is equal to your qualifications. Base your range on careful research. The employer will respect your confidence in the quality and worth of your work.
- ☐ **Do not discuss any other sources of income and do not whine about your expenses.** Stay focused on the negotiation.
- ☐ **Discuss the benefits** (insurance coverage, pension plans, paid vacations, and so on) during the discussion of salary.
- ☐ **Ask about the criteria used to determine compensation increases and the frequency of salary reviews.** Good benefits and salary increases can offset a somewhat lower starting salary.
- ☐ **If the salary offer is made in a letter and the salary is too low, arrange an appointment to discuss it right away.** Bargaining power is far greater in person than it is by letter or telephone.
- ☐ **If the salary isn't acceptable, state the salary you would accept,** and close by reaffirming your interest in the company and the job. If the interviewer says, "I'll have to think about your requirements," wait one week; then call back. You may receive a higher or compromise offer. If the interviewer gives you a flat "no," express regret that you were unable to work out a compromise. Restate your interest in the job and organization; then send a follow-up thank-you letter within two days. This could swing the decision in your favor.

complete *CareerActions*

12-2 Salary and Benefits Planning Sheet

Evaluate and Negotiate Job Offers

Because the decision to accept or reject a job offer affects your lifetime career plans, consider this important decision carefully. The following guidelines will help you assess job offers wisely.

Evaluate a Job Offer

Include the following factors in your evaluation of a job offer:

- ☐ **The job itself:** Is the scope acceptable? Is the work interesting to you? Will you work in teams or alone?
- ☐ **The organization and personnel:** Do you feel comfortable with the organizational structure and the people you have met?
- ☐ **The salary and benefits:** Does the salary match your education and abilities, and is it comparable with that of the competition? Does the potential for increases exist?
- ☐ **Career development opportunities:** Will you have adequate opportunities for professional growth (through training, continuing education, and experience)?
- ☐ **The values and philosophies of management:** Are they compatible with your own?
- ☐ **Expense considerations:** What expenses are required for relocation, housing, living costs, and so on?
- ☐ **How the job meets your goals:** Consider carefully how the job fits into your long-term career goals.
- ☐ **The job market:** Are jobs in your field plentiful or in short supply?

A job offer may be made by telephone, by letter, or in person. If the offer is made by letter, you have more time to think it over carefully and less emotionally than you do if it's made by telephone or in person. You may want to discuss the job offer conditions with a member of your support system, a family member, a career specialist, or all of these people.

Respond to the offer quickly so you don't jeopardize it in any way.

If the offer is made by telephone or in the interviewer's office, request time to think it over. Occasionally, interviewers will offer to increase the salary or benefits if that appears to be your main concern. This is particularly true if they believe you are the right person for the job and they don't want to interview other applicants. Even if this doesn't happen, though, it's still in your best interest to take at least one day to consider the advantages and disadvantages of the job offer.

Important: Be sure that waiting one day won't be an imposition. Don't put yourself in the position of returning the next day to accept the offer and finding that someone else has the job. Be sure you understand all the conditions of the job before you decide whether or not to accept the offer.

If you have absolutely no doubts or objections concerning the job offer, accept the offer on the spot with enthusiasm. This will reinforce the employer's confidence in your suitability for the job.

Accept the Offer Professionally

If you accept the job offer verbally, follow up immediately in writing, summarizing your understanding of the conditions of the offer and stating the position title, starting date, salary, and other pertinent items. (Your employer may do the same, but this helps ensure mutual agreement about all the conditions of the offer.)

Contact other organizations with which you have interviewed, and tell them that you have accepted a job. You may deal with these people in your new job, or you may want to contact them in the future regarding employment.

Contact your references and other people who helped with your job search to tell them about your new job and thank them for their help. People you thank are more likely to help in the future when you seek a new position or advancement in your career.

Reject the Offer Professionally

If you decide that this is not the job for you, notify the employer by telephone first, if possible. Then politely decline the offer in a letter, thank the employer for the job offer, and wish the employer future success.

Consider How Economics May Influence Your Decision

Your final decision may be influenced by economics—the need to earn a living. If the offer meets most of your requirements but is not a perfectly logical career step, you could still decide to accept the job. If so, take the job with a determination to excel. It is an opportunity for you to establish your reputation—all while taking home a regular salary. Accept the challenge and view it as preparation for the next step in your career development.

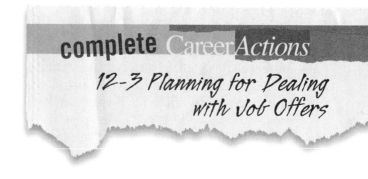

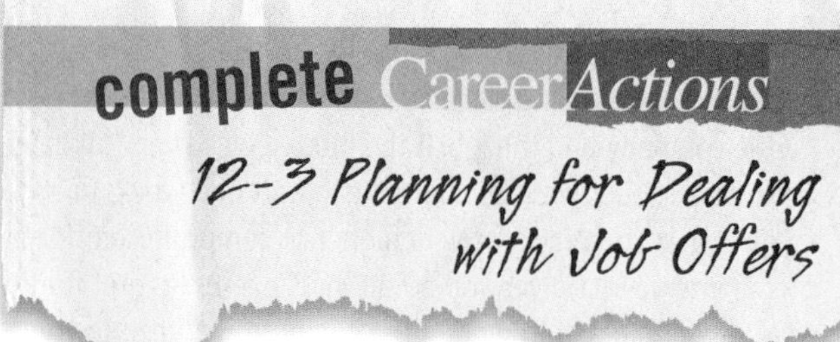

complete CareerActions
12-3 Planning for Dealing with Job Offers

Next Steps

Complete all the Career Actions in this chapter to ensure that you have a plan for responding to job offers professionally and can negotiate the best compensation package before you accept a job. File the completed Career Actions in your Career Management Files Binder. In Chapter 13 you will learn strategies for turning rejection into a type of success, by actively learning from every interview, whether or not it leads to a job offer.

Chapter Checklist

Check each of the actions you are currently taking to increase your career success

- Researching to learn what types of tests are given by target employers.
- Practicing beforehand to sharpen my performance in skills tests and studying concepts for technical tests.
- Postponing salary discussions until after I have received a job offer.
- Considering all aspects of a job offer—the job and company, the compensation package (salary and benefits), growth opportunities, and so on—and negotiating to improve any areas of concern before accepting a job offer.

Critical Thinking Questions

1. What specific strategies for acing employment tests apply to your job search campaign?
2. Is it more advantageous for the applicant or the interviewer to bring up the subject of salary first? Why?
3. What is an appropriate response when an interviewer asks what salary you are looking for?
4. If economic conditions require you to accept a job that is not exactly what you are aiming for, how can you best approach the new job? What are the benefits of doing so?
5. Base your answers to the following questions on your salary research: (a) What is the entry-level salary for the job you are seeking? (b) What salary range do you plan to seek in your job search? What is this range based on?

For convenient access to valuable career resources, study tools, activities, and job information links, visit the companion web site for this text: www.cengage.com/careerreadiness/levitt.

Trial Run

Pay scales and benefit packages are affected by larger economic issues. Divide into four teams and research the employment conditions in your area. Use anecdotal information and your own observations, and check the web sites of the local newspaper, business journal, chamber of commerce, and television stations.

Start by having a class discussion about what you want to learn from your research. For example:

- How have members of your group been affected by any economic changes?
- What can older workers tell you about past economic downturns or economic bubbles?
- What is the relative impact of national and local factors?
- What is the local unemployment rate? How has it changed in the last two years, one year, six months? How long do people report taking to find a new job in their field? Are people changing fields or taking contingency jobs?
- What are the elected officials predicting? What are business leaders predicting?
- What is your advice for your community leaders?

Team 1. Research the two or three largest employers in your area. How have they been affected by the national economic downturn? Have there been layoffs? If yes, have these jobs been shifted to other parts of the country, to other countries, or eliminated altogether?

Team 2. Research the local stores or branch offices of national companies. What is the reason behind any closures; for example, did the national company close low-performing stores or did they go bankrupt and close all the stores? Have any national chains opened new stores in your area? Have any openings been postponed? How many people have lost their jobs? How many new jobs have been created?

Team 3. Research small, locally owned retail businesses. Have any small businesses near your school closed? What about the neighborhoods you live in? Have new businesses opened?

Team 4. Research locally owned service businesses. Include companies that provide services to consumers (such as dry cleaners and nail salons) and business-to-business companies, such as janitorial services and restaurant supply companies.

As a class, decide how to share the findings of each team with the entire class. For example, you could hold a panel discussion with representatives of each team and/or each team could present its findings to the class in a PowerPoint presentation. Consider taking the assignment a step further and talk about how your school can help unemployed people and companies in your area. If you do this, consider sending or giving the presentation to a person or group at your school who can help implement your ideas, such as the staff of the career services center.

Career Action

12-1 Internet Research on Salary Information

Part 1 Directions: Compare the web sites Homefair.com and Salary.com. Use one site's salary calculator to compute the cost-of-living differences between two cities in which you would consider working. What are some other factors to consider? Print the results.

Part 2 Directions: Visit the *Occupational Outlook Handbook* at the Bureau of Labor Statistics site and complete the following steps:

1. Select the title of your occupational cluster.
2. Choose the title of your field (and a subtitle if necessary), and then click on "Earnings."
3. Print or summarize in writing the wage ranges listed for the occupation.
4. Find the wage ranges for at least five more occupational clusters and career fields that interest you.

Part 3 Directions: For additional salary information, check out the valuable "Salary Info" section at the JobStar web site. Take at least one quiz or read one article.

Career Action

12-2 Salary and Benefits Planning Sheet

Part 1 Directions: Contact two employers in your field to learn about the salary ranges and benefits they offer for the type of job you are seeking. Ask the following questions.

Does this position have a fixed salary or a salary range?

____

If the salary is fixed, would you tell me the amount?

____

If the salary is in a range, would you tell me the range?

____

Is the salary negotiable?

____

What criteria are used for determining the salary for this position?

____

Are salary raises awarded for excellent job performance? If so, what criteria are used in this process?

____

What is included in the typical complete compensation package (salary and benefits)?

Part 2 Directions: Review the strategies in the section "Negotiate for Top Salary and Benefits." Use a separate sheet of paper to summarize, in your own words, the tactics you plan to use when negotiating a compensation package (salary and benefits). List any additional tips you have found in your Internet or other research.

Career*Action*

12-3 Planning for Dealing with Job Offers

Directions: Answer the following questions.

1. **List every factor you should consider when evaluating a job offer.** Be thorough in your answer. You may want to discuss this with a member of your support system network, a placement counselor, or both. Include the factors that are specific to your personal job search, as well as general factors.
2. **Explain how you can best respond to a job offer made in person:**

   a. If you think you want the job

   b. If you are sure you want the job

   c. If you don't want the job
3. **How can you best respond to a job offer made by telephone?**
4. **List the follow-up steps you should take when accepting a job offer.**
5. **How should you professionally reject a job offer?**

For Your Career Management Files Binder

After completing the Career Action activities in this chapter, file the following documents in your Career Management Files Binder:

- ☐ **CA 12-1: Internet research on salary information**
- ☐ **CA 12-2: Salary and benefits planning sheet**
- ☐ **CA 12-3: Plans for dealing with job offers**

© STOCKBYTE/GETTY IMAGES

Chapter 13

Handling Rejection

Objectives

- Determine how to deal effectively with rejection in your job search.
- Evaluate your job search performance and identify methods of improving it.

Overview

Getting a good job often requires more than one interview; it may take several tries before you land the job you want. Getting a rejection notice is not a great ego booster, but it's not a reason to stop your job search campaign, either. Think of it as a learning experience, and continue with your job search activities. Chapter 13 highlights practical strategies for recharging your motivation, reversing a rejection notice, and trying new angles to land a top job.

chapter 13 Career*Actions*

13-1: Internet Research on Handling Job Search Rejection

13-2: Action Plans for Improving Your Job Search Campaign

Jump Start Excelling at What You Do

If you are reading this book, chances are high that you want to improve your employment situation. If the process is taking longer than you hoped, renew your career by using the opportunities available in your current place of employment. Brainstorm how you can apply the following strategies:

- Observe how the managers and the more senior people do their jobs. What can you learn for your own career?
- What are the most important technical skills in your workplace? What is your plan for acquiring these skills?
- Who are the most "popular" employees? How can you become a more positive and energetic force in your workplace?
- What does each department do? What do they need from your group?
- How can you help your organization succeed?

Persevere for Success

Winners in all fields agree: Perseverance is a major factor in their success. When they meet an obstacle, they find a way around it. Setbacks are not failures; you only fail when you quit trying.

No one can be right for every job. The right person for a job doesn't always get it. The best prepared and the most determined person often does, however. While you may be responsible in part for an initial rejection, you have the power to correct the situation and win the job offer. With belief in yourself, you can still succeed.

Get an Evaluation of Your Interview Performance

After receiving a rejection notice, if you're not sure where you fell short, call the interviewer and ask for an honest evaluation. If you are aware of the perceived shortcoming, though, prepare a strong written clarification you can refer to while making this follow-up call. Here is a way of asking for an evaluation:

> "Hello, Ms. Nguyen. This is Aaron Goldman. I received your letter stating that I had not been selected for the job, and I appreciate the prompt notification. Could you tell me which areas of my qualifications I need to strengthen, and could you suggest methods of improving in these areas?"

Some employers are reluctant to offer specific opinions and are justifiably cautious about being sued by job applicants for unfair hiring practices. Even if you don't get concrete help, express your thanks.

Prepare and Respond If the interviewer is willing to evaluate your performance and make suggestions for improvement, listen carefully and take notes. Accept the concerns expressed. Their validity is irrelevant. The important point is that they represent problem areas in the interviewer's perception of you.

If you like the organization and want the job, be prepared to *briefly* clarify your qualifications or clear up any misunderstanding. Use a friendly tone, and do not react defensively. Remember: You asked for the opinion.

Set Up Another Meeting If the interviewer seems receptive, explain that you didn't convey your qualifications as completely as you had planned and suggest that you meet once more to review them. Handled well, this approach demonstrates confidence, competence, and assertiveness.

Consider Other Departments

If your rejection response doesn't land you this job, emphasize your enthusiasm for working for the employer and ask whether you are more qualified to fill another position. This strategy encourages the interviewer to give you more consideration and may land a "hidden job." Ask for a referral to another employer. Employers are impressed by applicants who demonstrate initiative and confidence. If you project confidence and competence, you greatly increase your chances of convincing others of your potential.

Don't Be Afraid to Reapply

If you don't get a job with your preferred employer now, don't give up. Opportunities can develop later. If an opening comes up in the future, you have the advantage of being known by the employer because a known applicant saves valuable time in recruiting a new employee. Besides, you never know how close to being hired you were. You might be at the top of the list the next time an opening occurs.

Keeping your name in front of the employer can put you first in line for the next opening. One way you can do this is by calling the interviewer every couple of months just to check in. Keep the phone call brief and polite. Your purpose is to keep your name at the top of the list of applicants.

MAKE IT A HABIT

Counter Rejection with Success Strategies

To counter natural feelings of rejection, the best approach is taking immediate positive action.

- Maintain a positive attitude.
- Evaluate your performance and your self-marketing package.
- Connect with your network for support, and rework your contacts.
- Plan your next job search steps, and follow through.

Taking a short breather helps you renew your energy and enthusiasm. Allow yourself one day—but no longer—to do something you enjoy and to relax. And don't use rejection as an excuse for giving up. Regroup and rework your action plans.

Reread the success strategies in Chapter 1, focusing on the strategies that project competence and strengthen self-esteem. Visualize yourself performing successfully in your next interview and on your new job. Make a conscious effort to think and act positively and to use positive self-talk and affirmation statements.

Review your self-analysis forms from Chapters 2 and 3 (your talents, skills, qualifications, special accomplishments, and personal attributes).

Be Persistent

Be persistent in pursuing your preferred job. Stay focused on your goal, and consider all the factors that may affect the status of the position for which you have applied.

Changes in business conditions may affect the status of your target job. Consider how these changes may also present new opportunities to you as a job seeker.

Many organizations and businesses keep applications in their active file for a specific period of time (usually six months). If you are interested in a position with a particular company, find out the organization's policy for keeping applications active. You may need to call a prospective employer periodically to keep your application active and to remind the organization that you're interested in new job openings.

Stay Informed

Once a month, at your computer or at the library, read the local business journals. Know what's happening in your community and look for networking opportunities. Example:

Arthur wants to work in the financial world. He reads about a free seminar for people who plan to retire in the next two years. Arthur calls the registration number and asks if he can attend as an observer. He shows up early and takes notes during the seminar. After the seminar, Arthur thanks the presenter and right away mentions something specific that he just learned:

> "My parents are investigating Medicare supplemental insurance plans. I didn't know these plans may not cover all prescription drugs and I'm going to pass along your advice. I read about this event in the [name of local business journal] and wanted to learn more about retirement planning as a possible area to concentrate in. Thanks for letting me come."

The presenter asks Arthur what he does and agrees to meet Arthur for a career information survey.

complete Career*Actions*

13-1 Internet Research on Handling Job Search Rejection

complete Career*Actions*

13-2 Action Plans for Improving Your Job Search Campaign

Next Steps

Complete all the Career Actions in this chapter. Read what others are saying about handing rejection and develop an action plan to evaluate and recharge your job search. File the completed Career Actions in your Career Management Files Binder. In the next chapter, you will find strategies for succeeding in the job that you *will* find.

Chapter Checklist

Check each of the actions you are currently taking to increase your career success:

- Using positive thinking, action, visualization, goal setting, and self-talk to recharge my motivation and to improve my job search campaign.
- Asking each interviewer to evaluate my performance so that any areas that need improvement can be identified.
- Asking for referrals to other departments or organizations.
- Reapplying at a later date; calling back periodically to check the organization's hiring status.

Critical Thinking Questions

1. After a rejection, how should you approach your continuation of the job search?
2. Should you abandon your efforts to obtain a job with a particular prospective employer if, following your interview, you are notified that you were not selected for the position? Why or why not?
3. What can you gain from seeking an evaluation of your interview performance from an interviewer who rejected you?
4. If all your efforts fail to result in a job offer, what last request should you make of an interviewer?

For convenient access to valuable career resources, study tools, activities, and job information links, visit the companion web site for this text: www.cengage.com/careerreadiness/levitt.

Trial Run

The search for a new job is always challenging and too often frustrating. This activity may help you put things into perspective and renew your energy.

Take written notes during each part of the activity.

The activity starts in the present day. Jot down words and phrases that describe the general business climate in the country and in your community, the key issues in your career field, and your own career.

Turn back the calendar five years ago and repeat the activity.

Break into teams of people with related career interests. Take notes during the discussion. Reflect on the changes in your career field. How many of the changes were deliberately planned for and implemented? How many changes were unexpected? How did the larger business environment affect your industry? What things that seemed small five years ago turned out to have big consequences? What big things turned out to be not so big after all?

In teams or as a class, project ahead five years. Take notes during the discussion. What changes do you predict in the general business environment and in your career fields? Where do you expect the most changes? How confident are you about these predictions? What are the implications of these changes for the public and for the people working in the field? Where what you expect and what you hope for are far apart, what can you start doing to bring them closer together?

Think about these discussions for a few days and reflect on your own professional life five years ago and five years from now. Write yourself a letter to be opened in five years:

- Describe the circumstances leading to this letter: this assignment, your work situation today, your current plans, recent setbacks, etc.
- Record your predictions about your situation in five years.
- List helpful actions and "attitude adjustments" you have decided to take. Be specific about your plans so that in five years you can judge how well you succeeded.
- Include anything else in your letter that (you predict) you will enjoy reading in five years or that (you predict) will be helpful to reflect on.

Put the letter where (you predict) you will find it, or give it to someone who (you predict) can mail it to you.

13-1 Internet Research on Handling Job Search Rejection

Directions: Search the Internet for additional tips on persevering after being rejected for a job. Use the search phrase "job search persistence rejection" or go to job club sites and blogs you bookmarked in earlier research. Summarize your findings and file your research in your Career Management Files Binder.

Career Action

13-2 Action Plans for Improving Your Job Search Campaign

Directions: Review your complete job search campaign thoroughly. Answer each of the following questions in detail. Where necessary, include specific action plans you will take to improve your job search effectiveness. Check off each item as you complete the related actions.

After reviewing my self-analysis activities in the Career Actions in Chapters 2 and 3, have I overlooked anything important that supports my job target? (List the items, and describe any needed research or improvement.)

____
____
____

Have I checked with my support network members to find out whether they have any new job leads? (List them here, and follow up immediately.)

____
____

Could my resume be improved or tailored to a new job target? How could it be improved? Who could do a good job of helping me with it?

____
____
____

Should I make additional telephone calls/personal visits or write additional letters to prospective employers? (List details on a separate sheet of paper, and begin following up today. Don't put these actions off.)

____
____
____

Could my cover letters be improved? How could they be strengthened? Who can give advice?

____
____

Have I followed up on the cover letters and resumes I sent and on all job leads? Have I followed up on every interview? (List any follow-up needed in these areas.)

Have I done thorough research on my current job leads—enough to talk intelligently and persuasively about how I would fit in with the organization? (List any research that must be completed.)

Have I tried every possible job source? (Refer to the list of suggested job sources in the book. List any you could use now.)

Should I reapply with any employers? When?

Did I follow up on interviews thoroughly? What else can I do?

Have I scheduled my job search on my daily and weekly calendars?

For Your Career Management Files Binder

After completing the Career Action activities in this chapter, file the following documents in your Career Management Files Binder:

- ☐ **CA 13-1: Internet tips for handing job search rejection**
- ☐ **CA 13-2: Action plans for improving your job search campaign**

Chapter 14

Take Charge of Your Career

Overview

Chapter 14 presents guidelines for adjusting to and succeeding in a new job. Techniques are included for developing successful interpersonal skills, achieving top work efficiency, quickly mastering new responsibilities, and learning how to prepare for a successful job performance evaluation. The importance of taking responsibility for achieving a high quality and quantity of work and for being adaptable to change is also emphasized. Once you master your job and are performing at your peak, you will likely be interested in working toward career development and advancement opportunities. This chapter also provides clear guidelines for earning a promotion and achieving career growth.

Objectives

- Review guidelines for adjusting successfully to a new job.
- Learn strategies for achieving peak performance in a new job.
- Evaluate your previous or current performance in a job, in volunteer work, or in another responsible activity.
- Learn techniques for managing change and being adaptable.
- Research your industry for tips on job success, promotion, and making a job change.

chapter 14 Career*Actions*

14-1: Internet Research on Career and Job Success Tips

14-2: Job Performance Evaluation

14-3: Research Success Tips for Your Industry

Jump Start Your Successful Career

Congratulations on reaching the final chapter in *Your Career: How to Make It Happen.* One of the strongest messages in *Your Career* is that you are in charge of the success of your career search. On the job, you are in charge of the satisfaction you gain from your career. For this activity, talk to two or three older members of your personal support network. Ask each person the same questions:

© DIGITAL VISION/GETTY IMAGES

- What part of your career has brought you the most satisfaction and pride? Was it related to money or to "a job well done"?
- What was your best "career move"? Did you recognize it as a positive change at the time?
- What do know now that you wish you had known on the very first day of work? What mistakes do you see the younger people you work with making?

Reflect on how you can apply this wisdom in your own career. Share your reflections with a classmate. Did you hear the same things or different things?

1 Adjust to Your New Job

All workers who start new jobs have one challenge in common: adjusting to the job. This adjustment includes learning to perform specific tasks, learning how the job relates to the business as a whole, learning to work with others, and understanding the formal and informal rules and ways of doing things. Mastering these elements takes time and effort and training assistance from your employer.

Don't expect to achieve top efficiency overnight. It doesn't happen. Experiencing some anxiety while trying to learn so much new information and so many new procedures is normal. Maintaining enthusiasm, an eagerness to learn, and a positive attitude will help you adjust successfully.

Starting a new job is an important personal and professional step that helps shape your lifetime career. Successful careers are developed through planning and determination to succeed. You will achieve peak success by being persistent and by accumulating skills, knowledge, and experience.

Your employer will want you to succeed, and your coworkers will help you get off to a good start. The following techniques will help you adjust to a new job and achieve a successful lifetime career.

Project a Positive Attitude: The Most Important Success Factor

Employers hire and promote employees who have positive attitudes and demonstrate enthusiasm. Employees who demonstrate a defensive, negative, or disinterested attitude are not promoted and may eventually be terminated. Two employees with equal job skills but vastly different attitudes will develop widely different career paths. The one with a strong, positive attitude will progress steadily, while the one with a negative attitude will stagnate.

Approach new tasks, colleagues, and superiors with the attitude that you will do your best and that you expect the best from them, while being patient with their constraints. People most often live up to the expectations others have of them.

Project a Positive, Professional, and Competent Image

People perceive the image you project as a reflection of the quality of work you do. Your image projects from three sources: your inner confidence, your outward appearance, and your verbal and nonverbal communication. Review and practice the tips on self-esteem, appearance, and communication skills from Chapters 1 and 11. Maintain the professional appearance you had in your job interviews, but dress appropriately for your job duties and organization.

If you project an unsure attitude through your speech, appearance, and actions, you will be perceived as a tentative, unsure worker—even if your work is excellent. Purposely think, speak, dress, and act positively. This projects career-building confidence and competence.

Projecting a positive, professional, and competent image gives you a competitive edge. For example, if you make an error, your professional image may influence people to view the error as a part of learning rather than a sign of incompetence. Successful people act positively, practicing the success strategies presented in Chapter 1 until they become habits.

Emulate the habits of successful people. Think of yourself, see yourself, groom yourself, and talk about yourself as a winner.

Develop and Practice Good Interpersonal Skills: Be a Team Player

Job success depends largely on the ability to work well with others. Studies repeatedly verify that job failure is most frequently the result of poor interpersonal (behavior and attitude) skills—not lack of skill.

Be a Team Player Get along well with and assist others, show interest in their work, and work efficiently alone or with others. Team players are promoted first.

Be Tactful The world's most successful people have these qualities in common: They are tactful, diplomatic, courteous, and helpful in dealing with other people.

Treat People the Way You Want to Be Treated Help others accomplish their assignments, compliment them on work well done, critique their work tactfully only when necessary, and listen to what they have to say. This behavior encourages others to treat you the same way.

When you need help with a project or are in line for a promotion, your reputation for working well with others will more likely be rewarded. Treat all people (your employer, your peers, the custodian) with respect.

Get Off to a Successful Start

When you're hired, your employer expects you to have the basic knowledge and skills needed to do the job. You acquired these through your education and prior work experience. The challenge now is to apply them to the best of your ability in performing your job.

Be a good learner, and expand your abilities. You will be expected to become a productive employee within a reasonable training period. You can improve the quality and speed of your learning and performance by applying the following techniques for mastering a new job.

Learn About Your Company

It is important to learn as much as you can about your company or employer and its leaders. Read the annual report if the company has one. (Many are online at the Securities and Exchange Commission web site and are available through employers' investor relations or human resources departments. Your manager might also have one.) Read your company's web site thoroughly and/or visit your local library to research the company's history and news stories.

In addition to learning about your employer, learn about its industry and main competitors. Research the competitors' products or services and seek to understand why customers might buy them instead of your company's offerings.

Talk to long-time employees about their experience and recollections. Knowing the employer's history can help you understand its culture.

Embrace your employer's values and goals. Most places of business have a mission statement that includes their goals and values. Read the mission statement and think about it. How are the larger organization's goals and values reflected in your department? If there are gaps, what do you think accounts for them? How can you apply the mission statement in your own position?

Many employers sponsor volunteer or community service activities and organizations. Get involved! Participation provides many benefits, including expanding your network of contacts, developing leadership skills, and demonstrating your support for the employer's goals and related activities.

complete CareerActions

14-1 Internet Research on Career and Job Success Tips

Pay Attention to Your Job Orientation

Your employer is responsible for informing you of your job duties and for providing an orientation to the work procedures. You should also be told about work hours, parking requirements, and related information. Learn what the rules are, and follow them. Ask for copies of policies and procedures that pertain to your job and workplace.

Your employer should explain when and how your performance will be evaluated. To help focus your efforts and achieve the best possible performance evaluation, *find out immediately exactly how and when your job performance will be evaluated*. If your employer overlooks any of this orientation or job evaluation information, request the information yourself.

> **Focus on three goals to help you adjust successfully to a new job:** Keep a positive attitude; project a professional, competent image; and be a good team player.

Be Smart About Compensation and Benefits

Take the time to learn about employee benefits, and take full advantage of those that can save you money. Enroll in benefit programs at the start of your employment, and update your benefit selections during your company's annual benefit enrollment period.

In addition to insurance programs, many employers offer flexible spending accounts that allow you to set aside pre-tax income to pay for medical expenses and dependent care. Such accounts can lower the amount of your income that is subject to tax. Some employers also offer such accounts for using mass transit, for paying parking fees, and so on. If your new position doesn't have all the benefits you hoped for, you may need to make alternative plans for health and disability insurance. These are available through professional organizations, credit unions, auto clubs, alumni groups, etc.

Plan for Retirement Now

It is *never* too early to start saving for retirement, so take advantage of any savings plans that your employer offers. Many large companies offer tax-deferred savings plans—known as 401(k) or 403(b) plans—and will contribute to your retirement savings if you participate in the company-sponsored plan through payroll deductions.

Because you save your own money and contributions from your employer, this is one of the best ways to save for retirement. Depending on your savings plan, the amount you put aside can reduce your taxable income, the gains may not be taxed until you retire, and you may draw from the plan to pay for your education or buy a home. Also get investment and retirement savings advice from a financial planner or an investment banker who can help you establish your own individual retirement account (IRA), if needed.

Be Aware and Alert

Observe carefully the way work flows through your department, and be a good listener. Others appreciate good listeners and not having to repeat information. Also, pay attention to subtle attitudes and unstated policies that influence work operations.

Learn the Organizational Culture

Every organization has a unique personality and culture. To enhance your success, develop organizational savvy. Learn and adhere to the culture, including the expected work ethic and social norms. For example, are social activities in and out of the workplace the norm? Will you be considered aloof if you don't participate?

Pay attention. Not all cultural norms are spelled out. You will discover them through observation.

MAKE IT A HABIT

Use a Question-and-Answer Notebook

As you learn each aspect of your job, use a notebook or an electronic organizer to record all your questions and the instructions you receive.

Ask your supervisor and coworkers what times are best for discussing your questions (to avoid annoying them with poorly timed interruptions). Maintaining your notebook is important for several reasons:

- You will improve your efficiency by clarifying information that hasn't been explained fully.
- You won't have to repeat your questions.
- Your supervisor will appreciate your efficiency.

Remembering every detail required to master a new set of job tasks is impossible. A notebook provides a quick review and a reminder of tasks and procedures.

Be Dependable, Punctual, and Industrious

Be professional, hardworking, and accurate in performing your job. This sets a positive example for your coworkers. Employers value and look for these qualities when retaining and promoting people.

MAKE IT A HABIT

Manage Your Time

Managing your time effectively is one of the keys to becoming an efficient worker. Follow these time management tips to increase your productivity:

Be on time. Be at your desk ready to work on time (or a little early) every day. Being on time gives you an edge of preparedness and an unhurried mind-set that improves work performance.

Determine priorities and plan your work around them. Ask your coworkers and supervisor what tasks are most vital to the successful operation of your department. Prioritize your work based on their answers. Do your most important daily tasks first to avoid overlooking vital tasks during rush work periods. Reassess your priorities as new tasks are assigned, and review these with your team or supervisor periodically.

Use time management tools: calendars and job-tracking forms. Keep your work calendar current, coordinate it with your work team, and check it daily. Keep a reminder notebook of tasks to be completed. Prepare a daily to-do list, recording the tasks in order of importance. Do your best each day to complete as many tasks on your list as possible. Move any incomplete tasks to the next day's to-do list.

Develop good time management habits. Group all similar tasks and complete them in one block of time. This focuses your attention and task performance rather than fragmenting it. For example, schedule one block of time to prepare documents and another to place phone calls.

Keep your work area well organized. If your work area is well organized, you can locate and use resources efficiently; this increases productivity, decreases frustration, and enhances your professional image.

Expect that adjusting to your new job will take some time. Be alert, listen, and stay positive. Look, speak, and act professionally.

Go to Work Every Day Absenteeism causes work inefficiency, disruption of workflow, and lower productivity. It also places stress on workers who must cover for the absent employee, causing resentment and frustration. If you must be absent because of a severe illness, a serious emergency, or an unavoidable problem, let your employer know as soon as possible. Chronic absenteeism is not tolerated by employers and is an eventual ticket out the door. Patterns of questionable excuses raise questions in the employer's mind.

Be Punctual and Dependable Be on time for work at the start of the day and after breaks or mealtimes. Be punctual for meetings. Those who make an effort to be punctual will not appreciate your being late. Be on time! Being on time also means finishing projects and assignments when they are due.

Demonstrate Initiative Personal initiative is a major factor affecting your promotability. After you've finished your assigned duties, don't sit and wait for more work to be assigned. Find an appropriate task to perform on your own, notify your supervisor that you are ready for another assignment, or ask how you can help someone else. Think about better ways to do your job. Then research and plan how to implement your ideas. If a coworker is overloaded, offer to help.

Focus on People As Well As Job Duties

The way you relate to the people in your work will influence your career success as much as the quality of your job performance—no matter how skilled or educated you are. Make time for your coworkers, supervisors, employer, clients, and/or customers. Be courteous and helpful.

Get to Know Your Coworkers Spend time with your coworkers during breaks and meals. Network with others, and be friendly and approachable. Don't let yourself become a loner; it won't enhance your career success.

Be Aware of Organizational Politics Every organization has formal and informal politics. Learn who is respected—or even feared—in your place of employment. These people often influence office politics greatly and are usually powerful within the organization.

Note, however, that first impressions are not always accurate. Take time to observe and learn the office politics.

Be a Good Communicator

Good communication skills are important for career success. Effective verbal communication, listening, and written communication can improve your productivity and enhance your interactions with coworkers and managers.

Use Excellent Phone Manners Phone manners are important, especially in a customer-service economy. Greet callers pleasantly and promptly, listen carefully, and answer their questions patiently and thoroughly. Check your voice-mail messages frequently, and leave very brief, specific, and clear messages for others. Return calls promptly.

Listen Actively Active listening can be a powerful tool for gaining information and solving problems. In a conversation, give the other person your full attention. Focus on what is being said, look directly at the other person, and never interrupt. Ask questions to show that you want to understand. A good rule of thumb is to listen twice as much as you talk.

Recognize Communication Styles Even in the same culture, people have different communication styles. This means that they process information differently, approach problems differently, want information given to them differently, and socialize differently. A key to success in any organization is learning the different styles of the people you deal with (especially customers and managers) and adapting your style accordingly. This ability can be a key step in resolving disputes and avoiding conflicts in the workplace.

Use E-mail Appropriately E-mail is the most popular form of workplace communication today. Make your e-mail messages businesslike and brief, and always include informative subject lines. Do not use e-mail to handle serious

MAKE IT A HABIT

Use Strategies for Effective Writing

In most careers, you can count on writing being used frequently in your daily business. To make a good impression, your e-mails, memos, letters, and reports must be professional, precise, and error free. Follow the "4 C's" of effective writing. Make certain all your written correspondence is complete, concise, correct, and clear. Always use a businesslike tone, and proofread your work. Never use slang or inappropriate humor in business writing.

For important workplace documents, follow the steps of the writing process to achieve your best work and make writing tasks seem less overwhelming.

1. **Pre-write.** Identify your audience, purpose, and main topics. Generate ideas by brainstorming and making lists.
2. **Draft.** Start creating a rough draft by writing out your ideas in sentence form—on paper or on the computer.
3. **Revise.** Improve your draft by reorganizing paragraphs, adding details, and making your sentences more precise.
4. **Edit and Proofread.** Review your work and check your facts. Correct all spelling and grammar errors. If possible, have someone else review your work, too.
5. **Present and Publish.** Present your final work in a professional, properly formatted document.

issues or difficult problems that are best resolved in person.

The e-mail messages you write at work are not private and can be legally monitored by your employer. Don't use e-mail to send sensitive or personal information, to convey information that you would not want to be shared, or to send jokes or other non-work-related messages.

Because you are human, you will make an occasional mistake. The challenge is to learn from your mistakes and accept criticism maturely. When you work for someone else, you agree to perform according to that person's standards. Because your employer pays your salary, he or she has the right to criticize your performance or behavior if it doesn't meet established standards.

Show your maturity by thinking like a manager, acting like a leader, and being an example to others.

Manage Yourself

Learn to deal with difficult people, control your emotions, and manage stress and conflict. Maintain a good fitness program and a healthy life balance. Also, manage your family and transportation needs; anticipate and prevent problems. Many excellent classes, books, CDs, DVDs, videos, and web sites are available on all of these subjects.

Build a Network

Actively build a network of people who are willing to help you understand how to work most efficiently and effectively in the organization. Whenever possible, reciprocate by helping people in your network. Become involved in one or more professional, trade, or technical associations to expand your resources and networking opportunities.

Seek Feedback and Accept Criticism

Actively asking for feedback from your supervisor demonstrates initiative and professionalism. Periodically ask your supervisor directly if your performance is meeting his or her expectations or if you need to improve. Ask for specific recommendations for improvement where necessary.

If the criticism is deserved, don't deny fault. Don't react defensively or blame others. Accept the criticism professionally, and make improvements. To learn from your mistakes, request suggestions for improvement from the person who criticizes you. If you don't think the criticism is justified, tactfully present evidence that supports your opinion.

If your employer or supervisor continually criticizes you unfairly, particularly in front of others, request a meeting to discuss the reason for this behavior. If the criticism continues even though you make the recommended improvements, consider seeking a position in another department or looking for a new employer.

Make Your Supervisor Look Good, and Be Supportive

Find out what your supervisor needs to meet goals and excel, and do what you can to provide it. Regularly using your initiative to meet your supervisor's needs is a career booster.

In return for offering you a job and salary, the employer expects your support. Speak well of the firm and its personnel, products, and services. Speaking negatively about an organization harms the employer's reputation and may result in your being fired. If you're unhappy and see no way to gain satisfaction, move on.

Demonstrate Maturity

Be responsible for your actions:

- ☐ Perform at your best level, and expect the same from those you supervise.
- ☐ Be aware of your strengths and weaknesses. Capitalize on your strengths, and make efforts to improve your areas of weakness.
- ☐ Be self-reliant and self-disciplined.
- ☐ Maintain stable emotions in the workplace, leaving your personal problems at home.
- ☐ Show your maturity by thinking like a manager, acting like a leader, and being an example to others.

Know Your Customers You have two types of customers, internal and external. Internal customers are the people or groups that use your service or depend on you to help get their jobs done. For instance, a programming group is a customer of the training department that provides computer classes. Every group is a customer of human resources to provide employees who are qualified to fill open positions. Get to know your internal customers, what their needs are, and how they depend on you or your group, and then go out of your way to provide great service.

Set Goals Establish realistic yet challenging goals and deadlines. Manage your time carefully, and have a plan for meeting your goals.

Take Initiative Become proactive—especially in providing service to customers. Don't wait until your customers present a problem to offer a suggestion that could improve their business. Ask questions to improve your knowledge; then take the opportunity to make suggestions.

Take Risks Don't be afraid to take risks or to fail. Although success is rewarded, no one is perfect. Take appropriate, measured risks when needed, and always have a back-up plan for when things don't go as you intended. Learn from your mistakes, and don't repeat them.

Offer Feedback Take advantage of opportunities to give feedback to your employer, such as through online employee surveys and continuous improvement teams and task forces. Don't complain or criticize. Instead, offer creative yet practical suggestions for improving procedures, saving money, and exploring better ways of doing things.

4 Prepare for Your Job Performance Evaluation

Learn how and when you will be evaluated on your job performance so you know where to focus your efforts to achieve a good evaluation. This will also help you avoid overlooking an area considered important by your employer. You need to know how heavily the employer weighs each performance area so you can concentrate on the important ones. If you don't receive this information during orientation, ask your supervisor to explain the process.

If your employer uses an informal method of job evaluation, ask what is considered good job performance and what criteria are used in determining promotions or raises. This will provide guidelines for your successful performance. As you become more knowledgeable about your job, show initiative. Set your own goals and deadlines for performance improvement and growth.

Many employers schedule annual, biannual, or quarterly meetings to review their employees' job performances in writing, orally, or both. Usually, the purpose of these evaluations is to identify the strengths and weaknesses of the employees and to establish short- and long-term goals for the employer and employee.

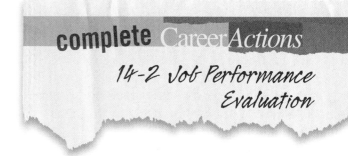

complete CareerActions

14-2 Job Performance Evaluation

Succeed in Today's Changing Workplace

Today's technology and increasing workplace competition are escalating the pace of work and changing the way work is performed. Employers need employees who are flexible, adaptable to change, and able to work independently when making decisions and solving problems. Competition requires increased efficiency.

Meet Your Employer's Quality Needs

Employers expect each worker to take responsibility for achieving maximum productivity while continuously looking for ways to improve quality. To meet your employer's expectations and achieve career success:

- ☐ Produce top-*quality* work. Produce the highest possible *quantity* of work.
- ☐ Be alert for problems, and take action to prevent or solve them.
- ☐ Contribute effectively as a team member.

Be Flexible and Manage Change

In addition to quality performance, focus on developing and improving your ability to be flexible and adapt to change.

Be Flexible Expect differences (some major) between the way your employer conducts business and the methods you learned in school or on another job. While schools often teach theories, employers interpret and apply theories and techniques (often developing their own) to accomplish specific work goals and tasks. Changing technology makes some textbook theories obsolete. Personalities also influence work methods.

A process that may seem inefficient or is different from the method used in your previous job may serve a purpose that is not immediately

Watch Out
Think Like a Free Agent

Career-long employment with one company is no longer the norm; in fact, today's workers can expect to change jobs about 10 times during the course of their careers. An employer and an employee are partners in a contract that has to work for both parties. Every job may be temporary, so you must keep an open mind, stay networked, and constantly be prepared to take the next step in your career.

Consider a portfolio career—a career made up of a variety of complementary activities that capitalize on your strengths and provide you with an acceptable level of income. These activities may include full-time work, part-time work, a temporary or contract work arrangement, a hobby that turns into a home-based business, or any combination of these.

Keep your ears open for new opportunities. Use your resume as a sales tool to highlight your relevant skills and successes—not just your jobs. Stay up-to-date in your fields and activities and take pride in the new skills you acquire.

apparent to you. Projecting a know-it-all attitude to your supervisor or others is a sure way to alienate yourself, perhaps permanently. If you think a technique could be improved, request a meeting with your supervisor to clarify the reasons for using it. Asking thoughtful questions is a good strategy for opening the discussion.

There is a right time, place, and method for presenting your ideas or suggestions to your supervisor. Learn by observing how others present theirs. If the clarification by your supervisor still doesn't convince you that a technique is the most effective option, explain the theory or technique you have learned or devised, offering it as a suggestion for consideration. Never try to bulldoze your ideas through.

Adapt to Change Rapid technological, global economic, and other changes require continual changes in work processes, tools, and equipment. Be flexible in evaluating the need for or adapting to changes in procedures, equipment use, and so on. Office automation affects the way business is conducted and the way work is performed. Keep an open, flexible attitude toward change. Don't make yourself obsolete through stubborn resistance; you may miss an open door to a career development opportunity.

Stay Up-to-Date

Continually update your skills and knowledge through education and training. We are living in an economy that is increasingly based on knowledge and service and less on manufacturing and goods.

In the late 1990s, for example, enormous wealth was created by ideas—many of which were applied to software and processes that increased productivity. Innovation (new ways of doing things) was the key.

Just as companies invested in new factories and machines during the Industrial Age, investment in employees with knowledge and information is the key in today's Information Age. That is why it's important for you to invest money and time in your ongoing training, education, and learning.

MAKE IT A HABIT

Be a Lifelong Learner

Rapidly changing technology and a global economy have created a fast-changing world. Jobs and careers are changing dramatically. To have a successful career and to distinguish yourself from the pack, you must update your current skills and add new skills quickly and continuously. In short, you must make learning a lifelong pursuit. You need to develop and sustain the habit of continuing your education to avoid being left behind.

You can become a lifelong learner by:

- Participating in workshops and training programs.
- Taking college- or graduate-level courses.
- Subscribing to journals and other print or online news and information related to your field.
- Joining professional associations related to your career.

Distance learning programs on the Internet make lifelong learning opportunities more accessible than ever. Online instructional services such as extremelearning.com, University of Phoenix Online, and Element K can help you find continuing education courses related to business and management, college studies, technology, training, graduate studies, and more. Links to these services can be found on the textbook web site at www.cengage.com/careerreadiness/levitt.

To ensure your continuous and future employability, make sure you have the skills required to meet the demands of the changing workforce. To remain a viable employee in the twenty-first century, you must make lifelong learning a part of your career management plans.

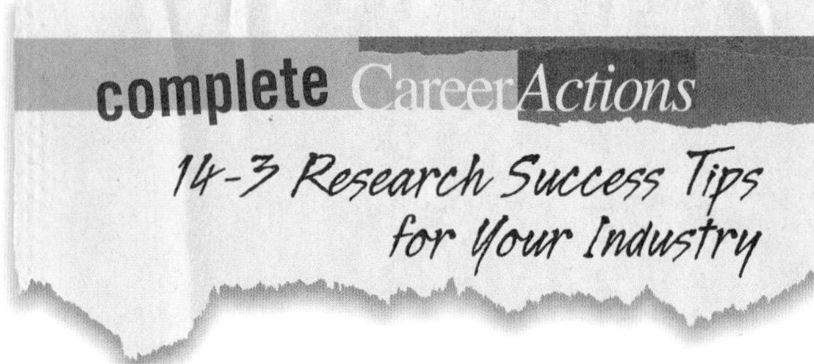

complete CareerActions
14-3 Research Success Tips for Your Industry

Manage Your Career Development/Advancement

Once you believe you've mastered your job responsibilities, you've overcome areas of weakness in your performance, and your employer is satisfied with your performance and understanding of the job, focus on managing your career development and seeking growth or advancement opportunities. You may want to work toward a new career goal—a lateral move or a promotion, for example.

Be Willing to Take on New Responsibilities

Find out what new responsibilities are included in any new growth opportunities or position you seek. Outline the required action steps; pursue them with an expectation of success; and be willing to accept, learn, and carry out all new duties. Get any training you need to perform at the levels required.

Earn Your Advancement or Promotion

Keep in mind that you must *earn* a promotion or advancement opportunity. When you know you're adequately prepared for advancement, start demonstrating your qualifications for it. The following guidelines will help you achieve this goal:

- ☐ **Seek a mentor.** A mentor is someone inside or outside your organization who can advise and coach you—someone who is respected and knowledgeable in your field. Seek advice from mentors who are experienced in the areas you need to improve. Don't limit yourself to just one mentor. Look for people who are sensitive to your concerns, who help you learn new skills, and/or who take time to explain organizational dynamics. Keep your relationship with a mentor professional. Strive to meet your mentors' expectations for your performance.
- ☐ **Develop expertise.** Identify your greatest working strengths and interests, and build on them. Take advantage of all training in these areas. Become known for your special expertise. This will help focus your career in a direction that best suits you and will expand your career opportunities.
- ☐ **Be professional.** Think, act, speak, and dress professionally. If you want a promotion, act as though you already fit the part.
- ☐ **Expand your knowledge and skills.** Keep current in your job and industry knowledge. Correct any deficiencies immediately through reading, involvement in professional groups, training, and education. Submit reports of what you have learned to your supervisor.
- ☐ **Do high-quality work.** Do the best possible job, and achieve the highest possible quantity and quality of work.
- ☐ **Increase your organizational awareness.** Learn all phases of the organization, its goals, and how each job is designed to meet the overall goals.
- ☐ **Increase your visibility.** Get involved in organizational committees and cross-team projects in which you can excel. Show extra initiative, and demonstrate leadership. Develop your speaking abilities.
- ☐ **Use subtle self-promotion techniques.** Sometimes it's not enough to perform well; you must also make your superiors aware of your achievements—without bragging. Focus on your experience, not on yourself. Whenever you talk with coworkers and managers, be positive and enthusiastic about your job and your projects. Speak with confidence about your experience and accomplishments, but avoid making too many "I" statements.
- ☐ **Seek a promotion.** Once you've accomplished most of the items in this list, tell your supervisor you're interested in progressing and learning more. Demonstrate your ability to handle additional responsibility.

Maintain Your Network

Networking is not a job search activity to be discontinued once you get a job. Once you're employed, send a thank-you note to all the members of your network who helped you or expressed interest in your job search. Tell them about your new position.

Keep in touch with your contacts for the next time you're ready to pursue a career goal. To achieve the greatest levels of career success, continual networking is a must. When you need important information or the time comes to seek a new job, you'll be leagues ahead of the competition that doesn't stay networked.

Maintain Your Career Management Files Binder

Keep your Career Management Files Binder current; don't abandon it. You've done a great deal of work in the activities in *Your Career: How to Make It Happen*. This information will be useful throughout your entire career. Save your work (this book, the written assignments, and your computer files); you'll be glad you did.

Maintain Your Career Portfolio

Continually add to the Career Portfolio you've developed through the activities in this text. This is your collection of documents and other items that provide evidence and examples of your work accomplishments, certifications, skills, qualifications, and more. Throughout your career, add records of all your work-related achievements, including samples of exemplary work; letters of recognition for a job well done; and other documents that support your good job performance, achievements, and related activities.

Next Steps

Complete all the Career Actions in this chapter. Find additional success tips for job and career on the Internet, and evaluate yourself using a typical job performance evaluation form. Talk to people in your career field about their advice for succeeding in this field. File the completed Career Actions in your Career Management Files Binder.

> **Networking is not a job search activity to be discontinued once you get a job.** Send a thank-you note to all the members of your network.

Chapter Checklist

Check each of the actions you are currently taking to increase your career success:

- Focusing on three goals to help me adjust successfully to a new job: keeping a positive attitude; projecting a professional, competent image; and being a good team player
- Learning about the company and culture, working efficiently, being dependable, focusing on people, and preparing for evaluation
- Being a good communicator, managing myself, building a network, and demonstrating maturity
- Being a high-quality, top producer; being a problem solver; learning to adapt to and manage change; and being flexible
- Taking on new challenges, broadening my skills and knowledge, seeking a mentor, developing expertise, keeping my portfolio current, networking, and increasing my visibility
- Keeping my job search network active and maintaining my Career Management Files Binder to use in future career development activities

Critical Thinking Questions

1. What is the most common cause of job failure?
2. How can you most effectively learn a new job? Name five things you can do to help yourself master a new job.
3. Why is it important to know how your performance will be evaluated?
4. Why is it essential to adapt to change, and how can you demonstrate adaptability?
5. Once you have mastered a new job, what specific actions can you take to increase your professional development and make yourself promotable? List additional training or coursework you could take to increase your knowledge and skills. Identify growth-oriented responsibilities you would be interested in pursuing. List other actions you could take to prepare for a promotion and increase your visibility.

For convenient access to valuable career resources, study tools, activities, and job information links, visit the companion web site for this text: www.cengage.com/careerreadiness/levitt.

Trial Run

How do you measure up to the traits that executives, managers, and business owners said they most admired in new workers?

Trait	Description	Recent situation where you showed (or should have shown) this trait
Willing to go the extra mile	Stays a little late or does a little more to see a project through	
Flexible	Can relate to different personality types of clients and coworkers	
Kind	A generally nice person, who does not talk about coworkers, bosses, or clients	
Poised	Presents herself or himself confidently and is at ease with others	
Cooperative	Pitches in and works as a team player	
Enthusiastic	Comes to work with a smile, full of energy and ideas	
Honest	Tells the truth, does not cover up mistakes	
Loyal	Concerned for the organization's welfare	
Disciplined	Keeps his or her work and priorities in order	
Conscientious	Thorough and hardworking	
Dependable	Arrives on time, misses as few days as possible, meets deadlines, keeps her or his word	

Career Action

14-1 Internet Research on Career and Job Success Tips

Directions: Search the Internet for articles related to the topics in this chapter. Some keywords to use in your search include *career advancement, promotion, time management, performance evaluation, adapt to change,* and *mentor/mentoring.* Write a summary of at least two articles that are useful to you, and file them in your Career Management Files Binder.

Career Action

14-2 Job Performance Evaluation

Directions: Career Action 14-2 is a sample job performance rating form that is representative of the forms used by many organizations. In the left column, rate your job performance in your current or past work experience, in volunteer or internship work, or in another significant task-oriented activity (O = Outstanding, V = Very good, G = Good, A = Acceptable, U = Unacceptable). On the line below each item, give one or two examples of your performance. Circle the items you rated acceptable or unacceptable; make these your targets for improvement.

Rating **Performance or Behavioral Category**

_____ **ABILITY TO ACQUIRE AND USE INFORMATION AND FOLLOW INSTRUCTIONS** (Uses initiative in acquiring, interpreting, and following instructions and using references)

List specific examples: ______________________________

____

_____ **INTERPERSONAL SKILLS** (Is tactful, understanding, and efficient when dealing with people)

List specific examples: ______________________________

____

_____ **BASIC SKILLS** (Is proficient in reading, writing, mathematics, listening, and verbal and nonverbal communication)

List specific examples: ______________________________

____

_____ **JOB SKILLS** (Demonstrates command of required knowledge and skills)

List specific examples: ______________________________

____

_____ **THINKING/PROBLEM-SOLVING SKILLS** (Generates new ideas, makes decisions, solves problems, and reasons logically)

List specific examples: ______________________________

____

_____ **ABILITY TO COOPERATE WITH OTHERS** (Works well with team members and under supervision, exercises leadership, and works well with people of diverse backgrounds)

List specific examples: ______________________________

____

_____ **QUANTITY OF WORK** (Does required amount of work)

List specific examples: ______________________________

____

_____ **QUALITY OF WORK** (Does neat, accurate, complete, and efficient work)

List specific examples: ______________________________

____

_____ **GOOD WORK HABITS** (Maintains good attendance and punctuality, is dependable, and follows safety/work procedures)

List specific examples: ______________________________

____

_____ **ATTITUDE** (Demonstrates enthusiasm, interest, and motivation)

List specific examples: ______________________________

____

_____ **TECHNOLOGY** (Works well with technology—tools, computers, and procedures)

List specific examples: ______________________________

____

_____ **PERSONAL QUALITIES** (Demonstrates responsibility, initiative, self-confidence, integrity, and honesty; practices good self-management; sets and maintains goals; exhibits self-motivation; and is cooperative)

List specific examples: ______________________________

____

OVERALL EVALUATION OF PERFORMANCE AND BEHAVIOR

Directions: Review the rating code (Outstanding, Very good, Good, Acceptable, or Unacceptable) you placed next to each category of your Job Performance Evaluation on the previous pages. Place a check mark below next to the rating you recorded the most frequently.

_____ **Outstanding** _____ **Very good** _____ **Good**

_____ **Acceptable** _____ **Unacceptable**

Employee's Short-Term Goals: (List your short-term job or career goals here.)

____

____

____

Employee's Long-Term Goals: (List your long-term job or career goals here.)

____

____

____

Suggestions for Improving Performance or Behavior: (List the steps you can take to improve your work performance or behavior.)

____

____

____

General Comments Regarding Employee's Job Performance: (Add any other appropriate comments to describe the quality of your work performance.)

____

____

____

Signature of Supervisor: (This is where your job supervisor would sign your performance evaluation.)

____

14-3 Research Success Tips for Your Industry

Directions: Arrange meetings with knowledgeable people in your field to learn (a) how the job performance of employees is evaluated, (b) what techniques help ensure success on the job, (c) how employees can earn promotions, and (d) what methods are recommended for making a job change. Use the following questionnaire, adding pertinent questions that are relevant to your field. Or, design and use your own questionnaire.

1. **What advice would you give a new employee (in a position similar to the one you are seeking) to help him or her adjust quickly to the job, the company, and the people the employee would interact with?**

2. **What are the most important things to learn about your company when starting employment there?**

3. **What advice would you give a new employee to help ensure the highest degree of job success?**

4. **How does communication affect productivity and success on the job in your company?**

5. **Does your organization encourage risk taking? In what ways?**

6. **What criteria do you use to evaluate the performance of an employee? Do you have a job performance evaluation form I could review?**

7. What advice would you offer employees to help them increase their visibility?

8. How can an employee earn a promotion here?

9. If an employee must leave your company, what steps do you prefer the employee take? How much notice do you expect? Do you prefer that the employee help train his or her replacement? Do you expect a letter of resignation?

For Your Career Management Files Binder

After completing the Career Action activities in this chapter, file the following documents in your Career Management Files Binder:

- ☐ **CA 14-1: Internet tips about career and job success**
- ☐ **CA 14-2: Your job performance evaluation**
- ☐ **CA 14-3: Success tips for your industry**

appendices

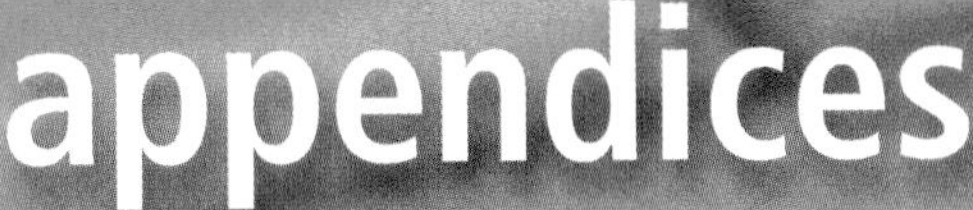

Appendix A

Sample Business Letter and E-Mail Formats

To project professionalism in your job search and career development written communications, use appropriate business formats. Listed below are guidelines for formatting a business letter and an e-mail message. Illustrations of these document formats follow the guidelines.

Business Letter Format (see model on page 303)

Use the following guidelines to format your business letters correctly:

1. Prepare standard business letters on 8 ½- by 11-inch letterhead. If you don't have your own letterhead stationery (not expected for an individual) use a high-quality bond stationery.
2. Use the block style letter format illustrated on the following page. General guidelines for the placement of the letter parts are indicated on the illustration. A few specific tips are emphasized below.
3. Place the return address and date based on the length of the letter.

   For an average-length letter, begin the return address at the left margin at approximately the 2-inch top margin point. If the letter is long, place this section higher on the page to achieve a more balanced placement. Place the date directly under the return address and at the left margin.
4. Microsoft Word 2007:
   - ☐ Use default spacing.
   - ☐ Remove extra vertical spacing within return address and letter address.
   - ☐ Insert one hard return after inside address, letter address, salutation, and each paragraph of the body of the letter.
   - ☐ Key two hard returns between complimentary close and name of sender.

   Microsoft Word 2003:
   - ☐ Key a double space (two hard returns) between salutation and body of letter.
   - ☐ Key two hard returns between each paragraph and between last line of letter and complimentary close.
   - ☐ Key four hard returns between complimentary close and name of sender.

E-mail Message Format (see model on page 304):

Follow the guidelines below to format an e-mail message correctly:

1. **Format:** Fill in the To and Subject lines in the form at the top of the message window. The date is added automatically. Use a descriptive subject line so recipients understand the purpose of the message quickly.
2. **Case:** Use the standard mix of upper- and lowercase letters. (Using all caps is like SHOUTING ON THE NETWORK!) Entire messages in all capital letters are also extremely hard to read.
3. **Brief but complete:** Keep e-mail messages short and focused on one subject, but be sure to include all information necessary for the recipient to take appropriate action and to reach you.
4. **Professional:** As with hard-copy documents, your professional reputation is reflected in e-mail:
   a. Plan and organize the message.
   b. Prepare a draft, proofread, and revise.
   c. Be courteous.
   d. Use correct spelling and grammar.

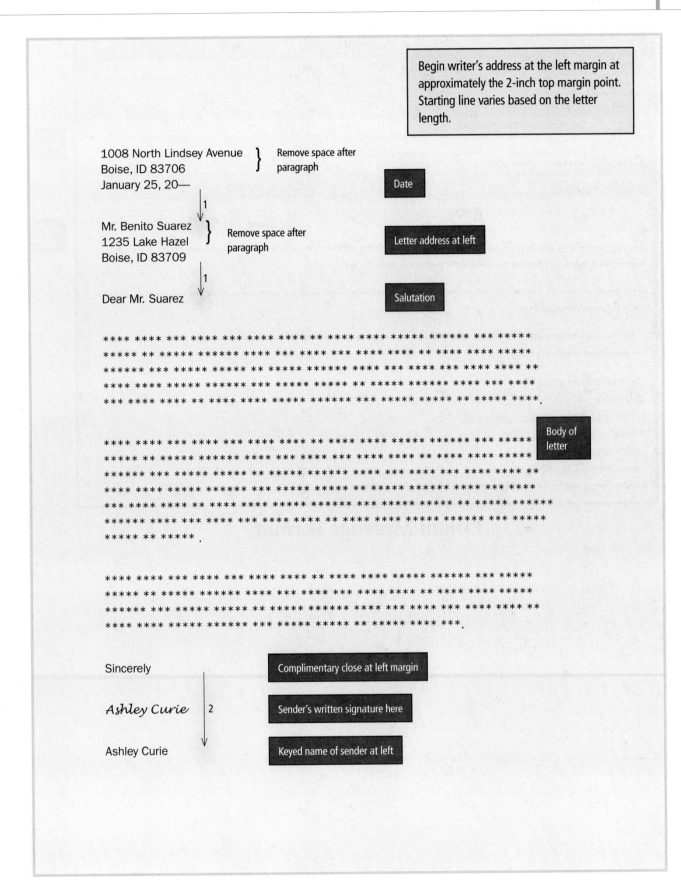

Begin writer's address at the left margin at approximately the 2-inch top margin point. Starting line varies based on the letter length.

1008 North Lindsey Avenue
Boise, ID 83706 } Remove space after paragraph
January 25, 20— — Date

↓ 1

Mr. Benito Suarez
1235 Lake Hazel
Boise, ID 83709 } Remove space after paragraph — Letter address at left

↓ 1

Dear Mr. Suarez — Salutation

**** **** *** **** *** **** **** ** **** **** ***** ****** *** *****
***** ** ***** ****** **** *** **** *** **** **** ** **** **** *****
****** *** ***** ***** ** ***** ****** **** *** **** *** **** **** **
**** **** ***** ****** *** ***** ***** ** ***** ****** **** *** ****
*** **** **** ** **** **** ***** ****** *** ***** ***** ** ***** ****.

**** **** *** **** *** **** **** ** **** **** ***** ****** *** *****
***** ** ***** ****** **** *** **** *** **** **** ** **** **** *****
****** *** ***** ***** ** ***** ****** **** *** **** *** **** **** **
**** **** ***** ****** *** ***** ***** ** ***** ****** **** *** ****
*** **** **** ** **** **** ***** ****** *** ***** ***** ** ***** ******
****** **** *** **** *** **** **** ** **** **** ***** ****** *** *****
***** ** *****.

Body of letter

**** **** *** **** *** **** **** ** **** **** ***** ****** *** *****
***** ** ***** ****** **** *** **** *** **** **** ** **** **** *****
****** *** ***** ***** ** ***** ****** **** *** **** *** **** **** **
**** **** ***** ****** *** ***** ***** ** ***** **** ***.

Sincerely — Complimentary close at left margin

Ashley Curie — Sender's written signature here

↓ 2

Ashley Curie — Keyed name of sender at left

Business Letter Format

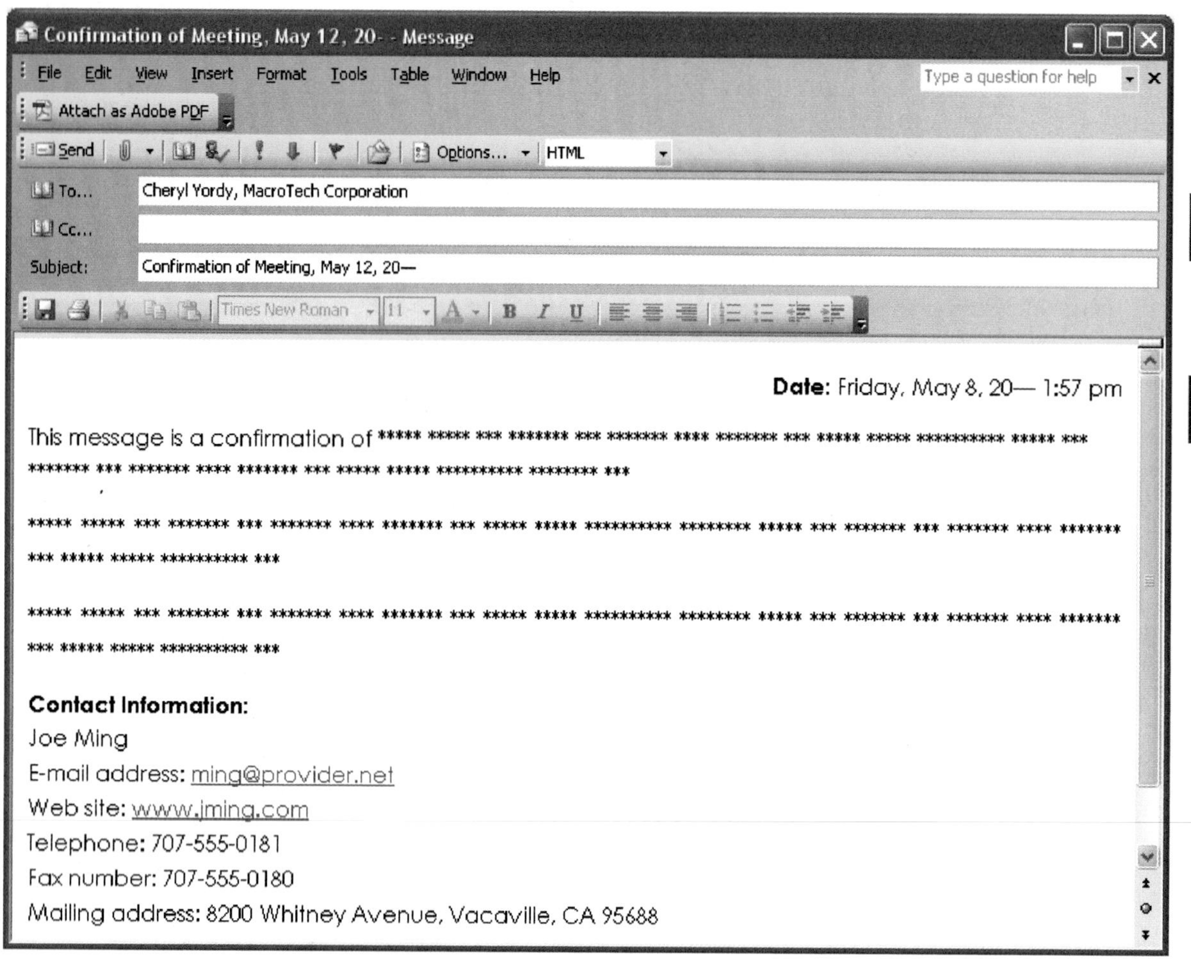

Confirmation of Meeting, May 12, 20- - Message
File Edit View Insert Format Tools Table Window Help
Type a question for help
Attach as Adobe PDF
Send
Options...
HTML
To... Cheryl Yordy, MacroTech Corporation
Cc...
Subject: Confirmation of Meeting, May 12, 20—
Times New Roman
11
Date: Friday, May 8, 20— 1:57 pm
This message is a confirmation of ***** ***** *** ******* *** ******* **** ******* *** ***** ***** ********** ***** *** ******* *** ******* **** ******* *** ***** ***** ********** ******** ***
***** ***** *** ******* *** ******* **** ******* *** ***** ***** ********** ******** ***** *** ******* *** ******* **** ******* *** ***** ***** ********** ***
***** ***** *** ******* *** ******* **** ******* *** ***** ***** ********** ******** ***** *** ******* *** ******* **** ******* *** ***** ***** ********** ***
Contact Information:
Joe Ming
E-mail address: ming@provider.net
Web site: www.jming.com
Telephone: 707-555-0181
Fax number: 707-555-0180
Mailing address: 8200 Whitney Avenue, Vacaville, CA 95688
Include a subject
Body of message

E-mail Message Format

Appendix B

Career Management and Marketing Tools

Three important career management and marketing tools are recommended to help you reach your full career potential: (1) a Career Management Files Binder, (2) a Career Portfolio, and (3) an Interview Marketing Kit. These tools are discussed in various chapters throughout this text and are further summarized below as a convenient reference.

Career Management Tool 1:

Career Management Files Binder

In using this textbook, you will develop information and documents you can use throughout your life to help achieve each new job and career goal. This material will consist of information you record in your Career Actions as well as drafts of job search documents you create in these assignments, such as your resume, cover letter, networking lists, and more. Altogether this valuable career data will form your **Career Management Files Binder**. This data provides the essential base of career information you will need throughout your career. This information will also be in a format that is easy to retrieve and update any time you seek a new position in your career.

Compiling Your Career Management Files

1. **Organize Your Data—Create a Career Management Files Binder**. Set up a system for collecting, organizing, and updating your career information. You will need most of this data whenever you seek a new job, an advancement, or a new career. Use a ring binder to serve as your Career Management Files Binder. Include 14 divider tabs, labeled Chapter 1 through Chapter 14.
2. **File Completed Career Actions**. Place all completed Career Action forms or other written assignments (such as your resume, cover letter, and other career documents you develop) behind the corresponding chapter tab in your Career Management Files Binder. You can also use tabs with topic labels, such as "network list," "references," "resume," "cover letter," and so on.
3. **Use Your Data CD or the Career Action Forms in Your Text**. Most of the Career Action Worksheets in the text are also available on the Data CD. Use the electronic version of these forms on the CD whenever possible (although you can use the paper forms included in your textbook). The Data CD increases the convenience of preparing Career Action Worksheets because the forms are interactive Word files you fill out using the keyboard.
4. **Back Up Your Career Action Work**. Save your completed Career Action forms from your Data CD as well as the other career documents you create in this course (resume, cover and other letters, reference sheet, and so on) onto your hard drive or network drive. Much of this information will be valuable to you throughout your career for use in revising and updating your career documents and reference data. Also back up your files on a CD or other storage media.

   File your Data CD and backup CD along with the printouts of your assignments in your Career Management Files Binder. In this way, you will be creating an electronic "Career-to-Go" of data you can take with you and easily update or revise any time you seek a promotion or a job or career change.

Career Management Tool 2:

Career Portfolio

The Career Portfolio is an organized master collection of items that demonstrate job-specific skills and work qualifications. Some examples of appropriate portfolio items include your resume; an official copy of your transcript(s); exemplary samples of your work, such as business writing, graphic arts samples, and printed samples from software presentations; evidence of sophisticated computer usage, such as desktop publishing and web site creation; awards and commendations; work performance evaluations; and letters of reference.

Portfolio samples can be from paid or volunteer work, internships, cooperative education, clubs, community activities, and more. A comprehensive list of appropriate items and ideas for building your portfolio is included under the heading "Sample Portfolio Items," starting below

Note: File original documents, such as school transcripts, in your Career Management Files Binder and include copies of these documents in your Career Portfolio. This way you will retain a clean master and still have a copy for demonstration during interviews.

Identifying Items for Your Portfolio

Begin by identifying your skills and experiences that relate directly to your job target. Then consider carefully what you have done or accomplished that best demonstrates those qualifications. For example, if you are seeking an accounting job, include your transcripts listing appropriate course work; a CD containing samples of budgets you developed or accounts receivable or accounts payable reports you prepared; a letter of recommendation from an employer for bookkeeping or accounting work you performed; and so on. See a comprehensive list of ideas for portfolio items under the heading, "Sample Portfolio Items," which appears below.

Assembling Your Portfolio

For a traditional portfolio, use a professional-looking folder or three-ring binder that holds 8½ by 11-inch pages. If you use a binder, file and categorize all of your portfolio documents behind tabbed sections in the binder. Whether you use a folder or a binder, use sheet protectors, CD inserts, and other accessories to display and protect your portfolio items. Larger portfolios (17 by 22 inches) are appropriate for art designers, journalists, advertising specialists, and technical writers to store and categorize oversized documents and credentials.

Sample Portfolio Items

Examples of portfolio components include:

- ☐ Paper documents
- ☐ CDs containing text-based documents
- ☐ Video- or audiotapes
- ☐ Multimedia CDs or DVDs containing sound or video clips and other presentation content
- ☐ Pictures/photographs
- ☐ Other items that can be used to demonstrate your qualifications.

Review the following list of suggested portfolio components, but don't limit yourself to these. Use your imagination and strive for a close match with your target job.

To Demonstrate Work Experience, Work Performance, and Credentials

- ☐ **Resume**: Include error-free copies of your resume printed on quality paper. This should be the first item in your portfolio.
  Also, include a CD with your scannable print resume and your electronic resume for employers who prefer those formats. Place the media in a protective jacket or case.
- ☐ **Employer or Internship Performance Reviews**: Include copies of all favorable reviews.
- ☐ **Licenses**: Include for professions requiring a license to work in the field.
- ☐ **List of References**: Include a listing of references' names, addresses, and phone numbers and their association to you. Past employers, direct supervisors, and instructors are all good references.
- ☐ **Letters of Recommendation/Commendation**: Include these letters since they speak for themselves.

Career Management Files	Career Portfolio
For personal use in record keeping and organizing during a job search	To show to prospective employers during interviews
Documents your job search progress and learning and serves as a reference tool	Showcases your skills and qualifications through high-quality documents and work samples
Includes all research, notes, document drafts, contacts, and work that is pertinent to your job search	Is a collection of your best work that represents your accomplishments and qualifications (including cover letter, resume, references, and work samples)

Education, Training, Degrees, and Certificates

☐ **Diploma/Degree**: Place a copy of your diploma(s) or degree(s) in your portfolio; place originals in your Career Management Files Binder.

☐ **Transcripts**: If your academic performance was good, keep copies of your transcripts in your portfolio to demonstrate this strength. Place your original transcripts in your Career Management Files Binder.

☐ **Certificates**: Include professional certification (CPA, CPS, CET, PE, teaching certificates, and so on) since this is evidence of lifelong learning. Certificates of completion for continuing education, specialized training, workshops, seminars, and so on, are important because they, too, demonstrate career development.

☐ **Awards**: Include awards showing perfect attendance on the job and in school; academic accomplishments; or employee of the month, quarter, or year. Awards are proof of outstanding accomplishments and are of interest to employers.

Samples of Work, Use of Technology and Information

☐ **Design Work**: Include computer or manual drawings in the field of drafting to prove technical ability in mechanical, architectural, structural, or electrical designs. Include computer-aided drafting design (CAD) examples where appropriate. Interior design work as it pertains to decorators can also be demonstrated through drawings, photographs, and videotapes.

☐ **Artwork**: Include samples of sketches, drawings, and paintings; photographs or video footage; or computer-generated items in your career portfolio.

☐ **Writing Samples**: Showcase your best work if you are an author, an editor, or a reporter. Include samples of technical writing, reports, articles, business plans, instructional or training materials, institutional improvement plans, proposals, written content for web sites, and mission statements you have composed. The ability to communicate is important to employers.

☐ **Software-Generated Documents**: Include your best examples from school if you're preparing to graduate and lack related job experience. Provide such items as electronic spreadsheets, database documents, newsletters, or presentation documents. If you have on-the-job work experience, include relevant copies of your actual work.

☐ **Publicity/Press Coverage**: Include articles highlighting your work, volunteer, community, or professional activities or other special accomplishments. Sources for these are school, employers, or professional publications such as newsletters, newspapers, journals, magazines, and so on. Use printed and online resources.

Other Portfolio Content

☐ **Examples of Community Service**: Include any materials that demonstrate active involvement in community service.

☐ **Forms of Identification**: Place front and back photocopies of a valid driver's license, social security card, or photo ID in your portfolio for easy retrieval. Many employers request at least two forms of identification to process your application.

☐ **Proof of Citizenship**: Include copies of your birth certificate, passport, visas, and/or immigration forms. These documents can be used to show you are eligible to work.

Web E-Portfolio

For some industries, a career portfolio developed as a web document is appropriate. This is called an **e-portfolio** or **web portfolio** and contains documents formatted for display on the Internet. Virtually everything you could assemble in a standard portfolio (described above) can be formatted as pages of a web portfolio.

Search the Internet for samples of web portfolios and articles on web portfolios that may provide useful ideas. Use the search string *web portfolio*.

If you develop a web resume or personal web site, include a link to your web portfolio. You can also include these web addresses in your cover letter and on your resume and business card.

Career Management Tool 3:

Interview Marketing Kit

The Interview Marketing Kit is a professional-looking folder containing items from the master Career Portfolio. You select the items from your master portfolio to meet the specific needs of each employer. In other words, your Interview Marketing Kit should be tailored and assembled using Career Portfolio items selected specifically for each interview. During interviews, you can extract appropriate portfolio items from your Kit that demonstrate your qualifications. This tangible evidence of abilities often gives candidates a winning edge in competing for a job. Choose items that match the needs of the specific target employer. After your interview, you can refile the items in your master Career Portfolio.

The kit should also contain an "Interview Survival Pack." These are supplies that can bail you out of a situation that could diminish your confidence and performance. They include rescue items such as a comb, a toothbrush, breath freshener, and a spare tie for a man or an extra pair of nylons for a woman.

Selecting Portfolio Items to Place in Interview Marketing Kit

Before each interview, select items from your Career Portfolio that best pertain to this specific job target. Don't use every item in your primary Career Portfolio for every interview. Place the items you select in your Interview Marketing Kit. Arrange the portfolio items in your Interview Marketing Kit in the order that best demonstrates how your abilities relate specifically to the employer's needs. Examples of appropriate items for your Interview Marketing Kit are as follows:

1. Items from your Career Portfolio that best support the needs of the organization with which you are interviewing:
   - Job-related samples of your work, if applicable (from your work, educational, or training experience)
   - Required certificates, licenses, transcripts, or other related documents
   - Forms of identification
   - Spare copies of your resume
   - Letters of recommendation
   - List of references appropriate for the job
2. Your 60-Second Commercial summarizing your qualifications for the job (see Chapter 8)
3. A list of pertinent questions you can ask during the interview (see Chapter 10)

Review items 2 and 3 just before your interview. Don't read from them during the interview.

Using Portfolio Items During Your Interview

Ask if the interviewer would like to see samples from your portfolio before displaying anything. Even if the interviewer prefers not to review them, having portfolio items conveys that you are professional and organized. During the interview, you may still have an opportunity to offer a portfolio sample if the topic suggests it. Employers typically ask questions about your resume. At this point, you can use your portfolio items to support your responses. Do not misrepresent yourself in the portfolio items; the work must be your own. Be prepared to reproduce the work if requested to do so.

To make a good first impression and to capture the interviewer's attention, refer to one of your most impressive accomplishments first. Provide evidence of the accomplishment with an appropriate portfolio item. Save another exceptional item for the end of your interview to leave a memorable final impression.

Have a friend conduct a mock interview with you, and practice referring to your portfolio items at key points during the questioning process. This will prepare you to make a smooth delivery during your actual interviews.

Appendix C

Reference Reading

Job Search and Career Management

Bolles, Richard N. *What Color is Your Parachute?* 2008: A Practical Manual for Job-Hunters and Career-Changers. Berkeley, CA: Ten Speed Press, 2007.

Johnson, Spencer and Kenneth H. Blanchard. *Who Moved My Cheese? An Amazing Way to Deal With Change in Your Work and in Your Life.* New York: G. P. Putnam's Sons, 1998.

Oliver, Vicky. *301 Smart Answers to Tough Interview Questions.* Naperville, IL: Sourcebooks, Inc., 2005.

Tracy, Brian and Campbell Fraser. *TurboCoach: A Powerful System for Achieving Breakthrough Career Success.* New York: American Management Association, 2005.

Yate, Martin. *Knock 'em Dead 2009: The Ultimate Job Search Guide.* Holbrook, MA: Adams Media, 2008.

Personal Motivation, Communication, and Assertiveness

Booher, Dianna. *E Writing: 21st Century Tools for Effective Communication.* New York: Pocket Books, 2001.

Briles, Judith and John Maling. *The Confidence Factor: Cosmic Gooses Lay Golden Eggs.* New York: Mile High Press, 2008.

Brown, Patricia. *Electronic Presentations, 10-Hour Series.* Cincinnati, OH: Cengage Learning South-Western, 2001.

Buckingham, Marcus and Curt Coffman. *First, Break All the Rules: What the World's Greatest Managers Do Differently.* New York: Simon & Schuster, 1999.

Buckingham, Marcus and Donald O. Clifton. *Now, Discover Your Strengths.* New York: Simon & Schuster, 2001.

Carnegie, Dale. *How to Win Friends and Influence People.* New York: Simon & Schuster, 1998.

Cloke, Kenneth, Joan Goldsmith and Warren Bennis. *Eight Strategies for Everyone on the Job.* San Francisco, CA: Jossey-Bass, 2005.

Covey, Stephen R. *The 7 Habits of Highly Effective People: Powerful Lessons in Personal Change.* New York: Free Press, 2004.

Covey, Stephen R. *The 8th Habit: From Effectiveness to Greatness.* New York: Free Press, 2004.

Frankl, Viktor. *Man's Search for Meaning.* Boston, MA: Beacon Press, 2006.

Goleman, Daniel. *Emotional Intelligence: Why It Can Matter More Than IQ.* New York: Bantam Dell Publishing, 10th Anniversary Edition, 2006.

Goleman, Daniel. *Working with Emotional Intelligence.* New York: Bantam Dell Publishing, 2000.

Gray, John. *How to Get What You Want and Want What You Have.* New York: HarperCollins, 2000.

Heim, Pat, Susan Murphy, and Susan Golant. *In the Company of Women: Turning Workplace Conflict into Powerful Alliances.* New York: J. P. Tarcher, 2001.

Hill, Napoleon. *Think and Grow Rich.* San Francisco, CA: Wilshire Publishing, 2007.

Knight, Sue. *NLP at Work*. Naperville, IL: Nicholas Brealey Publishing, 2002.

Leech, Thomas. *How to Prepare, Stage, and Deliver Winning Presentations*. New York: AMACOM, 2004.

Levitt, Julie G. and Jeff Craig. *Power Tools for Business Writing*. Cincinnati, OH: Cengage Learning South-Western, 2005.

Peale, Norman Vincent. *The Power of Positive Thinking*. New York: Random House, 1996.

Peters, Thomas. *In Search of Excellence: Lessons From America's Best-Run Companies*. New York: HarperCollins, 2004.

Phelps, Stanlee and Nancy Austin. *The Assertive Woman*. San Luis Obispo, CA: Impact Publishers, 2002.

Robbins, Anthony. *Unlimited Power: The New Science of Personal Achievement*. New York: Simon & Schuster, 2001.

Siegel, Bernie. *Prescriptions for Living*. New York: HarperCollins, 1999.

Tracy, Brian. *Focal Point: A Proven System to Simplify Your Life, Double Your Productivity, and Achieve All Your Goals*. New York: AMACOM, 2004.

Waitley, Denis. *The Psychology of Success: Finding Meaning in Life and Work*. Niles, IL: Nightingale-Conant, 2005. (Audio CD and MP3 download.)

Watson, Charles E. and Thomas A. Idinopulos. *Are You Your Own Worst Enemy?: The Nine Inner Strengths You Need to Overcome Self-Defeating Tendencies at Work*. Portsmouth, NH: Praeger Publishers, 2007.

Glossary

A

assertive behavior behavior that conveys self-esteem, capability, and qualifications.

attitude a way of looking at life; a way of thinking, feeling or behaving. A positive attitude is represented by a pleasant demeanor, good manners, a can-do spirit, willingness to try, and an ability to get along well with others.

B

behavioral interview an interview technique in which the interviewer asks questions aimed at getting the applicant to provide specific examples of how he or she has successfully used the skills required for the target job.

board or panel interview an interview in which the applicant talks with more than one person at one time, a panel that may have been selected to represent personalities and styles in the workplace.

C

campus interviews prearranged screening interviews that are generally scheduled through a school's career center.

career competencies specific skills, work values, and personal qualities necessary to be successful in an employer's organization. Employers look for these competencies during job interviews and expect employees to demonstrate them at work.

career information survey a meeting in which a job seeker interviews a contact about his or her job or career.

career management files binder career development and job search documents (completed Career Action worksheets, self-assessments, records of experience and skills developed, draft resumes, letters, job search organizational aids, and more).

career portfolio an organized collection of documents and other items that you will show to a prospective employer to demonstrate your skills, abilities, achievements, experience, and qualifications.

career target a job that is an ideal job for you right now. It completely suits your current qualifications and interests, matches your salary and work environment desires, and provides a challenging and interesting work situation. See also contingency target and stretch target.

chronological resume a traditional format used to show skills, work experience, and a logical career progression directly related to the job target.

combination resume uses the best features of the chronological and functional organizations to emphasize the match between your skills and a position's requirements.

computer-based interviews a timed interview on a password-protected web site typically consisting of 50 to 100 multiple-choice and true/false questions.

contingency target a "backup plan." You could easily get this job because you are possibly over-qualified or you have a good contact. See also career target and stretch target.

cover letter a letter of inquiry or introduction that you submit with an application and/or resume.

character questions interview questions asked to learn about your personal attributes, such as integrity, personality, attitudes, and motivation.

E

electronic resume a plain text document that is designed to be delivered via e-mail or an online form.

employment application a set of questions that employers use to get standard information from all applicants.

etiquette the expected professional behavior in the workplace based on common courtesy, manners, and cultural and societal norms.

F

functional resume a format that uses separate paragraphs to emphasize skill categories and show that you have the skills needed to do the job.

G

gatekeeper an administrative support person, receptionist, or human resources staff member who screens all job applicants.

general information questions interview questions asked to obtain factual information.

H

hidden job market job openings that are never published—personal searching is required to uncover them.

I

industry skills standards the skills employees are expected to demonstrate in a job interview and/or on the job.

J

job club a group of job seekers who meet regularly to share experiences and advice, set goals, and offer encouragement.

job reference someone who can vouch for your capabilities, skills, and suitability for a job.

job search network the network of people who can help you with job leads and contacts.

job-specific skills the technical abilities that relate specifically to a particular job.

K

keywords terms within resumes that represent the qualifications a company is seeking. Employers scan for keywords electronically using web-based applicant-tracking systems or in-house software programs.

N

networking the process of developing relationships with people who can assist with job search strategies and in finding strong job leads.

O

objective the section of the resume that is a statement of your employment goal.

online career portfolio contains your portfolio documents formatted for display on the Internet.

P

personal career inventory all the information you compile about yourself through the Career Action assignments. An important source of information when you develop your resumes, cover letters, and job applications and prepare for interviews throughout your job search.

personal references people who can vouch for your good character.

personality test a test designed to determine whether your personal and behavioral preferences are well matched to the work involved.

positive self-talk purposely giving yourself positive reinforcement, motivation, and recognition—just as you would do for a friend.

positive visualization purposely forming a mental picture of your successful performance and recalling the image frequently.

positive thinking making a conscious effort to think with an optimistic attitude and anticipate positive outcomes. Purposely acting with energy and enthusiasm.

power words action statements that use verbs to emphasize the applicant's qualifications (such as *build, prepare, test*)

print resume a printed, word-processed resume designed to be visually appealing and delivered as an e-mail attachment, by regular mail, in person, or by fax.

proactive approach focusing on solving problems, being responsible, and taking positive actions. Compare with reactive approach.

professional references people who can vouch for your work skills and personal qualities.

profile section the section of the resume that is a brief statement that describes a job applicant by stating his or her most relevant experience and qualifications.

qualifications section the section of the resume that is a bulleted list of skills that highlights why you are the ideal candidate for the job.

R

reactive approach focusing on problems and avoiding difficult situations. Compare with proactive approach.

references individuals who are willing to vouch for your qualifications, attest to your work abilities and personal qualities, and recommend you to prospective employers.

resume a brief, one-page document that details your qualifications for a particular job or job target.

S

screening interview an interview used to identify qualified applicants for the next level of interviews and to screen out those who do not have the basic qualifications for the job.

self-esteem belief in your abilities and your worth.

stress questions interview questions asked to determine how you perform under pressure—whether you are good at making decisions, solving problems, and thinking under stress.

stretch target the hard-to-get "dream job" that you would like to have in the near future. It might be in a competitive organization or field that does not hire many candidates; it might offer exceptional salary and benefits; or it might offer a desirable location. See also career target and contingency target.

structured interview an interview technique often used by professional interviewers in which the interviewer asks a predetermined set of questions, sometimes recording the applicant's responses on an interview rating form or checklist.

T

team interview an interview given by three to five employees, in which the applicant meets individually with each person. After the interview, the team members meet to discuss the applicant's performance.

telephone interview an interview format that is cost-effective for employers; if you have submitted resumes or applications, you must expect a call from an interviewer at any time.

transferable competencies abilities that can be applied in more than one work environment. The basic skills and attitudes that are important for all types of work.

U

unstructured interview an approach generally taken by people who are not professionally trained in interviewing—more informal and conversational in tone than a structured interview approach.

V

value that which is desirable or worthy of esteem for its own sake; the social principles, goals, or standards held or accepted by an individual.

W

web resume a document formatted in HTML so it can be posted on the Internet as a web document.

work experience section the section of a resume that lists the jobs you have, usually in reverse chronological order (most recent job first).

Index

C

D

E

F

G

Q

R

S

T

U

V

W